101 Performance
Projects for Your
Pickup and SUV

Rick Shandley

MOTORBOOKS

First published in 2007 Motorbooks, an imprint of MBI Publishing Company LLC, Galtier Plaza, Suite 200, 380 Jackson Street, St. Paul, MN 55101 USA

Motorbooks titles are also available at discounts in bulk quantity for industrial or sales-promotional use. For details write to Special Sales Manager at MBI Publishing Company, Galtier Plaza, Suite 200, 380 Jackson Street, St. Paul, MN 55101 USA.

To find out more about our books, join us online at www.motorbooks.com.

Library of Congress Cataloging-in-Publication Data

101 performance projects for your pickup and SUV / edited by Rick Shandley.
    p. cm.
  ISBN-13: 978-0-7603-3145-3 (softbound)
  ISBN-10: 0-7603-3145-6 (softbound)
  1. Pickup trucks--Customizing. 2. Pickup trucks--Performance. 3. Sport utility vehicles--Customizing. 4. Sport utility vehicles--Performance. I. Shandley, Rick, 1956- II. Title: One hundred and one performance projects for your pickup and SUV.
  TL230.5.P49A198 2007
  629.28'732--dc22

                      2006100833

ISBN-13: 978-0-7603-3145-3
ISBN-10: 0-7603-3145-6

Editor: Lindsay Hitch
Designer: Michael Cawcutt

Printed in China

About the author:
Rick Shandley's publishing experience spans more than 15 years, with almost 10 years in the automotive industry. As a former editor at publications such as *OFF-ROAD* magazine, *Four-Wheel Drive*, and *Sport Utility* magazine, Rick has a deep appreciation and understanding of the pickup truck and SUV aftermarket. In the 1996 Baja 1000 off-road race, Rick co-drove in a class-winning Pro-Truck; and again in 1998, in the same vehicle, he co-drove to a class win in the Race to the Clouds at the Pikes Peak hill climb in Colorado. Rick is currently director of business development at The Enthusiast Network.

On the cover:
A Superlift 8-inch system for current Super Duty models makes room for 38x15.50R20 Toyo Open Country M/Ts on 20x10 American Racing Trax wheels with 4.5 inches of backspacing. Visible options include the brushed-stainless skidplate, dual 3D stabilizer kit with stainless-bodied stabilizers, eXtreme Ring differential cover protectors, and Torque Max SS traction bars.

Inset:
This winch can be operated with a handheld remote control.

On the frontispiece:
This full billet grille look costs only $200.

On the title pages:
Twenty-four-inch American Racing rims truly fill the wheel openings without giving this Ford a lifted look.

On the back cover:
Common hand tools, a full day, and moderate mechanical abilities are all that's required to bolt on this late-model Hemi supercharging system.

CONTENTS

629.2873
5418

ACKNOWLEDGMENTS

As with any publishing effort, putting a book together takes more than one person. Many of the technical and "how-to" articles within this book have been written by automotive journalists you may have been reading for years in the traditional newsstand magazines. Most of the writers are also photographers, and their work spans from straightforward tech stories to feature articles, event coverage, and strictly opinionated editorials.

We want to thank some of the writers who contributed to this compilation of automotive upgrades. These contributors include: Justin Adams, Cam Benty, Lynn Guthrie, Courtney Halowell, Jim Harmon, Chris Hemer, Bob McClurg, Brian McCormick, Trent Riddle, Dan Sanchez, and Rick Shandley.

You know, we also have to thank the shops. Without the automotive aftermarket retail shops who sell, and the skilled technicians who install, most everything you'll find in this book, it would be much more challenging to bring these images and explanations to the readers. We should also mention the editorial archive we raided at The Enthusiast Network, a six-year-old media powerhouse with consumer sites such as www.fordtruckworld.com, www.chevytruckworld.com, www.dieseltruckworld.com, www.dodgetruckworld.com, www.jeeperz.com, and www.off-roadworld.net.

INTRODUCTION

Thanks for considering *101 Performance Projects for Your Pickup and SUV*, and welcome. In order for any project to get started, you've got to count the cost. Whether you are building a weekend cabin, a family home, or a ground-up restoration of your favorite make and model pickup truck, you must wrap your head around what it'll take to make your visualization of the complete vehicle come true. You need to take inventory of the components you'll need, how much they cost, and how much you can afford. Then you've got to make the purchase and get all your ducks in a row before you can even think of starting—provided you have all the tools, skill level, and facility to engage and complete your project.

This book will give you ideas and general procedures for many of the hottest light pickup truck modifications in today's market. It doesn't matter if you have a street truck that you want to rig for off-road or an off-road truck you want to build a little larger than life.

And for the enthusiast who owns a two-wheel-drive street truck, this book should give you plenty of ideas. Whether you own a gasoline- or diesel-powered hauler, power upgrades are straightforward and within most any skill level to install. You may want to keep things simple and do one project at a time, or you can string several projects together and completely change the look of your truck.

A little tip for you to consider: Try to determine whether or not you have the understanding, tools, and skill level to perform an installation yourself. If you have the skill to do the install, then any cost savings you enjoy by doing it yourself will be worth the effort. However, many shops both sell the upgrades you want and offer to do the installation in a packaged deal. All routes are worth considering, but not all routes lead to the same result.

Have a blast.
—Rick Shandley

SAFETY

It doesn't matter how minor the procedure you are working on, when you burn your hand or catch a metal chip in your eye, your Saturday is shot. By getting into the habit of working safely, you take the same precautions professional mechanics and fabricators take. The goal is to reduce or eliminate the chance of injury.

Hand Protection: Leather work gloves will protect your hands under most automotive work conditions, where the potential for bloody knuckles or burnt fingers is high. Even cloth work gloves offer a measure of protection over bare skin. But modern developments in design have brought work gloves to a new level in terms of protection and dexterity. Modern multi-fabric mechanics' gloves offer you protection from abrasion and heat, but they also allow you to handle small objects and let your fingers work with nimbleness close to that of your bare fingers. You can even get gloves with lighting built in to illuminate your work. Have gloves in your truck and with your tool kit.

Eye Protection: It only takes one time to learn this lesson. You might be shaking up a can of WD-40 and not notice the red nozzle pointing straight at your face when you push the spray button. Wearing safety goggles is a good habit to get into for countless reasons, but the point of wearing them whenever you work on or under your vehicle is for them to take the blow before your eyes do. Working under your truck and messing with your driveshaft can dislodge caked-on grime right into your eyes. Sometimes a speck of dirt in your eye is only an inconvenience, other times it could mean a scratched cornea and a trip to the emergency room. For readers who already know the value of eye protection, carry on. For people just starting out in pursuit of do-it-yourself truck building, take heed.

Jack Stands: For any work you plan that requires your truck's wheels to be off the ground, using sturdy jack stands is mandatory. You should own these safety items, and always make sure they are not bent or damaged in any way. Once you get your truck off the ground using a floor jack or bottle jack, you must place a jack stand—set to the proper height—directly under the frame of the vehicle closest to your work area. If you are upgrading your brake rotors, you can use two jack stands for the rear of the truck while it's off the ground; you will put wheel chocks behind the front tires still on the ground to prevent the truck from rolling back. When all four wheels are off the ground, you need four jack stands. Never rely on a floor jack or bottle jack to secure your truck off the ground while you are working under it.

Buddy System: Many projects will require an extra set of hands to help you hold a piece of hardware in place while you drill holes or get the first bolt started. You can usually find a friend to help measure and hold a component while you work on it. However, when you are taking on a project dealing with heavy components and the underside of your vehicle, it's our recommendation you arrange for a friend to work with you throughout the duration of the project. Trying to wrestle a transmission by yourself—with limited experience and even with a transmission stand—can be dangerous. Suspension components can be heavy and awkward, so evaluate your need for a second person while you evaluate the complexity of the project you are considering.

TOOLS FOR TRUCKS

It's probably safe to say most people who are inclined to work on their own vehicles already have a decent set of standard tools. Even so, it is always beneficial to review the types of tools you might need for the range of projects in this book.

Socket Set: A good complete set of ¾-inch and ¼-inch (or metric equivalent) sockets and socket drives are invaluable for the widest range of truck projects, maintenance, and repair. If you've been working with mechanical hand tools for years, by now you can look at a bolt head and instantly determine what size of socket or wrench to use on it. If you are new to tackling your own truck projects, you will eventually be able to determine the correct size socket by looking at the shape and size of the bolt you need to deal with. Sockets and drives are likely to be your primary go-to tools for most projects dealing with installation of suspension components, performance hardware, and drivetrain procedures.

Torque Wrench: Many engine, drivetrain, and suspension fasteners require specified torque values for proper installation and safety. Certain structural components are engineered to work correctly with consistent torque on each bolt holding the component in place. For example, if you change your cast-iron exhaust manifolds to stainless-steel headers, you will tighten the new headers to a torque value designed to maintain the seal and hold them in place so they don't vibrate loose. Learn to use your torque wrench and rely on it for accuracy.

Open-End Wrench Set: A small set of open-end wrenches are needed for times when you can't get a socket on a bolt because lack of space or the angle makes it difficult. A set ranging in size from ¾ inch down to ⁵⁄₁₆ inch (or metric equivalent) will work for most applications. When you need a wrench outside this range, that's when you invest in a couple more sizes. You can choose traditional open-end wrenches or ratcheting-type wrenches with one ratchet-driven closed end and an open end of the same size.

Pliers: Normally, three sizes of all-purpose pliers will serve you well for most applications: large, medium, and small. If you're starting out, invest in a medium-size pair of slip-joint pliers that can adjust from a small bite to a larger bite. Needle-nose, wire cutters, wide jaw, and any number of different purpose pliers will be useful at some point. Investing in a set of different purpose pliers is great if you can justify it. Often, when you are planning a project, you'll have an idea of the tools you'll need by reading the instructions for the components you are going to install. Many people build up their tool inventory one or two items at a time. You can buy packaged kits of various pliers; this will afford you a range of pliers designed for different purposes.

Screwdrivers: High-quality screwdrivers are economical to purchase as complete sets. You can find a range of screwdriver head designs like flathead and Phillips head in all sizes from $30 to $130.

Nut Drivers: Nut drivers are tools you'll need when you work on your electrical system, intake system, and fuel injection system. Nut drivers are designed to deal with small nut heads where the fasteners are not torqued to any specifications but are hand tight and usually found in tight quarters. Nut head sizes will range from ³⁄₁₆ to ⁹⁄₁₆ inch (or metric equivalent from 5 through 14 millimeters). You can choose nut drivers with ratchet handles and traditional fixed-shank nut drivers.

Hex Keys and Torx-Head Wrenches: Hex keys and Torx-head wrenches will be an asset when you are dealing with small fasteners in hard-to-reach locations. Hex-head and Torx-head screws and bolts are fasteners with multi-sided wrench pockets sunk into the bolt head or screw head. Hex-head bolt applications such as header bolts are used when the component to be secured is hard to reach with traditional sockets, or the component to be fastened needs to be flush on top with no bolt heads protruding from the surface.

Hammers and Mallets: Hammers are the universal persuasion tool. For automotive use, a ball peen metal-headed hammer is a good one to start with. However, you will find many uses for weighted rubber-head mallets. Rubber mallets will not mar most automotive metal surfaces while the component that needs to be removed is still coaxed away from the rust, corrosion, metal-to-metal torque, or seal it is bound by. For example, if you plan on upgrading your brake rotors from factory to an aftermarket style of brake rotors, you may have to take a couple hefty swings with a mallet to the back side of the rear brake rotor to dislodge it from years of corrosion buildup. Sometimes there is no way to finesse a piece of hardware from its position. You'll have to use some force, and a couple different sized

hammers and mallets will help you in a prudent use of force.

Measuring Tools: A flat-steel 12-inch ruler will serve you well in most cases when you need to accurately measure for a project. For longer measurements, a 25-foot or less steel tape measure will be an asset. Projects such as installing side steps on your truck will require you to measure across several yards of truck frame to determine where to drill holes for mounting. The old rule of thumb is to measure twice and cut (or drill) once.

Power Tools: Drilling holes and cutting sections from factory components to provide clearance for mount points will require power. Whether you choose to rent or own certain power tools, you must consider whether to go with electric power or compressed-air power. If you plan on doing lots of projects, an air compressor is a good place to start. With an air compressor, you have the advantage of an air hose (with air nozzle attachment) to clean your work area, fill up your tires, and run the gamut of automotive devices used by professionals for everything from fasteners to cutters.

Some tool manufacturers, such as Husky and Sears Craftsman, offer a lifetime warranty on the socket drives, sockets, and hand tools. You can invest as much or as little as your budget and enthusiasm will permit. For the sake of consistency, building your tool inventory through a single tool manufacturer's product line is a good idea but not mandatory. Keep in mind there will be times, even when it comes to the need for 1-inch-plus sized sockets and the correct driver, you can always rent a tool. In fact, unless you find your interest leaning toward a professional career, many of the gear-pullers, brake tools, and specialty tools will be more economical to rent as you need them.

HOW TO USE THIS BOOK

While it'd be ideal to read this book from cover to cover, we all know that our busy schedules will prevent that. So, the sections cover groupings of projects based on your truck or SUV's different systems. For the most part, the easier projects are listed at the beginning of the section. These projects offer novice mechanics an opportunity to get comfortable wrenching. To assist you in planning for a project, each one begins with an easy-to-read listing of information to give you an idea of what challenges you may face. The listed items are:

Time: Many projects can be finished in a couple of hours; others can take days. Wouldn't you like to know in advance? If you're a complete novice, you might want to factor in additional time. Old pros will probably breeze through some projects in significantly less time.

Tools: Although the majority of projects can be completed with the basic mechanic's tools listed in this section, each project requires a different subset of those tools listed here. Any special tools required will also be noted. You should still check your factory manual to make sure that your truck doesn't require a tool specific to it. Use this listing to justify forays into your local tool store.

Talent: While trucks and SUVs can vary from model to model, projects can be categorized into a broad range of difficulty. Each additional * marks an increased level of difficulty.

* This is a project that a novice could complete.
** Lets a novice know that a little help may be needed. A fair amount

of mechanical knowledge and comfort with complex assemblies would be helpful.
*** Implies that you are well versed in wrenching. Perhaps you've even had some training. A project at this level could be attempted with the assistance of a more experienced mechanic.
**** Marks a job best left to the pros, but those who aspire to professional tuner status could press ahead.

Applicable Years: Select projects apply to only certain makes or model years.

Tab: The approximate cost for components required for the project.

Tinware: The listing of parts required to perform the modification. However, you should still check your factory manual to ensure that your truck doesn't require anything special.

Tip: Knowledge comes from experience. The tip will have some information to make the project easier, keep you from overlooking a little detail, or give you information about how the modification may affect your truck. You won't find this information in your factory manual.

Performance Gain: What to expect from your time, money, and effort.

Complementary Project: This listing will point to other projects that could help you get even more out of the current project, including other projects to tackle while you have certain parts and systems exposed. Again, you won't find this information in your factory manual.

ENGINE

For Vortec applications, Smeding Performance uses all new castings and components to assemble the company's own heads. These heads feature screw in studs and stainless steel valves. Non-Vortec small-blocks can be had for cast-iron heads or Edelbrock Performer heads.

PROJECT 1 INCREASE AIRFLOW

TIME: 45 minutes

TOOLS: Small/medium socket set, screwdriver set, hex-head wrenches

TALENT: ★

APPLICABLE YEARS: Airaid manufactures intake systems for most popular late-model vehicles

TAB: Approximate costs are $100–$400 depending on your specific vehicle

TINWARE: Gear grease, gear oil, replacement gaskets

TIP: You can do it!

PERFORMANCE GAIN:
You'll notice a smoother throttle response in general driving conditions, and can expect an increase of about 10–18 horsepower.

COMPLEMENTARY PROJECT:
When you increase the volume of air, your intake system can pull in an aftermarket exhaust system, starting with a set of headers, which will help move the spent gases out quicker.

For easier access to the throttle body, remove the stock engine cover. Only one 10mm bolt holds it in place. The next step is to loosen the clamp that holds the mass air meter to the factory air box. With the engine cover out of the way, it's easier to access the coupler that holds the intake tube to the throttle body to loosen the clamp.

The factory intake tube has a support pin assembly that's attached to a bracket on the upper radiator hose. A screwdriver will separate the pin from the bracket. With the clamps loose, the factory intake tube, complete with the mass air meter, can be removed.

When it comes to engines, there is no question that better breathing means more horsepower and torque. More air in and more air out equals improved horsepower and torque. In order to fully understand this philosophy, you have to get down to basics.

First and foremost, an engine is essentially a giant air pump. The up and down motion of pistons moves a specific volume of air through the engine. The quantity of air depends on a lot of factors including the displacement of the engine, the size of the intake system, the camshaft configuration, and the efficiency of the exhaust side of the power plant.

On a typical four-stroke engine, the atomized fuel mixture is drawn into the cylinder past the open intake valve by the downward motion of the piston. As the piston moves upward, the air/fuel mixture is compressed and ignited. The force of the explosion pushes the piston downward. This is considered the power stroke. On the piston's return upward, the burned gases are pushed out through the open exhaust valve, and the process begins again.

But where's the additional power in this equation? By improving the efficiency of the engine in any one of the critical areas (intake, valve timing camshaft, ignition, exhaust),

you can make more power. For the purpose of this discussion, we will focus on the intake side of the engine.

Most manufacturers face quite a challenge when it comes to designing intake systems for today's trucks. First off, they have to fit the platform (model). More important, the intake system also has to thoroughly filter the engine's incoming air. In terms of noise, the intake system has to be somewhat quiet. The end result is what's found on today's trucks. Does it work? Yes. Is there room for improvement? There is always room for improvement.

On the stock intake system, the main airflow restrictions are usually the design of the intake box itself, the actual air inlet where the box meets either the inner fender or the radiator bulkhead, and the factory paper-style filter inside the box.

The easiest upgrade to any intake system is to simply change the filter from the original paper element to a high-flow-style filter. To extract the optimal performance from an engine, though, the next step to better breathing is to change out the

Because the mass air meter will be reattached to the new intake, it is separated from the factory accordion hose and the air box. The factory couple on the air meter will be reused.

With the ducting and mass air meter disconnected, the factory air box can be removed. The mounting plate that holds the factory air box is held in place by five 10mm bolts.

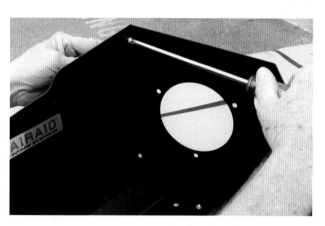

Remove the bolts and the box simply lifts out.

The next step is to assemble the intake's cold air dam as per the instructions using the enclosed hardware from the kit. Once the cool air dam is assembled, the 6-inch filter adapter is added.

The completed CAD assembly is gently placed where the factory air box was located. The box is bolted down using the supplied bolts and washers.

To ensure a proper seal at the throttle body, Airaid included a factory GM seal with the kit. The seal attaches to the kit's modular intake tube.

The mass air meter is attached to the back of the intake using the original factory coupler.

The Airaid modular intake tube attaches to the mass air meter with the supplied silicone coupler.

With the tube in place, all the connections are tightened. One of the final steps of the install is to add the Airaid premium high-flow air filter.

The finishing touch is the addition of the weather strip, which forms the seal between the cool air dam and the hood of the truck. You can also add the weather strip before you install the box in the vehicle.

complete air box for an aftermarket intake system.

Because the stock air box and the air box lid itself on most trucks are considered major restrictions, removing them and replacing the assembly with a high-flow air intake usually generates big improvements in not only horsepower and torque, but also throttle response.

We wanted to see this theory work in practice, so we decided to contact the Airaid Filter Company to help demonstrate how more power is made by improving the airflow on a typical truck intake system.

Airaid decided to demonstrate the performance benefits of a high-flow intake with one of its bolt-on air intake systems. We decided on one for the late-model GM trucks, as Airaid claims it yields an additional 18 rear-wheel horsepower. The system uses a computer-designed Cool Air Dam (CAD) housing that replaces the restrictive factory air box for maximum airflow. The heart of the CAD system is Airaid's Premium SynthaFlow air filter, which not only outflows the stock element, but it consistently filters dirt down to 2–3 microns in size.

The average driveway mechanic can accomplish installation of the smog-legal, bolt-on system in less than an hour. The late-model GM system is also offered with an Airaid modular intake tube for enthusiasts wanting a smooth tube to replace the factory "accordion" tube that directs air to the throttle body.

The following photos highlight a typical installation. The install was performed on a 2004 Chevrolet Avalanche fitted with the 5.3-liter V-8. The Airaid intake system fits all GM V-8s

Here's what the finished install looks like. The Airaid system flows a lot more air than stock and is good for about 18 additional rear-wheel horsepower.

including the 4.8-, 5.3-, and 6.0-liter power plants. The end result of this install was better breathing for the engine, which dramatically improved throttle response and power.

PROJECT 2 INSTANT THROTTLE-RESPONSE IGNITION

 TIME: Four hours

 TOOLS: Medium socket set, screwdriver set

 TALENT: ★ to ★★

 APPLICABLE YEARS: All years—automatic and manual transmissions

 TAB: $300

 TINWARE: Surgical gloves, flashlight, cover to protect car finish, gear grease

 TIP: Heed the tips and cautions presented in photo captions to keep you on the right track.

 PERFORMANCE GAIN:
Improvement in power, instant throttle response, and improved low-end torque

COMPLEMENTARY PROJECT:
Consider upgrading or replacing spark plugs and spark plug wires.

The engine bay of this truck is clean and tidy, however, there was no getting away from a big wiring loom and that unsightly coil mounted beside the gray distributor.

Although this side of the engine is fairly clean, the unsightly electronic control module is still mounted on to the firewall on the lower left. It soon will be removed, as it will no longer be necessary.

Would you put an HEI distributor in your Ford? Not many Ford owners would, but you can't beat the compact system that has been in GM trucks for many years. However, with a Davis Unified Ignition system (DUI), available from Performance Distributors, you can experience an improvement in power, instant throttle response, and improved low-end torque.

Designed as a simple remove-and-replace operation, Ford owners can now toss their coil, ignition module, and all the wires necessary to connect these items to the stock distributor. The DUI distributor features a coil-mounted cap and an internally mounted module. Wiring the unit requires just one 12-volt power feed, and it is ready to run. However, the distributor is wired for an optional tachometer feed. DUI eliminates all of the messy wiring found on stock Ford electronic ignition systems and really cleans up your engine compartment, especially with the distributor being positioned at the front of Ford engines.

The DUI distributor is available in either the Street/Strip version, up to 7,000 rpm, or the Racing version, which will supply spark up to 9,000 rpm. Both units are designed to deliver a more powerful ignition spark to plugs now gapped at .055 inch, generally .020 more gap than stock. This is the key to generating a more powerful spark and ignition of the fuel/air mixture. DUI's Dyna-Module is designed with more dwell time, thus producing a hotter spark. No ballast resistor is used as it is on stock Ford systems and many other aftermarket applications. Use of a ballast resistor reduces voltage, thus reducing spark. DUI allows full voltage into the ignition system, providing you with a better, cleaner spark, thus generating enhanced engine performance.

Each DUI distributor is custom curved on a distributor machine designed to complement the specs of your Ford motor and your performance demands. This process produces a super smooth curve, which will eliminate engine-damaging detonation while providing instant throttle response.

An added bonus is the custom appearance of the DUI distributor, which will enhance the engine bay of your Ford truck, as it is a work of craftsmanship. Uniquely designed, replacement parts are easy to find and install. High Energy Ignition (HEI) replacement parts will fit this DUI distributor. Built for extended life and durability, the DUI is polished and lubed during assembly, and it features both an upper and lower bushing, unlike the stock Ford distributors with only one bushing!

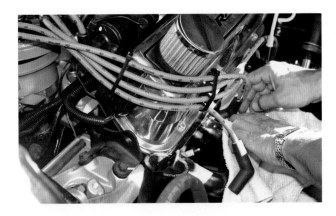

Be extra careful to ensure the stock wires are in fact installed according to proper engine timing before removing them.

Ford distributors come in several configurations, this one being relatively new. Now remove the cap and stock plug wires.

Say *adios* to the stock coil. Not only is it unsightly, but this will eliminate the need for several wires and the coil wire to the distributor as well. This will make a major under-the-hood improvement in appearance.

This is the original power feed to the stock Ford distributor. Remember the size of this plug and the change to come.

The key to ensuring the proper installation of the new DUI distributor starts here. Rotate the engine until the harmonic balancer timing mark is on top dead center (TDC). Next, locate the number one plug wire on the distributor cap, then mark this location on to the cap and intake manifold—before removing the stock distributor!

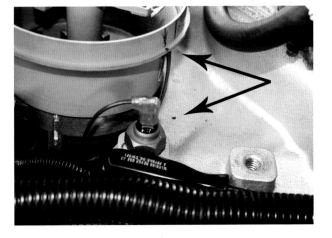

Take note of two items in this photo. First are the marks on the distributor and intake manifold indicating the location of the rotor pointing to the number one spark plug wire and the corresponding mark on the manifold. Also, we made sure the intake manifold water temperature–sending unit would clear the new distributor. It did!

DUI manufactures an HEI distributor for practically all Ford applications from the inline six to the popular 221-289-302 series, the Cleveland and Windsor series, and 330s through the 428 big blocks, even the 302 roller cam series. Performance Distributors has a full line of DUI distributors for all domestic and popular import cars and trucks from Chevy to VW as well. So, toss those unnecessary components and move into the new world of electronic distributors . . . designed specifically for your Ford!

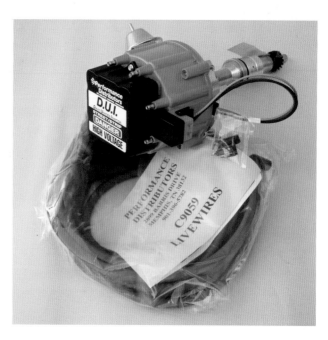

Out goes the stock distributor. Nice item to sell on Ebay.

Here is a close-up look at the DUI distributor with the coil-mounted blue cap and 135 degree high-temp covered blue Live Wires.

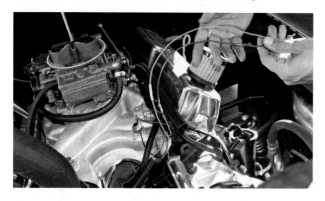

Tech tip here is to stuff a rag into the distributor hole while you modify the wiring harness, eliminating the big plug and extending the red and green wires, which will be the power and tachometer feeds.

The cap was removed to simplify the installation of the new DUI/HEI distributor. Cap is retained by spring-loaded L-fasteners.

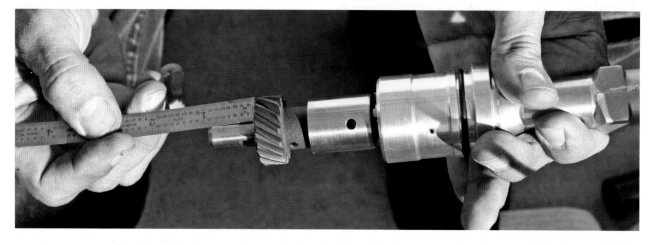

Installation tip is to ensure the distributor shaft is no longer than the distributor that was removed from your engine. It must be long enough to drive the oil pump but short enough to ensure the distributor seats all the way into the engine block. This unit measured the same as stock!

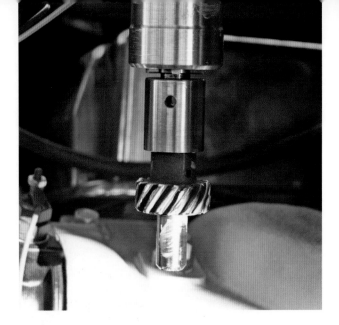

The plugs simply snap into the distributor receptacle. The distributor was installed with the rotor pointing exactly at the mark on the intake manifold indicating the location of the number one plug wire.

Light grease was then applied to the gear drive before installation.

The red and green wires are then fit with wire ends and plugs that are compatible with the DUI distributor.

Ah, those lovely, fat Live Wires were then installed, number one first then the firing order rotation. Live Wires are supplied cut to length and numbered and are a very functional, attractive addition to the installation. This truck owner had ordered this distributor with a mild-street/street curve to ensure full engine performance while eliminating engine detonation from using pump fuel. Timing was set to Performance Distributors specifications.

Billet aluminum wire looms from Performance Distributors were added to properly route the Live Wires over the valve covers. The truck owner reported his 351 V-8 Ford now starts quickly and has enhanced throttle response and improved fuel economy! It has also become a topic of discussion with his fellow Pickups Limited, OC truck club. After all, his is the first HEI-fired truck.

PROJECT 3 | 25 HORSEPOWER FROM A SIX-SHOOTER

TIME: Three hours

TOOLS: Full socket set, screwdriver set, torque wrench, Loktite

TALENT: ★★★

APPLICABLE YEARS: Chevy small and big block

TAB: $2,500

TINWARE: Replacement gaskets, masking tape to cover cylinder valley

TIP: If you have a small-block, carbureted, Chevy motor, this is a killer cool project that makes about 25 horsepower.

PERFORMANCE GAIN:
As mentioned, an increase of about 25 horsepower

COMPLEMENTARY PROJECT:
A new set of billet aluminum valve covers would add some pop to the already eye-catching good looks of the intake.

AFR 185 cylinder heads work with hydraulic lifters. Intake valve lift is .44 inch; exhaust is .454 inch. Also notice the enormous secondary bore size on the old cast-iron intake manifold.

They call it the Gladiator. At Westech Performance Group in Mira Loma, California, a dynamometer shop with guys who know what makes an engine scream, the Gladiator is a small-block Chevy motor of the cubic-inch genre. It's a 350 cid drilled .30 inch over, and it has been a test-mule motor since the mid-1990s with hundreds of pulls on the engine dyno. The engine has so many different combinations of cams, manifolds, carburetors, and heads that if it weren't documented accurately, it would be impossible to remember the list of parts making up the machine. You name it and it has likely been bolted on to this iron warrior and tested in increments of 500 rpm until it reached that apex called redline.

Carbureted engines continue to hold captive a huge number of automotive enthusiasts and competition-minded people who build and run V-8s from the analog generation. That's the generation where computers were unsophisticated, and muscle motors screeched like banshees, giddy with intoxicating quantities of high-grade fuel.

If you are planning on building a muscle motor for your truck or SUV, whether you live in a state that allows horsy motors on the street or you intend to tow your toy to a safe playground, you can take some ideas from the Gladiator platform. Then again, if you already have a carbureted small-block

Chevy in your rig, it may already have the kind of internal hardware that measures 300–375 horsepower at the flywheel. In any case, we attempted to measure the power increase by swapping a factory iron manifold and the old-style GM Quadra Jet carburetor with a Barry Grant six-shooter manifold. This manifold has three two-barrel carburetors designed to progressively deliver all the fuel your motor needs and maintain good everyday drivability.

In this session on the engine dyno, we ran a baseline test on the Gladiator with the factory manifold and Quadra Jet carburetor. Then we bolted on the Barry Grant six-shooter triple carburetor and manifold, and wound up the Gladiator past 6,100 rpm for a few consistent pulls on the engine dyno. What we discovered was a solid 25 horsepower increase and 18.5 lb-ft torque gains. Your specific Chevy small-block build might lie on any point of the modification continuum from just headers and an RV cam to sick and twisted. The Gladiator is somewhere in the middle and is ranked in the 400 horsepower range.

The Gladiator is a 355-cid motor with AFR aluminum cylinder heads (185cc bench flow; D ports) with a 10.1:1 compression ratio. A Comp Cams XE256H hydraulic camshaft—.44-inch intake lift; .212-inch intake duration—

The Quadrajet used to be a state-of-the-art fuel delivery system. Even on this motor, the Q-jet pulled its weight by getting fuel into the motor and showing respectable numbers.

Three two-barrel carburetors add up to about 650 cfm and running jet sizes 68/78. At partial throttle, the middle carburetor is in use. At half throttle and beyond, as more throttle is demanded, the linkage mechanism progressively opens up all three carburetors at the same time until full throttle is reached.

As tested on the Gladiator, this Q-jet delivered 354.6 horsepower at 6,100 rpm and 397.6 lb-ft of torque. The average production at 4,050 rpm was 278.8 horsepower and 365.4 lb-ft of torque.

As you can see, the six-shooter is a serious and well-finished piece of hardware. The fuel rail needs to be connected, and this motor will be ready to fire up.

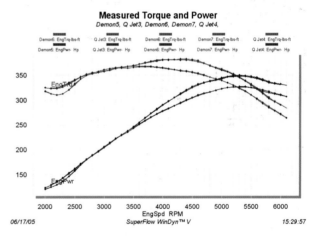

Measured Torque and Power
Demon5, Q Jet3, Demon6, Demon7, Q Jet4,

Left: At 6,100 rpm, the Gladiator produced 379.5 horsepower and 416 lb-ft of torque. The average output at 4,100 rpm was 296.6 horsepower and 382.1 lb-ft of torque. **Right**: Red denotes the torque curve and blue represents engine power. The Six-Shooter torque and power curve is at the top of each comparison. Note how big the torque increase is at the very bottom of the rpm range.

works with Comp Cams 1.5:1 ratio rocker arms, and AFR valve springs. Hooker headers with 1.75-inch diameter tubing routed the flames, and MSD ignition system started the fire. This setup ran on pump gas and, as close as is practical, presented the environment where the enthusiast can get a fairly accurate impression of performance increase with just a naturally aspirated change in carburetion.

Yes, the Quadra Jet is a mechanism that an entire generation of our youth has never heard of before. Bear in mind the Quadra Jet was the last carbureted induction system before General Motors and the field of automotive manufacturers switched entirely over to fuel injection systems. That being said, the old 350-cid Chevy small-block motor is perhaps the single most-popular platform for enthusiasts to build upon and therefore is a likely platform that you will start with, or have already. If so, this Barry Grant system is something to consider. Enter the Gladiator, packing a six-shooter.

PROJECT 4 TURBOCHARGE YOUR TRUCK

TIME: Eight hours

TOOLS: Full socket set, screwdriver set, torque wrench, appropriate jack, jack stands, Sawzall, die-cut, or metal cutting tool

TALENT: ★★

APPLICABLE YEARS: Late-model GM and Dodge Ram. Ford F-150 is in the works and a universal kit will be available.

TAB: $2,800

TINWARE: A new PCM will come with your turbocharger kit. Be aware that you will send your factory PCM back to Nelson Performance in exchange.

TIP: If you can get a friend to lend a hand, this project will go smoother.

PERFORMANCE GAIN:
146 horsepower increase and a gain of 124 lb-ft of torque

COMPLEMENTARY PROJECT:
For increased eye appeal, consider installing a stainless-steel exhaust system along with this project.

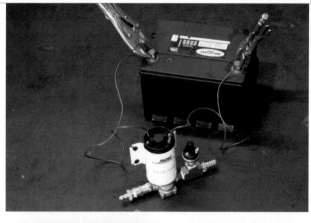

Above: Because oil is essential to the operation of the turbo, it made sense to test the STS-provided oil pump to ensure that it is working properly.

Left: The first step was to completely remove the Suburban's air intake system. This included the inlet tube, air filter box, and clamps.

If you could listen in on the conversations of truck enthusiasts as they are discussing ways to get big horsepower, you would more than likely find out which supercharger and nitrous system they are contemplating to add to their trucks. Rarely do you hear someone talking about turbocharging, as it is mainly thought to be used for small-displacement engines such as those found in sport compact cars.

In the past, turbocharging V-8 engines meant direct combat with detonation due to poor fuel, but with modern fuel injection systems and computer management, it is possible to add a turbo to your late-model V-8. We were recently introduced to the STS Turbo System, which surprisingly is not as complicated a system as we would have thought it would be. STS devised a simple kit that mounts the turbo back where the muffler should be and uses the factory exhaust to spool the turbo. The pressurized intake tubing intercools the air charge as it makes its way back up the chassis of the truck and goes up into the engine's throttle body.

This may sound like the STS system has a lot of turbo lag, but according to Rick Squires, who handles the research and development of the system, the exhaust tube pressurizes in a mere fraction of a second and the pressure is consistent. This means that the boost comes on quick and is typically fully on by 3,000 rpm in first gear and as soon as 2,000 rpm in higher gears. Squires explained that mounting the turbo at the rear of the vehicle actually allows the exhaust gas to cool a bit, resulting in denser gases to drive the turbine more efficiently and resulting in less heat under the hood. Because the turbo is not using any horsepower from the engine's crankshaft, it is more efficient, thus the reason why substantially more horsepower can be created from smaller amounts of boost.

This system typically produces five to seven pounds of boost and is enough to develop 100-plus extra horsepower and torque on most late-model Chevrolet V-8 engines. With a turbo upgrade, it will generate up to 15 pounds of boost. Squires says the system is simple to install as it is essentially like installing a new cat-back exhaust system on your truck or SUV. Only factory hangers and bolts are used, and the turbo is oiled via a supplied fitting that attaches to a high-pressure area of the engine block and the oil is returned via a frame-mounted electric oil pump. The return line simply attaches to an STS-supplied oil filler cap that has a quick-disconnect fitting attached to the top of it so no drilling of the oil pan is necessary.

A 90 degree high-temperature elbow is installed to the throttle body of the 5.3-liter V-8. This will receive the intake tube from the turbo. STS supplies a new oil filler cap that has a 90 degree fitting for the oil return line. This makes it very easy to install and is a simple way to feed oil back into the engine.

The turbo and assembly are clamped together and bolted to the inlet tubes. It is best to do this on a workbench, as the unit will be installed as a complete assembly. A waste gate is also part of the STS turbo system, and it, too, is put together with the proper line fittings.

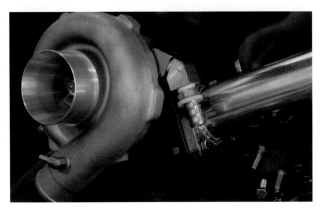

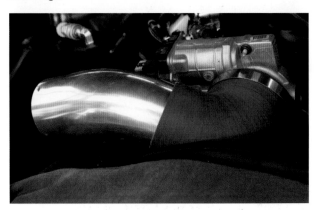

Both the oil inlet and return fittings are also installed on to the turbo. These are brass high-pressure hose fittings that are easy to work with. Most of the work is done under the vehicle, so it is lifted on a hoist. The factory muffler is cut off from the head pipe and removed along with the tailpipe. The wiring to the oil pump is routed from the vehicle's fuse box, where a 12-volt ignition source is used. The wiring harness also has a relay and a connection to the ground. These are attached to the firewall of the vehicle.

There are several pieces of tubing that make up the intake side that is pressurized from the turbo. Part of this includes mounting the factory MAF sensor, which is done with two silicone sleeves and clamps. There's a high-pressure area on the engine block where oil is taken to lubricate and cool the turbo. The fittings are included in the kit as is the proper length of hose.

Because the turbo sits at the rear of the truck, it makes sense to install portions of the inlet at the turbo as well as at the engine's throttle body. Once the turbo assembly and tubing are bolted together, the assembly can be lifted into position under the chassis. The rest of the air inlet tubing is clamped into place and runs alongside the driveshaft. The oil pump and safety switch are placed on a bracket and mounted alongside the chassis. Once the unit is mounted, the inlet and outlet hoses are attached to the pump. The wiring and hoses are carefully routed under the frame, making sure they stay away from the exhaust tubes. Other connectors on the wiring harness are attached following the instructions. From under the vehicle, the waste gate and tubing are installed making sure there's plenty of clearance.

Here you can see how the steel-braided hoses are attached to the inlet of the turbo.

A cotton-gauze air filter is used at the turbo inlet to gather cool air from under the vehicle.

Left: Because the turbo is powered by the engine's exhaust, it is attached to the down pipe of the factory system. STS uses a body mount bolt to support some of the turbo's inlet and outlet tubing.
Right: The air inlet tubing is then pieced together to meet up with the tubing under the vehicle reaching the turbo.

The factory PCM is removed from the vehicle and the harness is plugged into the tuned PCM. The old unit is then sent back to STS.

Once everything is clamped together, the engine is started and checked for any leaks.

With the unit installed, we achieved some impressive results. In this case, six pounds of boost yielded a corrected horsepower of 361.7 horsepower at 5093 rpms and 403.2 lb-ft of torque at 4,042 rpms at the rear wheels.

STS demonstrated an installation of the system on to a 2003 Chevrolet Suburban equipped with a 5.3-liter V-8. Most of the work involves bolting together the turbo assembly, which is done on a workbench. But the installation was much simpler than most supercharger installations. The only cutting that was required was a portion of the exhaust system to remove the muffler and rear tailpipe section. In addition, the STS kit supplies a new tuned PCM from Nelson Performance that replaces your factory unit. The customer simply sends his unit back to Nelson Performance as a core.

There is some wiring involved; the STS wiring harness attaches from the oil pump to the battery connections and to the 12-volt fuel pump relay wire in the factory fuse box. The system also comes with an alarm system in case of an oil delivery problem. Furthermore, if you wondered where the fresh air for the intake system comes from, it is the actual turbo inlet. STS supplies a high-flow cotton-gauze filter that fits over the intake side of the turbo, allowing it to take in cold air from under the vehicle's chassis.

So how's the performance? In our situation, the Suburban

was placed on the dyno and yielded an extra 146 horsepower and 124 lb-ft of torque from six pounds of boost. Sound too good to be true? We have the independent dyno results from Westech Performance Group in Mira Loma, California, which performed the tests on the company's Superflow chassis dyno.

The baseline runs on the Suburban netted 215 horsepower and 278.7 lb-ft of torque to the rear wheels. After the system was installed, the corrected horsepower jumped to 361.7 horsepower and 403.2 lb-ft of torque. The system with the tuned PCM runs about $3,995 (turbo system) and $599 (Nelson PCM 03 and up; 99-02 $499) and comes with everything you need to install within a matter of hours. Keep in mind that the system uses the factory fuel injectors and fuel pump, keeping the overall price of the system low.

We were pleased with the Suburban kit, and although it may be a little more difficult to install on some dramatically lowered trucks, the system does what it says it will do. STS also manufactures systems for full-size GM and Toyota trucks, and a Dodge Ram kit is soon to be released.

PROJECT 5 | INSTALL A SUPERCHARGER

 TIME: Eight to 10 hours

 TOOLS: Full metric socket set, screwdriver set, torque wrench, die cutter

 TALENT: ★★★

 APPLICABLE YEARS: Late-model Ford 5.4-liter V-8

 TAB: $3,500

 TINWARE: Fender cover, step stool

 TIP: Roush instructions are precise and the packaged hardware is complete. Take your time and be certain you understand the process.

 PERFORMANCE GAIN:
More than 100 horsepower

COMPLEMENTARY PROJECT:
Upgrading the air intake system from the air box to throttle body would upgrade and complement the supercharger install.

Unplug powertrain control module (PCM), remove, and prepare the FedEx package that comes with the kit. Do this right off the bat and get it under way first thing. Remove entire air box assembly. Remove throttle body. Remove radiator core-support cover. Unbolt and pull out the fan shroud and fan assembly. Unburden the serpentine belt and remove. Remove alternator.

Disconnect fuel rail lines from both sides of the plastic intake manifold. Disconnect all hoses and remove aluminum cross-over pipe, also referred to as a coolant bridge. Unbolt intake manifold. Slide it forward and tilt up to disengage brake booster hose attached on the bottom of the driver's side. Remove intake manifold. Cover intake head ports with masking tape to keep any loose debris from falling into the motor. Remove the two 15mm nuts attaching radio capacitors to the front cover of each cylinder head. You will trim 31mm of material away from the fan shroud to accommodate shifting the fan forward 31mm. Sandpaper works great to smooth the rough edges. As installation begins, notice that you will be using genuine Ford components wherever appropriate. Install boost bypass solenoid and control bracket to the bottom of the new Roush aluminum intake manifold. With the Roush aluminum manifold right side up on your workbench, install the ACT sensor and vacuum port fittings to the manifold. You will redeploy the factory head gaskets using the nine new crush limiters (spacers) supplied with the kit. To provide clearance for the front of the supercharger, this adapter is supplied for the factory alternator. This is a simple step but an important one.

A s light pickup truck engines go, the Ford 5.4L V-8 does a good job striking the balance between fuel economy and pulling power. But the general feeling among folks who own or have driven the F-150 running a Triton 5.4L V-8 is that the motor responds best when you wake it up. The 24-valve single overhead cam (SOHC) V-8 puts out 300 horsepower at 5,000 rpm and delivers 365 lb-ft torque at 3,500 rpm running 9.8:1 compression on common 87-octane pump gas through about 330 cubic inches of displacement.

Three hundred horsepower at 5,000 rpm is about that point in time when you are merging on to the freeway from a rolling start at the top of the on-ramp. Even the torque, which is significant, is at its strongest at the upper end of each shift point where engine rpm is highest. Improving the performance without giving up the reliability engineered into the drivetrain can be approached through several methods. You could gain efficiencies and performance by freeing up the air intake and exhaust paths. You can run a performance computer program or change the chip to recalibrate the electronic language that controls engine performance. Or you can look into a bolt-on supercharger that delivers 80–110 horsepower, similar torque increases, and throttle response that shifts your brain in its bucket.

Ah, wouldn't it be nice if that kind of performance were

Left: You will splice in the Roush charger bypass solenoid into factory CMCV harness. **Right:** Remove masking tape from cylinder heads and do a complete inspection for loose debris. Install the Roush aluminum intake manifold. Follow the torque sequence pattern for bolting down the manifold.

Left: Install coolant bridge and all hardware components. **Right:** Two metal dowels from the hardware kit will tap into the manifold and act as guide pins for proper seating of the supercharger.

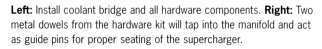

Left: Install fuel rails and related components such as the fuel injector wiring. Lay down the Roush charger gasket on to the intake manifold, over the dowels. Install the Roush supercharger on to the intake manifold. **Right:** Here's the Roush supercharger taking its rightful place in an otherwise nondescript 2006 Ford F-150. Imagine the sleeper effect on the Hemi Ram as you emolliate the rear tires at the stoplight.

Left: Hook up the throttle body. Install the alternator and reinstall first sheave serpentine belt. Here is the crank adapter to drive the supercharger pulley. Notice that it's a Ford part. **Right:** Front belt drive (FEAD) bridge is installed using the studs where the original radio capacitors were located. Install the supercharger drive belt. Reinstall the fan and fan shroud at same time. Notice the result of trimming the fan shroud to provide correct clearance. Install new intake system provided with the kit. A K&N filter charger is provided with your Roush supercharger. Replace radiator core cover. You're running super unleaded from here on out.

okay with the state you live in and, as a bonus, the performance modifications didn't void your new vehicle warranty? Well, that's where the Roush Performance group has endeavored to establish a competitive advantage in the automotive aftermarket for the Ford 5.4L V-8 with the ROUSHcharger, which features six PSI of boost in a nonintercooled supercharger. This hardware is legal in all 50 states and keeps the factory warrantee for the drivetrain intact.

If you have the confidence, tools, and know-how to tackle this install, it will take about eight hours to complete.

You will have to remove your factory electronic control module (ECM) and FedEx that to Roush on a 48-hour turnaround to reprogram the factory ECM to the performance tune compatible with the supercharger. For the record, we found this Roush Performance supercharger to be one of the most complete systems of any kind we have dealt with . . . ever. From the packaging of the hardware kit to the installation instructions, to the fit and clearance of every piece, this supercharger system is of the highest quality. Everything you'll need is included in this kit.

PROJECT 6 POWER UP WITH NITROUS

TIME: Seven hours

TOOLS: Full socket set, screwdriver set, volt meter

TALENT: ★★ If you can install a stereo system, you can handle this project.

APPLICABLE YEARS: Most model year vehicles can adapt to nitrous systems.

TAB: $950–$1,200

TINWARE: Nitrous gas fill, friend for a second pair of hands

TIP: Decide beforehand if you have the space to mount a 10-pound nitrous bottle in your vehicle. It's not cool to have a baby seat sitting next to a bottle of nitrous oxide.

PERFORMANCE GAIN:
Horsepower boost depends on size of nitrous dose and engine. This system added 70 horsepower.

COMPLEMENTARY PROJECT:
Upgrade intake system to increase air volume

We used universal kit number 05130NOS. A 10-pound nitrous bottle means 10 pounds of nitrous oxide gas fills the storage chamber. All together, the bottle weighs 24 pounds when full. The delivery lines, solenoids, valves, and hardware come complete with the system. First, choose the mounting place for the nitrous bottle. Mark holes for the short bracket to the rear. A unibit works great for drilling bracket-mounting holes through the carpet and floorboard of the vehicle.

With the help of a friend underneath the vehicle to hold the bolts, secure the brackets. Test-fit the bottle to determine where to drill the ⅜-inch hole for the nitrous line leading from the bottle up to the engine bay. After drilling the hole for the nitrous line, run the line through and prepare to mount the bottle. Note: You want to position the bottle so the valve handle faces up, is within reach to open and close, and the nose of the bottle is angled slightly toward the front of the vehicle. The rear of the bottle should have a slight kick toward the back of the vehicle. This positioning allows the liquid nitrous pickup tube in the bottle to deliver all available nitrous.

We've all heard the stories and seen the movie in 2001, *The Fast and the Furious*, where the moment of glory repeatedly revolves around flipping a switch and riveting the throttle to the firewall in a small sport compact. For others, that black Dodge Charger launch was the high point of the movie. Anyway, in that instant, the little aluminum motor is screaming for all it's worth and the drama builds to a peak as the driver prepares for liftoff when the dose of nitrous oxide hits the throttle body and the vehicle surges forward with the explosive force of 150-plus more horsepower. Instant horsepower, that's it . . . give it to me.

"*Fast and Furious* did more for the nitrous oxide performance industry than any multimillion-dollar advertising campaign could," says Mike Flynn, of Nitrous Supply in Huntington Beach, California. Demand for nitrous oxide systems grew rapidly as guys with every sort of vehicle went looking for a nitrous supply of their own.

"I need NOS," the hopeful stranger would tell the guy at the counter of the local speed shop. His expression vacuous, like the face of a bewildered pit bull, recovered, but forever stunned by the effects of distemper. Kind, but somehow . . . lost.

"Do you mean you need Nitrous Oxide Supply?" the counter guy would reply as helpfully as he could. "We are not them, but we have this."

"I need NOS," was all that the stranger could utter, his eyes glazed with the excitement of getting a little black switch of his own to flip. So the guys at the speed shops sold what they had to sell, and the liquid nitrous industry took off in a new upward growth direction.

As if socked by the hammer of a thousand anvils, scores of normally levelheaded consumers simply had to have their own supply of canned horsepower, and a few automotive aftermarket suppliers were standing on the shoreline when the groundswell of demand for nitrous oxide kits hit the market.

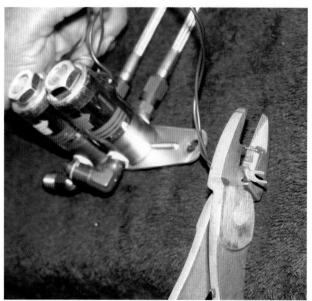

Left: With the bottle in its correct place, go ahead and bolt it down. Attach the nitrous line to the bottle. As you feed the nitrous line up toward the engine bay, loosely support with zip-ties. After you have all the hardware in place, and the nitrous line is in its correct position, tighten up the zip-ties to hold the line firmly. We were fortunate that the factory fuel line had a test port installed to aid in testing the fuel pressure in the system. Rather than tapping into the fuel line, we threaded on the fuel supply elbow and attached the AN fitting to run the fuel pickup over to the fuel solenoid. The nitrous line is on the left and routes up through the passenger side of the engine bay and over toward the driver's side where it will also tie into the nitrous solenoid and on into the throttle body. **Right:** Preassemble the fuel and nitrous solenoids on to the bracket and connect appropriate wiring before mounting the bracket.

Well, the demand for nitrous oxide systems is still pretty strong around the country, but the expectations and mystery surrounding the vaporous, injectable, and exciting power increases liquid nitrous oxide will provide are equally strong.

Just so you know: modern liquid nitrous oxide systems activate only under full-throttle conditions. When you jump out of the throttle, the nitrous stops. The amount of nitrous that feeds into the fuel delivery system depends on the size of the gas delivery jets, nozzle capacity, and bottle capacity. Normally, a full-throttle run is over in a handful of seconds; a full 10-pound bottle will last a bit more than a minute. But, oh what fun you'll have in that minute.

The liquid nitrous oxide used to fill automotive systems has a trace amount of sulphur-dioxide in it that renders one's nostrils inflamed and sets one's lungs on fire should one try to ingest it as if it were dental-grade laughing gas. The only laughs you're going to get with this stuff are when you blow the doors off a Porsche Boxster on a hole shot at the traffic light with your sleeper.com daily driver. But you will get that laugh. Imagine the look on the dentist's face when—having leased the Boxster six months ago, he was just now finding the time and feeling confident enough to take on a few lesser-profile transporters—you paste the throttle on your stocker with a four-banger and grab second gear in a flurry of tire chirping: see ya; so long!

Yes, almost any nitrous oxide injection system can be calibrated to throw down 150 horsepower, or more, enough to sky the crank out of an improperly selected host vehicle. The trick is—for most people who value their vehicle yet want the excitement from those occasional blips of wide-open throttle—to take a moderate approach and work up to larger doses of nitrous (that leads to huge power increases) if that is truly the direction you want to go.

For this install, the host vehicle was a 1998 Chevrolet S-10 with a four-cylinder motor that eked out 118 horsepower at best. It's a clean, pristinely maintained family vehicle that is relied upon to get dad to work and back home to his wife and children. Dan Sturgeon of Rosamond, California, owns this S-10. Rosamond is a little town out in the vastness of the Mojave Desert where Sturgeon lives and works as a government contractor who supports navigation systems for the United States Air Force at Edwards Air Force base. Sturgeon is a member of the *Chevy Truck World* website community and his interest in things automotive was immediately apparent by the lack of any visible wear, tear, dust, or fingerprints anywhere in the engine bay. The motor, the truck, and the installation were spotless.

Holley Performance Products supplied this nitrous kit; Eric St. Andre of St. Andre's Automotive Accessories in Westminster, California, handled the installation, and Mike Flynn of Nitrous Supply provided the technical support. St. Andre has installed lots of nitrous systems as well as handled complete frame-off restorations of high-end musclecars and late-model buildups. St. Andre's rule of thumb is: "If you can install a stereo system by yourself, you can install a nitrous kit." You can get started on a Saturday morning and complete the install in about six to eight hours.

The four-cylinder motor in this S-10 is stock, with the exception of a K&N air filter. A guideline for choosing a nitrous system is to err on the side of modesty with consideration for the size of the motor. For example, a V-6 gives the nitrous system two more cylinders to spread the increased power load on to, so a 70-horsepower nitrous boost may be the way to go, and a V-8 would be a good candidate for even more. Given the size of the motor in the S-10, and the relative use of the truck, a 40-horsepower increase was thought to be adequate, not too much and not too little. But, ultimately, the boost is a whole lot of fun when the nitrous system is armed and the way is clear.

Mount the solenoid bracket. We were able to use a pre-existing bracket, so no additional hole needed to be drilled.

Connect the fuel and nitrous lines with AN fittings from the solenoids to the soft plume nozzle at the throttle body. In this case, we connected the soft plume nozzle into the air box, just across from the throttle body.

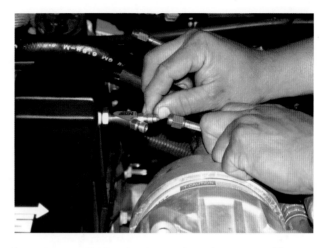

Insert the correct jet into the nitrous valve and connect the AN fittings (nitrous and fuel) to the soft plume nozzle. Each jet and AN connection will be clearly marked on the nozzle. Connect wires from ground, power, and throttle body to the throttle body activation switch. This switch reads when the throttle body is at full throttle, thus sending the signal to the solenoids to open up.

The full-throttle switch can be screwed in or attached to a convenient mounting surface using Velcro with glue-backed mount pads.

Mount the in-cab on/off switch at a convenient point within reach on a lower dashboard panel. With the on/off switch in place, test the system: listen for clicks when the solenoid activates; listen and feel the connection for gaseous leaks when the nitrous bottle is opened; smell for fuel leaks. Check each component of the system. It's a good idea to add some octane booster to regular gasoline, which turns up the combustion dial for greater performance. Here is the completed system. You can see the nitrous line coming up from the left, the fuel line joining the nitrous line around the front of the engine bay and terminating at the solenoid bracket at the right side of the engine.

PROJECT 7 INSTALL NEW INTAKE AND EXHAUST FOR YOUR HEMI

TIME: Three hours

TOOLS: Medium socket set, screwdriver set, appropriate jack, and jack stands

TALENT: ★ to ★★

APPLICABLE YEARS: AEM and Flowmaster have products for most makes and models of pickups

TAB: $700

TINWARE: Fender protection, step stool

TIP: Lashing your truck to a dynamometer just to prove a 12-horsepower increase is not recommended. We used the dyno to show gains for a particular motor.

PERFORMANCE GAIN:
Approximately 12 horsepower

COMPLEMENTARY PROJECT:
Stainless-steel headers

The air-cleaner lid and inlet hose are removed from the system. This is done by loosening the retaining clamps and the clamps that hold the lid to the filter box. With the filter out of the way, the entire air filter box lifts out from the plastic bracket that holds it to the fender. To remove the filter box bracket, the plastic inner fender must be removed. This allows access to the bolts on the underside of the bracket. The two top bolts of the bracket are removed from the inner fender first. Once the bottom bolts are removed, the entire bracket is freed from the engine compartment. All of the vacuum and PCV tubing is then removed from the engine and the rest of the intake near the throttle body. The throttle body cover is unbolted and removed. It uses three bolts that secure it to the intake manifold.

With the cover removed, it exposes the throttle body. The orange seal around the throttle body is also removed. Four bolts hold the throttle body to the intake manifold; these are removed in order to install the AEM spacer that comes with the kit. The spacer provides extra plenum volume for the system and comes with an O-ring seal and new hardware. The spacer is placed between the intake manifold and the throttle body. It is then bolted in place using the AEM provided hardware.

Searching for the right combination of parts to make more power can often lead to some impressive gains. But more important, the search helps us learn how our engines operate and that not all of the advantages of aftermarket parts are shown on the dyno chart.

Everyone knows that an air intake system and a cat-back exhaust should make more power, right? For the most part, they do, but not all engines are affected in the same manner. Take for example our test truck: a 2005 Dodge Quad Cab outfitted with a 5.7-liter Hemi engine. The truck, with less than 10,000 miles, is owned by Chad Case. The Ram was absolutely stock and made a perfect candidate for our test.

We wanted to see what the effects, if any, would be on an engine with an air intake system and a cat-back and no other changes. For our test we decided to use AEM's Brute Force air intake system and match it to a Flowmaster cat-back exhaust system that would be installed by Greg Nakano at AEM's facility in Hawthorne, California. The Brute Force air intake system replaces the factory tubing and filter by using a polished aluminum tube and a cone-style cotton-gauze air filter that is situated within a heat shield. The shielding blocks out engine heat, but it also gathers cold air from under the fender and directs it to the filter.

The system comes with a heat shield that must have the seals attached to the top and the center opening of the shield. The shield is bolted to the engine compartment from various locations. One is under the fender using the original fender bolt. The shield blocks any engine heat from entering into the intake and a small insulated stud bolts on to a factory hole on the fender. The factory air temperature sensor is removed from the throttle body cover by twisting it from its mount, and it is installed on to the AEM inlet tube with the provided grommet.

The inlet tube is then inserted into position on the engine. The tube slips into a silicone sleeve on the throttle body and is held in place with two clamps that are provided in the kit. The tube also attaches to the insulated stud and is bolted in place to secure it into position. Finally, the conical air filter is slipped into position from underneath, and the clamp is tightened to hold it in place on the intake tube. Some of the vehicle's wiring is routed through the heat shield, and the coolant overflow hose is rerouted under the air filter. The air temperature sensor is also plugged back into the factory harness. A new crankcase ventilation hose is supplied in the kit, and the hose is attached to the intake tube with the provided clamps.

With all of the clamps tightened, this is what the Brute Force system looks like installed.

The Flowmaster exhaust system comes with the company's 50-series muffler and a host of aluminized tubing.

When tested, the dyno showed that the addition of the AEM Brute Force intake system developed an additional six to seven rear-wheel horsepower and seven to eight rear-wheel lb-ft torque across the entire rpm band; a substantial difference, no doubt, by merely improving the airflow into the engine. The fact that the engine will also receive additional cold air will also benefit in better throttle response, and the polished intake tube adds a performance look under the hood.

If we were able to make a few more horsepower with intake air, would we make much more with the air exiting out of the engine? We bolted on the Flowmaster exhaust system, which came with the company's 50-series muffler, and a dual-exit

tubing system that is fully aluminized. The system also came with the necessary hardware to hang it on the factory hangers, and it gives you the option to allow the exhaust tips to exit straight out from under the bumper or behind the rear wheels.

Case decided he wanted the tips to exit out behind the rear wheels, and after the factory muffler and resonator were removed from the truck, it became evident that the exhaust would not only give the truck a nice exhaust tone, but it would also afford some substantial weight savings. Nakano managed to bolt together the system while the truck was still

The factory muffler is clamped in place from the factory, and it is easily unbolted and removed from the truck.

At the rear of the exhaust system, Dodge utilizes a resonator that adds weight and more restriction to the system.

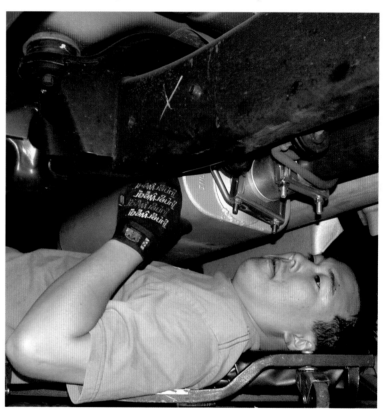

Left: With both the muffler and resonator removed, we could figure that the Flowmaster exhaust would also benefit us by providing weight savings. **Right**: The Flowmaster muffler slips into the Ram's existing tubing and is clamped into position.

on the dyno and, aside from having to bolt on an additional bracket to an existing hole on the frame (this was for the driver-side exit tubing), the system bolted together fairly easily.

Once the truck was restarted and we could hear the awesome tone from the dual-exit system, the Ram was once again run on the dyno to observe the results. In this case we noticed a small improvement of one to two horsepower and a torque increase that was only slightly above the results of the AEM Brute Force unit alone. Nevertheless, the combination seemed to work very well together and it managed to

improve the stock Ram with an additional seven to eight horsepower increase and an additional 9–10 lb-ft of torque over our initial baseline.

Although these results may not seem overly impressive, they are actual numbers; and with the addition of a power programmer, the air intake and exhaust would increase the breathing benefits of the engine for even greater results. The test also demonstrated that the factory intake and exhaust are pretty efficient, but the other benefits of the aftermarket items are also evident.

The muffler has two outlets; the tubing slips into place and its clamps are used to secure the system.

One side of the tubing exits out of the passenger side of the truck and exits out behind the rear tire.

The other side of the exhaust is routed around the spare and a hanger bracket is bolted on to the frame using an existing hole.

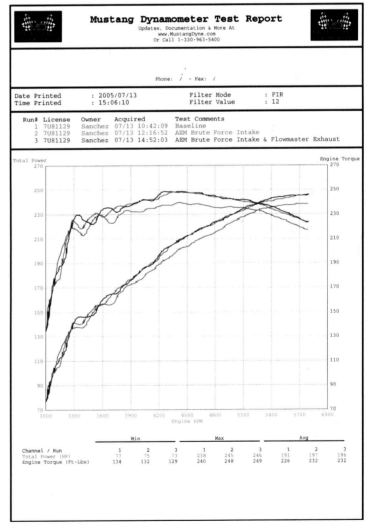

Mustang Dynamometer Test Report
Updates, Documentation & More At
www.MustangDyne.com
Or Call 1-330-963-5400

Phone: / - Fax: /

Date Printed	: 2005/07/13	Filter Mode : FIR
Time Printed	: 15:06:10	Filter Value : 12

Run# License Owner   Acquired   Test Comments
 1   7U81129 Sanchez 07/13 10:42:09   Baseline
 2   7U81129 Sanchez 07/13 12:16:52   AEM Brute Force Intake
 3   7U81129 Sanchez 07/13 14:52:03   AEM Brute Force Intake & Flowmaster Exhaust

	Min			Max			Avg		
Channel / Run	1	2	3	1	2	3	1	2	3
Total Power (HP)	77	75	73	238	245	246	191	197	196
Engine Torque (Ft-Lbs)	134	132	129	240	248	249	226	232	232

This is what the rear exit system looks like fully installed. The system can also be installed with the tips exiting straight out from under the bumper.

The graph shows the three dyno runs. These include the baseline run, the run with the AEM Brute Force intake, and a run with the intake and Flowmaster muffler combination. The result was an 8-horsepower and 10 lb-ft of torque increase over the stock intake and exhaust.

PROJECT 8 GET MORE HORSEPOWER WITHOUT THE HIGH PRICE

TIME: Two days to install motor

TOOLS: Full socket set and hand tools, cherry picker, jack stands

TALENT: ★★★

APPLICABLE YEARS: All makes and models of trucks

TAB: $4,000

TINWARE: Headers, exhaust

TIP: Be familiar with the installation process and take your time.

PERFORMANCE GAIN:
Fresh motor

COMPLEMENTARY PROJECT:
Deep sump oil pan

Here you see the technician removing a block that has just been bored and decked to blueprint specs. A Smeding Performance block is machined with care to tighter tolerances than the original factory block. The diamond hone operation provides a superior finish on the cylinder bore. This allows for faster and better ring seating and longer engine life.

The small-block GM block is clearanced to allow for the rod bold clearance required with the stroker motor. The front of the block must be clearanced to allow for use of a double roller timing chain. All blocks are cleaned after machining. Then cam bearings, brass freeze plugs, and dowel pins are installed in the block.

In just about every city in America, you can find an engine rebuilding firm that will take your old worn-out motor and return it to almost-new condition. We say almost-new because the typical rebuilder will go over your old motor, repairing or replacing the bare minimum to provide you with a functional engine to drop back into your truck or car. Although this can sometimes be a viable option for getting your vehicle on the road again, it hardly constitutes a new engine, let alone a high-performance one.

If you are looking for a truly all-new, high-performance engine for your performance and towing needs, you ultimately want an engine that will produce more horsepower than stock and yet meet all emissions standards. Although this sounds expensive, it doesn't have to be. We found a performance crate engine from Smeding Performance, which builds a 383 TBI crate engine with plenty of power.

The company's 383 small-block Chevy engine produces 310 horsepower and is emissions legal. It is made to fit into 1987–1995 Chevrolet and GMC model pickups and sport utility vehicles, and it retails for less than $4,000. We also discovered that Ben Smeding and his crew are going into their fourteenth year of building truly superior high-performance engines. The first thing to note is that the company offers crate motors that are built with 100 percent new parts.

We were able to visit Smeding Performance and found it has a complete self-contained engine machine shop. This equipment is top of the line as are all the parts Smeding uses. The company's Cylinder Head Center uses the same machine that a majority of the formula one, CART, and NASCAR teams use. Smeding Performance uses this equipment to provide a Super Stock valve job that is second to none. In the Block Machining Center, the company turns out "true blue-printed" blocks. This means that the bores, deck height, and cylinder alignments are held to standards that are often tighter than OEM engines. Your local machine shop can't match this type of precision. Once a block has been through the Block Machining Center, it then goes to the Smeding Performance Honing Center. This computer-controlled Honing Center features a diamond hone and superior control of the cylinder surface. In fact, the finish of the cylinder walls is so superior that only a few years ago it would have been unheard of. This superb finish means quicker breaking, enhanced ring sealing, and a longer engine life.

Perhaps the most important piece of equipment in the Smeding

Left: Here the motor is precision balanced to provide smooth operation even at high rpm. An added bonus is that this balancing potentially extends the engine's operating life. **Right:** When balancing an engine, the weight of the rods, pistons, and even the pins must be measured. Here you see a standard GM 350 small-block piston on the right compared to a shorter deck height piston for a 383-stoker motor on the left. This is a view of the standard GM 350 small-block rod on the right compared to a longer rod for a 383-stoker motor on the left. A special setup is required to weight the rod's small-end weight for proper balancing of the assembly. This is what the screen looks like when balancing the crank. The information here tells the operator where to take material off and how much to remove. If the crank is light, it will also tell how much weight to add.

Left: Smeding's cylinder head center can machine a race quality head in less than 30 minutes. **Right:** Once a head has been machined, the guides are checked and matched to the valves. Assembled heads are checked for leak-down before being installed on an engine. Here you see a raw pair of heads on the left and an assembled pair of Smeding Performance Vortec heads on the right. Ben Smeding likes to personally handle the assembly operation at the shop.

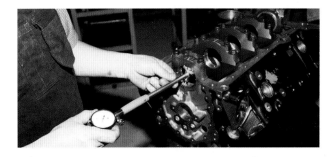

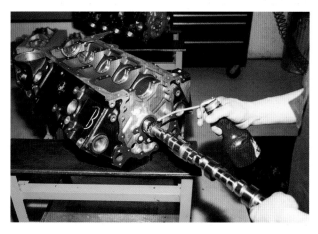

Above: The first step is to install the main bearing caps and check the crank bore diameter. **Right:** The camshaft is lubricated and installed into the block. On the Vortec 383, Smeding Performance uses a special grind that is made to its specs.

Left: The crank bearings are installed in the block, and then the crank is dropped into place. The crankshafts that Smeding Performance uses are all polished and chamfered. **Right:** Once the crank has been installed, the piston, rod, and ring assembly are inserted into the cylinders. Smeding Performance takes care to be sure the ring gaps are all even and as small as possible. Additionally, the piston clearance is as small as practical to prevent piston slap. This is imperative in a computer-controlled application as the computer can read piston slap as knock or detonation.

The timing chain is installed along with a crank trigger wheel for the crank-positioning sensor used on Vortec engines. TBI or carbureted applications don't require this trigger wheel. A new timing cover is installed on all crate motors that Smeding performance builds. Each lifter is lubricated and then inserted into the lifter wells. Vortec engines use a roller tip rocker and as such require rocker retainers to keep them from rotating in the lifter bores. For Vortec applications, Smeding Performance uses all new castings and components to assemble the company's own heads. These heads feature screw-in studs and stainless-steel valves. Non-Vortec small-blocks can be had for cast-iron heads or Edelbrock Performer heads.

The final step to building the motor, at least for Vortec applications, is to install the balancer. Non-Vortec engines will also receive a new Edelbrock intake manifold.

Once the heads are torqued to specifications, the rocker arms and lifters are installed. Smeding Performance uses roller tip rockers on its Vortec truck engines as well as most of its other applications. Full roller rockers are used in all other cases, except for restoration engines. Smeding Performance uses only the best quality, high-volume oil pumps on its engines. To be sure that you don't have any oiling problems, weld the pickup to the pump body and use a solid oil pump drive. The stock oil pump drive uses a plastic sleeve that can lead to trouble over time. Once the oil pump and pickup are in place, the oil pan can be installed. As advertised, an all-new oil pan is used.

This is an example of a completed small-block GM Vortec 383 engine from Smeding Performance. Smeding Performance can ship your engine to you by truck or you can pick it up at the company's location, if you're in the Sacramento area. Be sure you have a way to get the engine out of your truck once you're home. Smeding Performance offers more than just Vortec small-block GM motors. The company also has 540 GM big-blocks, Ford 347 stroker small-blocks, 427 Ford Windsor motors, Vortec 383 GM small-blocks, and 383 GM TBI motors.

Performance gallery is the Balancing Center. This computer-aided, digital, high-speed balancer allows Smeding Performance to balance its performance engines to within as little as 1 gram. By comparison, your typical GM or Ford factory crate motor is typically balanced within 30–40 grams.

We looked on as Smeding employees built a 383 Vortec truck motor. This is a stroked version of the venerable GM 350 small-block, bumped up to 383 cid. We show you this motor for practical purposes only; as it is typical of the work Smeding does

on a daily basis. While the crew at Smeding Performance was working on mostly small-block GM motors the day we arrived, they also put together 540 GM big-blocks as well as Ford 347 stroker small-blocks, 427 Windsor motors, non-Vortec 383 GM small-blocks, and 383 GM TBI motors. Of course, they can put their expertise into rebuilding your original motor and provide as many of the available upgrades as you want.

TIME: Eight hours

TOOLS: Full socket set, torque wrench, appropriate jack, jack stands

TALENT: ★★★

APPLICABLE YEARS: All years—automatic and manual transmissions

TAB: $700–$1,200

TINWARE: Step stool, good lighting, flashlight

TIP: The challenge with installing a set of headers in a tight engine bay is common across all automotive brands. However, headers and cat-back exhaust are also common performance components you can install on your truck, regardless of make or model.

PERFORMANCE GAIN:
Approximately 13 horsepower

COMPLEMENTARY PROJECT:
Aftermarket intake system

A pair of shorty headers are a popular upgrade with today's late-model, computer-controlled engines. These ceramic-coated headers are from Gibson Performance. We installed them and the company's cat-back exhaust on to this F-150. The factory exhaust manifolds work fine, but the airflow can be improved by replacing them with headers. The method to do so is to unbolt and remove the studs.

Gibson's R&D technician Shawn Seidelman began the F-150 installation by unbolting the factory Y-pipe from the manifolds. Each bolt and stud had to be removed meticulously from the engine's cylinder head. Seidelman had to remove the truck's 4WD input shaft to remove the driver's-side manifold from the vehicle. With the studs removed, the cylinder head was exposed, and the area needed to be cleaned before bolting on a new Gibson gasket and the header.

A long-held belief exists that headers and a cat-back exhaust are good for making additional horsepower and torque. The theory is that by reducing exhaust back-pressure, additional performance gains can be had. However, does this hold true with late-model, fuel-injected engines that are totally controlled by the vehicle's computer system?

Furthermore, late-model engines are more compact and fit into tighter engine compartments that are part of the vehicle's design for shorter and smoother hood lines. The idea is to create more aerodynamics. The result, however, is that it is harder to install a set of headers on to these engines, and many aftermarket header manufacturers have moved from long-tube headers to shorty styles that have many enthusiasts wondering if they are actually worth the cost of installing.

We decided to try to test this theory with a 2004 Ford F-150 that is equipped with a 5.4-liter, three-valve modular engine. Compared to previous year model trucks, the 2004 and 2005 models have a much tighter engine compartment, and installing a set of headers on this truck is a full-day task that requires additional work.

To help us with this test, we contacted Gibson Performance, which manufactures a shorty-style header and a full-flow cat-back exhaust system for this application. According to Shawn Gibson, head of research and development, the goal for the F-150 was to produce as much useable horsepower as possible. "It makes no sense to build a race exhaust system for a truck that will see between 1,800 rpm and 4,000 rpm most of the time," says Gibson. "We try to design a system that allows the vehicle to make a maximum amount of power from 2,500 through 3,800 rpm where it is more useful for towing and daily driving performance."

Of course, we had to pick the most difficult installation possible. According to Gibson, installing the headers into the late-model F-150 requires removal of the starter, and on four-wheel drive applications, we also had to unbolt the engine mounts and lift the engine up a few inches. This is done to make additional space for inserting the headers from underneath the vehicle. In this case we also had to remove the transmission crossmember in order to move the factory Y-pipe back enough to remove the driver-side exhaust manifold. The front axle driveshaft also had to be removed for additional clearance.

Once the exhaust manifolds and studs were unbolted from

Removing the passenger-side manifold was a bit more difficult. Seidelman had to move the starter aside and lift the engine a couple of inches before gaining enough room to remove the manifold.

Once the headers are secured, the factory Y-pipe is bolted to the header flange. In addition to replacing the exhaust manifolds, we also wanted to replace the restrictive factory exhaust system. The entire system was clamped together, so Seidelman simply unbolted the clamps so that the exhaust could be removed. Unhooking the muffler and tubing from the exhaust hangers allowed Seidelman to remove the muffler. One problem we faced in trying to reconnect the factory Y-pipe was that there wasn't enough room to maneuver it. Seidelman had to temporarily remove the transmission transfer case shield. With the transfer case shield out of the way, it was easier for Seidelman to maneuver the Y-pipe to fit together and fit the Gibson system on to the end. The head pipe was slipped into the rear of the Y-pipe that exits out from the catalytic converters.

the engine, the Gibson headers were installed. These headers are designed with thick flanges and come with hardware. The headers that were used for this application were ceramic-coated stainless steel. They bolted on to the engine with the gaskets provided by Gibson. Once this was done, the factory Y-pipe was bolted back to the collector flanges on the headers.

With the transmission crossmember, starter, and driveshaft back in place, the engine once again rested on the engine mounts and was bolted down. With that accomplished, bolting on the cat-back exhaust system was a breeze to install. The system is completely slip-fit and uses C-clamps to hold it in place. Gibson's muffler is a baffle design that absorbs sound but flows a large amount of exhaust through it. The company tunes the inner baffles of the muffler to provide the best airflow for the application and to eliminate all resonance in the cab.

Once the entire exhaust system was put together, the truck was placed on the dyno to see the results. The baseline runs showed that the 5.4-liter V-8 produced 147.2 horsepower and 241.8 lb-ft of torque at the rear wheels. Most of the power was made from 1,800 rpm all the way to 4,000 rpm. With the addition of the Gibson shorty headers and cat-back exhaust system, the engine produced a peak of 160.3 horsepower and 263.4 lb-ft of torque. Most of the power gains were in the 3,000–3,800 rpm range, where the truck netted a 13 horsepower gain and an additional 21.6 lb-ft of torque.

With enough space between the engine and the frame, the Gibson header is maneuvered into the passenger-side position. Once the passenger-side header was in place, Seidelman reinstalled the starter motor, which was removed to make additional room. It's a tight fit, but the headers bolt on to the factory cylinder heads with the supplied gasket and hardware.

Seidelman marked 2 inches on each pipe to ensure that it slipped up to that point. This allowed the system to fit together properly. The muffler was slipped on to the head pipe up to the 2-inch mark, and the rest of the system was assembled in the same manner. The rear tailpipe section was slipped into the muffler and the system was checked to make sure it all fit together.

Gibson's exhaust systems can be clamped together, but Seidelman recommends adding a tack weld to ensure it stays that way—even in case of vibration. The remaining piece of the tailpipe was installed, along with a polished, stainless-steel tip. Once this was done, the truck went on the dyno, and it gained an additional 13 horsepower and 21.6 lb-ft of torque.

The results of this test do show that a well-tuned header and exhaust system can definitely make a difference. The headers typically retail for around $420 for a chromed set. Ceramic-coated headers, like the ones we used here, cost about $700. The aluminized, single-exhaust system sells for around $375. So, how about the sound? Surprisingly, the truck didn't sound much different than stock. There was a hint of a deeper tone, but the truck was extremely quiet in the cab. The performance, however, was evident as the truck could now spin the tires from a standing start, demonstrating that it's not the peak performance that counts but performance over a wide range that makes the most difference.

PROJECT 10 | INSTALL AN ALUMINUM RADIATOR

TIME: Four hours

TOOLS: Full socket set, pliers, vise-grips

TALENT: ★★

APPLICABLE YEARS: All years and models of pickup trucks—automatic and manual transmissions

TAB: $600 (with two electric fans—$1,200)

TINWARE: Marker chalk, tape measure, new radiator hose, coolant

TIP: Consider mounting an electric fan on the radiator with this project.

PERFORMANCE GAIN:
Superior cooling ability

COMPLEMENTARY PROJECT:
Electric fan

Truck owner Jeff Hornsby loosening the core support bolts after the whole one-piece nose assembly was removed. Hornsby's truck is equipped with a Ford 302 V-8 that refused to be cooled by the stock, down-flow radiator. Hornsby's 1956 Ford has been fit with a Volare front suspension clip, which placed the engine about 2 inches forward to clear the steering box. The old radiator was mounted in this original core support, which will no longer be used.

Flex-a-lite now manufactures its own all aluminum cross-flow radiators called Flex-a-fit. Although no direct replacement is available for the 1956 Ford F-100 down-flow style, this fits Hornsby's highly modified custom Ford pickup. Those T-bracket channels on the ends of the radiator will work perfectly for mounting this unit. A look at the flip side of the Flex-a-fit radiator reveals the 180-style Cyclone S-blade fan and 100 percent coverage shroud, which only draws 17 amps but moves 2,500 cfm of air through the radiator. This Flex-a-fit cross-flow radiator is designed to be installed on the vehicle using the T-channel bolts and two L-brackets as shown. These two brackets were test-mounted to two existing vertical brackets, which formerly retained the old crossmember.

Jeff Hornsby drives a neat-looking 1956 Ford F-100 short-bed pickup, painted to match a Mattel model, cream with red graphics. Try as it may, the truck's 50-year-old radiator would no longer keep up with the cooling demands of his 302-ci Ford engine. Hornsby did what all of us do; had the radiator flushed, then rodded out, installed a new thermostat and new hoses, and even dropped big coin on a set of aftermarket fans that would suck the dust off the truck in front of him, but the temperature gauge would hit 220 and keep climbing in city traffic! What to do now?

Turns out that one of the most famous manufacturers of aftermarket radiator fans has stepped up to the needs of hot-rod truckers and now markets the all-new Flex-a-fit cross-flow radiators. These aluminum radiators are designed with internal fins that perform as heat sinks, which absorb heat more quickly from the engine coolant, then radiate it through external fins that increase the tank's radiant surface area threefold. The unique external-fin design integrates limitless fastening points into the tank itself, transforming the radiator into a convenient bracket for attaching expansion tanks, electric fans, oil coolers, and so on.

Flex-a-fit radiators are all aluminum with two-row core, 1-inch/26mm tubes, and three different core sizes with inlets on either the left or right side of the tank. Inlet is 1.5 inches while the outlet is 1.75 inches. Radiators can be purchased separately or included with the Flex-a-lite electric fans to cover 100 percent of the core surface with a trick-looking shroud.

With that said, the really cool part of the cosmetics of the new Flex-a-fit radiator is the side tanks, which make for an easy installation. The side tanks have T-channels, like ribs, top to bottom

Left: Hornsby and friend, Chris Travers, then dropped the Flex-a-fit radiator into place for a test fit. With the radiator's unique, universal T-channel mounting system, this baby was practically going to bolt right up! **Right:** The existing top holes worked perfectly for the mounting of the top of the L-bracket, while new holes were drilled to mount the bottom bolts. This is where you will have to measure and come up with a mounting system if you wish to install a similar radiator into your truck. Hornsby held the radiator steady as Travers installed T-bolts into several channels until the optimum radiator angle and mounting was achieved. As you can see, there are a variety of options.

Left: Check out the T-bolt locations that are in two different channels on each side. Worked great and the radiator is as level as a pool table. Hornsby had to remove the cardboard protection for a look! Flex-a-fit radiators from Flex-a-lite are not available with built-in trans coolers, so an external cooler will be added to the front of this radiator using these supplied trick-mounting brackets. Hornsby and Travers opted to mount the cooler high on the radiator to avoid a conflict with the rotation of the gravel pan. The supplied hardware and cross-brackets that mount to the T-channels made this a quick job. All was left loose until the lines were attached. One of the major hurdles in mounting a custom radiator is to ensure everything clears, especially the water pump pulley and harmonic balancer. Hornsby's engine is mounted forward and has inches to spare! **Right:** Stock 1956 radiators have the top return line centered. Being a cross-flow, this Flex-a-fit radiator has the feed line on the passenger side and return on the top left. Using measurements, Hornsby found this double-S radiator hose to be a perfect fit! Now he has more under-hood bling and the overheating problem cured.

on three sides, which allow the radiator mounting brackets to adjust up and down, or front to back on each channel. And you can use one channel for the top mount and another for the bottom mount creating endless adjustments and mounting options. This came in real handy for Hornsby's truck, as the vehicle's tilt front end meant that everything, including the radiator, was mounted on custom brackets. Because of those T-channels, the installation turned out to be a breeze.

The good news is, anyone with a traditional cross-flow radiator can order a replacement unit, which will pretty much be a direct replacement, because all Flex-a-fit radiators are cross-flow with end tanks. For classic truckers, with the old-style down-flow radiators where the cans are on the top and bottom, Flex-a-lite does not have a direct replacement

radiator for you. However, with some ingenuity, such as we used on Hornsby's '56, you can install a Flex-a-fit radiator if you have the space. Hornsby's engine is actually mounted forward due to the use of a Volare suspension install but had room for this fat radiator. And, he was not looking to retain the traditional classic Ford radiator look. Now, the engine bay looks more like a race truck with a lot of bling-bling and a big, wide cross-flow radiator with an attractive full coverage shroud and fan! Topping it off is the external trans cooler, as the Flex-a-fit radiator is not available with a built-in cooler.

You've spent a fortune on building your truck and engine, so why would you rely on a $10 radiator to keep it from overheating? So, check out this custom installation!

PROJECT 11 BOLT ON A SET OF HEADERS

TIME: Six hours

TOOLS: Full socket set, screwdriver set, and appropriate jack

TALENT: ★★

APPLICABLE YEARS: All years—automatic and manual transmissions

TAB: $700

TINWARE: Mechanic's gloves help

TIP: Gibson Performance exhaust makes headers and complete exhaust systems for most popular vehicle makes and models.

PERFORMANCE GAIN:
15–20 horsepower

COMPLEMENTARY PROJECT:
Cat-back exhaust system

The Gibson headers that were used on this install were ceramic-coated stainless-steel units. The ceramic coating contains the heat and improves the longevity of the headers.

Gibson also uses a reinforced center cone that prevents the area from getting crushed when the Y-pipe is reinstalled. A 3/8-inch-thick flange also prevents warping that can cause gasket leaks and can gradually loosen the header bolts.

The first part of the installation was to remove the Y-pipe from both sides of the factory exhaust manifolds.

For someone who is not familiar with Dodge trucks, it might seem that the only two engines that Dodge makes are the 5.7-liter Hemi and the 5.9-liter V-8. For the Dakota owner with a 5.9-liter, there is an abundance of aftermarket parts, which allows for someone to pick and choose the performance levels that they are looking for. Unfortunately, for Dakota owners with the 5.2-liter V-8, not as many parts are available. However, if you look hard enough, some parts can add performance to the 5.2-liter.

One of the most popular, and one that the engine responds to, is a high-flow exhaust system. Many dyno tests have shown that Dodge Dakotas and Durangos equipped with a high-flow exhaust will yield as much as 15–20 horsepower. Much of the restriction on these engines comes from the factory exhaust manifolds that can be eliminated with the use of a quality set of headers.

Headers work well to alleviate back pressure and help to efficiently evacuate the cylinder chamber, but many truck owners have dreaded installing them due to limited space in the engine compartment and the possibility of reoccurring leaks that require constant retorquing of the header bolts.

Some of these problems are common misconceptions with headers that do not necessarily apply to truck headers intended for street use. To demonstrate how a set is installed into a 5.2-liter Dakota, we observed an installation at Gibson Performance in Corona, California.

Gibson's solves some of the problems associated with headers

by offering ⅜-inch-thick flanges to prevent leaks and 14-gauge steel tubing that improves the header's longevity. The headers are also available in 409 stainless steel and can be ceramic coated to provide improved thermal protection and to maintain a clean appearance. The headers used in this install were ceramic-coated stainless steel to improve the longevity of the headers and truly offer a maintenance-free operation.

The system came with a set of headers, hardware, and high-temperature gaskets to make installation as easy as possible. The headers are designed to bolt on to the factory Y-pipe and feature a reinforced collector to avoid any leaks in this area. The installation required the removal of the factory Y-pipe connection to the exhaust manifold collectors. Then the exhaust manifolds are removed, which often requires a shot of WD40 or other lubricant to remove old rusted studs.

With the exhaust manifolds out of the way, the exhaust ports on the cylinder head are cleaned with a wire brush to ensure that the surface is flat and free of any silicone or gasket material. The Gibson headers are installed from underneath the vehicle. Two bolts are used to secure it in place, and the gasket is inserted in between the header and cylinder head.

Left: Here you can see how the Y-pipe flange fits into the donut-style collector. **Right:** The factory exhaust manifolds are restrictive and are often rusted, as they were in this situation.

Left: Carefully removing all of the bolts and studs allows the manifold to be released from the cylinder head. **Right:** In comparison, the header offers individual tubes for each cylinder, which improves the scavenging effect, enhancing performance.

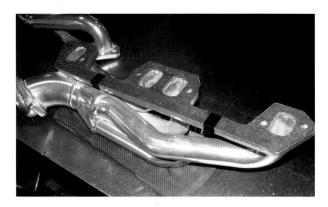

Left: The installer taped the gasket to the headers, which made the installation a bit easier to handle when trying to maneuver the header up from under the vehicle. **Right:** The headers are then bolted into the cylinder head with the provided hardware. This may take some time but the end result is well worth the effort.

The rest of the bolts are installed and both driver and passenger sides are bolted tight. Once this is done, the Y-pipe is bolted up to the header's collector. New hardware is also provided, and once everything is in place, all of the bolts are tightened and checked. The engine is started to listen for any leaks in the area.

With the headers in place, the 5.2-liter engine sounded great, and although we were not able to test this system on the dyno, we did notice improved throttle response and power on the road.

PROJECT 12 | THREE BOLT-ON HORSEPOWER UPGRADES

 TIME: Two hours

 TOOLS: Small socket set, screwdriver set

 TALENT: ★

 APPLICABLE YEARS: All years—automatic and manual transmissions

 TAB: $400

 TINWARE: Rubber gloves for your hands

 TIP: This is an excellent project to increase your vehicle's performance and your confidence level.

PERFORMANCE GAIN:
10 to 15 horsepower

COMPLEMENTARY PROJECT:
Stainless-steel exhaust

Jay LaRossa from STS Performance wanted to show that not every modification had to be so complicated that it took a team of professionals with specialized tools to complete it. All of the modifications were something that could easily be finished by one person in a single day with standard tools. Previously, he dropped the Ram with a McGaughys lowering kit, he added a roll pan from Street Scene Equipment, and he installed a set of billet door handles from Grippin' Billet.

Here, LaRossa is going to install a series of performance goodies to help both the horsepower and the economy of this 5.7-liter Hemi V-8-powered Ram. To meet the need for more horsepower, using a group of components that can be easily installed in a matter of a few hours using only standard hand tools, LaRossa decided on a JET Performance Dodge module, JET Powr-Flo throttle body spacer, and a high-performance open-element air intake from STS Performance. All of these parts are easily installed and effective to add horsepower to your already impressive Hemi power plant. And the best part is that everything was installed, including having to wait for the photographer to shoot the photos, in less than two hours.

Above left: The first things to be removed are the air box and the intake system. Not only are they going to be replaced, but Jay LaRossa needs to remove them so that he can remove the throttle body to install the JET Performance throttle body spacer. Here he is popping the lid off the air box. Once the lid of the air box is out of the way, the factory-style filter element can be removed. Then the bottom section of the air box can be unbolted from the inner fender. **Top right:** The bolts that hold the upper section of the intake and the mass airflow sensor to the intake are then removed. **Bottom right:** Next, the wiring harness is unplugged from the mass airflow sensor to free it up completely. And the upper section of the intake system can be easily lifted out of the way. The plug for the wiring that connects the throttle body to the truck's electronic control unit is the next item to be removed. Then the four bolts that hold the throttle body to the intake manifold are removed.

Left: Once the bolts are backed out, the throttle body is easily removed from the manifold. Be careful not to drop anything into the manifold because this could cause damage to the inner workings of the engine. **Right:** LaRossa unpacked the box from JET Performance and removed the throttle body spacer and the new piggyback ignition module. Before the throttle body spacer can be installed, the new O-ring seal has to be pressed into the groove in the front of the spacer to ensure it will seal to the bottom of the throttle body when it is reinstalled. To install the spacer, just line up the holes and slide it into place. Then drop the new mounting bolts into the base of the throttle body, and slip it into place.

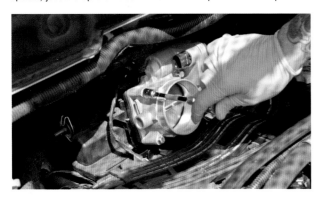

While the STS Performance intake is waiting to be installed, LaRossa takes advantage of the added room to install the JET Performance piggyback performance module. Here, the harness is unplugged from the factory ECU. The JET module is simply plugged into the ECU right where the factory harness plugs in.

Once all of the new mounting bolts have been installed, they are torqued to specifications. The upper section of the factory intake that houses the mass airflow sensor is reinstalled next.

The factory wiring harness is then simply plugged into the new JET module, and the installation is complete. After LaRossa gets out of the way, you can easily see where the new JET module is plugged in between the factory ECU and the wiring harness. With the throttle body spacer and module installed, it is time to install the new STS Performance cold air intake system. To start things off, the silicone adapter is clamped to the mass airflow sensor.

The chrome-plated intake tube with the open-element air filter already installed on the end is then slipped into the other end of the silicone adapter. After a little adjusting, the clamps on the silicone adapter are cinched down.

The breather hose is then slipped into place on the new STS Performance intake tube. One of the factory bolts that held the air box to the inner fender is reused to bolt the STS tube into place.

PROJECT 13 BUILD A RELIABLE SMALL-BLOCK CHEVY

 TIME: One to two weeks—depends upon your time

 TOOLS: Full socket set, appropriate hand tools, assembly bench

 TALENT: ★★★

 APPLICABLE YEARS: Any year model

 TAB: $3,000–$4,000

 TINWARE: Gasket kits, compounds

 TIP: Take your sweet time.

 PERFORMANCE GAIN:
You decide horsepower range and choose parts accordingly.

COMPLEMENTARY PROJECT:
Upgrade or rebuild transmission to match a fresh engine.

The main bearings are Federal Mogul standard issue, but engine builder Brian Baugh cut a slight chamfer in the rear thrust bearing to help direct more oil to the rear seal area to keep it lubricated. The stock cast crankshaft needed nothing more than a good bath and brushing out of the oil passages before it was ready to drop back in the block.

Main bearing clearances were checked by laying Plastigage strips on the crank's main journals. The caps were torqued down, and then removed to measure the Plastigage. The factory manual calls for .002–.006 inch of clearance; ours were .003–.004 inch. The main caps were torqued to 75 lb-ft, then crankshaft endplay was checked. It came out to .003–.004 inch, well within the factory .002–.007 inch tolerance range.

Everybody loves big-horsepower engines, covered with the go-fast stuff like hot fudge on a sundae. However, the reality is that for every person who builds one of those flash motors, there are probably 10 guys assembling basic, beer-budget street truck engines. Although these motors won't set records or gather admiring glances, they do the job they were built to do: make reliable, budget-friendly power.

Billet cranks, aftermarket aluminum heads, big cams, or electronic fuel injection need not apply. These "basics" engines are built with proven, affordable parts—stuff like two-bolt blocks, cast cranks, hydraulic cams, and carburetors.

That doesn't mean a budget engine has to be a slug. By carefully selecting factory and aftermarket components, doing basic machine work, and paying attention to assembly procedures, you can put together an engine that will make more than enough power for a daily-driven truck or mild off-roader.

Plucked from the remains of a 1977 Malibu wagon, our subject small-block Chevy 350 is the quintessential low-compression, smog-era engine. But after we're through with it, the small-block will be more than enough motor to get anyone where they want to go. And for those of you who can't resist turning the wick up a little, we have a list of upgrade parts that'll hot up this 350 quite nicely.

The freshly scrubbed stock four-valve relief pistons were treated to a new set of Summit piston rings. The machine shop checked the connecting rods for cracking and egging of the big and small ends; they passed with flying colors. The rods received new Federal Mogul bearings and were reassembled with the stock rod bolts. The piston and rod assemblies were tapped into their respective bores with a Summit billet aluminum ring compressor. The rod caps were then torqued to 45 lb-ft.

43

The Summit high-volume oil pump bolted into place. The pump comes with the pickup welded on instead of just pressed on, which is good insurance against a pickup coming loose and destroying the engine. A Summit hydraulic cam and lifter set will control the motion of the valvetrain. The grind chosen for our 350 specs out at 194/204 degrees duration at .050 inch and .398/.420 inches lift. That is plenty of cam for a mild street truck or daily driver engine. A Summit double roller timing chain will keep the crankshaft and the cam in sync. The chain has three keyways (straight up, 4 degrees advanced, 4 degrees retarded) and a solid bushing to eliminate chain stretch. The cam was installed in the standard (straight up) position. The Summit steel oil pan is a stock replacement piece. If you look closely, you can see the dabs of silicone sealer where the rubber end seals meet the pan rail gaskets. An additional bead of silicone was run between the pan and the timing chain cover for extra leakage insurance. The stock cast-iron cylinder heads were cleaned up and reassembled with the original 1.94/1.60-inch valves, 1.25-inch valve springs with new umbrella seals, and rocker arm studs. Nothing trick, just reliable factory parts and good assembly work.

An Edelbrock Performer 600 cfm four-barrel carburetor tops off the Performer intake. The Performer is a great street carburetor, providing good power and all-around drivability. Plus, it can be run practically out of the box, requiring just some minor tuning. Feeding the Performer carburetor is the job of a Summit chrome mechanical fuel pump. The lower portion of the pump housing can be rotated so the inlet and outlet fittings can be positioned to meet the fuel lines from the tank and to the carburetor. The distributor is a factory GM HEI upgraded with a Summit cap and rotor kit. The high-quality alkyd cap has brass inserts that conduct spark and resist corrosion better than the aluminum inserts used in ordinary stock replacement caps.

Rocker arm preload is adjusted by tightening the locknut until the pushrod starts to bind, then tightening the nut an additional half-turn. The rockers are the stock 1.5 ratio stamped steel items; the pushrods are new Summit pieces. With the intake manifold gaskets in place, beads of silicone are laid down on the end rails. Traditional end rail gaskets have a tendency to squeeze out when the intake manifold is bolted down. Silicone is also used around the water jacket openings on the head and the gasket to prevent coolant leaks.

The Edelbrock Performer aluminum intake is lowered into place. The dual plane, four-barrel manifold is designed to make power from idle to 5,500 rpm, making it a fine upgrade from the stock two-barrel intake.

Here is the finished 350 in its new home, a 1950 Studebaker. It has been outfitted with factory rams-horn exhaust manifolds, a new water pump and alternator, Accel 300+ ignition wires, powder-coated factory pulleys, a Summit flexplate, and a Summit air cleaner. Best guess on power? Around 200 horsepower and 250 lb-ft of torque—not a lot these days, but still good, reliable motivation. You can make the 350 sit up and bark with the parts in the Upgrades sidebar.

UPGRADES

Want to give your 350 a little more get up and go? These components will help turn a mild-mannered mill into a very healthy street performer running on pump premium gas.

- Summit 355 engine kit (includes new cast crank, Summit stage I rods, Keith Black hypereutectic pistons, sealed power rings, Clevite bearings, Summit high-volume oil pump, roller timing chain, Trick Flow engine gasket set): SUM-CSUM355KIT*

- Trick Flow hydraulic cam and lifter set (228°/234° @.050, 480-inch/.494-inch lift): TFS-31401001

- Trick Flow 23 degree aluminum cylinder heads: TFS-30400001**

- Summit 1.6 Ratio Aluminum Roller Rockers: SUM-G6920B

- Moroso Street/strip oil pan, 7 quart with crank scraper and windage tray (pre-1980 block): MOR-20191

- Edelbrock performer RPM air-gap intake manifold: EDL-7501

- Holley Street Avenger carburetor, 670 CFM: HLY-0-80670

- Summit HEI distributor with coil (black cap): SUM-850001R

- MSD 6A ignition: MSD-6200

- StreetDampr harmonic damper (internal balance): FLU-670100

- Milodon high-volume cast-iron water pump: MIL-16212+

- ARP main cap bolt kit: ARP-134-5001

- ARP head bolt kit: ARP-134-3601

- ARP engine accessory bolt kit, stainless steel/hex head: ARP-534-9601

- Summit die-cast valve covers, ball milled: SUM-G3303

PARTS LIST

Short Block
1977 Chevrolet 350 2-bolt block
Stock cast crankshaft, connecting rods, and pistons (8.0:1 compression)
Summit piston ring set, standard bore: SUM-133-M139-00
Federal mogul bearings: FEM-4663M (main), FEM-2555CP (rod), FEM-1235M (cam)
Sealed power gasket set: SLP-260-1000
Summit high-volume oil pump: SUM-121155
Summit cam and lifter set: SUM-K1100
Summit true roller timing chain set: SUM-G6600

Induction/fuel System
Edelbrock performer intake manifold, non-EGR: EDL-2101
Edelbrock performer carburetor, 600-cfm/manual choke: EDL-1405
Summit Chrome mechanical fuel pump: SUM-250000-1

Ignition System
Summit cap and rotor kit for GM HEI: SUM-850010
Summit HEI wiring harness: SUM-G5210
Accel 300+ ignition wire, universal fit for HEI: ACC-7031

Other Items
Summit pushrods, 5/16-inch diameter: SUM-G6400
Summit oil pan, bare steel: SUM-G3500X
Summit SFI Flexplate, 168-tooth: SUM-G100SFI

Tools
Summit adjustable ring compressor, 4.00–4.090–inch bore: SME-90A4000
Summit plastigage kit: SUM-MPG1
ARP assembly lube: ARP-100-9903

* Kit builds 9.6:1 compression engine with 64cc chamber heads.

** 64cc chamber, 2.02-inch/1.60-inch valves. 1.25-inch valve springs, good for cams up to .520-inch lift.

\+ Fits 1977-88 small Chevy except 1982 305. Other small Chevy applications available.

PROJECT 14 | IMPROVE BIG-BLOCK TORQUE AND POWER

TIME: Three hours

TOOLS: Full socket set, jack, jack stands

TALENT: ★★

APPLICABLE YEARS: Exhaust and performance systems for all years, makes, and models of light trucks

TAB: $1,700–$2,200

TINWARE: Rubber gloves, cleaning solvents, gasket sealer

TIP: You can perform this total performance upgrade in several steps, thus keeping the costs in line with your budget.

PERFORMANCE GAIN:
Increased performance and potential fuel efficiency

Banks Technician Kevin Hannah began with the installation of Banks' TransCommand module. After bolting it down to the frame's stringer rail, Hannah simply connected the wires and zip-tied the wiring harness to the frame in several places. Hannah cut off the entire factory exhaust system in about 10 minutes. The only part of the factory exhaust that gets saved is the catalytic converter. After removing it, Hannah will set it aside for replacement later. Removing the factory exhaust manifolds comes next. Hannah noticed when he was removing the manifold that one of the studs was already broken off. And it looked to have been broken for a long time. It would prove to be a huge pain, and it would take a major effort to remove it. Banks engineers had to redesign the factory Y-pipe to work with its TorqueTubes, but it fits perfectly. *Tim Gavern*

Diesel trucks seem to be all the rage right now, but the fact is, there are millions of gasoline-powered trucks on the roads that are used for towing and heavy-duty applications. If you own a diesel truck, chances are you'd like it to have more power to tow your boat, horses, or racecar with greater ease while saving some fuel in the process.

One of the best ways to do this is to upgrade the intake and exhaust system. Although Banks has been engineering power-enhancing products for diesel trucks for more than 20 years, the company also has power systems for many late-model gas-powered Ford and General Motors trucks—including sport utilities.

In order to gain additional power from big-block gas engines, Banks has developed a line of products that can be purchased separately or as a complete power unit. Banks' first level of power products is its Monster Exhaust system, which is a catalytic converter-back (cat-back) system, built from 3-inch or 3½–inch (depending on application) constant-diameter stainless-steel tubing. Each application is different, but most Monster Exhaust systems generally include the pipe between the converter and the muffler (intermediate pipe) and the tailpipe. Monster Exhaust systems also include either a stainless-steel Banks dynaflow or Monster muffler. Both have efficient, low-restriction designs that significantly reduce back pressure and have a nice throaty sound—all while being nearly as quiet as a stock muffler. Monster Exhaust systems

also include polished stainless-steel tailpipe tips. Some models even include a double-wall stainless-steel tip to protect it from discoloring from exhaust heat.

According to Banks, its Monster Exhaust systems typically add from 8 to 14 rear-wheel horsepower when installed on stock vehicles. Although this might not sound like much, Banks takes pride in providing honest rear-wheel horsepower numbers derived from real testing. Furthermore, the system produces a nice mellow rumble and all of the Monster Exhaust systems carry lifetime limited warranty.

For more horsepower and torque, Banks engineered its line of Stinger systems, which typically add a Ram-Air filter to the Monster exhaust. Some Stinger systems also add Ram-Air intakes—for even more horsepower—depending on application. Stinger systems include a Ram-Air filter service kit and have lifetime-limited warranties. Depending on application, Stinger systems produce anywhere from 21 to 40 additional rear-wheel horsepower, and 29 to 50 lb-ft of additional rear-wheel torque and up to 15 percent better mileage.

This additional power is a direct result of the Ram-Air filter providing additional airflow into the engine. Secondly, the Monster Exhaust system has the capacity to flow the additional exhaust away more efficiently.

For truck owners looking for the most horsepower and torque gains possible, Banks engineered its top-of-the-line

Banks includes quality hardware and anti-seize with its TorqueTubes. Banks' TorqueTubes fit well and installed easily in this application. Some trimming of each plastic inner fenderwell was necessary to provide clearance for the larger TorqueTubes and the heat they would give off. Hannah easily trimmed them with a large utility knife—and he didn't even have to remove them. The remainder of the Banks Monster Exhaust system looks great and efficiently replaces the stock dual-outlet muffler and dual-pipe tailpipe. Banks' Monster exhaust pipes are stainless steel for a long life. Tailpipe diameter is a hefty 3½ inches with a 4-inch polished stainless-steel tailpipe tip finishing it off. Banks' PowerPack system is so complete that it includes a heat shield to protect the starter from the heat from the TorqueTubes. Installation is simple and uses a large radiator hose–style clamp. *Tim Gavern*

In Banks' PowerPack system, Banks provides a Ram-Air air filter inlet top for Ford's dual-inlet air box–equipped trucks 1987–97. Henson's truck is one of the 1996–97 California trucks that came equipped with a different air intake system. Banks does not have a Ram-Air Intake available for the 1996–97 California-model trucks. *Tim Gavern*

After the TorqueTubes were installed, it was a simple matter for Hannah to connect the rest of the exhaust. Banks' exhaust is well engineered. Every part fit well, and the system uses factory-style clamps to hang the stainless pipes and muffler. Banks' Dynaflow mufflers are heat-shielded, low-restriction, stainless-steel construction mufflers that provide a nice mellow exhaust note. After Hannah hung the muffler, all that was left to install under the truck was the tailpipe. Although it isn't necessary and a clamp is included, Hannah welded the polished stainless-steel tip on to the tailpipe for Henson. *Tim Gavern*

The final step of the Banks PowerPack system installation is the replacement of the stock air filter element with Banks' lifetime air filter element. *Tim Gavern*

PowerPack systems. PowerPack systems typically add stainless steel TorqueTube exhaust manifolds (headers) and stainless steel Y-pipe assemblies (again, depending on application) to all of the goodies included in its Stinger systems. According to Banks, its PowerPack systems produce gains of 24 to 77 rear-wheel horsepower, rear-wheel torque increases of 26 to 94 lb-ft, and mileage increases from 2 to 15 percent.

Obviously, this is a lot of stuff to install on your truck, and we wanted to see how these modifications work on an older Ford truck. Banks found a 1996 Ford 7.5-Liter (460 cubic inch) F-350 duallie pickup. In testing, Banks engineers saw best gains of 68 rear-wheel horsepower, an 85 lb-ft increase in torque at the rear wheels, and a 15 percent increase in mileage in this application.

Banks PowerPack Installation

As we witnessed the PowerPack install on this truck, it's important to note that spraying penetrating oil (WD-40, and so on) on the exhaust manifold bolts prior to their removal will help the job go quicker and easier. If possible, allow the penetrating oil to soak overnight before trying to remove the exhaust manifold bolts. If you've ever broken an exhaust manifold bolt, you'll understand why we're so adamant about this. While you're at it, you might want to spray penetrating oil on the exhaust hanger bolts and exhaust clamp bolts to make their removal go easier too. That is, unless you have a cutting torch in your garage.

This particular vehicle belongs to Sara Henson, who uses her Ford as her daily driver and also tows her three horses to shows in and around southern California. She and her husband, Bill, bought the truck in 2001 as a test to see if Sara would like driving a truck every day. They didn't want to jump into a $50,000 truck until they knew if she even liked trucks. After putting 20,000 miles on her rig (it had 125,000 miles on it, when they bought it), Henson loved it. Her "Cowgirl Cadillac" license-plate frame is a good indicator of what she thinks about her truck.

Henson's truck may have some miles on it (it shows 145,000 miles on the clock), but it was well taken care of. It didn't smoke and ran well during our initial test drive. The Hensons also had a Banks TransCommand installed on their truck while it was at Banks' facility. Of course, this was the reason for the more positive (i.e., firmer) shifts. Banks TransCommand works in conjunction with the factory computer to sense load conditions, and it increases line pressure to the transmission's clutches accordingly—providing more positive shifts. TransCommand works especially well when towing heavy loads as it senses the heavier loads and increases line pressure accordingly taking throttle position, engine rpm, and miles per hour into consideration in its decision making.

One thing we noticed after the PowerPack installation was complete was that the truck was quiet. Even with the truck "floored" during our after-installation test drive, the noise didn't overpower our conversation in the cab.

PROJECT 15 INSTALL HEADERS FOR YOUR HAULER

TIME: Six hours

TOOLS: Socket set (metric sizes also), open wrench set (metric sizes also), appropriate jack, jack stands

TALENT: ★ ★

APPLICABLE YEARS: All years—automatic and manual transmissions

TAB: $700

TINWARE: Fresh header bolts and header gaskets are recommended, and so is an extra set of hands.

TIP: If you have them, plan on reinstalling the factory insulator plates (heat shields) to protect the ABS hose and other lines from the exhaust heat.

PERFORMANCE GAIN:
Look for 10 to 15 horsepower increase. Put your truck on a dyno to determine your actual performance increase.

COMPLEMENTARY PROJECT:
Upgrade to aftermarket air intake system

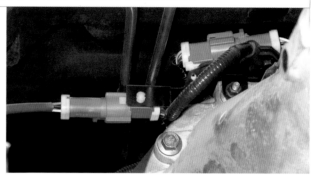

After Bassani Exhaust technician Ara Trujillo places Lonnie Ritchey's truck on the hoist, he begins by removing both right- and left-side front tires. This procedure is followed with Bassani R&D chief Del Dalrymple removing the factory plastic inner fender panels. This is accomplished by removing approximately eight "Christmas tree fasteners" and one lone ¼-inch sheetmetal screw behind the front lip of the lower valance panel. Shown are the factory Harley Hauler O2 sensors, which have to be removed prior to unbolting the stock system.

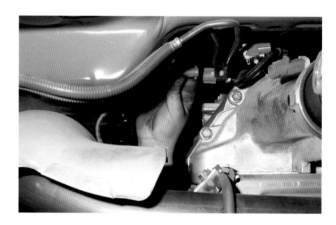

This is accomplished using a ⅞-inch open-end wrench. Be careful not to scrape the tips or get any dirt on them upon removal, or you can run the risk of ruining these rather costly sensors. While all this is going on, Dalrymple is at the other end of the truck removing the OE factory tailpipes. Trujillo removes the passenger-side oxygen sensor in the very same manner as the driver-side unit was removed and sets it aside for safekeeping. Dalrymple begins unbolting the factory cross-over pipe using a 15mm socket and wrench. A little shot of liquid penetrant makes the going easier. Next comes the removal of the factory F-150 cat pipes.

Ford's F-150 Harley Edition pickup is equipped with a 5.4L, Triton V-8 engine, which, in itself, is a strong performer in stock configuration with its supercharged two-valve mod motor rated at 340 horsepower and 425 lb-ft of torque. But there's always room for improvement, and what better way to improve performance than to add a set of four-tube headers and a high-performance catback exhaust system?

Recently, Ford Truck World member Lonnie Ritchey decided to upgrade his 2002 Harley Edition truck's exhaust system and paid a call on the folks at Bassani. The opportunity gave us an inside look at how to install the company's header and exhaust system. Bassani recommended using its Optimum Length (four-tube) headers, p/n 54150L, which fit the 1999-03 5.4L 2WD Ford SVT Lightning and Harley Hauler, and 1997-03 5.4L 2WD Ford F-150 and F-250 standard models, so check with Bassani to dial in the correct headers for your make and model truck.

The headers are constructed from 1⅝–inch-diameter 14-gauge mandrel bent mild steel tubing, and feature equal length primary tubes along with Bassani's exclusive "Wave Isolation Collector," which induces a scavenging effect and further improves performance. The headers can also be

ordered with Bassani's exclusive "SS Comp" header flange gaskets (p/n 5850G), which feature (replaceable) graphite seals that conform to the inner portion of the header flange to ensure a leak-proof operation.

Bassani offers the headers in a flash chrome finish or optional ceramic coating. Both feature a lifetime warranty. Ritchey also chose to install the Bassani cat-back exhaust system, p/n # 54154H-4. This system features ceramic-coated 2½-inch–diameter Bassani exit tubes aft of the OE catalytic converter and cross-over pipe, which connect to a lone dual-tip Bassani exhaust "X-Muffler." At the other end

Left: This comparison photo clearly illustrates the difference between the F-150 Triton cast-iron intake manifold and Bassani's optimum length header. And the performance value will underscore it all the more. **Right:** After loosening a series of 12mm nuts (the factory exhaust manifolds are bolted to studs), the driver-side OE exhaust manifold is removed. Shown are Bassani's exclusive "SS Comp" header gaskets (P/N 5850-G), which feature replaceable graphite "seals" that conform to the inner surface of the header gasket to ensure a leak-proof fit.

Because you're bolting steel to aluminum, a small dab of anti-seize is applied to the header bolt threads prior to installation to prevent the threads from galling. Because the Harley-Hauler uses a solid-mount steering shaft, space is somewhat restricted, so our installers decided that it was necessary to unbolt the driver-side (only) motor mount and jack up that side of the 5.4L Triton V-8 engine 3 inches to allow for sufficient clearance. For the very same reason, it was also decided to install the Bassani SS Comp header gasket to the cylinder headfirst to prevent knocking out the replaceable graphite seals while negotiating the header into place.

With the driver-side header in position, it's time to bolt the header up, leaving the bolts finger tight for final systems alignment. With both driver-side and passenger-side headers installed, Dalrymple is seen reinstalling the factory cat pipes.

This procedure is followed with the installation of Bassani's 2.5-inch stainless-steel inlet pipes, which are secured in place using a pair of Bassani torquer clamps with 15mm nuts. After placing Bassani's "X-Muffler" up in position, the next order of business is the installation of the forward muffler hangar bracket to the underside of the OE exhaust heat shield using the supplied 12mm bolts. Next, the system is final-tightened making sure that the X-Muffler is properly aligned. Next comes the installation of the 2.5-inch Bassani side-exit tailpipe assemblies. Two people will be required to properly set the units in place, final-tighten, and align them.

In the process of final-tightening and aligning the system which also includes the headers, a pair of aluminum heat shields are installed on both passenger and driver side to keep header heat safely away from the ABS flexible brake lines. Heading into the home stretch, Trujillo begins hooking up the 1-inch, EGR air injection tube to the headers. It may be necessary to loosen the tube from the top of the engine to facilitate easier installation. Because this truck was already lowered, it was necessary to fabricate a custom rear exhaust hangar to clear the rear shock. This hangar, however, is bolted in the same rear position as the Bassani factory rear exhaust hangar would be installed were the truck not lowered.

of the system is a pair of Bassani dual rear-side exit pipes with 3-inch stainless steel tips that exit on the passenger side. This system comes with all the mounting hardware necessary and includes Bassani's heavy-duty band clamps and hanger brackets.

How easy is this system to install? Ideally, it should take from four to six hours using common hand tools, a jack, and jack stands. Header installation is as simple as removing the front wheels and the factory plastic inner fender panels. However, having a hydraulic lift at your disposal would obviously make the going much easier.

If your vehicle is lowered, Bassani has taken that into account by offering optional rear outer exhaust hanger brackets to clear the passenger-side rear shock absorber.

Some F-Series trucks such as the SVT Lightning also feature a removable or collapsible steering shaft with retaining bolt. Of course, temporarily removing this shaft (and bolt) makes driver-side header installation easier. However, for whatever the reason, the Harley Hauler F-150 does not have this feature, so loosening the driver-side engine mount and jacking up the engine approximately 3 inches to clear the one-piece steering shaft is necessary.

Finally, Bassani recommends installing the sheetmetal "insulator plates" provided with the headers. These sheet-metal plates protect those delicate ABS flexible brake lines from thermal meltdown! Bassani research and development chief Del Dalrymple and technician Ara Trujillo demonstrated the installation and showed us step by step how it can be done in about a day.

And this is how the newly installed system looks from an ant's-eye view. The sound and performance is great.

PROJECT 16 WIRE YOUR HEMI

 TIME: One and a half hours

 TOOLS: Full socket set, spark plug socket

 TALENT: ★

 APPLICABLE YEARS: All years—automatic and manual transmissions

 TAB: $90–$160

 TINWARE: Anti-seize lubricant, step stool, fender protection

 TIP: Remember: change one plug wire at a time.

 PERFORMANCE GAIN:
Optimize spark energy to spark plugs. Minimize electromagnetic interference.

COMPLEMENTARY PROJECT:
New spark plugs

In the world of new coil-pack technology, truck enthusiasts have to look elsewhere for increasing engine performance rather than the traditional methods for improved distributor tuning and ignition systems. The MSD 8.5mm super conductor wire set is one way to improve performance as well as dress up the engine bay of your truck, whether it be a Ford, Dodge, Chevy, or any popular brand pickup truck.

Why does this work? First, spark plug wires have two main objectives. The first is to transfer the spark energy to the plugs. The second is to suppress the electromagnetic interference (EMI) that exists with high-energy ignition systems. Too much resistance in the spark plug wires decreases the spark energy, which is needed to properly ignite the air-fuel mixture in the combustion chamber. If the resistance is too low, a greater amount of spark energy, in the form of radio waves and EMI, will leak out of the wire and interfere with sensitive electronics on the vehicle.

The right set of wires will ultimately allow the maximum amount of spark energy to reach the spark plug and combustion chamber without bleeding off any excessive radio waves and EMI. Furthermore, a good set of wires also utilizes highly conductive terminals that are properly crimped to prevent the wire from coming loose. The end result is greater efficiency in your engine's combustion process, which can lead to increased throttle response and slightly more power—especially if your current wires are in need of changing.

Because most Dodge 5.7-liter Hemi owners are concerned with performance, we opted to look for a set of high-quality

Close-up of stock wires in the looms running across the engine. The looms will not be reused with the larger 8.5mm MSD wires. To gain access to all of the wires, the hose clamps on the True Flow intake are loosened to begin removal. We also loosen the hose clamps on the throttle body. The same methods will have to be used if your truck has a factory air intake.

We also removed the air temperature sensor and the oil breather line from the intake. Once the True Flow intake is removed, we can easily access the wires.

This is another shot showing the wire looms on top of the 5.7L Hemi engine. We begin by removing one factory wire at a time and replacing each with an appropriately sized MSD 8.5mm wire. The coil pack wire also is removed by pulling it out from the terminal.

Left: Here is the same coil pack with the new MSD 8.5mm wire installed. **Right:** Each cylinder has two plugs, making for a total of 16 spark plugs for the engine.

Left: Once all the wires are in place, we started it up to make sure it fired correctly. **Right:** This is the coil pack on the 5.7L Hemi with the new 8.5mm MSD wires installed.

wires that will enhance the vehicle's performance. We found a new set of MSD performance wires that feature dual crimp terminals and durable boots. Dual crimping allows the wire to have some of the strongest connectors on the market. They also contain a special locking tip that "clicks," letting you know that they are installed correctly on to the spark plug. By inspecting the wires and boots of the MSD wires compared to the stock wires, you can see the quality work that was done. The fit and the feel is perfect, and it's better than stock.

We installed the MSD 8.5mm super conductor wire set for the 5.7L Hemi engine on a 2003 Dodge Ram 1500 Off-Road Laramie. This truck currently has 67,000 miles on it along with a True Flow intake, Aero Turbine muffler, and Superchip's programming. Installing the precut set of ignition wires is a simple enough modification. Each cylinder on the 5.7L Hemi engine has an ignition coil pack and a regular plug wire connected to the other spark plug. The coil pack also has a plug wire attached to it that extends to

the opposite cylinder bank. It appears that each cylinder shares a coil pack with another cylinder. The dual spark plugs in each cylinder fire just about simultaneously. This does not cause detonation, because the flame front from each spark promotes a controlled burn designed for more effective combustion, good emissions control, and stable idle quality.

For this install, the wires were changed from the stock ignition wires to the new MSD 8.5mm super conductor wires. To perform the wire upgrade, the intake was removed and the hose clamp was loosened on the True Flow intake at the throttle body and the air box. The same would have to be done if your vehicle had the factory air intake system as well. We also had to remove the oil breather tube and the air temperature sensor that both attach to the intake system.

We chose to start the replacement from the backmost wire on the wire loom. The wire looms on the 5.7L are integrated on top of the engine; because the stock air hat covers all of

Left: Each coil pack has two screws to remove in order to gain access to the spark plugs. **Right:** We then installed the oil breather tube after we replaced the True Flow intake tube.

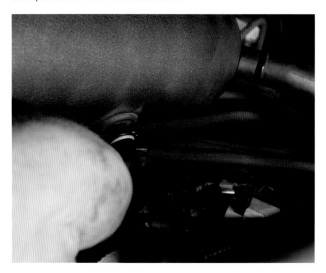

We then reinstalled the air temp sensor into the Trueflow tube, taking care not to break the sensor.

that area, it may have to be removed. In our case the True Flow intake allowed easy access.

We removed one wire at a time to make sure we connected each one to the proper cylinder and proper coil pack on the opposite side of the engine. We continued this method for each wire crossing over the engine, taking one wire off and directly comparing it to the MSD wires. This makes for a perfect fit and better look. The MSD wires are the same size as the stock wires, so be sure to compare the length of the factory wire to the MSD wires and select the most appropriate wire with similar length.

Because the new MSD 8.5mm wires were larger diameter than the stock wires, we could not use the wire looms that crossed over the engine. We chose to use the MSD pro-clamp wire separators to hold the wires in place. They really dress up the installation nicely.

We continued and replaced all the wires, making sure that the connectors of the wires were securely attached to the plugs and the coil pack by listening to ensure that the terminals

"clicked" into position. Then we test-fired the engine to make sure that there were no problems.

Once we were through replacing the wire set and the test, we reinstalled the air intake in reverse order, replacing the tube and tightening it, and then the air temp sensor was reinstalled. That was followed by the installation of the oil breather tube. We then took the truck for a test drive. Right away, it was noticeably smoother throughout the power curve at acceleration. We also picked up about three-quarters of a mile per gallon fuel economy improvement.

The next step was to replace the factory spark plugs with NGK 5306 factory replacement plugs. We gapped the new plugs to 0.050, instead of the factory gap of 0.045. The best way to change the plugs is one at a time, removing only the plug wire or coil pack at one time. Each coil pack has two small bolt screws to remove. Also, with the limited space we had with the 5.7L Hemi on the project truck, we removed the driver-side front tire and wheel well liner. The liner had eight screws to remove. Once out, we could get to the wires and plugs easier. Make sure all plugs are gapped the same, even if the box states that they are pregapped. Sometimes the plugs can lose the factory gap when shifting around during shipment. We also added some anti-seize to the threads of the new spark plugs, which is recommended to prevent gouging in the Hemi's aluminum cylinder heads. You need a good plug socket with a rubber washer inside to hold the plug once you've loosened it. Also, a good knuckle connector is a great tool to have in order to maneuver the socket into the plug holes in the tight places. A small extension connector and a good-quality socket wrench will round out the tools needed for this.

Once all 16 spark plugs were changed and the plug wires were reinstalled, we again took the truck out for a drive. We noticed a considerable difference, and we gained 1.25 to 2.5 mpg average.

All in all, with a little work in removing the air intake and removing the wires and plugs, we gained, on the average, almost 1.8 to 2.9 better mpg gas mileage with the change of these items, along with a smoother acceleration curve. The MSD wire set for the 5.7L Hemi combines quality workmanship, great acceleration, and improved fuel mileage. It is an easy way to dress up the engine compartment and to get a small performance lift.

PROJECT 17 INSTALL THE ULTIMATE SERPENTINE BELT ACCESSORY DRIVE SYSTEM

TIME: Eight to 10 hours

TOOLS: Full medium-sized socket set (include metric), screwdriver set, and medium torque wrench

TALENT: ★★

APPLICABLE YEARS: All years—automatic and manual transmissions

TAB: $2,500

TINWARE: Anti-seize compound

TIP: Take heed to the notes and cautions presented in this article. They will spare you headaches down the road.

PERFORMANCE GAIN:
Efficient design, easy to replace serpentine belt

COMPLEMENTARY PROJECT:
Install new serpentine belt.

One of the most respected names in the custom aluminum products business is Billet Specialties. For years it has supplied every facet of the custom automotive industry with a wide range of aluminum products, a line that largely began with its popular CNC machined billet wheels. As the company's product lines grew, so did the creativity of Billet Specialties engineers to craft high-quality aluminum products. One such product that Billet Specialties is very proud to introduce is the Tru Trac Serpentine System, designed for small- and big-block Chevy, Ford, and Dodge V-8s with or without air conditioning and power steering. Even more impressive is that the company has designed this system to also include the Dodge Hemi, which we will be addressing in the following installation steps.

The idea was to craft the ultimate accessory drive system for the engine using the popular late-model serpentine belt. The system contains everything needed for a complete package. It includes pulleys, brackets, air-conditioner (A/C) compressor, alternator, power steering pump, and even the water pump and housing. It's all right there in one kit ready to be bolted on. Even better for Dodge owners is that the Hemi kit also works with 383/440 B/RB motors. The innovative mounting system allows any type of cylinder head or manifold to be used.

Some of the direct features of the Hemi version of the

Remove all existing accessory drive brackets and components from motor. Remove water pump and housing, scrape away any existing gasket material with a gasket scraper, and dress surface with a Scotch Brite pad. Clean and prep threads on engine block at water pump; use a ⅜-16-inch thread chaser if necessary. Thread chasers are available at local auto parts store and tool dealers and are different from a thread-cutting tool. Apply RTV sealer to one end of the ⅜-16-inch x 3-inch threaded stud and thread stud into the driver-side top water pump mount hole. Next, apply RTV sealer to one end of the ⅜-16-inch x 4¼-inch stud and thread into the lower driver-side mount hole and tighten. Apply RTV sealer to one end of the remaining ⅜-16-inch x 3½-inch stud and thread into the bottom passenger-side mount hole and tighten. The studs can easily be tightened by threading two ⅜-16-inch zinc-coated nuts on to the stud and tightening them against each other to act as a drive nut. Apply anti-seize to the exposed threads of the studs at this time. Check installed height of studs by sliding water pump housing on to the studs. There should be ½ inch of exposed threads on the top stud and 1 inch of exposed thread on the bottom studs.

Tru Trac system include:
• Polished billet aluminum compressor manifold

• New polished Sanden SD-7 A/C compressor

• Polished 105 amp one-wire Powermaster alternator

• Polished one-piece billet aluminum alternator fan and pulley

• New Mopar Performance water pump and housing and polished aluminum water pump pulley

• Patent-pending polished billet aluminum tensioner and pully designed specifically for the Tru Trac system

- New Sweet Mfg. power steering pump with AN fittings
- Polished billet aluminum power steering, crankshaft, and idler pulleys featuring anodizing on high-wear surfaces for added durability
- Polished aluminum bridge brackets
- Polished 12-point ARP stainless fasteners throughout

Ultimately there are four different configurations per kit depending on what you require. As you will see in the following installation steps, the kit is really very easy to install and not only makes your engine look impressive, but works great too.

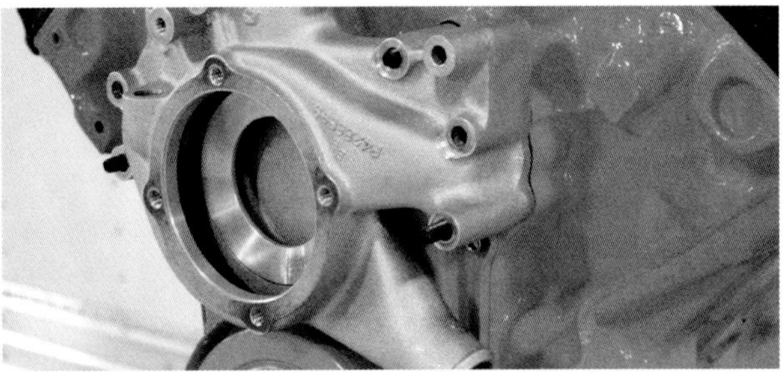

Apply Permatex Hylomar gasket dressing to both sides of the water pump housing gaskets and slip over studs on block. Install water pump housing on to studs while making sure top passenger gasket is still aligned.

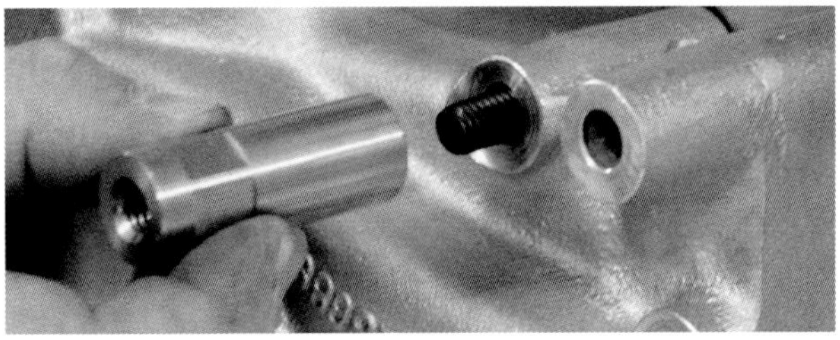

Apply anti-seize to the ⅜-16-inch x 2½-inch socket head cap screw with ⅜-inch washer and thread through water pump housing and into block only finger tight. Thread the 2-3/32-inch-long spacer nut to the driver-side top stud and finger tighten. Apply gasket dressing to both sides of the water pump and install water pump on to the housing and firmly tighten. Seep hole on the pump should point down. Place A/C bracket (14806) on passenger side of the water pump housing and align with the two left-mount bosses. Thread the 1½-inch-long spacer nut to the lower stud and finger tighten. Apply anti-seize to the ⅜-16-inch x 3-inch socket head cap screw with ⅜-inch washer and thread through A/C bracket, pump housing, and into the block, finger tight. Attach the power-steering pump bracket (P/N 14807) to the back of the alternator bracket (14801) with the 5/16-18-inch x ¾-inch socket head cap screws and tighten firmly. For kits without power steering continue to step 10. Place alternator bracket on driver side of the water pump and thread the 1 1/32-inch spacer nut on to the bottom stud and finger tighten. Apply anti-seize to the ⅜-16-inch x 3¾-inch socket head cap screw with ⅜-inch washer and thread through upper hole in the bracket, then through the water pump housing and into the block. Tighten all fasteners firmly at this time.

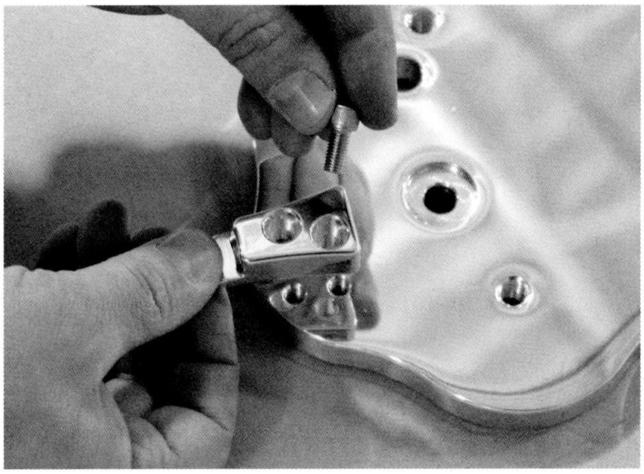

For kits with power steering, attach the power-steering support bracket to the back of the driver-side bridge bracket with two ¼-28-inch x ½-inch socket head cap screws and tighten firmly. Place bridge bracket on to the face of the motor and align bracket mount holes with spacer nuts and water pump bosses. Apply anti-seize to the ⅜-16-inch x ¾-inch flat-head cap screw and thread through the lower driver side of the bridge bracket and into the spacer nut and finger tighten. Apply anti-seize to the ⅜-16-inch x 1-inch flat-head cap screw and thread through the top driver-side bridge bracket and into upper spacer nut finger tight. Apply anti-seize to the ⅜-16-inch x 1¾-inch flat-head cap screw. Place the 13/16-inch stainless-steel spacer between the bridge bracket and the top of the water pump housing. Thread the ⅜-16-inch x 1¾-inch flat-head cap screw through the bridge bracket spacer and into the housing. Apply anti-seize to the 5/16-18-inch x 1-inch flat-head screw and thread through the lower passenger side of the bridge bracket and into the spacer nut and finger tighten. Apply anti-seize to the M10 x 2¾-inch ARP 12pt cap screw, then place and align the alternator between the bridge bracket and the alternator bracket with the long mounting boss at the bottom. Then thread the screw through the bridge bracket and alternator into the alternator bracket, just finger tight. Apply anti-seize to the M8 x 1-inch ARP 12pt cap screw, align top alternator box with the bridge bracket, and thread cap screw through bridge bracket and into the alternator. 10mm shim washers are provided to shim the alternator if needed at the bottom. Do not tighten fasteners at this time. Apply anti-seize to the compressor shoulder bolt threads. Attach the SD-7 compressor to the compressor bracket using the compressor shoulder bolt and washer. The compressor shoulder bolt and washer install through the lower back ear of the compressor and thread into the compressor bracket only finger tight. Apply anti-seize to the two 8mm-1.25 x 25mm 12pt ARP cap screws. Thread on cap screw through the bridge bracket in the bottom ear of the compressor and finger tighten. Swivel compressor up and line top compressor ear with the top bridge bracket ear and thread second 8mm-1.25 x 25mm 12pt ARP cap screw through bracket and into the compressor and finger tighten. Apply anti-seize to the thread of the 5/16-18-inch x 1-inch set screw and thread into the back of the tensioner body only finger tight. Apply anti-seize to the remaining exposed threads. Thread the 2 13/32-inch long spacer nut on to the set screw and tighten firmly. Apply anti-seize to the two 5/16-18-inch x 1-inch flat-head screws. Place tensioner body with spacer nut between the bridge bracket and the A/C bracket. Align tensioner holes with the bridge bracket and thread the two 5/16-18-inch x 1-inch flat-head screws through the bridge bracket and into the tensioner only finger tight.

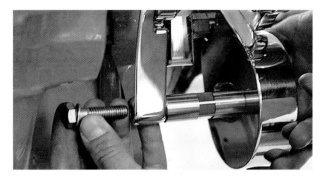

Apply anti-seize to the ⅜-16-inch x 1½-inch hex-head cap screw. Thread the hex-head cap screw with ⅜-inch washer through the back of the compressor bracket and into the spacer nut and tighten firmly.

Apply anti-seize to the two ⁵⁄₁₆-18-inch x 2¾-inch socket head cap screws and to the M8-1.25 x 25mm socket head cap screw. Place the power steering pump between the bridge bracket and the alternator bracket aligning the pump ears with the mount holes in the power steering bracket. Thread the two ⁵⁄₁₆-18-inch x 2¾-inch socket head cap screws with ⁵⁄₁₆-inch medium-split washers through the power steering pump and into the small support bracket and finger tighten. Thread the M8-1.25 x 25mm socket head cap screw through the bracket and into the power steering pump and tighten firmly. Tighten the two other power steering fasteners and all bridge bracket fasteners and accessory hardware firmly at this time.

Attach the manifold by removing the protective cover and placing the manifold on to the compressor. Apply anti-seize to the two M8-1.25 x 25mm socket head cap screws and thread through the manifold and into the compressor and tighten firmly. (Note: Billet Specialties recommends having your air conditioning charged and serviced by an automotive air conditioning service center with the proper equipment to ensure many years of trouble-free service.) Install and route the belt as shown in the diagram while allowing the belt to rest on the pulley boss. Place a ⅝-inch box end wrench on the tensioner nut. Align belt on to pulley groove above the tensioner boss.

Pull up on the wrench until tensioner pulley is able to slip on to the tensioner boss.

Thread ⅜-16-inch x ¾-inch 12pt ARP bolt and washer on to the tensioner pulley and tighten firmly.

Place the crankshaft pulley on the damper and align holes. Apply anti-seize to and thread the six ⁵⁄₁₆-18-inch x 1-inch socket head cap screws with ⁵⁄₁₆-inch Belleview washers through the pulley and into the damper and tighten firmly to 26 lb-ft. Place the water pump pulley and nose cone on the water pump shaft. Apply anti-seize and attach with four ⁵⁄₁₆-18-inch x 1-inch socket head cap screws and tighten firmly to 26 lb-ft. Apply anti-seize to the three ⅜-16-inch x 1¾-inch ARP 12pt cap screws. Thread the ⅜-16-inch x 1¾-inch ARP cap screw through the idler pulley polished cover, idler pulley, and boss, and into the bridge bracket and tighten firmly to 46 lb-ft. Repeat the previous step for the other two idler pulleys. Install the compressor clutch cover by applying anti-seize to the three ¼-20-inch x ¾-inch socket head cap screws and thread them through the compressor cover into the compressor. Tighten firmly. Remove sealed cap on compressor only if you plan on charging your A/C system. Leaving the compressor open to outside air can introduce moisture into the system and cause the cooling system not to operate properly. Never connect the compressor clutch wire and run the compressor unless the system is completely charged.

PROJECT 18 | POWER FOR YOUR TIRED ENGINE

TIME: Five hours

TOOLS: Full socket set, screwdriver set, torque wrench, appropriate jack, jack stands

TALENT: ★★★

APPLICABLE YEARS: All years—automatic and manual transmissions

TAB: $700 for Corsa exhaust system, $300 for Jet Performance chip

TINWARE: Access to a hydraulic truck lift is an asset here.

TIP: A second pair of hands can be a big help.

PERFORMANCE GAIN:
8–20 horsepower increase

COMPLEMENTARY PROJECT:
Aftermarket air intake system

Our F-150 features a tired but still capable 4.6-liter V-8 that has 90,000 miles on it. One of the main components that we wanted to change in this power upgrade was the factory exhaust. We opted to try a Corsa stainless-steel exhaust system. The truck had the factory exhaust still on it, and we worked with A+ Performance exhaust to remove the old system and install the Corsa unit.

Although the factory exhaust is held with a clamp, it took some effort to get it off. Ultimately, the clamp had to be heated with a torch, and the exhaust was removed from that point.

How does a truck with more than 90,000 miles get a second wind? The answer is: with some aftermarket performance items that can help it regain some of its strength. We've looked at a variety of combinations, and we wanted to find out what the JET Chip and a Corsa cat-back exhaust system would do to improve the performance of a 2000 model Ford F-150.

We took the F-150 to JET Performance in Huntington Beach, California, where we conducted our baseline dynamometer tests. On the company's Mustang Dyno, the 4.6-liter made a maximum of 181 rear-wheel horsepower. With this baseline information we then went on to the next step to improve the truck's exhaust system.

Although the truck was well maintained, the engine was as stock as the day it rolled off the showroom floor. The factory exhaust system was rusted and ready to be replaced. For this first stage of the truck's transformation, we took it to A+ Performance Exhaust where a Corsa Performance cat-back system was installed. The system is manufactured from 304 stainless steel and features the Pro Series single side exit with a polished twin exhaust tip. Corsa uses a reflective sound cancellation technology (RSC), which is a patented design that eliminates any resonance in the cab, yet allows full flow and sound to exit out of the tailpipe.

The Corsa exhaust went on to the truck with only one hard spot in removing the front clamp of the tube that extends behind the factory catalytic converter. The rest of the system is bolted on and clamped into place. Aside from the high-flow muffler, the Corsa system also uses 3-inch, mandrel bent tubing and the factory hangers. Once the exhaust was clamped together on the truck, Harry Chelebyan at A+ Performance tack welded the sections together to avoid anything from coming loose over time.

The truck sounded great, and once we got it back to the JET dynamometer, it showed a peak gain of 13 horsepower at 5,000 rpm and an average horsepower gain of 8 to 10 horsepower across the entire rpm band.

Even though the truck is a 2000 model, Ford still incorporated a PROM chip in the factory Electronic Control Module

The rest of the tailpipe is put into place as were the clamps provided in the kit. Where necessary, the exhaust system hooks into the factory hangers. The dual tip is then inserted and clamped into position.

Here you can see the difference between the factory exhaust on the left and the Corsa exhaust on the right. The Corsa has a limited lifetime warranty, and because it is made from 304 stainless, it will never rust. The new head pipe on the Corsa exhaust is slip fit into the factory Y-pipe.

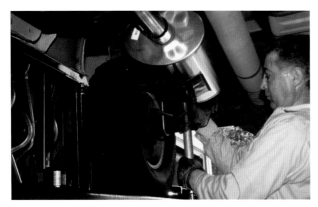

The high-flow muffler and the rest of the system is slip fit into position. The Corsa system comes with wide, stainless clamps that are similar to the factory units, and they are tightened on each of the slip-fit joints.

Once the truck was off of the lift, this is all that was visible of the Corsa exhaust system. Nevertheless, it sounded great and provided no noise in the cab. With the ECU out of the vehicle, the factory chip is removed and the contacts are cleaned. The new JET reprogrammed chip simply plugs into the port. An indicator decal is used to alert anyone working on the vehicle that the chip is a JET product.

(ECU). On this truck, the ECU is located behind the passenger kick panel inside the truck's cab. Once removed, the ECU has a connector cable that is easily unplugged, and the ECU can be removed from its retaining bracket. On the outside edge of the ECU, there is a computer chip panel that can be pulled out by pushing in on the retaining tabs on the chip holder. Once the chip was removed, the connector was cleaned and the new JET chip was inserted into the ECU.

JET provides a decal that goes over the new chip to indicate it is not the factory PROM in the computer. The chip provides increased fuel and timing to the engine and, along with improved fuel economy, JET claims increased horsepower with the program updates; and the chip is emissions legal in all 50 states.

With both the JET chip installed and the Corsa exhaust system on the truck, the truck improved again with a peak horsepower gain of 20 rear-wheel horsepower. Across the rpm range the combination provided an average 15 to18 horsepower increase.

This combination easily brought this tired F-150 back to life, and with some customizing, the truck would be perfect for a high school student or a daily driver who sports some attitude. So, what's it going to cost to get an extra 18 to 20 horsepower? The stainless-steel Corsa exhaust retails for less than $700 and the JET PROM chip sells for a bit more than $300.

With the chip installed, the ECU is then plugged back into the vehicle's factory harness and placed back in its position behind the kick panel.

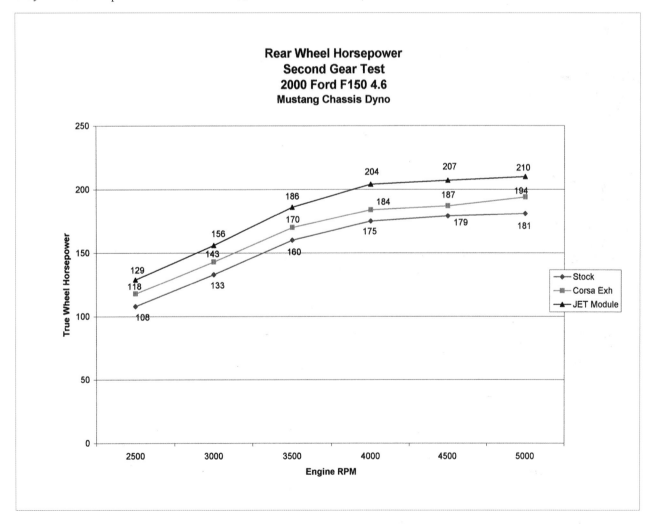

Rear Wheel Horsepower
Second Gear Test
2000 Ford F150 4.6
Mustang Chassis Dyno

The dyno chart shows an impressive horsepower gain with the JET/Corsa combination. This is one that is well worth the cost and effort as both units will last the life of the vehicle and give it an extra 18–20 horsepower as well.

PROJECT 19 INSTALL A DUAL BATTERY TRAY AND HIGH-OUTPUT ALTERNATOR

TIME: Three hours

TOOLS: Basic socket set, basic open-end wrench set, screwdriver set

TALENT: ★

APPLICABLE YEARS: All years—automatic and manual transmissions

TAB: $400—kit plus the cost of a second battery. If you choose to install a new alternator, the cost will increase.

TINWARE: Second battery; quality of second battery will affect total cost of project.

TIP: If you run lots of lights or stereo equipment, this is a must-do project.

PERFORMANCE GAIN:
Backup battery to provide starting power and supplemental battery for running auxiliary electronics

COMPLEMENTARY PROJECT:
Auxiliary lights, winch, audio video equipment

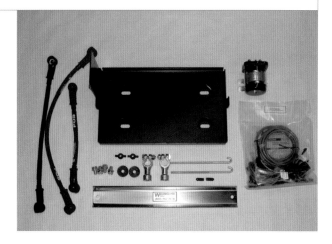

The dual battery tray is included in this Hummer H2 kit and comes with everything necessary to install.

The original setup included an aftermarket battery and plenty of cables from amplifiers for a high-end stereo system on this H2. The factory alternator was not sufficient in providing amperage to properly recharge the battery and left this H2 stranded several times without enough power to turn over the engine. The system's isolator helps to maintain proper charging and maintains the charge of the secondary battery. The isolator in this instance is mounted to the H2's firewall where the connections can be easily accessed. The next step was to replace the factory alternator and to install the dual battery tray. In order to do this, the factory air intake system had to be temporarily removed. The tension on the serpentine belt is loosened, and the bolts that hold in the factory alternator are removed. The alternator is unplugged from the wiring harness, and it is removed from the OEM bracket. There are no modifications necessary to bolt on the larger-case alternator to the factory alternator brackets. Even the factory bolts are reused. Although there is a size difference, the large-case alternator on the right will fit perfectly into the factory bracket. It also provides 190 amps to power the H2's accessories.

Off-road lights, television monitors, and high-watt amplifiers are some of the more common items that often get installed on our vehicles. In fact, it almost seems mandatory that high-end sport utility vehicles, such as Hummer H2s and Cadillacs, should be equipped with these pieces of aftermarket equipment. Once one or more of these items are installed on your truck or SUV, the first problem that arises is the lack of battery power.

Dead batteries are not necessarily a function of high-watt lights or a multi-amp stereo system. The problem comes from the vehicle's inability to recharge the battery and the amount of power that is drawn from it when your accessories are turned on. The way to solve this problem is to upgrade your charging system. Factory alternators usually put out anywhere from 45 amps to 105 amps. But given the fact that a 1,000-watt stereo system can draw more than 71 amps and a 9,500-pound winch can draw more than 500 amps, you get the idea on the amount of drain accessories can have on your charging system. High-output alternators can deliver as much as 200+ amps, and when combined with a dual battery setup, your charging system

can handle big amp draws without any problem.

To get a better idea of how this works, we spoke with Wrangler NW Power Products, which manufactures a line of dual battery trays and high-output alternator systems. The components are designed for specific vehicle makes and models, and when we visited Wrangler NW Products, the company happened to be installing a dual battery and high-output alternator on a modified Hummer H2, owned by Casey Miser of All American Truck & SUV Accessory Centers. Miser's H2 is equipped with several television monitors, a high-end stereo system, and off-road lights that his company sells and installs in his All American shops, which are located throughout the Portland, Oregon area.

Miser's recharging problems stemmed from the high-watt stereo system and HID lighting system, which drew huge amounts of amperage from the factory GM small-case alternator. Wrangler recently developed an H2 system that includes a dual battery tray and a 190-amp alternator. All of the components fit in the factory locations, and the installation took a couple of hours to complete.

The installation began by removing the factory air intake system, followed by removing the serpentine belt from the engine's idler pulley. The factory alternator was then unbolted from its bracket and removed. Then the connections to the battery were removed and set aside. A battery isolator unit was mounted to the H2's firewall, and the wiring was left loose until the rest of the system was installed.

The battery is removed, followed by the original battery tray. The new Wrangler tray has the relay bolted on to its side before it is installed in the factory tray location. This system used dual

Odyssey PC1200 dry-cell batteries that, together, are the same width as the original battery. Once installed, the batteries are wired according to the instructions. The kit comes with large cables and high-quality clamps that are also installed. The wiring from the isolator to the battery manager is put in place. The battery manager is a switch located on the inside portion of the dash next to the fuse panel. This turns on the dual battery system. If one of the batteries goes dead, the manager is switched to the emergency "on" position where enough power is stored in the secondary battery to start the vehicle. Because the switch would mostly be on the "dual on" mode, Miser wanted to keep the switch hidden and out of the way.

Once the rest of the connections were made, the system provided plenty of amps to power all of the H2's accessories. This particular system #100-600 costs about $210 and is a great way to ensure that you'll be able to enjoy your stereo and other accessories without getting stranded.

The new batteries were then installed on to the Wrangler tray. Two battery hold-down J-hooks and a retainer bracket are included in the kit.

All this wiring looks complicated, but the instructions tell you where to mount the large positive and negative cables.

The new alternator is installed using the original bolts, and the serpentine belt is also reinstalled. The large-case alternator fits perfectly in the OEM location, and all of the wiring attaches to this alternator. Before the new battery tray is installed, the relay is bolted on to it. All of the connections to the original battery were removed. These will be added on after the new system is installed. By removing the bolts at the bottom of the OEM tray, it can be removed from the fender. In this application, the alarm siren also had to be relocated. The new Wrangler tray is installed in the factory location. Make sure to include the J-hooks for the battery hold-down bracket.

Using the factory bolts, the Wrangler tray is installed. To make room for the larger tray, a small portion of this computer module shroud had to be trimmed.

The two positive cables are also routed to the relay, mounted to the battery tray. The large-gauge alternator wire also has a fusible link to prevent any damage to the system should something go terribly wrong.

PROJECT 20 | INSTALL A REMOTE SECURITY SYSTEM

TIME: Three hours

TOOLS: Small socket set, screwdriver set, torque wrench, appropriate jack

TALENT: ★★★

APPLICABLE YEARS: All years—automatic and manual transmissions

TAB: $400

TINWARE: Wire connectors, shrink sleeves, electrician's tape

TIP: Because of the circuitry, it's recommended this system be installed at a shop that does this kind of project all the time. However, if you can stick to detailed directions and you're not afraid of cutting wires, go for it.

PERFORMANCE GAIN:
Remote engine start

COMPLEMENTARY PROJECT:
Backup monitor

The Stellar STRS9950 security system and remote start combo comes with the microprocessor, two-way LCD remote, siren, relays, and all necessary hardware and instructions. The first step is to pop off the top of the dash, followed by the side and bottom panels. Just give them a sharp tug, and they come right off. Next, the metal bezel beneath the steering column is removed to gain access to the dash wiring.

For most of us, there's nothing worse than the thought of some low-life stealing our truck. It's bad enough that you lose the truck itself, but in most cases, there's so much more at stake. A killer stereo, a stack of your favorite CDs, maybe even a DVD player could be inside. You may have performed untold modifications to your truck that won't be covered by your insurance, because you'll be reimbursed only for its Bluebook value (unless you've purchased extra coverage, which most of us don't). With this in mind, it's no wonder that automotive security systems have become so popular in recent years. With a push of a button, you can secure your truck and your belongings, or at least deter thieves from choosing your truck as their next target.

The problem is, many of the security systems on the market today have been around for years, and thieves are usually quite accustomed to the way the more popular systems function, making them easy to disable. Living in a port city, where vehicles can be stolen and on a container ship by the time we wake up in the morning, we wanted to equip our 2000 Chevy Silverado extended cab with a state-of-the-art security system—and found what we were looking for at Stellar Vehicle Security. Stellar is one of

the Hoffman Group brands that include AutoLoc accessories, Zirgo cooling fans, and Keep It Clean wiring systems, with the main office located in Tigard, Oregon, just outside of Portland.

Stellar offers a variety of security systems and related products, but the system that caught our eye is the new STRS9950 security system and remote start combo. "This system was developed in response to some of our customers who had been requesting a vehicle security system using the latest technology," explained Hoffman Group president, Drew Hoffman. "So, we sat down and designed a very high-tech security system that is modular in design and can be upgraded with a variety of available accessories."

A key feature of the STRS9950 is its two-way LCD remote, which offers real-time monitoring in the palm of your hand. Unlike most remotes, which simply send a signal to your vehicle to lock or unlock the doors, arm the alarm, and so on, the STRS9950 uses FM transmission technology, and can therefore send and receive a signal. What difference does this make? Well, instead of being a lump of plastic that sits in your pocket, this LCD remote receives a signal from your vehicle, so you know what is happening with it at all times. A small LCD display on the remote depicts a vehicle (in this case, a BMW X5). That remote, then, can alert you to the fact that your alarm has been triggered and how it has been triggered.

For example, if someone were to gain access to your truck by opening the door, the door of the vehicle in the LCD display would turn dark and its lights would flash on and off, indicating that the alarm had been triggered. If someone tries to break a window, a small hammer striking the rear window is displayed. A signal strength indicator, similar to those used on cell phones, tells you if your remote is still in range. In addition, you can select a silent arming mode that causes the remote to vibrate in your pocket (rather than triggering an audible alarm), or you can also set it to sound an alarm and vibrate. You can stop the alarm and reset it via the remote as well; the LCD display will confirm with a padlock icon in the locked position and a tiny dot on the windshield that indicates the "armed" LED will be blinking.

Pull down the driver-side pillar cover, then install the antenna that receives messages from and sends messages to the remote. Installing the antenna in this area makes for a clean installation and does not seem to affect remote performance. The car call sensor is preassembled with an adhesive tape ring and is affixed to the lower right-hand corner of the driver-side window. The LED in the middle serves as the arming indicator.

Sheets says it is very important to use a digital multimeter when checking the wires, not a test light, as you run the risk of sending a ground signal to the airbag system and setting them off. That would be bad.

The valet switch that allows you to control many of the system's functions can be mounted virtually anyplace of your choosing, but the technician mounts it in the fuse box because it's hidden, yet easy to access.

It is also very important to diode-isolate the door triggers; they can't be wired together, or it can confuse the microprocessor.

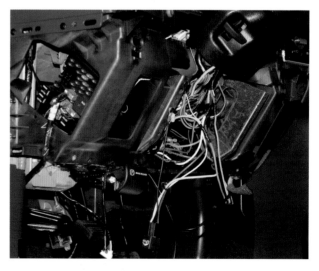

The microprocessor slides neatly into place underneath the steering column, next to a steel dash support bracket.

Here, the completed wires and relays have been soldered and taped and are ready to go back up in the dash.

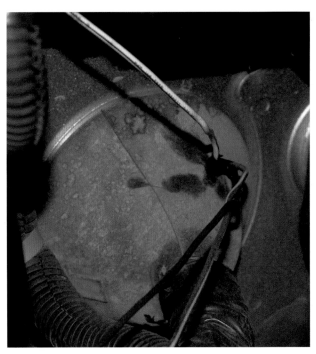

Sheets uses nylon ties to secure all of the wires, then tucks them neatly under the dash.

The wires for the siren run through a large grommet in the driver-side firewall; a hole is poked in the grommet, and the wires are pulled through.

The STRS9950 is what you might call an "intelligent" security system. Employing "fuzzy logic" technology (the same used in the Tomahawk Cruise Missile, according to Stellar), the system's microprocessor is programmed to "think" and decides if the impact is the proper signature for a break-in or if it is just the vibration from a passing truck. It also allows the use of a unique feature called "Car Call." Let's say a friend was supposed to meet you at a car show, but he was late, so you walked away and now he doesn't know where to find you. He can simply tap the system's sensor on the windshield, and your remote will page you and display the Car Call logo of a phone on the vehicle's windshield, instead of an intrusion alert. Fuzzy logic knows the difference between a light tap on the windshield and a thump on the side glass, for example.

One of our favorite features of the STRS9950, of course, is the remote start—and again the unique LCD two-way remote plays an important role in the success of the system. Press the number four button on the remote, hold it for two seconds, and your truck can be started from up to a quarter mile away (sometimes more, depending on the circumstances). And because you may be too far away to confirm that the truck has actually started, the LCD display will indicate your truck is running with little puffs of smoke coming from the vehicle's exhaust. An anti-grinding feature makes sure that the starter will not be engaged any longer than necessary by monitoring engine rpm and voltage drop, and an auto restart feature will attempt to start the engine up to three more times if it fails on the first attempt.

When you arrive at your truck, simply press the number two button to unlock the doors, then step inside and put the key in the ignition. We don't have to tell you how invaluable this system is for those who live in very hot or cold climates; you can set the A/C or heater before you leave the vehicle, and find the interior at the perfect temperature when you return. If you change your mind after you've started the vehicle, no

problem—simply press the number four button again, hold it for two seconds, and the engine will stop.

There are other cool features as well. For example, an auto start program can start your truck automatically on a 24-hour clock, so it will be ready for you each morning before you leave for work. And if you've got a diesel truck, you'll love the Turbo Timer feature. As you know, a diesel engine should idle for several minutes after having been under load (driving a steep grade or towing a trailer) before you shut it off to prevent turbocharger "coking" (deposits left on the turbo from burned oil). The Turbo Timer feature allows you to turn off the engine immediately, get out, arm the security system, and walk away; the engine will continue to idle for five minutes before shutting down. How 'bout that?

One of the greatest concerns enthusiasts have with remote start systems is that someone will be able to break the window, get inside, and drive away—and even if you are alerted to an intruder by the remote, you won't be able to get there in time. Well, Stellar has thought of this scenario too. Because contemporary automatic transmission-equipped vehicles won't let you put the transmission into gear without first stepping on the brake pedal, a sensor in the system will kill the engine the instant the brake pedal is touched if the key is not in the ignition. Once the engine stops, it cannot be restarted without the key.

Stellar has also included an anti-carjacking feature in the STRS9950. If you see a suspicious character approaching your truck, press the number three button on the remote once. If the would-be carjacker opens the door within eight seconds, the anti-carjacking feature is triggered; when he shuts the door, he'll have only 30 seconds behind the wheel before the alarm begins to sound every two seconds. Twenty seconds after that, the parking lights will begin flashing continuously. The siren will stop sounding and the lights will stop flashing when the key is

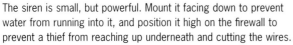
The siren is small, but powerful. Mount it facing down to prevent water from running into it, and position it high on the firewall to prevent a thief from reaching up underneath and cutting the wires.

Last but not least, plug in and adjust the two-stage shock sensor, which features adjustable sensitivity.

turned off; however, the starter and ignition kill circuits will be enabled, and the vehicle can't be started again until you push a button on the remote (we're not going to say which one!). Of course, there are also more common features such as a panic mode that sounds the siren and flashes the lights for 30 seconds and a "car finder" mode that also sounds the siren and flashes the lights, but only for 8 seconds.

Moreover, the STRS9950 is completely programmable to suit the owner's needs. Stellar includes a chart that lists numbered system functions and tells you how to enable/disable them using a valet button that can be hidden in the area of your choice. To change a function, simply disarm the system, turn the key to the "on" position, and press the valet button seven times within eight seconds. Then, press the valet button the same number of times as the function number you would like to change, and press the number one button on the remote to select the default value or the number two button to select the variable value. The system's siren will "chirp" accordingly, one or two times to confirm your selection.

The modular design of the STRS9950 means that a variety of different accessories can be added to the system for an even higher level of security. For example, there are a number of ways a thief can break your side glass without much impact, and therefore will not trigger the motion sensor or the alarm. The

GS1 glass sensor contains a microphone that is tuned specifically to "hear" the sound signature of breaking glass and will trigger the alarm. If you want to deter thieves before they even have a chance to look in your window, then perhaps you'll be interested in the RM2000 two-stage radar motion sensor. It "chirps" the alarm when an intruder approaches and will trigger the alarm if motion is detected in the vehicle's interior, like someone reaching in an open window to steal your CDs.

Then there's the UT1000 two-head bi-directional ultra sonic sensor, which allows you to set an invisible line inside the vehicle; if that line is crossed, the alarm is triggered. And, if you'd like to add some redundancy to your security system, you can opt for the BKSR battery backup siren—which will still work even if the power supply to the system's primary siren is cut.

Having lived with the STRS9950 for about two weeks now (as of this writing), we can tell you that it has been a pleasure to own. The remote is powerful and reliable, and the displays are very helpful when we can't see our vehicle to confirm that it is started, locked, secure, and so forth. It has issued only what we believe were two false alarms in that time, which is great, compared to some cheap security systems that issue false alarms twice an hour.

If you've been considering a security system or a remote start system, then Stellar's STRS9950 is a great way to get both in one small, well-engineered package. It costs $349.

PROJECT 21 UPGRADE YOUR PLUG WIRES

 TIME: Two hours

 TOOLS: Medium socket set, screwdriver set

 TALENT: ★ to ★★

 APPLICABLE YEARS: Ford 4.6-liter V-8: Performance Distributors makes kits for Chevy, Dodge, and most popular vehicle applications.

 TAB: $328

 TINWARE: Fender protection cloth while you lean into the motor bay

 TIP: Pay close attention to your plug-wire fire orders.

 PERFORMANCE GAIN:
More spark for higher fuel-burning efficiency

COMPLEMENTARY PROJECT:
Aftermarket air intake system to draw in more air

In order to get to the spark plugs, we have to remove the air intake system. We began by unplugging the air temperature sensor. We loosened the air filter clamp in order to remove the inlet tube and air filter box. Once the clamp was loosened, we could remove the air filter box from the intake. We simply set it aside and left the MAF sensor plugged in. We then removed the throttle body cover by unscrewing the three bolts that hold it in place. The clamp to the throttle body intake tube was loosened, and the rest of the intake could then be removed. We carefully pulled out the air intake tube, making sure to unplug it from the two breather hoses near the throttle body.

The hardest part is to reach and pull out the factory spark plug boots. We unplugged all of the wires first, but left them attached to the OEM coils. It was also necessary to unplug the coils from the wiring harness. The coils use four bolts that attach it to a bracket. These were removed.

If you need a little more spark out of your Ford 4.6-liter V-8, then it may be time to upgrade your truck's ignition system. Ford uses a dual-coil system that fires directly from the coil to the cylinder. The problem is that over time the coils and wires can deteriorate due to vibration and heat.

Upgrading is an option, and Performance Distributors recently introduced a Firepower ignition kit specifically for the 4.6-liter V-8. The kit includes the company's Screamin' Deamon coil packs, which can deliver a higher spark for a more efficient burn of air and fuel in the engine's combustion chamber. Performance Distributors claims you can open up your spark plug gap to 0.065 inch. The coils are epoxy filled, which dissipates heat and are vibration resistant.

The kit also comes with the company's Live Wires and has a nice heat sleeve affixed to the half-inch spark plug wires. The wires feature a spiral-wound core that prevents electronic interference with radios and computers, and allows maximum voltage to get to the spark plug. The kit also comes with billet aluminum wire looms because the larger wires won't fit in the factory looms.

This kit fits 1997–99 Ford trucks and retails for around $328. The hardest part of the installation is removing and reinstalling the spark plugs into the cylinder head. We tried a kit on our 1998 F-150 and found that the wires were custom cut to the proper length and fit perfectly. To avoid mixing up the wires, we left them connected to the factory coils, and once the new coils were in place, we attached the new ones one by one. The wires were long enough to be routed under the fuel injector wiring harness alongside the intake manifold, and they fit nicely under the radiator hose, just like the factory wires were routed.

Once complete, we noticed a slight improvement in the idle and a snappier throttle response. It will take some time for us to note any mileage change as well as noticing any horsepower improvements. If we were to later add more performance to this engine, such as supercharger or nitrous oxide, the addition of the improved spark would also help in overall performance gains.

The new coils fit in the exact same position as the factory units, making sure that the harness plug faces out toward the front of the vehicle. The original bolts are used to secure the new coils to the coil brackets. Don't forget to plug the wiring harness back on to the new coils.

The coils were then removed from the bracket but were left with the wire attached. This helped us to remember where the new wires plug into the Performance Distributor coils.

Once all of the wires were swapped out, it was time to decide where to install the billet aluminum wire separators. We double-checked the wiring and made sure the wires were all in the correct position on the coils.

The wires plug into the coils with a locking mechanism that is removed by squeezing the locking arms at the top.

The finished installation improved the throttle response a bit, and our idle smoothed out.

A rule of thumb is to measure twice and cut once. A local driveshaft service is then used to resize the driveshaft, which has to be shortened by some 14 inches. Finally, the driveshaft can be removed from the truck. In some instances, a two-piece driveshaft will be changed to a single shaft.

PROJECT 22 SUPERCHARGE YOUR HEMI

 TIME: Four to six hours

 TOOLS: Full socket set, hand tools

 TALENT: ★★★

 APPLICABLE YEARS: Late-model Hemi

 TAB: $5,500

 TINWARE: Fender protection

 TIP: N/A

 PERFORMANCE GAIN:
Approximately 100 horsepower

COMPLEMENTARY PROJECT:
Boost gauge

With the serpentine belt removed, you will simply reroute the EGR solenoid plumbing out of the way of the supercharger head unit. The 2004–05 Dodge Hemi Ram 1500 is equipped with an EGR solenoid located on the front of the passenger-side cylinder head. You will remove the factory EGR tube, then cut and relocate with the high heat blue hose and clamps supplied with the kit.

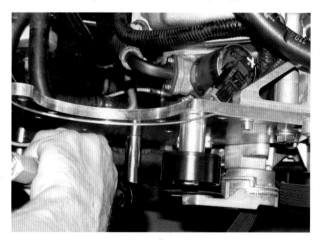

With the ½-inch aluminum plate assembled with the small idler-pulley bracket, and the bracket designed to clear your EGR solenoid, mount the plate to the engine block. Reinstall the radiator overflow tank and washer assembly. With the throttle body disassembled according to instructions, you will install the supercharger injector plate between the throttle body and the manifold with the O-ring facing the throttle body.

Sometimes Dodge loyalists feel like they get overlooked when it comes to aftermarket performance products for their late-model trucks. That's understandable, and it took a couple lifelong Mopar purists to figure out a solution to give these loyalists the ability to bolt on more than 100 horsepower to a 5.7-liter Hemi engine.

Scott Quaranta of GS Motorsports and his small band of colleagues designed a quality supercharger, intercooler, and software management program designed expressly for a factory-stock motor operated at sea level and in a warm climate.

Common hand tools, a full day, and moderate mechanical abilities are all that's required to bolt on this supercharging system that uses a Paxton centrifugal blower head unit and half-inch-thick aluminum plate mounting bracket. At half-inch thickness, the aluminum mounting plate provides a sturdy platform for mounting a supercharger that won't bend or wobble under a load. The instructions are straightforward, and the wiring steps are well documented.

At one-quarter throttle, the 5,400-pound Ram pickup stepped right up and moved off the stoplight like a vehicle half its weight. Half-throttle roll-offs give a full-size truck a power-to-weight ratio that makes the pickup a blast to drive. By design, there is a lag-time between gear shifts in the transmission to allow gears to change smoothly and prevent excessive strain on the driveline when the supercharger spools on. This supercharger lives from mid- to upper-range engine speeds. So, a 2,000-rpm roll away from the stoplight will help you sink into your seat.

If you are interested in tackling this project, we highly recommend that you put your truck on a chassis dyno to document the performance your Hemi is turning out with the supercharger onboard. Once you experience this basic supercharger platform, you can dial in more with a set of GS Motorsports stainless-steel headers and advanced-tune programming. Keep in mind that GS Motorsports can dial in your specific tuning needs depending upon the operating conditions and the climate you actually live in.

Here are the highlights of the installation process to give you an idea of what it takes. You will use your factory intake manifold and throttle body with all additional components supplied with the system.

Mount the Hemi fuel and timing box on the right side (on driver's right) inner fenderwell. With the control box installed, you will follow the wiring instructions to tie the system together electronically. We all know there is no easy way to change spark plugs, but you need to do it. The factory spark plug at top is noticeably longer than the new plug at bottom. There's plenty of spark-throwing capability with this system without the need for the electrode to spew fire right on top of the piston. These new plugs are readily available at all automotive supply stores.

Install the Paxton centrifugal head unit (supercharger) to the mounting bracket and thread bolts finger tight to secure the head unit.

Bolt down the head unit and connect hoses and lines.

Install the intercooler and ducting to the top of the supercharger head unit. Install the serpentine belt.

Install the ducting tube from the supercharger to the air cleaner box. Make sure everything is tightened down and that the wires are all connected.

Load the software into your laptop, then download the Hemi GS4 programming. Once the base tune is installed, you have unlimited options for tuning your vehicle.

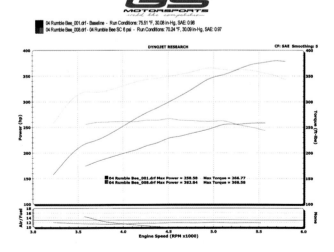

When you fire up your Hemi and take it to the dynamometer, look for numbers like this. This yellow Rumble Bee Hemi Ram turned out 382.84 rear-wheel horsepower and 368 lb-ft of torque at about 5,300 rpm. That's about 124 ponies more than stock horsepower.

TIME: Eight hours

TOOLS: Full socket set, screwdriver set, torque wrench, transmission jack

TALENT: ★★★

APPLICABLE YEARS: All years—automatic and manual transmissions

TAB: $2,300

TINWARE: Transmission oil

TIP: Line up a driveline shop in advance to resize your vehicle's driveshaft. Access to a hydraulic lift is an advantage.

PERFORMANCE GAIN:
Fuel efficiency, wider power range

COMPLEMENTARY PROJECT:
Transmission cooler and temperature gauge

Weighing in at about 40 pounds, this Gear Vendors under/overdrive will increase performance and fuel mileage. The first order of business will be to measure the stock transmission's tail shaft, which will be figured into the equation for shortening the stock driveshaft.

With the ring gear removed, the bearings were taken out from the carrier assembly with the use of a bearing puller. The carrier was then cleaned up in preparation for reassembly.

Would you believe me if I told you that a full-size diesel-powered pickup can get 30 miles per gallon while being driven at 75 miles per hour? Like you, I might believe it, but I would still want to see some proof with my own eyes. True, this project summary walks you through a typical Gear Vendors under/overdrive auxiliary transmission installation; however, I want to share the test drive experience and results with you first.

First thing to understand is that a gasoline engine requires more rpm to accelerate and to maintain freeway speeds than a diesel. Gas engines, from my experience, have a sweet spot at about 2,400 rpm while the diesel engine loves about 1,700 rpm. Either way, to get the best fuel mileage possible, you have to operate your truck within the engine's optimum torque range.

The Dodge used in this installation has a factory 3.73:1 rear-end gear ratio, which put the tachometer at approximately 2,200 rpm at 70 mph. Rich Johnson, president of Gear Vendors, then clicked the Gear Vendors unit into overdrive, and instantly the engine dropped to 1,700 rpm. Because we were well within the torque range of the diesel engine, there was no

noticeable loss in power, and speed remained the same. However, the cab became quiet as the rattle of the diesel engine was almost eliminated. The added bonus was fuel economy, which soared to almost 30 mpg!

Johnson added that Detroit is getting much closer to designing a precision transmission with multiple gears, allowing for higher rear-end gear options, which reduce engine rpm at highway speeds. But this Dodge six-speed manual transmission setup came closer to perfection with the addition of a Gear Vendors under/overdrive unit! Johnson added, "When the trucks came off the dealer's lot with three- and four-speed auto and stick transmissions, installing a Gear Vendors was the perfect solution to filling gear gaps and slowing engine rpm in all gears, especially high gear.

"If they hadn't changed to five- and six-speed transmissions, we would be on some island somewhere sipping margaritas

The only modification to the driveline will be the removal of the transmission's tail shaft housing, which will be replaced by the Gear Vendors unit and adapters. With the stock tail shaft housing removed, the Gear Vendors adapters are selected and test-fit to ensure correct bolt patterns and length.

The first of the two transmission adapters is cleaned and prepared for installation by creating a gasket of Permatex Ultra Blue.

A dummy Gear Vendors auxiliary transmission is then positioned to ensure all truck components are clear, and it is positioned far enough away to not heat up the unit. The meat and potatoes of the install is the Gear Vendors auxiliary transmission, which is very compact and self-contained. It does not share the transmission's fluids.

with little umbrellas. But even with a six-speed, our gear splitter corrects for the spacing between gears, which allows the engine to comfortably operate within a tight, controlled powerband." Make it easy on the engine, and the engine will reward you in fuel savings. Think about it and you will agree that 90-plus percent of the time you are driving your truck, it is being used empty, not towing a trailer or hauling a full load. This is when the Gear Vendors unit really pays for itself, as you can now slip the truck into "double overdrive." With double overdrive, you are driving at 75 mph, and the engine is running just above idle!

Gear Vendors has been in the business of building under/overdrive gear splitters for 27 years, and they currently manufacture units for more than 250 automatic and stick-shift applications; everything from vintage enclosed driveshaft vehicles to trucks and cars that rolled off the dealer's lot yesterday.

To best understand the accompanying gear chart, we have to go back to the test drive that we took in a Gear Vendors–equipped, turbocharged, Cummins diesel-powered Dodge standard cab pickup. Without towing a load, there is no need to use first gear. So, I took off in second gear. As the engine reached 1,700 rpm, I depressed the clutch and actuated the Gear Vendors shifter-mounted button, and it instantly went into second-over. Then as I shifted to third gear, I clicked off the Gear Vendors.

I reached 1,700 rpm, and then actuated the GV unit for third-over, and so on. Johnson commented, "Fifth and fifth-over are now for those times when you are hauling or towing a load. By running this gear, you will have a slightly higher torque

One of the few pieces that will be visible inside the cab is this on/off rocker switch with an indicator light.

Everything today works off of some sort of computer including the Gear Vendors under/overdrive unit. Input plugs are typical telephone/computer style. Popular position for installation is under and above the pedals against the firewall. Wiring to the transmission is then routed through a floor port.

multiplier, and the transmission will run as much as 100 degrees cooler than in sixth gear, the weakest gear, so you will now use sixth and sixth-over only when empty. When you are running empty, sixth-over will get you better fuel mileage and far less engine wear at today's 70-mph speed limits. Not only is the engine turning slower, but so are all of the engine drive accessories, which cuts down on parasitic losses and wear to these components. Turning the air conditioner compressor and alternator slower greatly reduces their work and load on the engine."

Check out the gear ratio chart to get a clear idea of how the Gear Vendors unit fills the ratio gaps when installed in a Dodge six-speed manual transmission.

NV5600 SIX-SPEED MANUAL TRANSMISSION	TRANMISSION RATIO	FINAL DRIVE RATIO W/3.73 REAR GEARS
First	5.63	21.00
Second	3.38	12.61
Over	2.64	9.85
Third	2.04	7.61
Over	1.59	5.93
Fourth	1.39	5.18
Over	1.08	4.03
Fifth	1.00	3.73
Over	0.78	2.91
Sixth	0.73	2.72
Over	0.57	2.13

Do the math and you will find that the Gear Vendors auxiliary transmission reduces the drive ratio by 22 percent (0.78:1), which reduces wear and tear on the engine and drivetrain. The key is reduced rpm while traveling the same freeway speed, producing a major savings in fuel economy.

In a nutshell, the installation requires the replacement of the transmission tail shaft with an adapter, then bolting up the Gear Vendors unit. The driveshaft has to be shortened to the length of the Gear Vendors auxiliary transmission and the adapter, generally about 14 inches.

The GV unit is self-contained and does not share fluids. An internal pump produces the necessary pressure (more than 30 mph), so when the activating switch is on, the unit reacts by having a solenoid redirect fluid, which activates a clutch pack that drives planetary gears. These gears reduce the drive ratio by 22 percent, which can be used to split gears to reduce engine load or to work as a double overdrive. Just in case you are curious about durability, similar units have powered dragsters to

two world records and race trucks to four off-road championships using this close ratio multiplying aspect: Torque x rpm / 5252 = horsepower. Interesting aspect—slow your rpm, go faster, and burn less fuel!

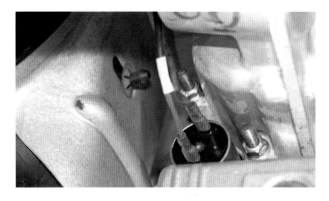

Wiring from the computer and switches is then attached to the Gear Vendors unit, this being attached to the solenoid, which triggers the shifting to under/overdrive. With the unit now in place, the wiring is checked to ensure nothing is close to a heat source and that all mounting bolts are firm.

A cutaway view of a Gear Vendors under/overdrive unit reveals the inner workings of this auxiliary transmission. Bottom line is a 22 percent reduction in engine rpm. A flip of the rocker switch activates a solenoid, which redirects pressurized gear oil to activate a clutch pack that drives these planetary gears. This produces a ratio of 0.78:1 for the final drive.

Out back on the rack, the Dodge truck is receiving a new and slightly shorter driveshaft, which fits perfectly.

Back underneath the truck, a splined shaft is installed to extend the driveshaft length of the transmission, being shimmed to tolerances. Finally, the Gear Vendors under/overdrive can be installed into the driveline of the truck, using a gasket. A special fluid is then installed as well, which should be frequently changed.

On a closed course, Johnson showed what the torque of a diesel engine can do, pushing the truck to near 95 mph while staying under 2,400 rpm, thanks to the truck now being equipped with a sixth double overdrive.

PROJECT 24 | RECALIBRATE YOUR SPEEDOMETER

 TIME: Two hours

 TOOLS: Soldering iron, screwdriver set, heat gun

 TALENT: ★ If you're willing to try, you can do this!

 APPLICABLE YEARS: All

 TAB: $150

 TINWARE: GPS, mile markers, or friend to help verify calibration

 TIP: If you have changed your wheel/tire size in any way, this project is a must. If you still have stock wheels and tires on your vehicle, this project will not have an impact.

 PERFORMANCE GAIN:
Speed accuracy decreases the chances of a speeding ticket due to ignorance.

COMPLEMENTARY PROJECT:
New tires and wheels

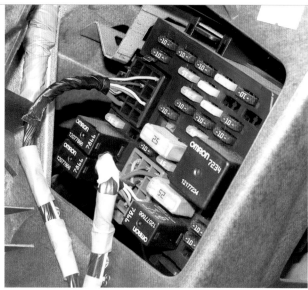

Mount the TruSpeed close to the fuse box if possible. (The unit is water-resistant and can be mounted under the hood if necessary.) On this Duramax, the under-column area works well. Refer to the instructions to help find a fuse that's hot in Start and Run (the 10-amp cruise control fuse for this truck). Use a test light to confirm power, and then disconnect the truck's batteries. Pull the fuse with the appropriate tool. Install the supplied tapper connector and press the fuse back into place (far left, second fuse from the top here).

"Do the math" is one of today's most overused clichés. Truth is, if most of us were disciplined enough to do the math, we'd be Microsoft millionaires—and possibly paying others to fix our trucks.

Along these lines, most of us are good at putting performance tires on our trucks. But we're too dumb or lazy to estimate how far off our speedometers become after adding big meats. For example, if the stock tire diameter is 30 inches and we bump up to 33s (a 10 percent increase), does that mean that the speedometer is now 10 percent slow? So, when the needle reads 55, are we actually traveling closer to 61 mph? "Sorry, officer, but I don't have any clue how fast I'm actually going."

Once again, modern technology saves us from ourselves. An Icelandic invention called TruSpeed offers a straightforward way to correct the speed signal in many late-model, computer-controlled trucks. TruSpeed intercepts the speed signal between its source (such as the ABS sensor-circuit) and the PCM, modifying the pulse waves so that the truck's computer receives accurate information. Each quarter-turn of the TruSpeed's dial changes the speed signal by 1 percent for highly accurate calibration. It also stores settings for two different tire sizes.

In addition to controlling the speedometer reading, the vehicle's speed sensor can have an impact on these other systems: anti-lock brakes, auto-transmission shift points, fuel delivery, timing, and other emissions-related functions. Fixing the speed signal to register actual speed and distance traveled restores these functions to their stock parameters. Maintenance, resale, and warranty issues are also affected: taller-than-stock tires cause the odometer to register fewer miles than actually traveled, and smaller, low-profile rubber will make the speedometer spin faster than it should.

TruSpeed installation involves only four wires and can be done by anyone with basic skills who can also solder. For calibration, the TruSpeed instructions provide approximate settings based on the difference between new and stock tire diameters and/or axle gears. Calibration should be verified by using roadside mile markers, a GPS, a radar system, or by pacing with another vehicle.

These photos show a TruSpeed installation on a Chevy Duramax (TruSpeed applications are available for many 1992-and-newer Chevy/GMC, Dodge, Ford, Jeep, and Toyota trucks). The main installation differences among vehicles are the locations of their fuse box and speed-sensor wires.

Our leisurely installation took about two hours. A nearby speed-survey radar trailer helped us dial in and verify speed calibration. A few passes were necessary because our initial "dial in" was off—this truck's stock tires were long gone and we guessed at their diameter. Once we zeroed in on the correct setting, the speedometer was incredibly accurate.

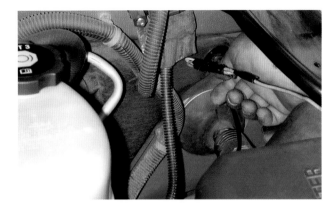

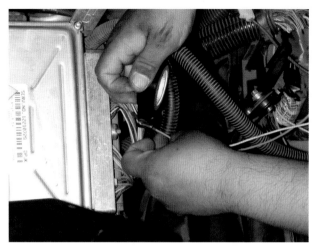

Crimp the supplied spade connector on to the TruSpeed's red wire. This connection mates to the tapper in the fuse box. Route the TruSpeed's green and yellow wires through the firewall and into the engine compartment to the PCM. (We used another wire to fish them through the firewall grommet.) Sensor wire locations vary among vehicles. This Duramax's speed-sensor wire is in the PCM, which is under the hood on the driver's side. Release the mounting clips to free the PCM. Refer to the TruSpeed instructions and isolate the correct sensor wire. Cut it. Strip the factory speed-sensor wire. Slide the kit's heat-shrink tubing over the wires, then crimp-connect the TruSpeed's yellow and green wires to the truck's speed sensor, following the instructions.

Superlift recommends wrapping electrical tape over the heat-shrunk connections before returning the PCM to its mount. Then, use the kit's zip-ties to secure the green and yellow TruSpeed wires away from hot and moving parts. Crimp the supplied eyelet connector on to the TruSpeed's black wire. This ground lead secures under an existing bolt that's grounded to the vehicle. Use the supplied hook-and-loop fastener to mount the TruSpeed unit. Secure all excess wires with kit's zip-ties.

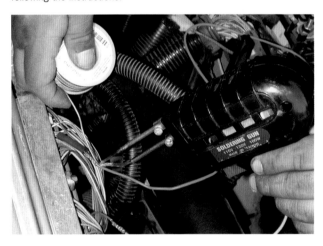

Solder each crimped connection for added insurance. The kit's heat-shrink tubing provides a third line of defense. (A heat gun is recommended, but a hair dryer will work in a pinch.)

Refer to the instructions, and then use the calibration key to dial in the approximate speed sensor signal. Fine-tune the speed signal (each quarter-turn equals 1 percent correction) using a GPS, radar, or by pacing alongside a vehicle that has an accurate speedometer.

From the street speed indicator, we could determine how accurate our speedometer actually was. After a couple of tries, our speedometer was pretty accurate.

PROJECT 25 | UPGRADE YOUR VEHICLE'S REAR END GEARS

TIME: Five hours

TOOLS: Full socket set, screwdriver set, torque wrench, appropriate jack

TALENT: ★★★

APPLICABLE YEARS: All

TAB: $700

TINWARE: Gear grease, gear oil, replacement gaskets

TIP: Although setting backlash on a new set of rear-end gears is challenging, if you have the confidence in your skills to handle this project, tackle it. You can acquire a specific video from www.badshoeproductions.com on the Ford 9-inch that will demonstrate setting backlash and dealing with crush sleeves on any type of differential.

PERFORMANCE GAIN:
Correct gearing for tire size

COMPLEMENTARY PROJECT:
Upgrade U-joints

To gain access to the original 3.73:1 ring-and-pinion gears, the factory differential cover was first removed; this can be messy as the stock differential covers don't come with a drain plug, so be prepared when the cover comes loose.

Building the perfect off-road rig (or any truck with larger than stock tires) is a passion of sorts for some people, but it can be an arduous task that not only consumes immense amounts of your time but a large portion of your pocketbook as well. Lifting your truck to support a set of 40-inch wheels is just a part of the natural progression many people set out to do when they first envision their truck as a trail-ready hauler. Even though a lift and a large set of off-road wheels and tires is a great start, much more work is involved in making a truck capable of handling the rough and tough conditions of a mud-soaked trail. Although the lift makes your truck look awesome, it does little more than increase the amount of wheel travel and ground clearance between the trail and your truck. There are several more things to consider than just modifying your suspension and wheels.

Increasing your vehicle's tire size greatly complements the overall look of your off-road machine. The larger diameter, however, wreaks havoc on the final drive ratios of your truck's transmission, speedometer, and, in some cases, the anti-lock braking system. So changing the differential gear ratio is a criti-

cal step in the buildup of your rig, which can bring back the final gear ratios to a more comfortable level, similar to stock. It can also make the difference between having the power to muscle through a sloppy mud hole and having to be pulled out of it by your friends.

The size you select for your off-road tires makes all the difference. If they are much larger in diameter, you can also count on them being heavier too, especially if you have to use larger wheels to match. The problem is that a larger diameter tire requires considerably more torque to keep those mammoth wheels turning as you navigate your favorite off-road 'wheelin haunt.

Just in weight alone, off-road tires can add 70-plus pounds to each wheel for a combined weight of at least 80 pounds—and that's not even a big wheel. Some tires like Toyo's Open Country M/T weigh in close to 110 pounds apiece. The same tire in the company's 38-inch-diameter model adds more than 400 pounds to the driveline. Once you combine the added weight of your truck's new rubber with the greater amount of torque required to keep those wheels churning through the mud, you will find out the hard way that your truck no longer has the torque needed to get you back on to dry land. This makes for a long day of wading through the mud to your buddy's truck in order to hook up the tow line.

Modifying your truck's differential gear ratio is the best way to restore torque multiplication that is lost when using larger diameter tires and wheels. Furthermore, this modification can improve the dynamics of your truck's suspension, breathing new life into your truck's tired original driveline.

Before you delve headfirst into overhauling your truck's rear-end gears, you should know that a ring-and-pinion gear replacement is not an easy task to accomplish. If you don't have all the tools, you are going to end up stranded on your driveway. Furthermore, if you don't get it right, your gears won't last very long. We would recommend leaving this modification to the pros. For an example of such an installation, we observed how a set of Superior's 4.56:1 gears were used to replace the stock 3.73:1 gears on a truck that uses 38-inch-tall tires. This modification will really help restore lost power to the wheels, transforming the truck into an off-road performer. Bear in mind, rear-end gear selections may change according to how you use your vehicle. In NASCAR races, each speedway or road course requires different gear setups. Although you will try to match the best gear ratio to meet most of your on-highway and off-highway needs, depending on the tire size you run, the ability to change your own differential gear set allows you to try different gear ratios with different sizes of tires.

A gentle amount of persuasion on the ring gear will allow the whole carrier to be removed from the differential housing. Depending on the make and model of the differential, you might not need to force out the carrier.

Remove the axles from the differential, which will disengage the axles from the carrier, allowing the carrier to be removed from the housing. In order to gain access to the pinion gear, the rear driveshaft must be removed first.

Once the oil has finished draining, which should easily be done in the amount of time it takes to remove the driveshafts and axles, the carrier bearing supports are removed. Take note of which carrier bearing is on what side. They will need to go back exactly as they came out.

To gain access to the pinion gear, the driveshaft yolk must be removed; this allows for the removal of the stock pinion gear. The pinion gear bearing races were replaced; this should be done with any new gear set that is installed. With the third member and differential housing all cleaned up, attention was shifted to preparing the new pinion gear and third member for reinstallation. First, the new pinion gear was outfitted with the new bearing that was supplied by Superior.

The pinion gear was reinstalled, but not tightened down all the way, as the carrier assembly still needs to be installed and shimmed correctly to set the backlash to the correct tolerances. Setting the backlash correctly keeps the gears from making a whining noise and wearing prematurely.

Turning our attention to the carrier, the ring gear was first removed from the assembly. All of the bolts were removed, with a little bit of coaxing from a hammer and punch.

With the ring gear removed, the bearings were taken out from the carrier assembly with the use of a bearing puller. The carrier was then cleaned up in preparation for reassembly.

Using an air-impact wrench, the new ring gear was mated to the carrier assembly. Prior to final assembly, the bolts were all torqued to manufacturer's specs.

Once the carrier is reassembled, the new bearings are pressed on to the carrier bearing ends.

The carrier assembly is reinstalled into the differential housing, and the carrier bearings caps are torqued to the correct specifications. Marking compound is applied to the outer ring gear to aid in meshing the ring and pinion gears correctly. The backlash is then measured and adjusted by moving the pinion gear in and out. Getting the gears set up correctly is a very time-consuming process, as these steps must be repeated until the measurements are correct.

With the cover on and the axles in place, the differential was filled with Superior's gear oil, and friction modifier was added to ensure long-lasting performance of the limited slip unit.

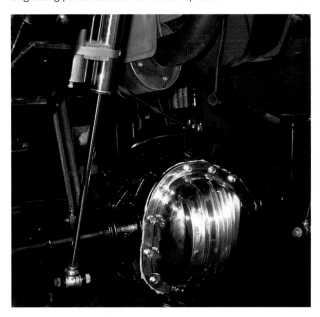

Once the alignment of the pinion and ring gear is correct, your tooth pattern in the marking compound should look similar to this example.

The completed differential with its new gear set is now ready for the trails and will look great doing it.

The axles were then installed into the carrier and bolted to the hubs. A generous bead of silicone was applied to the differential cover-mating surface. With the new gears installed, an ORU polished differential cover was added to give the rear end a little bit of spice and to help the gears stay cooler.

SECTION **3**

SUSPENSION

With the factory bar out, we set it next to the new Hellwig anti-sway bar, so you can see the dramatic difference in size.

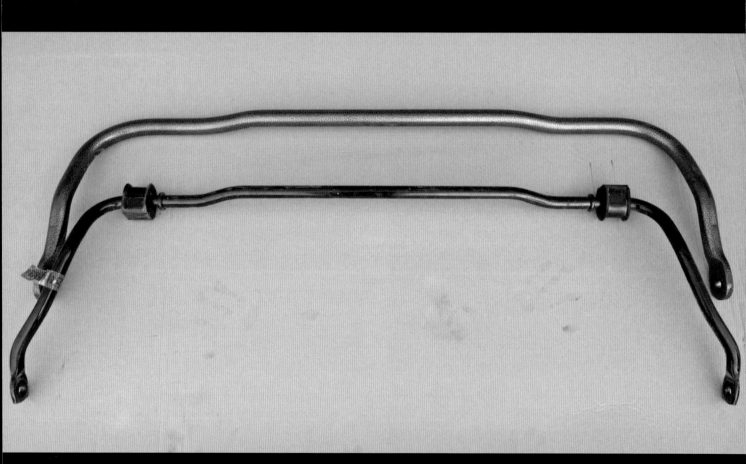

TIME: Two hours

TOOLS: Full socket set, flathead screwdriver, box-end wrench set, wire cutters, appropriate jack, jack stands

TALENT: ★★

APPLICABLE YEARS: All makes and models of spring-suspended pickup trucks

TAB: $500

TINWARE: Drop cloth, spray paint

TIP: While you have the wheels off, freshen up the brake hubs with a can of black spray paint. Check your brake wear.

PERFORMANCE GAIN:
Better weight distribution on the suspension

COMPLEMENTARY PROJECT:
New shocks

First, raise the vehicle until the rear wheels are off the ground, then use a pair of properly rated jack stands on the frame, so that the rear suspension is fully extended. Next, you simply install one of the supplied over-the-axle blocks made from a high-strength urethane composite. Amtech supplies two sets with each kit; one set is for vehicles with the leaf springs located under the axle, the other, larger set of blocks is for vehicles with the leaf springs located above the axle, like this Suburban. In this type of application, the block is simply placed on top of the leaf spring over the axle's center, as shown.

Place the preassembled RG Stabilizer leaf on top of the over-the-axle block.

For many, towing a heavy load can be a harrowing experience. Suddenly, the capable truck or SUV you were once accustomed to has become a laboring, ill-handling beast. Furthermore, the trailer in tow seems to have as much influence on your vehicle's direction as the steering wheel itself. It doesn't have to be that way, however. In addition to proper tire inflation pressure, a correctly adjusted weight-distributing hitch, and a well-matched truck and trailer, there are things you can do to improve your rig's handling—especially when towing.

A stabilizer kit works wonders on problems like truck/trailer sway, bounce, and body roll. And it's so simple to install—all that is required is a floor jack, a C-clamp, and some common end wrenches—no drilling, welding, or grinding is required. The kit not only makes the product easy to install, but also to remove if you'd like to install it on another vehicle with the similar leaf-spring arrangement and weight-carrying capabilities. For this example, we looked at a stabilizer kit available from the Amtech Corp. The company offers a RollGard (RG) stabilizer system, which works great on vehicles using a rear leaf-spring suspension system.

The concept of this and other stabilizer systems is simple. When a leaf-sprung vehicle enters a corner, the spring on the inside of the corner extends, while the spring on the outside of the corner compresses. The stabilizer, which has a similar appearance to a leaf spring itself, provides opposing resistance to these motions, resulting in flatter cornering. In other words, as the inside spring extends, the stabilizer pushes it back down; and as the outside spring compresses, the stabilizer pulls it back up.

This simple but effective design also works to help the driver maintain control of the vehicle in an emergency lane change situation like this one: The driver jerks the wheel to the right suddenly to avoid an obstacle, which sets the suspension into motion. The left leaf spring compresses under the force of the sudden steering input, then rapidly rebounds, shifting the weight to the other side of the vehicle. To compensate, the driver then turns the wheel quickly in the other direction—and the process repeats itself. These unsettled suspension motions can result in a loss of vehicle control and can possibly cause an accident. With the stabilizer in place, however, counter-active force applied to the leaf-spring pack prevents suspension oscillation and helps bring the vehicle under control quickly, without drama.

We recently visited Amtech Corp. in Las Vegas, Nevada, to drive the company's 1999 Chevy Suburban, first with the stock suspension, then with the RG stabilizer installed. Sales manager Mark Colford rode along, taking us through the kind of maneuvers that can upset the average SUV or truck. First, we drove through a private parking lot at about 40 mph and began sawing the steering wheel back and forth as quickly as possible. As we did so, Mark says, "Now let go of the wheel." As we did, we noticed that the vehicle continued to sway from side to side several more times—with no steering input at all. Next, we drove in a straight line at about 40 mph, and then applied the brakes as hard as we could. Predictably, the Suburban nose-dived severely as its substantial weight was shifted forward. Finally, we went through a series of simulated corners at the same speed and noted substantial body roll.

We then drove back to Amtech's shop, where Mark immediately went to work installing the RG Stabilizer on the

When the front of the stabilizer leaf is pushed down, the rear raises up, so a C-clamp is required to compress the stabilizer and bring the shackle down over the stock leaf spring.

Pull the front of the leaf spring down and insert the pin/roller assembly through the highest possible hole in the shackle, as shown.

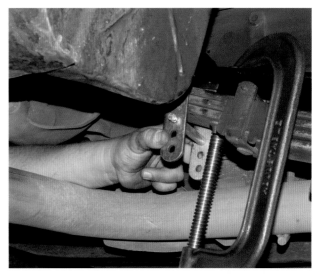

Once the pin/roller assembly is in place, secure it with one of the supplied cotter pins.

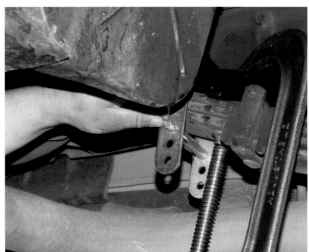

Once the stabilizer leaf is compressed and the shackles are properly located, the pin/roller assembly is inserted through the highest possible point on the rear shackle, and the cotter pin is installed.

Suburban. In no more than 20 minutes, the job was finished and we were back in the parking lot conducting the same battery of tests. But this time, when we whipped the wheel back and forth then let go, the vehicle moved to one side, then the other, then became completely stable. And because the RG stabilizer prevents the rear leaf springs from extending under hard braking, dive was considerably reduced as well. We also noticed a significant improvement in cornering—something that we could really take advantage of with some good aftermarket wheels and tires.

The RG stabilizer is available for any leaf-spring-equipped car, truck, SUV, van, or RV, and it is adjustable to achieve the perfect fit. It is made in the United States, is affordably priced ($395 retail for light-duty applications, $495 for heavy-duty applications), is easy to install, and really works as promised. What's more, it comes with a 30-day money-back guarantee and a lifetime warranty against defects in workmanship.

Whether or not you tow a trailer or boat, the RG stabilizer is a good investment in both handling performance and stability. Follow along with us now as we go through the installation of an RG stabilizer system on the shop's '99 Suburban.

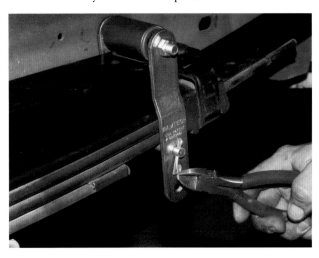

Once the stabilizer leaf is installed, use a pair of pliers to bend the cotter pins at both ends, keeping them secure.

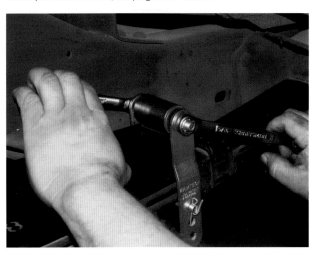

A pair of 3⁄16-inch end wrenches are used to tighten the shackle bolts until they are snug.

When you think of handling, odds are good that your camping, horse, or boat trailer doesn't come into the picture—but it should. A bouncing, swaying trailer exerts unwanted forces on to the tow vehicle, which in turn affects the vehicle's handling. This is especially true in high winds or when a large truck passes creating what is known as "bow wave."

Most trailers use a very simple leaf-spring suspension system—in fact, many trailers don't even have shock absorbers at all! The thinking behind this is that because no one is riding in the trailer, it doesn't have to ride well—but this is not the case. In addition to producing poor overall handling characteristics, a bouncing trailer suspension can upset the contents of your trailer (if you've ever arrived at your destination only to find many of your belongings on the floor, you know what we mean).

Fortunately, the folks at Amtech Corp. have developed a product for your trailer, and it's called the RG trailer stabilizer. Like the RG stabilizer for leaf-spring-equipped trucks, SUVs, vans, and other vehicles, the RG trailer stabilizer attaches to your trailer's existing leaf-spring suspension in just minutes per side—and works on single-, double-, or triple-axle trailers. By counteracting the forces of the stock leaf springs, the RG trailer stabilizer results in smoother, more confident towing.

Here is what the finished side looks like. Repeat the process on the other side, and the job is complete. Total time is around 30 minutes.

SUSPENSION

83

PROJECT 27 | KEEP YOUR LOAD LEVEL

TIME: Three hours

TOOLS: Full socket set, jack, jack stands, welding equipment

TALENT: ★★★

APPLICABLE YEARS: Kits for all years, makes, and models of light trucks

TAB: $350 for rear axle on most trucks

TINWARE: Air-line cutting tool, electrical pliers, wire connections

TIP: Measure twice, cut once.

PERFORMANCE GAIN:
Ability to manage suspension stiffness and load carrying ability

COMPLEMENTARY PROJECT:
New shocks

The kit includes every component you need for the installation.

With the rear end raised off the ground and safety stands under the axle with wheel chocks in place, remove the rear wheels. Assemble the upper bracket with the swivel air fitting facing toward the front of the truck. Position the lower mounting bracket on the leaf spring. Check for any obstructions that might interfere with the tire/wheel.

John Rago, co-owner of Mac's Springs in Highland, California, has a long-standing deal with his teenage daughter, Theresa. The father/daughter negotiations came about as a solution to academic performance in high school. Since she was a child, Dad has taken his daughter to car shows and truck shows in support of his business and love for custom rides of all kinds. Naturally, Daddy's girl spent every spare minute at Dad's spring shop in Highland, California, hanging out and helping get things done when she was not in class. So it was no surprise that her first car would be a truck, soon to be a show truck.

The deal is for Theresa to achieve A's and B's in return for Dad's help in building her own customized pickup truck. This strategy may not work for every family, but it lit a fire under little Miss Rago. Getting the truck in the first place required an academic performance that convinced the senior Rago that his one and only daughter was serious about school and her determination to build a truck. So, even before she was ready to take her driving test for her driver's license, Theresa took delivery of her own late-model Chevy S-10 after raising the bet and throwing down a royal flush–like report card.

Then came the 3-inch spindle/spring drop at the front end and a 4-inch Western lowering spring at the rear. Doetsch Tech shocks at each corner probably explain the A in English. Another round of high marks earned the teenager four high-end low-profile tires on 20-inch wheels; the show truck buildup had begun. As the S-10 was slightly lowered and getting closer to the ground, the need to retain the load-carrying utility of the truck bed needed to be addressed.

Any half-ton pickup truck that gets loaded with the occasional Jet Ski, snowmobile, car parts, or any of the innumerable uses of a square box, is subject to sagging springs once you load it up. Even trucks that are not lowered or customized to any extent can benefit from a set of air bags to assist the load-carrying capacity of a pickup truck. Well, with a fresh report card and outstanding grades, Miss Rago put her order in for a set of rear air-adjustable Slam Air air bags by Air Lift (P/N 59104). The installation takes a couple hours and is very doable for any enthusiast with moderate mechanical skills and the ability to figure out how to position the kit components and route the air lines and wires so the install looks seamless.

As we follow this installation, the first thing you need to do is to measure the ride height of your truck. Ride height is determined as the distance between the bottom of the bumper and a flat surface with no weight in the lowered vehicle. Measure this distance before you begin the installation and note it. Air Lift kits are designed to be installed and operated at ride height.

Set the entire lift assembly on the leaf spring. Make sure the air fitting is pointed forward and that the entire upper assembly is parallel and perpendicular to the lower bracket. Holes are provided so you can drill and bolt the assembly to the truck frame. As you can see, this install was welded. Whether you choose to drill holes or weld it, make sure you have a clean mounting surface on the frame to secure the upper bracket.

Here is the entire driver-side install. If you weld it, keep a Dixie cup full of water ready to splash-cool it down. Connect the air line and spray paint the weld to prevent corrosion.

This application runs both Firestone air bags off a single air compressor. Air lines from the air bags intersect at a T-fitting, which routes to the compressor. Be sure to route all air lines well away from exhaust pipes or sources that might bind or pinch. Assemble the air compressor to the universal mounting bracket.

We located the mounting bracket along the driver-side frame rail just below the truck cab. This is where you need to decide what's best for your application. Weld it up! Route air lines along with the electrical wire from the compressor up into the truck cab, under the doorsill molding and carpet, up to the location where you elect to mount the pressure gauge. We ran the wiring from an unused fuse port on the fuse panel.

This is how the wiring is linked to the fuse panel. We're hooked up to the number 20 fuse. The key to a nonleaking air line fit is straight and square cuts on the air line.

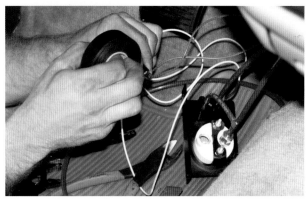

Here we prepare the wiring harness from the fuse box to the back of the pressure gauge. Pick your location for the pressure gauge and install it.

PROJECT 28 AIR LIFT YOUR TRUCK

 TIME: Five hours

 TOOLS: Full (medium and large) socket sets, screwdrivers, torque wrench, appropriate jack, and jack stands

 TALENT: ★★★

 APPLICABLE YEARS: Late-model three-quarter- to one-ton light pickup trucks (Ford, Chevy, Dodge)

 TAB: $2,400

 TINWARE: Many existing mounting holes in the frame are used for this installation. You will have to drill a few new holes and make a couple of cuts.

 TIP: This kit is designed with 3-inch rear lift blocks in mind and longer U-bolts. Longer U-bolts are included in the hardware kit. However, if your rig is a two-wheel drive (2WD), it's a good idea to acquire factory 3-inch lift blocks before you start your project.

 PERFORMANCE GAIN:
Better control of suspension and ride comfort

COMPLEMENTARY PROJECT:
Consider investing in the options that are available with this system.

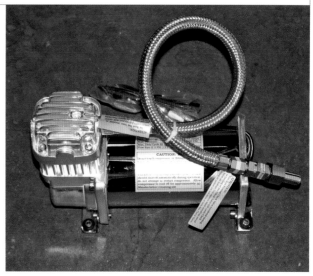

Surprisingly, the kit came with a popular Viair compressor system. The compressor is quiet, and all of the hoses and fittings are included in the kit. The factory rear suspension on this 2004 F-350 uses heavy-duty leaf springs that can lead to a rough ride when the truck runs unloaded. Chris Malek of Ranch Truck begins the installation by removing the rear tailpipe. This would later have to be modified because the air bags will be in the way of this part of the exhaust. With the exhaust out of the way, Malek removed the tires, exposing the leaf springs and factory shocks.

Everyone who's owned a duallie, crew-cab, or long-bed pickup of any manufacture knows how the ride can become rough; especially when you're not loaded down with any weight in the bed. The rough ride comes from oscillations due to the length of the truck and the conditions of the road. Removing the overload springs is one popular way to cure the problem, but unless you're building a lowered customized truck, removing them will limit the truck's overall towing capacity. Air springs would seem to be another method for smoothing the ride. However, most air bag systems are not rated for the heavy loads of a three-quarter- or one-ton truck.

After some research, we found Air Lift's Road Tamer kit was designed to smooth out the ride and yet maintain the factory's towing capacity. The system seemed quite different from most air-spring kits we've seen, and we wanted to see how well the Road Tamer kit worked on our 2004 Ford F-350, crew-cab duallie. The truck is owned by our friend Kenny Wayne Shepherd, who uses it to tow his cars and a horse trailer. Shepherd asked us to help him upgrade his

truck so that it would have more power and tow and ride better. Over the course of a few months, we've upgraded the power by adding a Granatelli Big G module, Billy Boat stainless exhaust system and Airaid high-flow intake system. The next step was to improve the ride without decreasing the truck's towing capability and the Air Lift Road Tamer seemed like a good candidate to do this.

The Air Lift Road Tamer looked as though it would do the trick and the company sent us its system for the Ford F-250/350 that fits on 1999–present pickups, P/N 39010. The Road Tamer system is also available for the Dodge Ram and Chevy Silverado heavy-duty pickups. The kit replaces the factory rear leaf springs with a full rear air suspension that uses two trailing arms with heavy-duty air bags at the end.

The kit also has an optional kneeling system that allows the vehicle to be lowered up to 3 inches, helping to load and unload the truck on to a trailer. A switch inside the cab lets you dump the air from the bags, and an onboard compressor pumps up the bags to the correct ride height, using the optional Air Lift leveling system. One of the nice aspects of this kit is that it includes a high-quality Viair compressor.

Another option is Air Lift's Select-A-Ride shocks. These nine-position shocks can dramatically help dampen the ride and help tune the suspension to match road and load conditions.

For the installation, we elected to use the leveling system with the Road Tamer suspension and asked Ranch Truck Accessories in Temecula, California, to install the entire system for us. Ranch Truck is an Air Lift dealer and has expertise in installing Road Tamer kits. Chris Malek of Ranch Truck made the installation look easy and began by properly supporting the F-350 on to the lift.

Malek unbolted the factory spring perches and hangers and removed the leaf springs from the truck's rear axle. The spring perches have a hole in the center that was drilled out to fit around the centering bolt on the Road Tamer trailing arms. The front of the trailing arm bolts on to the front leaf-spring perch before it is attached to the rear axle. Air Lift supplies longer U-bolts in the kit, but we discovered that it was designed on a four-wheel-drive (4WD) system and requires the use of the factory 3-inch blocks. Ranch Truck supplied the blocks, and the trailing arms were secured to the rear axle.

The system also has several brackets that bolt on to the frame. Many of the frame's existing holes are used, but a few need to be drilled. The brackets are used to house the top of the air bag and to mount the Panhard rod. Once Malek attached these brackets, the rod and bags were assembled and attached to the system.

The instructions on the Road Tamer kit explain how to properly set the ride height of the truck. Malek carefully

Malek removes the factory leaf-spring bump stops. New bump stops will be added to maintain a proper ride height. With a jack or stand, the rear differential is supported before the shocks are removed from the suspension. Removing the springs requires unbolting the perches from the axles.

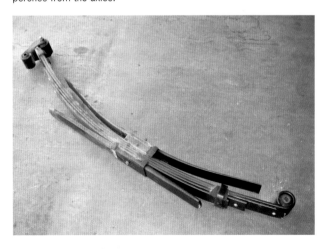

Malek also unbolted the spring eyes from the vehicle's hangers and removed the leaf springs from the vehicle.

measured the system with air in the bags and set the ride height of the vehicle to slightly lower—to its original stock height. This helped to give a more level appearance to the truck. Malek also adapted a new set of urethane bump stops that were supplied by Ranch Truck. These were set in place to ensure that the suspension would not hit the differential or damage other components when the air bags are fully deflated.

The next step was to properly attach and route the air lines from the air bags to the compressor and actuator. As mentioned earlier, we incorporated Air Lift's self-leveling mechanism, which adds or releases air to maintain a preset ride height. This is done with Air Lift's magnetic trigger, which can also be adjusted to set any height you wish.

Once all of the lines and wiring were done, the system was fully activated and we watched as the air bags filled with compressed air and raised the rear of the truck to the ride height we set. We flipped the dump valve from the in-cab switch and released all the air. This allowed the bags to deflate, allowing easier loading of cargo and trailer hitching.

Flipping the switch back on, the system quickly inflated and set the rear to the correct ride height. Minor adjustments were made while driving but, more noticeably, the ride smoothed out considerably. The system did not eliminate any of the oscillations that occur with these long trucks, but it did dampen the harshness to make it more comfortable than it was.

With a smoother ride and good towing capacity, the only thing left was to upgrade the truck's factory wheels. Although we were very tempted to use a set of big-rig-style 22.5 wheels, we decided to stick with a quality set of wheels that offered a high load capacity with a great appearance. We selected a set of Alcoa #GA363282 wheels. These feature a big-rig look that fit the factory 16-inch-diameter tire size. The wheels are lightweight, forged, fully polished, and feature fluting along the face of the wheels, giving them a custom appearance. The large chromed caps fit over the lug nuts, and a smoother and smaller center cap looks much sleeker and cleaner than the factory wheels.

The Road Tamer trailing arms have a spring perch mount, but the larger bolt necessitates drilling out the center hole on the factory perch.

The top air bag mounting bracket is also bolted into position.

The front of the trailing arm is bolted directly to the front spring hanger. The rear of the arm rests over the factory rear axle. In order for the suspension to align perfectly, a set of 3-inch blocks had to be used on our two-wheel-drive application. Four-wheel applications use the factory blocks. The perch, U-bolts, and blocks are all bolted together to the trailing arm and axle.

Two of the existing holes are used but one has to be drilled for a third bolt. The bottom of the air bag mounts also requires drilling to mount the bolts. Backing away from the truck, you'll see the space between the trailing arm and the top mount. This is where the air bag will be mounted.

Mounting brackets for the air bags must also be bolted on to the frame and may require some drilling. In this instance, the top of the Panhard rod mount is bolted to an existing hole in the frame. In some instances, the factory holes can be used but must be enlarged.

Before the bags are inserted, Malek bolted in the Panhard rod. This keeps the axle from moving side to side with the air suspension. With the axle nearly resting on the frame, the air bags are inserted into position with the proper fittings already attached. The kit comes with all of the necessary fittings and hoses to connect the air bags to the compressor. Air Lift also provided its automatic leveling system, which allows you to set the desired ride height. The sensors automatically allow filling and dumping of air to reach the selected height.

This is what the system looks like fully installed. At this point, the air bags are inflated to set the ride height and need to be connected to the compressor. Air Lift also uses a heavy-duty cycle Viair 380C compressor for this system. The compressor includes two spare filters and comes with the necessary hardware to mount it to the vehicle's frame.

Malek installed all of the wiring and hoses to attach the system to the compressor and electronic solenoids. Malek fabricated two brackets to mount the compressor to the frame.

The wiring from the system's solenoids is routed to the switch that was mounted under the dash in the vehicle's cab. Because the rear passenger-side air bag now takes up the room used for the tailpipe, we had to cut the pipe off of the rear end of the B&B muffler. A simple solution was to cut the tailpipe and turn a portion of it into a turn-down. Ranch Truck also mounted and installed our new set of Alcoa wheels. The forged-aluminum wheels are lightweight and have a heavy load capacity.

SUSPENSION

TIME: Four hours

TOOLS: Full socket set and hand tools

TALENT: ★★

APPLICABLE YEARS: Kits for all makes and models

TAB: $300 per axle

TINWARE: N/A

TIP: N/A

PERFORMANCE GAIN:
Ride control

COMPLEMENTARY PROJECT:
Anti-sway bars

On this heavy-duty air spring kit for the 2006 Dodge, the stock bump stop mounting point will be used to mount the top air spring bracket to the frame. As such, the bump stops are removed and discarded, but the factory fasteners will be reused. The air spring is first preassembled with the upper and lower brackets and air line connections before it is installed in the truck.

For most of us, a half- or three-quarter-ton truck is more than capable enough for our needs. Whether using it to haul goods from the local home improvement superstore or to pull a boat or trailer, the number of times you wish for a heavier-duty truck are likely rare. The exception to this, of course, is the truck owner who uses his truck for two distinct purposes—such as personal use and on the job site. For these truck owners, the stock suspension is likely perfect for around town, typical usage, but maybe not quite stiff enough when it comes time to haul a load of cinder blocks. Adding extra leafs can help, but this modification will also make the truck ride stiffer the rest of the time.

The best solution to this problem is an auxiliary air spring suspension. These systems use air springs (or "bellows") between the axle and the frame that can be inflated as much as needed to support the payload and keep the truck riding level. The rest of the time, the bags can be deflated to the minimum recommended pressure, and the truck rides as it did stock.

Air Lift Company of Lansing, Michigan, has been building air suspension systems for more than 50 years. Today, the company has a variety of air suspension systems for different applications, but its Load Assist product line is most likely of

greatest interest to dual-use truck owners. Its RideControl air spring kit provides up to 2,000 pounds of leveling support for pickups, while its SuperDuty kit can provide up to 5,000 pounds of leveling support. Both kits come with air springs, inflation valves, air lines, fittings, mounting hardware, and instructions, and are inflated manually when needed. If you want onboard inflation capability, Air Lift also offers several choices, including its SmartAir automatic leveling system, LoadController I heavy-duty onboard compressor system, LoadController II light-duty onboard compressor system, and its latest system, the SureSet with digital control.

The SmartAir is the only system Air Lift offers that doesn't require a controller in the cab—it's all automatic. The rest of the systems allow the user to set the air pressure manually, but some offer the option of independent adjustment of the driver-side and passenger-side bags. This is a great benefit for those times when you might be carrying an uneven load; you can simply inflate one bag more than the other to compensate for any weight-induced lean.

The big difference between the LoadController units and the SureSet is the controller readout and how it functions in the vehicle. The LoadController units use analog gauges, which take a reading from air lines that must be plumbed into the vehicle, which can make mounting a challenge. The SureSet system, on the other hand, is a digital control module that interfaces with the compressor through a single electric cable—so no air lines need to be plumbed into the cab. In addition, the controller is very lightweight and compact (about the size of a deck of cards) and features a digital readout. As with all Air Lift onboard compressor systems, the SureSet system is programmed to maintain a minimum of 6 psi air pressure, which prevents pinching or bottoming and subsequent premature air spring failure. As a result, Air Lift offers a limited lifetime warranty on its air springs when installed with any of its compressor systems. The SureSet system comes with the digital controller, wiring harness, air compressor, and air manifold.

Our 2006 Dodge 2500 Quad Cab is used as daily transportation but also sees occasional duty hauling heavy landscaping materials and a truck camper on the weekends. As such, we contacted Air Lift for its SuperDuty air springs and its SureSet controller, and then called Central 4 Wheel Drive, an authorized Air Lift dealer/installer, for the installation. Central stocks a complete line of Jeep and four-wheel-drive (4WD) truck and SUV accessories and offers factory-direct discounts on thousands of products, with free shipping on many items. Its stores also offer installation on any product the company sells.

Central 4 Wheel Drive has three locations in central California, one in Portland, Oregon, and two locations in Washington State—Kent and Spokane. Because the truck is located in the Seattle area, we chose the Kent store, where manager Bill VanTuyl arranged for the installation with Central's tech, Kevin Mock.

Installation was pretty straightforward and took only about four hours. When the job was completed, we didn't notice much difference in the ride quality over stock, but when we loaded it with roughly 2,000 pounds, the difference was phenomenal. It took only about 20 pounds of air pressure (max is 100 psi) to make the truck ride level, and the ride quality was smooth, yet very controlled. Instead of bouncing and wallowing several times after a dip in the road, it recovered quickly and predictably, and it cornered much easier as well.

If you're a dual-use truck owner who's looking for added control and stability when carrying a heavy load, then an Air Lift air spring system with an onboard compressor is a great option.

The top of the air spring is mounted to the old bump stop mounting point using the factory fasteners—no drilling required. Trick!

The bottom air spring bracket is attached to the rear axle tube using a pair of metal straps and carriage bolts/nuts. You'll note that the bottom bracket is actually offset to the inside in order to provide adequate clearance from the leaf-spring assembly. The air spring actually overhangs the bottom of the bracket and, though it may appear odd, is normal. The next step is to find a mounting location for the tiny air compressor and air manifold. These components can be mounted anywhere under the truck, so long as the location prevents exposure to water spray or exhaust system heat. Space is tight under new trucks these days, but we found a good location on the inner passenger-side frame rail, just behind the transfer case. This area is inboard from the front wheel, so water splash won't be an issue, and the exhaust is routed on the opposite side of the truck, so it won't be affected by heat. With the location established, two holes were drilled and the air compressor was mounted.

Next, the manifold was mounted adjacent to the air compressor, and the air hose from the compressor plumbed into the manifold. Air Lift's instructions recommend that the manifold's pressure transducers face upward, but because we had to mount the manifold vertically for space considerations, they are located on their sides. The important thing is that these transducers are not mounted facing down, as this can cause condensation and/or debris to collect in them. Just in case of an air compressor system failure, there must be an external Schrader valve for each air bag, so they can be inflated manually. These can be mounted anywhere, but because we wanted the cleanest installation possible, Kevin Mock recommended we run them through the license plate mounting holes. First, the plate was removed and the holes enlarged slightly; then the valves were run through the bumper and through the plate. The plastic air lines are run from the manifold, to a T-fitting at each air spring; the other end of the T is routed to the air valves at the bumper. The Air Lift fittings require only that the line be pushed in; an O-ring assembly holds the line in place. Air line routing is different in every truck, but the idea is to keep the lines away from anything sharp or hot, keeping things neat in the process. Mock ran the air lines from the passenger-side spring across to the driver-side manifold using a hollow channel under the bed.

Here, the air springs are shown mounted in place, with air lines plumbed. With the mechanical part completed, the wiring was up next. The compressor relay wire was run into the engine compartment, to the truck's fuse box under the hood. Mock used a test light to determine which open terminal functions only when the key is in the On or Accessory position. The supplied Air Lift harness is then routed from the fuse box, through a grommet in the firewall. It is then connected to the controller, which can be mounted anywhere in the cab. The wiring harness is then connected to the air compressor/manifold assembly. Air Lift supplies a wiring harness that is more than long enough for most applications, so the excess wiring was tied in a bundle and tucked away on top of the compressor assembly.

The SureSet controller is very small and lightweight and can be mounted virtually anywhere in the cab. Controller features a digital readout that tells you how much pressure is in each side; the independent inflation feature allows you to easily compensate for uneven loads.

PROJECT 30 | DROP YOUR TRUCK

 TIME: Eight hours

 TOOLS: Full socket set, screwdriver set, torque wrench, appropriate jack, jack stands

 TALENT: ★★

 APPLICABLE YEARS: Lowering kits are available for most late-model brands of pickup trucks.

 TAB: $700

 TINWARE: Mechanic's gloves

 TIP: You don't need air tools for this project, though an extra pair of hands will make it go much smoother. Double-check your work.

 PERFORMANCE GAIN:
Lower center of gravity improves cornering and general side-to-side stability.

COMPLEMENTARY PROJECT:
Tires and wheels

After measuring the stock ride height at 21 inches in the front and 23 in the rear, technician Mark Futino put the Ram on the lift and removed the wheels. Tie rod ends are removed from the spindles. Bolts are removed from the lower ball joint. Stabilizer end-link shings are removed. Futino removes the brake caliper.

Using a floor jack, the lower control arm is lowered to remove stock coil spring. Futino prepares to install the new coil spring. Stock coil spring is removed. The difference in the spring rate of the stock coil spring (left) compared to the Ground Force coil spring is not obvious to the naked eye.

Stock bump stop is removed. The Ground Force bump stop (left) is considerably longer than the stock bump stop.

Getting your Dodge Ram, or any pickup truck, to the place where low-profile tires on 20-plus-inch billet wheels look like they belong requires a shift from stock ride height. We followed the installation of this lowering kit on the Jet Performance 2004 Dodge RAM Hemi. Here's one way to get your Dodge Ram lowered to where it looks fine and handles great. Bear in mind, if you own a Ford, Chevy, Toyota, Nissan, or most any brand of truck, there is a system to lowering your truck just like this one. All late-model and early model pickup trucks will take a similar path to sinking the ride height.

One drop kit by Ground Force is for the 2004 Dodge Ram, which is designed to lower the truck about 4 inches in the front, and 5 inches in the rear. Thanks to technician Mark Futino at A+ Performance in Huntington Beach, California, the kit installation was straightforward and went smoothly.

Before we began, the Ram's stock ride height was 21 inches in front and 23 inches at the rear. After the installation, coil springs in front and a flip kit with new hangers and shackles in the rear, the Ram measured a much more attractive 18.5 inches in front and 19.5 inches in the rear. After installation of the kit, the actual drop

in this case was 3.5 inches in the front and 4.5 inches at the rear. This truck has the Hemi motor, and each truck, depending on the motor, will be different. But what's half an inch between friends?

Of course, you are the judge when it comes to your truck. We think the final result this kit achieved gave this Dodge Ram a greatly improved stance and more the look of a show truck. Check out the photos and captions showing the highlights of the installation and see for yourself.

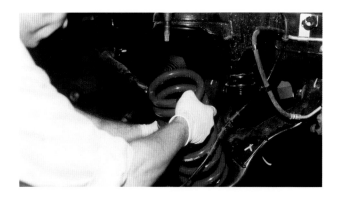

Futino installs the Ground Force coil spring.

Spindle is then reconnected to upper control arm. A comparative look at the stock front shock (right) and the Ground Force shock.

Brake caliper is reattached. New front shock is installed.

After removing the stock rear shock, Futino unbolts the inner wheel-well shroud. Stock shock is removed. Next, the shackles are removed.

Futino removes the U-bolts that secure the shackles. He then removes the center bolt securing the leaf pack.

Leaf spring is removed. Ground Force bump stop is installed.

Futino prepares the Ground Force hardware and shackles. Leaf spring is reinstalled with the new bolts.

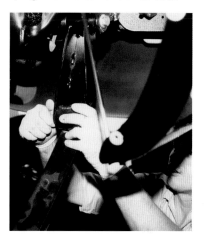

Ground Force shock mount extensions are installed. Extension hardware for securing the leaf springs is installed. Futino completes reinstalling leaf springs. Spacer plate for transmission mount is installed to complete the drop.

SUSPENSION

TIME: Eight hours

TOOLS: Full socket set, screwdriver set, torque wrench, appropriate jack, jack stands, die cutter or plasma cutter

TALENT: ★★

APPLICABLE YEARS: All years—automatic and manual transmissions

TAB: $700

TINWARE: Mechanic's gloves

TIP: Read through the instructions of your specific lowering kit before you break out the jacks and wrenches. Double-check your work.

PERFORMANCE GAIN:
Lower center of gravity, improved cornering

COMPLEMENTARY PROJECT:
High-performance shocks, new tires and wheels

With the truck up on jack stands, the wheels and tires are removed to allow access to the suspension. The technician starts off by removing the factory bump stops and shock absorbers. Next, he removes the tie rod ends from the steering arm of the spindles. The technician also removes the anti-sway bar from the end links to allow the lower control arms to swing all the way down so he will be able to remove the coil springs once the factory spindles are removed. Now it's time to remove the calipers and caliper brackets from the factory spindles. The nut is loosened on the upper ball joint and a hammer is used to shock it free. Then the nut can be carefully removed to free the top of the spindle and allow access to the coil spring. The coil spring can be dropped out of the coil cup in the frame, and then the nut is removed from the lower ball joint to allow the factory spindle to be removed.

The three bolts that hold the spindle to the hub assembly are removed, and it allows them to be separated. The hub mount on the McGaughys spindle has been relocated 2 inches higher on the face of the spindle.

There is all of this craziness going on in the truck world with air bags, long-travel off-road suspensions, drop-down-style lift kits that offer 16 inches of lift, and all of the other over-the-top suspension modifications that fill every page of every magazine on the planet, and we decided to ignore all of it. We want to show you that a solid foundation for any sport truck always starts with a top-quality suspension drop. Regardless of the make and model truck you own, there is a drop kit that will work for your truck.

In fact, just the installation of a kit, such as the 4/6 McGaughys drop kit that we're installing on this 2005 Dodge Ram with new low-profile Nitto 420S tires will automatically improve the truck's handling. Not only will the lower center of gravity keep the truck from leaning hard during cornering, but the new 265/50R20 Nitto tires that we're installing on the factory 20-inch wheels offer better grip to the road because of a softer rubber compound and less sidewall flex than its factory counterpart. And all of this is achieved without even having to incur the added expense of a set of high-performance shocks.

So, just imagine the kind of handling improvement you could expect if you added a set of gas-charged shock absorbers, aftermarket anti-sway bars, polyurethane suspension bushings, and a brake upgrade into the mix. But the funny thing is that none of those handling upgrades would be as effective if they were installed without the lowering kit. That's how important selecting the right lowering kit is for your truck!

And to make the story more "hands-on," we decided to make it part of the do-it-in-the-driveway theme. So we limited ourselves to one day to simulate having to do the job on a Saturday when you're not using your truck to get back and forth to work, and we used fairly basic tools. About the only thing we cheated on was using a plasma cutter to trim out the rear frame rails for the bolt-in C-notch, but it was only because we were out of cutting wheels for the grinder. Other than that, though, the job was very straightforward, and, on a difficulty scale of 1 to 10, installing the McGaughys kit was pretty easy, ranking about a 5.

In a side-by-side comparison of the coil springs, it is easy to see how much shorter the McGaughys coil spring is than the factory unit. In the instructions it says to trim the brake backing plate even with the front edge of the spindle, so mark the backing plate and trim it with a pair of sheetmetal shears.

Then the factory bolts are used to install the factory hub and backing plate to the new drop spindle. The new McGaughys coil spring is slipped into the factory coil spring pocket in the frame and the control arm is pushed up to pin it in place. Reinstall the anti-sway bar to hold the lower control arm against the coil. Slide the spindle over both the upper and lower ball joints at the same time and install the lock nuts that hold everything together. All that's left is the installation of the brakes and the outer tie rod ends to finish off the front suspension.

The kit to drop the back of this Dodge is straightforward. It comes with a bolt-in C-notch, axle saddles, U-bolt plates, and all of the necessary hardware needed to install everything. With the wheels and tires out of the way, start by removing the U-bolts that hold the axle assembly to the leaf springs. Then the shock absorbers are unbolted from the rear axle assembly.

The bolts that hold both the front and rear of the leaf spring in place are removed, allowing the technician to pull the leaf spring out from its factory position over the axle and move it to its new position under the axle.

At this point, the technician unbolts the factory rear bump stops to give him more room to jockey the rear end around and move it into position. The bump stops had to be removed eventually anyway, and this just seemed like a logical time to do it.

Next, the new spring saddles are slipped around the bottom of the axle, and the factory U-bolts with the new McGaughys leaf-spring plate are installed. Because the kit uses the factory-length shock absorbers, the McGaughys kit comes with a pair of shock extenders to keep the shocks from bottoming out before the suspension is compressed. With the flip kit installed, the technician centers the bolt-in C-notch over the axle and marks the frame where it is going to have to be cut.

Because we were out of cut-off wheels, we decided to use a plasma cutter to trim out the frame, then we cleaned up all of the slag with a grinder. Then the 1/2-inch holes were drilled into the frame rails for the inside support that also houses the mounting hardware for the bolt-in C-notch. This piece slides inside the frame rail, and the bolts that hold everything together are actually part of the support, killing two birds with one stone.

The bolts simply slide through the holes that were drilled in the frame, and then this spacer is slipped into place on the side behind the axle on both sides of the truck. The outer notch support is then bolted into place, and the new low-profile bump stop is installed into the threaded hole in the new notch.

PROJECT 32 ADD AN AUTOMATIC ADJUSTING AIR SPRING SUSPENSION SYSTEM

 TIME: Eight hours

 TOOLS: Full socket set, power drill, drill bits, torque wrench, appropriate jack, jack stands

 TALENT: ★★

 APPLICABLE YEARS: All

 TAB: $1,000

 TINWARE: Air hose cutting tool

 TIP: Take your time. Double-check your work.

 PERFORMANCE GAIN:
Better ride control when towing and daily driving

COMPLEMENTARY PROJECT:
New wheels and tires

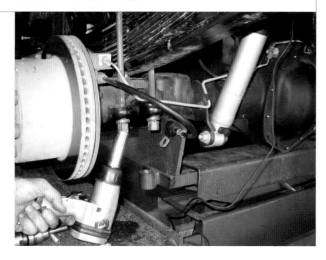

To begin the installation, the factory leaf springs must be removed. This is done by first unbolting the factory U-bolts.

With the axle supported, the rear leaf-spring bolts were removed from the leaf-spring hangers. Then the front hanger bolt on the leaf springs was removed to free the leaf spring from its hangers. Carefully, each side of the truck's heavy leaf springs was removed from the axle. The instructions show where to measure and install the brackets on the frame. These were placed into position in order to drill the lower bolt holes on to the frame.

Balancing and leveling your three-quarter- or one-and-a-half-ton truck while maintaining comfort and stability can often be a challenge with factory leaf springs. Although many ways exist to improve the ride, such as using heavier-duty leaf springs and helper springs, many truck owners don't want the firmer ride that these add-on springs cause when their trucks aren't towing anything. For this reason, air spring systems have become extremely popular among truck owners who occasionally tow heavy loads, but who also use their trucks for daily driving.

Air springs offer the advantage of having the ability to stabilize trucks under towing conditions and also maintain the correct ride height. Air springs also provide added comfort when driving under normal conditions and can be adjusted to improve handling or to help smooth out the road.

While adding or decreasing the amount of air pressure adjusts most air spring systems, the Air Lift Company has recently come out with a new system that can do this automatically and electronically. The Air Lift Road Tamer uses an automated control system, called SmartAir, which tweaks air spring pressure to certain degrees to improve handling, braking, and cornering in varying road conditions, such as aggressive wind and sharp curves.

The SmartAir system regulates the air bags' spring rate to match the load in the vehicle through hands-free electronic control. The system's automated functions even include a 25-second delay, which keeps the system from reacting to single bumps in the road to provide an even ride. As an added bonus, the system does not rely on gauges, so drivers don't have to spend time monitoring air pressure or cluttering dash space with gauge equipment.

Although Road Tamer air springs do not increase a vehicle's weight rating, they do address a multitude of load-balancing issues that better equip a vehicle to bear an acceptable load. This air spring system replaces the factory steel rear leaf springs on a vehicle and replaces them with formed steel beams, rugged air bags, and the SmartAir automatic control system.

According to the Air Lift Company, installing Road Tamer air suspension will drastically reduce and eliminate rough ride, sag, roll, bounce, bottoming out, trailer sway, side-to-side tipping, hitch misalignment, and headlight misalignment. Most important, the air springs will cushion road shock to reduce the stress on a vehicle, trailer, and cargo, and any passengers who may be inside the cab.

In addition, Road Tamer systems are designed to work with a kneeling option that allows drivers to temporarily override the automated height control system when parked. With the ease of flipping a switch inside the cabin, drivers can disable the compressor and height control, open the dump valve, and drop the rear of the truck up to 3 inches. As a result, campers and trailers can be safely connected.

Other options for the Road Tamer system include Select-A-Ride shocks, a digital controller, and an expansion tank. The Select-A-Ride shocks feature a nine-position damping dial, which allows the fine-tuning of a vehicle's suspension travel to match the road conditions and load. The digital controller easily mounts inside the cabin of a vehicle for touch-key adjustment of the shocks. Features of the digital controller include a clear display, user-friendly buttons, automatic leak detection, and automatic ride height after starting the vehicle.

An expansion tank can also be purchased separately to further improve the ride of any Road Tamer system. The expansion tank acts as an add-on volume for Road Tamer air springs while also decreasing stress on the springs under rough road conditions. The result is a smoother ride without altering Road Tamer's carrying capacity.

Currently, the Road Tamer system is available for Chevy, GMC, Ford, and Dodge model trucks. Air Lift demonstrated how the system is installed and used basic tools to do the job. According to Air Lift, the entire system can be bolted on in about six to eight hours by an experienced home mechanic or a professional.

After the bolt holes are drilled, the nuts and bolts are inserted into the upper air bag bracket to hold it in place. The process is repeated for the system's Panhard rod. The brackets are set in place and ½-inch holes must be drilled for the bolts. Heavy-duty hardware is installed to hold the Panhard rod bracket in place. The front of the Air Ride beam uses the factory hanger as a pivot point. New hardware is provided for this attachment point. The height control magnet bracket is attached to the inside of the passenger-side beam with self-tapping screws. On the passenger side of the vehicle, the electronic control module (ECM) is mounted to the frame with self-tapping screws. The magnet is adjusted to the centerline on the ECM to achieve the static ride height.

Because the front of the beam is attached to the factory hanger, the rear of the beam can now be bolted to the axle. New U-bolts are provided to secure the beams to the axle using the factory bottom brackets.

At this point, the Panhard rod is placed into position on the frame, above the axle. The provided hardware is inserted into the top Panhard bracket to hold it into position. Once the bottom of the Panhard is attached to the bracket on the axle, the bolts are tightened.

Once everything is in position, the air springs can be inserted between the frame mount and the Air Ride beam. The bottom of the air bag is bolted in first, using the hardware provided in the kit.

At the top, the hardware secures the air bag to the top bracket. One of the bolts also functions as a valve that will be connected to the air line. Standard nylon air line and compression fittings are used and are routed to the air springs and the onboard compressor. Due to the extreme motion of the system, Air Lift recommends relocating the parking brake cable and includes this bracket to hold it in place on one of the U-bolts. An optional kneeling switch mounted in the cabin allows the vehicle to be lowered up to 3 inches for safe and easy hitching.

The finished installation looks great and adjusts automatically with the SmartAir computer control system.

PROJECT 33 ADD ANTI-SWAY BARS TO IMPROVE HANDLING

TIME: 40 minutes per axle

TOOLS: Medium socket set, bottle jack, jack stands

TALENT: ★

APPLICABLE YEARS: All years—automatic and manual transmissions

TAB: $200 per axle

TINWARE: Drop cloth or mechanic's creeper if you are working on the ground.

TIP: Use sealable sandwich bags to organize the hardware you will use again.

PERFORMANCE GAIN:
Superior road handling compared to stock suspension

COMPLEMENTARY PROJECT:
High-performance shocks such as Bilstein

Many of the 2005 Ford F-250/350 trucks (this includes all brands, makes, and models of light pickup trucks) come equipped with only a front anti-sway bar, and this bar alone is pretty tiny compared to the massive truck it is supposed to stabilize. To put it bluntly, the factory bar is too small to do the job it should be doing. With the truck on a lift and the parking brake set, the first step is to remove the bolts holding the U-clamp and bushings.

Many components of a suspension contribute to the handling and ride of a vehicle. Most of the time, the best ride and handling occur when all of the specific suspension equipment works together. The problem is that often the factory equipment doesn't meet these requirements. It seems there is always room for improvement. One product that has the greatest impact on how your vehicle handles is anti-sway bars.

Anti-sway bars do just that; they keep a truck from swaying. They help to stabilize your vehicle's center of gravity and actually increase the function of the suspension. Every facet of suspension performance benefits from good anti-sway bars, be it a race car or the truck you use for towing. The function is the same—to allow the suspension to actually work, while stabilizing the body and chassis motion from side to side.

One of the biggest names in anti-sway bars is a company called Hellwig. For more than 50 years, Hellwig has been designing and manufacturing anti-sway bars as well as performance- and duty-enhancing springs for cars and trucks. The company's goal is to give customers the key products to allow them to achieve their handling and suspension performance results. Thanks to most

truck manufacturers "underdeveloping" their anti-sway bar components, Hellwig has grown its product line to include just about every truck on the market. And two truck models in dire need of a set of good anti-sway bars are the 2005 Ford F-250 and F-350 Super Duty trucks. These trucks were designed for tough jobs like towing and hauling, yet they have only a small front anti-sway bar and no rear bar at all.

To help owners of these new Ford trucks greatly improve the stability and handling of their purchased vehicle, Hellwig has recently introduced an anti-sway bar package that contains new front and rear bars as well as the hardware and brackets necessary to get the job done. Hellwig's bars are made from heat formed and coined 4140 chrome moly spring steel to ensure strength and durability. Hellwig's bars are much thicker than the factory bars, which help translate into less body roll, improved traction, and even weight distribution to all four wheels. The front Hellwig bar is a direct replacement and includes new polyurethane bushings. The rear bar kit comes with axle housing brackets to position the thick rear bar over the housing. Two long end links attach to the frame dropdown and meet the bar ends next to the leaf springs. As you will see in the following photos, this anti-sway bar combo is very easy to install. We completed the swap in less than 30 minutes.

Even with the bolts removed, you'll probably have to pull a bit on the U-clamp to free it from the frame. Make sure not to discard the factory U-clamps. These, along with all of the hardware from the end links, will be reused with the Hellwig bar. The end links are in a pretty accessible location, which makes it pretty easy to get a couple of wrenches on the hardware. Again, make sure to not lose the factory hardware.

You will probably have to turn the front wheels to the left or right to get the bar out because there are several items, such as the radiator return hose, that run under the bar. The new Hellwig anti-sway bar is much thicker and made from heat formed and coined 4140 chrome moly. The end link pads are nearly twice as large as the stock pads. At this point we installed the provided new polyurethane bushings on to the Hellwig bar. Even the bushings are bigger but will still fit the factory U-clamps.

With the wheels turned to the left, the new Hellwig bar is installed in the same manner in which the factory one was removed. Make sure the bar goes over the radiator return hose. With the bar in place, the factory U-clamps are installed over the new bushing and secured, but not permanently tightened just yet. The Hellwig bar dimensions are exactly the same as the factory bar, so the original end link and hardware can be reused.

As you can see, the steps are pretty easy, and I think anyone would immediately notice the dramatic difference in appearance of the new bar as opposed to the factory one. At this point you can permanently tighten the mounting hardware. Some of the 2005 Fords come with a rear bar, but even those that do have a little tiny bar as opposed to the much larger Hellwig bar. This truck didn't have a rear bar so we will install the entire Hellwig rear stabilizer kit. The first step is to remove the emergency brake cable support from the passenger-side shock mount. Save the hardware to be reattached later. Now the new rear bar is installed over the rear end housing. It should rest on top of the housing once it is positioned correctly. The key to making stabilizer bars work is the end links. The rear kit comes with long end links that will attach to the frame.

Remove the frame bolt from the top of the end link and insert it through the factory hole in the frame, which is located just in front of the four frame rivets that hold the rear frame clip in place. This bolt should be pointing outward. Once the end link is loosely installed on to the frame bolt, the end of the bar can be loosely attached to the end link. You will know if you have got it right if the end link is hanging straight down.

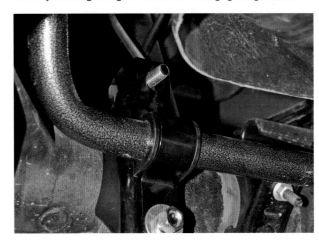

The key to making the rear bar kit work are the two housing brackets, which provide a flat surface for two U-clamps and bushing to mount to. The brackets are designed to fit on to the ends of the differential housing where it meets the axle tubes. One U-bolt is used to secure the bracket in place. Position the U-bolt between the saddles located on the bottom edge of the differential housing. With the U-bolt hardware holding the bar in place, swing the bracket assembly upward from the front side to move the bar up above the housing.

Once the proper placement is determined, the bracket hardware can then be tightened. If the end link of the bar is horizontal, the position of the axle brackets is accurate and the end link hardware can be permanently tightened.

With only a few minutes of work, your truck can now have strong, well-designed anti-sway bars that will greatly enhance the towing and hauling duties.

SUSPENSION

TIME: Two to three days

TOOLS: Full socket set, screwdriver set, torque wrench, appropriate jack stands, air line cutter, acetylene torch, die cutter, mig welder—ability to cut and weld

TALENT: ★★★★

APPLICABLE YEARS: All years—automatic and manual transmissions

TAB: $700

TINWARE: Tape measure, grease pen, work space, level

TIP: If you have the skill and confidence to cut, measure, weld, and work accurately, this is a doable project for the automotive enthusiast working on a project vehicle.

PERFORMANCE GAIN:
Greatly improved traction when level of customization when using high horsepower engine

COMPLEMENTARY PROJECT:
High performance shocks and rear-end differential

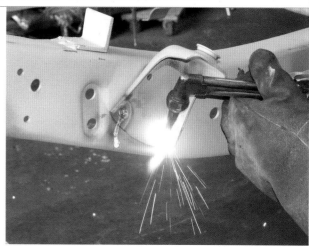

Though this frame has been stripped, it is not necessary to go to these lengths. Although it is necessary to remove the bed, the Fat Bar 4-link kit can be installed on a road-ready vehicle. The first step is to remove all of the stock suspension and shock brackets. An acetylene torch makes this job much easier, but this job can also be done by grinding off the heads of the rivets and then pounding them out with a drift and single jack. The torch also makes quick work of this factory E-brake bar. The rest of the extraneous brackets are removed. Because a new shock crossmember is used with the No Limit kit, the stock one is also removed at this time. With the frame stripped of all unnecessary pieces, the install can begin.

When classic trucks were simply trucks, they were built for a purpose. That purpose was not to smoothly cruise down the highway at high speeds, it was to carry heavy loads. They did this with heavy leaf springs and they did this well. The result was what the original designers were looking for, but the ride is sure not what modern owners want.

Rob MacGregor, owner of No Limit Engineering in San Bernardino, California, knows what the owners of classic trucks want. And thanks to an engineering degree, he is in a position to give them what they want as well as need. And for those who want to have a smooth ride, the choice is No Limit's Fat Bar four-link suspension kit.

Unlike other kits, the No Limit Fat Bar four-link is designed specifically for pickups. The difference with the approach that No Limit takes and some other manufacturers don't is that No Limit designs parts for a specific application rather than trying to adapt what the company has to fit as many vehicles as possible.

The No Limit Fat Bar four-link suspension system can be equipped with myriad shock options as well. Do you want to run coil-over shocks, or are you a fan of air bags? Or maybe not just air bags, but Air Ride Technologies ShockWaves? No problem. No Limit offers kits to satisfy all cravings. Also included in the kit is a Panhard bar and related bracketry, so no one will accuse you of having an out-of-center rear end.

We watched as MacGregor installed one of his Fat Bar four-link systems on to a 1951 Chevy pickup. The job is one that is not for the novice wrench, so we recommend that a reputable shop do this job for you. It is an install that needs to be precise, but the results gained are just as precise.

It is imperative that the frame is level both front to back and side to side. If the frame is off now, the suspension system will be off when the job is done, and nobody wants his or her truck to crawl while going down the road or to sit lopsided. Clean metal means strong welds, so the steel is prepped for the boxing plates.

A template is made from construction paper, and from that the boxing plate is fabricated.

The plate is then welded in. Be certain that the piece is welded in using a rotating pattern so that no one spot gets too hot. The welds are then ground smooth. The front mount for the four-link sits where the triangle brace is, so that is the next piece to go. By cutting along the top of the brace and removing the rivets that hold it in place, the triangle brace is removed. A grinder cleans up the edges of the cuts.

Needless to say, it is important that the axle centerline be properly located. The way to determine this centerline is by measuring 36 ½ inches from the end of the frame rail, then the mount location is determined by measuring 35 ½ inches from the centerline to the rear edge of the bed-mounting hole.

Once you have measured twice to be sure, a mark is placed where the leading edge of the 4-link mount will sit.

With the 4-link mounts held by C-clamps, the space between them is measured. The mounts need to be 26 ½ inches apart. A mark is placed exactly at the center of the rear crossmember.

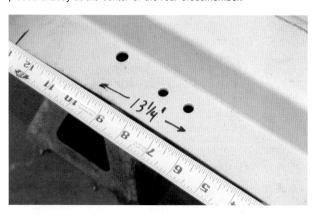

Using this center mark, a measurement of 13 ¼ inches is marked on the frame. This mark will be used to determine the proper angle of the mounts. An easy way to line up the mounts with the marks is to clamp a long piece of straight stock to the mount. With the angle determined, the mount is welded to the frame. Again, a series of short welds (1–2 inches) are applied using a rotating pattern so that no one spot gets too hot. Care is taken not to weld up the bed-mounting hole, however, as it will be needed later.

With the mounts on, attention is focused on the axle housing. A measurement is taken to determine the exact distance between the backing plates. This number is 53 ½ inches. Remember that 13 ¼-inch mark placed on the rear crossmember? Well, it is the same measurement needed to determine the rear four-link mount location on the axle housing. This measurement is taken from the backing plates as well. Use a level to determine that the axle housing is sitting with the U-joint cup straight up. Then use it to determine that the 4-link mount is perfectly level and at an exact 90 degree angle to the snout of third member. A few tack welds hold the mount in place. Measurements are taken to determine that the area between the mounts is exactly 26 ½ inches, just like the area between the mounts on the frame. Do you see a pattern here? The importance of these numbers matching cannot be overstated as the angle of the four-link bars must be precise to avoid binding or other things equally as bad for handling characteristics.

A mark is placed at the top center of the shock mount. With the axle housing spun so that the snout is pointed exactly down (again, precision counts), a measurement of 5 ¾ inches is made from the original 13 ¼-inch mark. The shock mount is tack welded in place. Again, all measurements are double-checked. With everything determined to be perfect, final welding is completed. To ensure strength, welds are also placed along the inner edges of the mounts, not just to the exterior edges. With the bushings installed into the bars, they are measured to determine that they are all at 30 inches on center. The live ends of the bars are installed into the front mount, and the rear end housing is set into position and on to a set of jack stands. The dead ends of the bars are bolted to the rear mounts. Time to place the upper shock mounts/crossmember. A measurement of 41 ½ inches is taken from the leading edge of the forward four-link mount. Due to the variations of frame widths, No Limit sends out the crossmember a little long. This way the crossmember can be cut to fit exactly with the frame, which in this case is 39 ¾ inches. With the crossmember cut, it is installed, and tack welds are placed at the upper/leading edge of the crossmember. By placing the tacks there, the crossmember can be rotated using a screwdriver to get it exactly level. Call it a trick of the trade.

With the crossmember in the correct location, it is welded in. After installing the lower spacer, the Air Ride Technologies ShockWaves are installed. Next comes the Panhard bar. After measuring from the backing plates to the frame rails to get the housing centered, the axle mount of the Panhard bar is tacked in place—after determining that it is completely level, of course.

With the Panhard bar mounted up, the frame mount of the Panhard bar is placed beneath the frame rail and tacked in place. Note that the Panhard bar is aligned so that it is perfectly parallel with the rear end housing. As the frame rail turns up, there is a gap around the frame mount of the Panhard bar. To fill in this space, pieces of flat stock are cut, and the gap will be boxed out.

With that, the shocks are removed, and the final welding is done to the Panhard mounts. Always remove the shocks (especially air-type shocks) before any welding is done, so that flying bits of slag do not damage them. Once the welding is done, the shocks can be bolted back up.

Once the axle housing is perfectly aligned, the jam nuts on the bars are tightened.

And with that, the No Limit Fat Bar 4-link System is in and ready.

TIME: One and a half hours

 TOOLS: Full socket set, hand tools

 TALENT: ★

 APPLICABLE YEARS: Most light pickup truck years, makes, and models

 TAB: $200–$250 for each axle

 TINWARE: N/A

 TIP: If you plan to color-match or use accent colors on suspension, plan to powder coat or paint anti-sway bars before you install them on your vehicle.

 PERFORMANCE GAIN:
Better, flatter handling and cornering

COMPLEMENTARY PROJECT:
Consider replacing your shocks at this time so you enjoy a more complete suspension improvement.

SUSPENSION

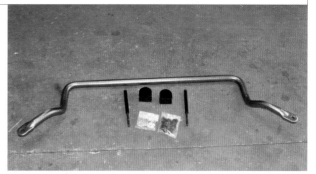

With the vehicle in the air, remove front wheels. Disconnect the end links.

Remove bolts on central mount points. Have a friend assist you as the front sway bar is removed. Install new rubber mounting U-blocks on to the new anti-sway bar. There is a slit in the rubber allowing you to slip the rubber U-block over the bar. Have a friend assist you in positioning the front anti-sway bar in place while you position the rubber U-blocks over mounting holes.

Improving the handling of a half- or three-quarter-ton light pickup truck is one of the most rewarding performance upgrades you can do. Aside from lowering the center of gravity and upgrading the coils and shocks, you can start with controlling your side-to-side body rolling in curves and turning maneuvers by adding front and rear anti-sway bars. Your pickup might have come with a factory anti-sway bar up front, and that helps. But you can do substantially better by increasing the gauge of the bar and adding one at the rear.

Hellwig has been in the suspension business for many years, and improving the handling of a vehicle is what it does best. In addition to increasing the suspension's ability to flatten your truck's cornering ability via anti-sway bars, Hellwig also provides a means of bolstering your factory half-ton rear leaf springs to handle the load better in the form of helper springs. Helper springs support the load rating of your vehicle's factory springs with the addition of one longer main leaf and a shorter secondary leaf spring. When you are running without a load on your truck bed, the Hellwig helper springs are not engaged and your softer leaf springs continue to provide a softer ride. But

when you add 400 pounds to your bed load, the two springs engage with the primary factory spring pack and keep the load from sinking the truck suspension.

Installation time for all three suspension upgrades took about two hours and can be installed with common tools on the floor. It would be ideal if you have access to a drive-on lift

103

so that as the sway bars are being positioned and secured the vehicle will be resting on its own weight making adjustments more accurate. That's the big tip; make sure the vehicle is sitting on the ground before tightening all bolts related to the anti-sway bars. This will avoid binding of components and potential pressure on a misaligned installation. Front anti-sway bars run about $200 and rear bars cost about $250. Helper spring kits are about $230.

Handling improvement is instantly recognizable with the anti-sway bars. Cornering is flat with no wallow or side-to-side weight shifting in tight and less-than-gradual curves. Lane changes are flat and the truck stays planted on the highway. You gain a sense of control and assuredness.

We worked with Custom Motor Sports to pull three suspension upgrades together in a few hours; a project you can handle in a Saturday afternoon. Installation instructions are thorough, so we're going to hit the highlights and you can see how this upgrade will work for you. We'll move through the sway bars first, then show the helper spring install.

Here's the front Hellwig anti-sway bar as a direct factory replacement to a more robust handling and suspension component. We first installed the end-link frame brackets on each side of the truck. A J-hook at the lower portion is used to provide a secure anchor.

Once rubber blocks are in place, note you will reuse metal factory U-plates and bolts. Load up new anti-sway bar end links with new hardware. Position correct grommets and washer combination as you loosely mount up your Hellwig. To help collapse the front suspension so the end-link bolt assemblies could be snugged down, we used an adjustable floor stand and then mounted up the bolts. Likewise, a stout long-shank screwdriver helps to compress the front suspension assembly from the top.

Ryan places the stabilizer bar up and over the rear differential housing. Note any possible contact with brake lines, cables, or electric wiring. With the stabilizer bar somewhat in position, you will loosely orchestrate where U-bolts and mounting brackets will be located. Don't cinch down any bolts at this point.

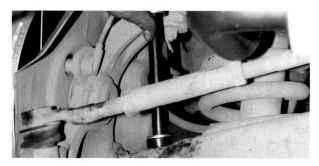

Double-check your link assembly and bolt/washer patterns. As you snug down the bolts at the front Hellwig anti-sway bar, wait until you have the truck on the ground before final cinching and setting torque.

Here's what a correct installation looks like. Make sure the stabilizer bar does not go over any brake or electric lines. Note: A long end link is used for four-wheel-drive vehicles. Two-wheel-drive trucks will use a shorter end link. Both lengths of end links come with this kit.

Here's the completed Hellwig rear anti-sway bar. Wait until you have the truck back on the ground before you torque down the bolts. Torque values for bolts used on this application are: ⅜ inch = 30 lb-ft; ⁷⁄₁₆ inch = 45 lb-ft; ½ inch = 70 lb-ft; ⁹⁄₁₆ inch = 90 lb-ft.

Rubber silencer bushing sets up like this. You might want to trim some length off U-bolt ends. We found using a C-clamp the best way to keep spring assemblies in place while you are lining springs up and mounting U-bolts.

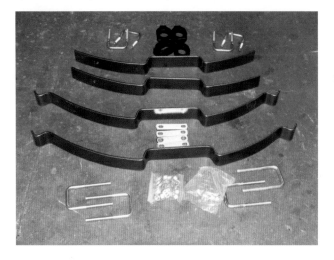

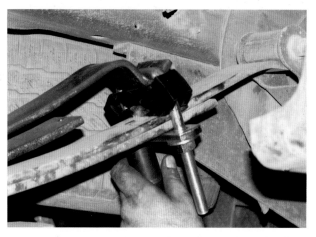

Here's the entire kit. Shorter springs will nest under longer springs. Longer top spring will point toward rear of the vehicle. Assemble offset U-bolts so kick of each U-bolt angles in toward the axle. Note that every bolt will use two nuts.

Expect to compress the silencer bushing when you snug down the bolts. Note double nuts on each bolt end. This pattern repeats for all bolts on this application.

Close-up of the silencer bushing compressed. You're finished.

SECTION 4

OFF-ROAD SUSPENSION AND HARDWARE

Front SSR shocks and Bulletproof brake hoses are two of the available upgrades. Tom Morr

TIME: Two hours

 TOOLS: Full socket set, jack, jack stands

 TALENT: ★

 APPLICABLE YEARS: Kits for all years, makes, and models of light trucks

 TAB: $150 plus coil spring compression

 TINWARE: N/A

 TIP: If you need new front shocks, this is a good time to install them while you have the tires off.

 PERFORMANCE GAIN:
Tire clearance

COMPLEMENTARY PROJECT:
New shocks

Before: This F-150 work truck needed a little more ground clearance up front. *Jim Cole*

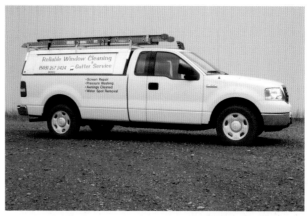

After: Once the CAGE Off-Road spacers were installed, you can see the difference in the front-end ride height. *Jim Cole*

Although some methods of adding inches to your truck or SUV are easier than others, CAGE Off-Road recently found a simple way to add 2 inches to the 2004-05 Ford F-150 pickup. Two inches may not seem like enough, especially when you compare it to 6-to-8-inch-lifted 4x4s that roll on 35- to 38-inch-diameter tires.

But many people who don't necessarily want to severely lift their trucks are simply looking for a way to add a 33-inch wheel and tire package to gain additional ground clearance over stock. Others also like the fact that lifting the front suspension 2 inches will also keep the truck level, as it typically has a higher ride height in the rear than in the front. Furthermore, a 2-inch lift will also keep the ball joints and CV joints within their proper range of operation without binding or causing excessive wear.

But while many begin to lift the F-150 with new coil springs and shocks, CAGE found that a simpler way to lift the truck would be to use a set of spacers between the top of the coil pack and the spring cup. The company uses a machined 2-inch, T-6 billet aluminum spacer that is simple to install. Although removing the strut itself is a simple procedure that many home

mechanics can do themselves, it is important to stress that to remove the coil spring, a strut compressor must be used. If you don't have one or can't rent a heavy-duty unit, take the strut to a local alignment or suspension shop that has one, as those shops can do it for you at a minimal cost.

The process simply involves compressing the coil spring so that the top spring cup can be unbolted and removed. Once this is done, the spacer fits on top of the spring and the spring cap is then reinstalled by again using the spring compressor. After

OFF-ROAD SUSPENSION AND HARDWARE

both right- and left-side struts are reassembled, they are simply bolted back into the vehicle. The new ride height is immediately visible, and there's no change to the ride of the truck.

CAGE Off-Road demonstrated a typical installation on a 2004 F-150 work truck, in which the owner wanted to get more clearance under the bumper for some job sites that required additional height to access. The CAGE Off-Road spacers retail for around $150, and if you do the work yourself, it would cost only about another $25–$30 to have a shop compress the springs and install the spacers.

The spacers for the F-150 measure 2 inches and are made from T6 billet aluminum. *Jim Cole*

To install the spacers, the struts have to be removed. First, use a floor jack and jack stands to raise the vehicle and begin by removing the wheels. Then remove the tire rod end. *Jim Cole*

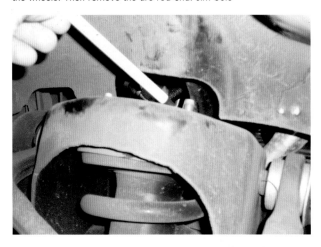

In order to remove the strut, the top strut bolts need to be removed. These secure the strut to the frame mount. *Jim Cole*

At the bottom of the strut, a single bolt holds it to the bottom A-arm. This, too, must be removed in order for the strut to be taken out from the suspension. *Jim Cole*

The installation instructions recommend taking the struts to a shop with the proper compressor too. We went to a local shop, Eaton's Tire & Service Center, which did this for us for only $30. *Jim Cole*

Here you can see the shiny aluminum spacer barely peeking out from under the top strut cup. Note that this kit retains the factory rubber coil-spring isolator for a squeak-free ride. *Jim Cole*

Once the spacers are installed, the struts are put back into the truck. Note that the kit requires removal of the dust shield. According to CAGE this is not a problem with strut life and seals and actually helps clean out any mud that may accumulate around the strut shaft. *Jim Cole*

TIME: Four hours

TOOLS: Full socket set, jack, jack stands

TALENT: ★★

APPLICABLE YEARS: Shocks for all years, makes, and models of light trucks

TAB: $600–$1,500 depending upon vehicle and amount of lift desired

TINWARE: N/A

TIP: Have your wheels and tires mounted, and test the tire clearance at earliest possible time.

PERFORMANCE GAIN:
Better control running rough terrain and capacity to run taller tires with more ground clearance, and potentially more wheel travel

COMPLEMENTARY PROJECT:
Consider installing bump stops and new longer-travel shocks.

After we get the truck up on a lift, and the front wheels and brake calipers are removed, the calipers can be hung off the frame during the work.

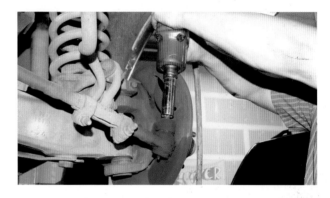

The steering control arms are removed as well as cotter pins and the castle nuts. A good solid hit with a sledgehammer dislodged the pins from the spindle and allowed the removal of the control arms.

The sway bar end links are disconnected to allow easy access to the spindles during this process. With the upper retaining clip removed, the spindles were gradually lowered to take the pressure off the front springs.

Grown from a desire for 4x4 enthusiasts to gain more ground clearance, the lifted truck has never been so popular. Both four- and two-wheel-drive truck owners have gone to great lengths to lift their trucks as a means of gaining more performance, and also as a means to have something different than the lowered pickup. Several manufacturers specialize in lifting trucks, and if your intent is to move upward, there are some things you will want to know.

First, lifting a two-wheel-drive (2WD) truck is easier than lifting a four-wheel-drive (4WD) truck. Most aftermarket manufacturers raise a 2WD by using taller coil springs and by actually lowering some of the internal components in relationship to the frame. Thus, lowering the position of the suspension will ultimately raise the height of the frame and give more lift. The most common 2WD lift uses this approach and can be raised anywhere from 2 inches to 10 inches, depending on the spring and control arm.

Observing an installation of a Fabtech kit on to a 2WD, 1995 Ford F-150 club cab, it was surprising to see how easily one could lift a pickup with the right components. The Custom Truck Shop in San Dimas, California, and owner Louis Morosan, performed the installation in stages, and what seemed like a lot of parts were actually installed in a very short period of time. The entire installation took a few hours.

When completed, the F-150 had 4 inches more height, huge in comparison to stock height. After the installation, the truck was taken to an alignment shop and the truck drove great. The added height gives not only a more commanding view of the road, but it also smoothed out the ride and was more intimidating to other traffic.

OFF-ROAD SUSPENSION AND HARDWARE

 To get the springs off the spindle, a socket extension that would fit the length of the spring had to be used. This also allows access to the bottom retaining bolt for the spring. Once it was removed, the spring came right out. With the springs out of the way, the I-beams are adjusted to handle the travel of the lifted suspension. Fabtech supplies a new set of I-beam brackets that replace the stock brackets on the frame.

New spacer blocks are placed between the axle and the spring pack. The Fabtech kit comes with new U-bolts and hardware to accommodate the longer length. With the new Fabtech shocks installed, the rear end was buttoned up. The attention was turned back to the front installation of the new 4-inch springs. After tightening down the base hold-down nut, the spring is squeezed into place.

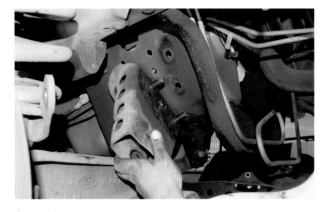

The bracket for the driver-side I-beam was simple to remove. The other side, however, wasn't so easy. Only three additional holes need to be drilled in the frame to completely attach the bracket.

 The spring was reduced in height to allow for an easy install with a specialized spring compressor tool. Before the spring pressure is released, the upper spring retainer clip is put in. The spring tension is then gently released. With the springs installed, the new shocks are bolted on to the front. Because the ride height of the suspension is altered, the steering system components are not at the proper angle. The kit comes with a dropped pitman arm to restore the proper working angles of the steering control arms. Once the pitman arm–retaining nut is removed, it is pulled off with a special puller.

 With the new bracket in place, the driver-side I-beam was reattached. The passenger-side I-beam bracket was a bit more difficult. The rivets had to be removed by a drill and cutting wheel. They can also be torched out. After torching off the bracket and rivet heads, the rivets are simply punched out. The holes from the rivets were only ⁷⁄₁₆-inch diameter.

 The new pitman arm went in very easy, and it was a simple job to put the retaining nut back on and tighten it up.

The Fabtech kit comes with ½-inch hardware, so the holes must be opened appropriately. All the nuts for the attachment of the brackets were nylon locking nuts to ensure a tight and safe fit.

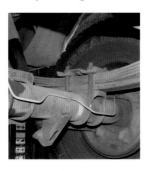 The stock rear end of this Ford F-150 two-wheel-drive truck is standard with shocks and leaf springs. Once the shocks were removed, a jack supports the rear axle. The springs detach from the axle by removing the stock U-bolts. Once the U-bolts are removed, the jack is let down a bit to allow for the axle to drop away from the spring pack.

With everything put back in place, the new attitude of this Ford F-150 is definitely apparent.

TIME: Three hours

TOOLS: Full socket set, jack, jack stands, cutting die, welding equipment

TALENT: ★★

APPLICABLE YEARS: Two-wheel-drive suspension lifts are available for all years, makes, and models of light trucks

TAB: $2,200

TINWARE: Safety glasses

TIP: Use new nuts, bolts, washers, and cotter pin

PERFORMANCE GAIN:
Better control running rough terrain for longer periods of time

COMPLEMENTARY PROJECT:
Consider installing bump stops and larger brake rotors if you are going to run a taller tire.

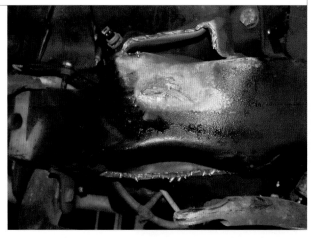

As you can see, the top of the upper A-arm stop bracket was removed. This is done to clear the new tubular A-arm of the system. The lower spindle stop is also removed by grinding the rivets to remove the stop. The area was cleaned up with a grinder and was prepared so that a support plate could be welded to box in the cut mount.

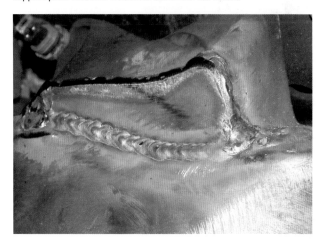

This is what the area looks like after it has been properly boxed and welded together. In order to use the CST tubular control arms, the factory alignment bars must be removed from the OEM stamped steel A-arms. The alignment bars are inserted into the tubular A-arms that include new urethane bushings. New ball joints are also included and must be bolted on to the tubular A-arms. CST provides a new lift spindle, which replaces the factory spindle on the left.

Although a large majority of Chevrolet S-10s and GMC Sonoma pickup trucks are lowered to the ground, there are a few of us who like the lifted look on this popular small-size truck. The lifted look on these vehicles not only offers a rebellious appearance from the norm, it also provides a smooth ride and a greater amount of ground clearance.

Most of the time, performing a moderate 3-inch lift to these vehicles is a simple task. This is especially true with two-wheel-drive (2WD) versions, which can be accomplished in several hours. Most 2WD lift systems incorporate a new spindle and/or a redesigned upper control arm. In some cases, however, there is some cutting that is required to gain added clearance for the shorter arm. What parts need to be cut and modified? We asked White Motorsports in Riverside, California, to demonstrate the process and show us the techniques they use to accomplish this.

The company was beginning the process of lifting a 2WD Chevy S-10, using a CST lift kit. The CST kit comes with a new lift spindle, coil springs, shocks, and a rear shackle kit. Once installed, the system will lift the truck approximately 3 inches and will allow the use of a set of 31-inch-diameter tires.

The process demonstrated where cuts were made to the frame, but were done only to the top of the control arm mount to make clearance for the CST tubular control arm.

Because the truck would use a larger diameter set of wheels and tires after the lift, the owner also wanted to upgrade the brakes with a Stainless Steel rotor and caliper upgrade kit, which was also installed.

Overall, it took approximately five hours to fully install the kit, but unless you are handy with a cutting torch and some mild welding, a professional should install this kit. The results were well worth the effort. The ride is smooth and the taller profile of the truck gives it a new attitude.

OFF-ROAD SUSPENSION AND HARDWARE

The new A-arm is installed on to the truck. With the factory stop bracket removed, there is more room for the A-arm to move up and down. The lift spindle is installed on to the factory bottom A-arm. New coil springs are used to also lift the truck. These must be installed with the proper spring compressor tool.

The front and rear bolts holding the spring eyelets are removed first, as are the U-bolts holding it to the axle. The factory shocks are also removed from the axle brackets.

With the spindle assembly installed, you can see how much more lift the system can provide this S-10. The owner of this truck wanted to upgrade the brakes with a Stainless Steel brake system. This involves removing the factory bearings and installing them into the new rotors. The disc backing plate is trimmed slightly and installed on to the new spindle. Stainless Steel's rotors are axial vented and are installed on to the CST lift spindle. The company also provides a new two-piston caliper that provides improved clamping force for better stopping power. New stainless-steel braided brake line is also included in the kit. These were installed and the system was properly bled.

The rear shackles are easily removed and the new CST units are installed and will help raise the vehicle. GM uses rivets to hold the factory hangers in place. These must be removed by grinding or heating with a welding torch. In this instance, the White Motorsports crew used a welding torch to heat and remove the rivets. The CST hanger is put into position to mark one of the bottom bolt holes, which must be drilled into the frame. Once the position is marked, the hole for the attachment bolt is drilled.

This is the finished front CST system with the Stainless Steel brake upgrade installed.

This is what the front hanger looks like finally assembled. Using the factory U-bolts, the leaf spring was reattached to the axle.

White Motorsports lifted the rear of the truck using CST's shackle and hanger kit. This involved securing the axle to the frame so the leaf springs could be removed.

CST also provides new shocks for the lift system. These were also installed at the front of the vehicle. To accompany the lift, the owner installed a set of Yokohama 31-inch-tall Geolander M/T tires mounted to a set of American Eagle aluminum wheels to finish off the look.

TIME: Eight hours

 TOOLS: Full socket set, jack, jack stands

 TALENT: ★★★

 APPLICABLE YEARS: Lift kits for all years, makes, and models of light trucks

 TAB: $2,000

 TINWARE: $180 per shock

 TIP: Use new nuts, bolts, washers, and cotter pin

 PERFORMANCE GAIN:
Better control running rough terrain for longer periods of time

COMPLEMENTARY PROJECT:
Consider installing bump stops.

Remove four bolts holding the crossmember. You will use a reciprocating saw to cut off the driver-side crossmember bracket by 3.125 inches.

Differential drop brackets secure the front differential to the frame. Two sturdy bolts on each side provide strength and make it much easier and lighter for the installers. You will square off the rounded inside corners of the lower control arm front brackets. With help from a friend, Rancho's master R&D wrench Cliff Molina positions the lift cradle up on to the lower control arm frame brackets.

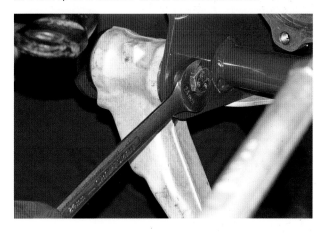

With the lift cradle in place, loosely attach lower control arms. Use a spring compressor (rent it/own it) to compress factory coil and install longer coil spring and shock. (You must purchase shocks separately and should consider the cost in your overall decision.)

For the 2007 model year of the Chevy Tahoe, General Motors moved away from torsion bars up front to an all-new coil-over front suspension. The new front suspension design allowed product engineers at Rancho Suspensions to fabricate a system that keeps the factory alignment and performance characteristics intact. The front-wheel-drive differential is attached to the chassis directly so the lift cradle is much lighter and easier to install.

According to Chris Batsch, product engineer for Tenneco Automotive, the parent company behind Rancho suspensions, the new coil-over suspension for the 2007 Chevy Tahoe provides a better ride quality and better handling characteristics. New GM tolerance guidelines also help engineers design components with the best fitment results. One of the engineering criteria was to design a lift system that is installation friendly while providing 4 additional inches of suspension lift and the continued use of factory 17-inch wheels.

For approximately $2,000, this kit comes with all the hardware, bracketry, and components you'll need. There are only three holes to be drilled, one instance of squaring off rounded

OFF-ROAD SUSPENSION AND HARDWARE

factory bracket corners, and one cutting procedure requiring a sawzall. You'll need access to a coil spring compressor as well. Hand tools and a weekend day is plenty of time to install front and rear lift components on the 2007 Chevy Tahoe.

Keep in mind that the greatest tip for installing this suspension kit or any type of load-bearing components for automotive use is to leave all bolts slightly relaxed until the vehicle's full weight is back on the ground before you torque them down. The reason is alignment. Once the vehicle weight is fully on the ground, all hardware assemblies will shift and adjust. If bolts are cinched down before the vehicle weight is back on the ground, components tend to bind.

Here are the highlights of a "reverse" install on the 2007 Chevy Tahoe Rancho brought to the Specialty Equipment Manufacturers Association (SEMA) in November 2005. Because of the efficiency of design and economy of hardware, this system is doable for any person able to follow directions, acquire access to a lift and needed tools, and persuade a friend to lend a hand when needed and a running commentary for moral support.

Install front coil/shock and connect to lower control arm. Leave upper bolts relaxed so you don't have to fight the shock when installing it to the lower control arm. With axle spacers in place, reinstall half-shafts to the front differential. New steering knuckles are bolstered in certain places, but otherwise retain factory GM steering geometry.

With hub assembled, insert half-shaft into hub. Bolt up steering knuckle to upper and lower control arm. Install half-shaft washer and nut and torque down to 165 lb-ft.

New sway bar drop brackets use factory holes. Aft brace uses nut bracket to facilitate installation using existing hole. Bolt-up front aft braces to front lift cradle. Compare Rancho coil (red) with factory coil on right. Install front wheels and lower Tahoe to ground. With full weight of truck on ground, tighten all snug bolts and nuts to specified torque values. After removing end links, shocks, and brake lines, lower rear axle and remove coil springs.

Install link drop bracket (red) using existing holes. Note that the precision fit of this piece allows all links to line up accurately. Loosely bolt up the upper and lower linkages to the drop bracket. You will drill one additional mounting hole (⅜ inch) for each new bump stop spacer. Bolt 'em up. Using original insulators, install new springs into spring pockets. Install rear shocks. Install new trac bar bracket.

You will drill a third hole (7/16 inch) through the trac bar axle bracket. Wait until vehicle is on the ground before you torque down bolts.

Assemble and install extended link assembly to rear sway bar, install extended rear brake line bracket, and you are almost in business.

Here's the full-dress rear end assembly to give your Tahoe 4 more inches of lift.

INSTALL A 4-INCH LIFT ON YOUR SOLID FRONT-AXLE 4X4

TIME: Eight hours

TOOLS: Full socket set, jack, jack stands

TALENT: ★★★

APPLICABLE YEARS: Kits for all years, makes, and models of light trucks

TAB: $2,500

TINWARE: Red Loctite anti-seize compound is recommended for this project.

TIP: Consider installing aftermarket steps or rock slider bars. With more ground clearance, you have to climb into your truck. Steps will help.

PERFORMANCE GAIN:
Better tire clearance, wheel travel, and axle articulation. Articulation improvement serves to keep tire contact patches on the traction surface.

COMPLEMENTARY PROJECT:
This is a good time to install the optional front sand bar/light bar that is available for this lift.

Remove trac bar while truck is on level ground. Use a socket leverage multiplier if you can to break the 20mm trac bar bolt loose. You do this on the ground, so the trac bar lines up properly with the bolt hole when you bolt it back up.

As automotive trends have expanded in recent years, truck owners have pushed the envelope in how they use their rigs and how they want them to look. Truck owners increasingly started to run larger tires and used backyard ingenuity to get the suspension high enough to shoehorn those tires into the wheel wells. There are more wheel and tire size combinations available today than ever before, and you can run any size tire you dare. But if you intend to use your rig off-highway, even occasionally, and you want to run tires that will look great and benefit you in four-wheel-drive situations, then you need a suspension that works.

This Rancho 4-inch lift kit was designed for 35-inch-diameter tires on 20-inch rims, which accommodates the current trend of truck owners running larger diameter wheels. For your tires to tuck properly within the wheel wells, a 6-inch backspace is recommended. Not just for looks, this system is built to perform in four-wheel-drive, low-range, driving conditions. The suspension must articulate and allow the truck to negotiate the terrain without binding or grinding out the wheel wells and gouging the tires.

A look at the massive forged pitman arm and sector shaft (18 percent larger than previous years) coming out of the steering box of the 2005 Super Duty trucks will tell you Ford has beefed up some of the front-end hardware. Well, the Rancho kit No. RS6511 uses an equally massive extended pitman arm and competition-grade tubular radius arms. The replacement coil springs are precision-calibrated specifically for the weight of the Ford Super Duty trucks. When ordering this Rancho lift kit, you will specify whether your Super Duty runs the gas or diesel motor. You will also choose which Rancho shocks you want.

Because Rancho's parent company, Tenneco Automotive Inc., owns Clevite, the company that makes original equipment (OE) bushings for Ford, this kit uses Ford factory rear radius-arm bushing. The bushing reduces bump-steer and maintains factory steering performance. Rancho's relationship with Ford is long and proven, but pulling off a factory rear radius-arm bushing is something that no other suspension kit manufacturer has been able to do. That's the competitive edge for Rancho on this kit.

Installation is fairly straightforward for you folks with access to an impact wrench, hydraulic hoist, and underhoist jack stands for safety. This is a straight-axle Dana 60 front-end so you're looking at roughly four to six hours to get 'er done. You will add a spacer to the center carrier bearing of the driveshaft. This carrier-bearing spacer will lower the driveshaft, keep it inline at the proper angle, and eliminate any chatter when you take off from a stoplight. At the rear axle, you will simply support the rear axle with underhoist stands, insert block spacers on each side, replace U-bolts with longer ones, and replace the shocks. The Rancho RS9000 shocks are the recommended shocks for this 4-inch lift.

A couple of things to bear in mind when you are tightening the bolts and setting proper torque specs: Use Loctite "red" on

115

all bolts. As you are installing the primary suspension components such as the radius arms, snug the bolts down. If you cinch down the bolts while the truck is still up on the hoist, the bolted components will tend to bind when the truck gets back on the ground. The recommended way is just to slightly tighten the bolts until you get the full weight of the truck on the ground, then torque down the bolts.

Also know that all brake and vacuum lines are long enough from the factory to work at full droop of the suspension. You will have to adjust the line protectors, install the brake line bracket extension at the front coil buckets, and re-zip tie those lines to secure them. All you need to adjust the line protectors is to slip a small Phillips-head

screwdriver between the protector and the brake line, put a drop of silicone to loosen it up, and move the protector where you need it.

This install hits the highlights of bolting up the Rancho 4-inch lift for 2005 Ford Super Duties. You won't have to cut, weld, or drill any new holes. The instructions you get with the Rancho No. RS6511 lift kit are comprehensive and well illustrated. Check out the photos to see how we bolted on this lift kit.

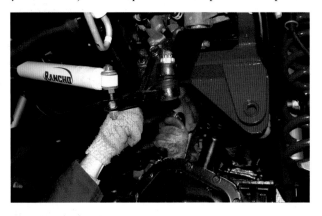

Remove stock trac bar bracket and install the new Rancho extended trac bar bracket. You can use an air wrench on the three bolts of the crossmember, shown in the previous step. Make sure you use Loctite and cinch them down tight. Use a handheld socket wrench to tighten the trac bar bracket bolts on the frame rail because the bolt clips could break.

Disconnect drag link on lower pitman arm and remove stock pitman arm from the vehicle. Install new Rancho pitman arm and bolt up the drag link. When reassembling the drag link to the pitman arm, be sure to use a new cotter pin. Remove factory end link (top and bottom) and install new Rancho extended end link. Disconnect ABS brake line from the bottom of the coil spring seat and the radius arm on each side. At this point, be sure to have your underhoist jack stands supporting the front axle beneath each coil spring. Remove factory shocks. Carefully lower axle to relieve tension on the coil springs. Don't let the front axle hang from any hoses, lines, or cables. Use a breaker bar and deep socket wrench to remove the bolt holding the lower spring seat to the front axle on each side. Remove the coil spring with the spring seat as a unit. Support both radius arms with jack stands. Remove rear mounting bolts and lower factory radius arm out of the frame brackets about 5 inches to allow for the extra upward kick in the new Rancho radius arms. Remove the driver-side radius arm from the front axle first. Be careful to support at least one radius arm to prevent the front axle from rotating downward.

Attach left side radius arm to the front axle on the driver side, leaving the bolts loose. Then loosely bolt up the right radius arm (shown in photo). You'll be using original hardware and one new 18 mm nut from the kit. Notice how the jack stands are used to support the front axle. Lift rear of radius arms into frame bracket and reinstall original bolts and nuts. Keep the nuts loose until you get the truck back on the ground. Remove factory bump stops and frame brackets. Replace with Rancho bump stop bracket extension and bolt it down tight. Replace rubber factory bump stop. While the coils are out of the buckets, bolt up the Rancho extended brake hose brackets and reinstall on the buckets using the factory holes. Use original rubber washer on top and install coil back in the bucket. Align the pigtail and install lower spring on the bottom of the coil seat. Repeat on other side. Now slowly raise the front axle until the springs are snug. Be careful not to lift the truck off the supporting jack stands. Reconnect ABS wires to lower spring seat and secure wire to radius arms with zip-ties. Repeat on other side. Install front wheels and tighten lug nuts to 150 lb-ft. Tighten all radius arm bolts to torque specifications listed in instructions.

While the truck is in the air, remove bolts on center carrier bearing and insert spacer extension. Bolt it back up. With the jack stands under the rear axle, remove the rear shocks. Remove top spring plate bolts and remove U-bolts and factory lift blocks (if equipped).

Insert new Rancho 4¾-inch block. Put in the top spring plate bolts and insert longer U-bolts. Do one side at a time. Install the shock absorbers. Install rear wheels. Snug bolts enough to hold, but do final torque-down when truck is on the ground.

INSTALL AN INDEPENDENT FRONT SUSPENSION LIFT KIT

 TIME: Six hours

 TOOLS: Full socket set, jack, jack stands, gear puller

 TALENT: ★★

 APPLICABLE YEARS: All

 TAB: $2,000

 TINWARE: You will need to rent or borrow a special gear puller for the project. No worries, these gear pullers are not rare.

 TIP: Although shocks are an extra expense item, it's a good idea to plan on investing in new shocks and combine two or more of these projects at the same time, without increasing estimated total project time.

PERFORMANCE GAIN:
Better control running in rough terrain for longer periods of time

COMPLEMENTARY PROJECT:
Consider installing bump stops.

Adding 6 inches of lift to a Chevy Tahoe usually required some trimming of the front differential, but Skyjacker lifted this Tahoe without any cutting at all. For the install we turned to the guys at Off Road Innovations, located in West Monroe, Louisiana. Josh Cooper, owner and operator, performed the installation along with Luke Sanford. With the front of the vehicle properly lifted and supported, the torsion bars are unloaded and removed. A special puller or tool is required for this step. *Lee McGuire*

With the torsion bars removed from the crossmember, the factory torsion bar crossmember is removed. Next, the front shocks, sway bar end links, and front skid plates are removed. *Lee McGuire*

With the brake caliper removed, the tie rod is disconnected from the steering knuckle. Next, disconnect the upper and lower A-arms and CV shaft from the factory steering knuckle. *Lee McGuire*

One of the drawbacks to many independent front suspension (IFS) lift kits is the fact that the front differential case must be grinded down or cut. Although many people do this modification to lift their GM IFS truck or SUV, this grinding or cutting often prevents the vehicle from ever being put back to stock condition. In reality, most lifted trucks stay lifted, but we wondered if there was any limit to the design of lift kits that would allow a simple bolt-on installation?

When we began searching for a way to lift a GM IFS system without any cutting, we came across Skyjacker's "No Destruction" kits for the IFS GM 1500, 1500HD, 2500HD, and Hummer H2. Skyjacker has recently released the same unique kits for the Avalanche, Suburban, and Tahoe. These systems do not require any grinding of the differential case, which allows the housing to retain its structural strength, making the installation of the lift completely reversible.

We took a closer look at Skyjacker's No Destruction 6-inch lift for the 2000–04 Tahoe 4x4, which includes all of the necessary components to install the system in about a full day. The system is impressive as it comes with a cast-iron CNC machined

Remove the six bolts that attach the CV shaft to the differential. Next, the lower A-arms are removed to make room for the new front and rear crossmembers. *Lee McGuire*

pair of spindles, front and rear crossmembers, lower skid-plate braces, full-front skid plate, bump stops, sway bar end links, CV shaft spacers, driver and passenger upper-differential relocation brackets, and torsion bar drop brackets. The rear is lifted via full-height replacement Softride rear coil springs, or in the case of some earlier models, full-length leaf springs.

As you can see in the accompanying photos, the lift is straightforward, but some of the components are unique, which allow a much simpler installation that does not require any cutting or welding.

After disconnecting the driveshaft, remove the differential from the vehicle. After installing the new differential drop brackets, the differential can be installed along with the new front crossmember. *Lee McGuire*

The lower A-arm attaches to the new front and rear crossmembers using the factory bolts. A machined aluminum spacer is used in between the CV shaft and the differential. The spacer is used to set the proper CV angle and travel. *Lee McGuire*

The factory hub assembly is unbolted from the original steering knuckle and bolted on to the new heavy-duty Skyjacker steering knuckle. The upper and lower A-arm attaches to the new knuckle using the factory hardware. *Lee McGuire*

The torsion bars are reinstalled and adjusted to the factory settings. Finishing up the front portion of the lift, the new shocks are installed along with the new sway bar end links. Moving on to the rear, the rear shocks, trac bar, and sway bar end links are removed. *Lee McGuire*

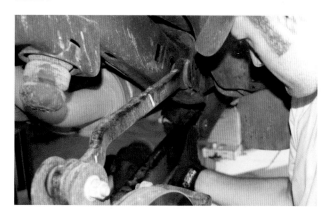

The rear upper and lower control arms are disconnected from the frame to make room for the new control arm relocation bracket. The new relocation bracket bolts into the factory control arm position. The rear pinion angle is automatically set with the new mounting position for the control arms. *Lee McGuire*

The new trac bar relocation bracket attaches to the factory frame mount. A new bump stop extension is supplied for the rear axle and bolts directly to the factory bump stop pad using ⅜-inch hardware. *Lee McGuire*

The new coil is now installed along with the new rear shocks and sway bar end links. The coil is a full-height factory replacement, no spacers. *Lee McGuire*

TIME: Eight hours

TOOLS: Full socket set, jack, jack stands

TALENT: ★★★

APPLICABLE YEARS: Kits for all years, makes, and models of light trucks

TAB: $1,800

TINWARE: N/A

TIP: An extra pair of hands can make certain procedures less cumbersome when you are dealing with the eight components coming off the truck and bolting them back on.

PERFORMANCE GAIN:
Tire clearance and ground clearance

COMPLEMENTARY PROJECT:
Consider electric steps or stout tube side bars to aid the climb into the truck.

Skyjacker's 6-inch Ram kit includes everything you need to install the system. It incorporates cast-iron CNC machined knuckles/spindles, front and rear crossmembers, and lower skid plate braces. Rear lift is available with full-height replacement rear springs or with a 4.5-inch block and U-bolt kit. *Lee McGuire*

The front and rear crossmembers are constructed of heavy wall tubing and ¼-inch die-formed steel. *Lee McGuire*

If you're serious about taking your Dodge Ram off-road, but are hesitant because of its independent front suspension system, rest assured that with the right combination of parts, your late-model Ram could handle the abuse. It's true that solid front axle trucks can handle off-road situations much better, but many Dodge owners love the handling and ride quality of their late-model Rams and would simply like to install larger tires and have the capability of greater ground clearance.

There are several kits available for the half-ton Ram with independent front suspension (IFS), and we took a close look at one of them, available from Skyjacker. Skyjacker has a new Ram 1500 lift system that offers a full 6 inches of lift and incorporates some unusual features to its design.

The kit is made to work on 2002–04 Dodge 1500 model trucks and can clear 37-inch-tall tires. How can the kit get so much lift? Skyjacker combined the use of new cast-iron lift spindles for the front, and a set of full rear leaf springs with 4 ½–inch blocks to achieve the total ride height at the rear. The Skyjacker Ram kit also uses a heavy-wall steel crossmember with a full steel skid plate. The crossmembers are constructed from heavy

wall tubing and quarter-inch die-formed steel. Furthermore, there are side skid-plate braces that are .1875-inch thick that bridge the extension between the two crossmembers, giving additional support.

Although the front skid plate looks great, it is there for more than simply show. It is die-punched and is .125-inch thick and ties back into the lower crossmember. This gives the entire front IFS system complete protection against rocks and damage.

Because driveshaft angles are critical to the proper operation of many IFS kits, Skyjacker also incorporated a new indexing ring that simply rotates the transfer case clockwise to allow for an improved driveshaft angle. This eliminates the need for any driveshaft modifications and is patent pending.

When installed, the Skyjacker Ram kit allows the use of a set of 37 x 12.50 x 17-inch tires with plenty of fender clearance. The kit is strong, and the full skid plates provide plenty of

OFF-ROAD SUSPENSION AND HARDWARE

119

protection and improve the crossmember's rigidity. The modified suspension system also offers a full 6 inches of suspension travel, and the CV joint angles are not too extreme. With the Skyjacker 6-inch lift system for the Ram, you can go where other IFS-equipped trucks may not be able to.

The stock A-arm bushings remain in place and no special tools are required with this system, only nimble fingers and tool control. The rear crossmember is stout, and the "sandwich" method of limiting the compression/give of this bracket's design works. Grade 8 bolts and nylon lock nuts hold the six steel spacers into place for strength. *Lee McGuire*

This is what you see from under the truck. Use ⅜-inch Grade 8 hardware to outline the attaching points that lock this assembly into place. *Lee McGuire*

From the driver side, this is the installed knuckle and crossmembers overview. The upper A-arm is maintained in the stock position via the steering knuckle. With the knuckles, crossmembers and differential lowering bracketry, you gain a full 6 inches of lift. *Lee McGuire*

New torsion bar drop brackets, built from 0.1875-inch and ¼-inch steel plate and die-formed for accuracy, lower the factory torsion bar crossmember from the frame rails. This allows the torsion bars to be reinstalled to maintain the factory ride. *Lee McGuire*

The passenger-side differential drop bracket relocates the diff down into position. This is one of three; there are two for the driver side— to securely brace the diff from all factory mounting points. *Lee McGuire*

This patent-pending indexing ring rotates the transfer case down to allow for a better front driveshaft angle. It mounts in-between the transmission and the t-case. The kit includes a seal adapter for the transmission output seal, hardware, and even a tube of silicone. *Lee McGuire*

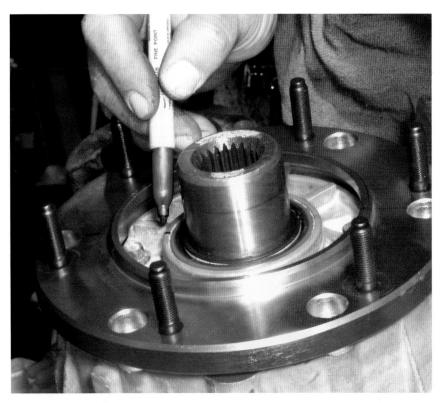

With the studs installed on to the indexing ring, align the ring into position. Mark your spot, remove the ring, apply a hefty bead of silicone, and install the ring back into position with the supplied Allen-head bolts. This will ensure that the silicone bonds properly. *Lee McGuire*

A 2002 Dodge 1500 Ram 4x4 with Skyjacker's 6-inch suspension running 37-12.50-17 Goodyear MTR's on Raceline Monster Crawler wheels with simulated bead locks—17 x 9 with 5-inch back spacing. *Lee McGuire*

OFF-ROAD SUSPENSION AND HARDWARE

TIME: Six hours

TOOLS: Full socket set, jack, jack stands, drill, drill bits

TALENT: ★★★

APPLICABLE YEARS: Kits for all years, makes, and models of light trucks

TAB: $1,500

TINWARE: Rent a pitman arm/tie-rod end remover

TIP: Use new nuts, bolts, washers, and cotter pin.

PERFORMANCE GAIN:
Better control running in rough terrain for longer periods of time

COMPLEMENTARY PROJECT:
Consider installing bump stops.

Taking proper safety precautions, remove the necessary stock components, referring to Superlift's detailed instructions.

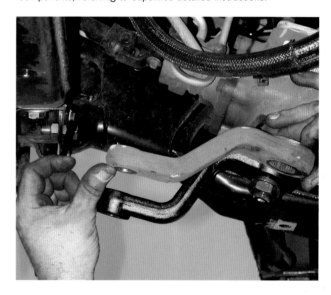

The kit's dropped pitman arm returns the drag link/tie rod angles to spec so that the lifted Dodge won't wander at road speeds.

Dodge has been at the forefront of exterior design, with bold, "big-rig" styling on the Ram light-duty pickup trucks and the use of 20-inch wheels and tires. Yet, the company has stayed to its mechanical roots, when compared to the competition. As independent front suspension systems became the 4x4 rule rather than the exception, Dodge stuck to its tried and true live-axle guns, only recently going independent in its full-size half-ton Ram 4x4s. Thankfully for people who like to drive off-road, Dodge still has live axles under its three-quarter- and one-ton HD 4x4 trucks.

BOLT-ON KITS
For the do-it-yourselfer, this means that new Dodge HDs can be lifted at home by anyone with average or better mechanical skills. Superlift is one company that designed its new Dodge HD kits to capitalize on the truck's suspension simplicity. We wanted to take a closer look at the new Superlift kit for the Ram HD and found that the company's three basic systems (2-inch, 4-inch, and 6-inch), require minimal to no drilling. About the only specialized tool necessary to install these kits is a pitman

arm/tie-rod end remover (which can be borrowed or rented from many auto parts stores).

According to Superlift, its Dodge HD system includes replacement Superide front coil springs instead of using spacers with the OE coils, as is the norm with other lift kits. The difference provides optimal ride and handling. Superlift does this by matching the spring rate to the engine weight, as V-10 and diesel applications are stiffer than the Hemi springs. Furthermore, we learned that all of the brackets in the Superlift kits are made of quarter-inch-thick plate steel, and that the system allows for factory-offset wheels to be used.

The factory trac bar must be lowered to compensate for the lift. Superlift's lowering bracket uses two factory holes and requires drilling a third one.

Superlift's progressive three-stage bump stops and mounting brackets keep the front axle from rebounding too far upward and damaging the springs.

This Superlift triple-shock front hoop catches two factory holes; a third is drilled for extra mounting strength.

Dual stabilizers help absorb road irregularities when running big tires. Installation requires cutting off the factory mount on the passenger side.

OPTIONAL EQUIPMENT

Because none of us wants to leave well enough alone, Superlift also offers some accessories to the Ram lift kit. One example that is shown here is the use of the optional Rockrunner lower-trailing arms. These units swivel inside themselves and function as a higher-articulation alternative to arms with Heim joints on the ends. The Rockrunner trailing arms also allow more caster adjustment, and if you are using large tires, another option might be the use of the company's dual stabilizer system. Super-lift offers it with either a standard center bracket or the racy Superlift "3D flaming logo" effect, which showcases the company's inhouse, computerized laser-cutting capabilities.

Superlift demonstrated an install of its system on to a 4x4 HD Ram that also includes optional Superlift select series (SS) shocks. These units are manufactured for Superlift by Bilstein and feature seamless, extruded-steel monotube bodies to dissipate heat. They also have a unique piston/valve assembly that permits independent damping between compression and rebound cycles. All SS shock bodies have a brushed finish and are silver zinc-plated to resist corrosion and look impressive. In multishock applications like this one, lighter-valve shocks are included for improved ride and control. Other available mounting systems are hoop-style dual or triple in front and duals on brackets in the rear.

If you want a remote reservoir shock system, a third shock option is the Superlift select series remote (SSR) by Edelbrock. Furthermore, Torque Max traction bars control wheel hop through an internal-swivel system (similar to the Rockrunner arms) and offer optional brushed stainless-steel dress-up panels. Rail Wraps frame panels, and a front skid plate continue the brushed stainless/Superlift logo theme. You can also use Superlift's line of stainless-steel braided brake hoses that are Department of Transportation approved. Need to protect your vehicle's rear axle? Then consider Superlift's eXtreme Rings, which protect the diff covers. Additionally, Superlift's TruSpeed unit corrects the speedometer when using non-stock-height tires.

INSTALLATION

Highlights of Superlift's 6-inch kit are shown here on a 2003 Ram 2500 4x4. Installed by the pros at Robby Gordon Off-Road, the job took less than a day. (The Superlift 2-inch kit is purely bolt-on, while the 4-inch and 6-inch kits require minimal drilling.) The end result is more ground clearance, thanks in part to the 37 x 13.50-20 Toyo Open Country M/T tires used on 20

x 10 ProComp Xtreme Alloys. After the system was installed, the Ram had improved off-road articulation, a road ride that was surprisingly supple, and an even-heavier-duty appearance.

KIT SPECIFICS

2-inch–33-inch tires: includes taller Superide front coil springs and extended front bump stops.

4-inch–35-inch tires: includes proper height and rate front Superide coils, extended front bump stops, upper- and lower-trailing arms, a dropped pitman arm, extended sway bar links, a trac-bar lowering bracket, rear blocks, and four Superide shocks.

6-inch–37-inch tires: adds appropriate-length coils, extended factory-style sway bar links (as opposed to bar drop-down brackets), transfer-case lowering brackets, front and rear bump stop spacers, and an e-brake cable-lowering bracket.

Instead of using drop brackets, Superlift includes extended factory-style sway bar links.

TIME: Eight hours

 TOOLS: Full socket set, jack, jack stands, Sawzall, vise-grip clamps, and die cutter

 TALENT: ★★★

 APPLICABLE YEARS: Suspension lift kits for all years, makes, and models of light trucks

 TAB: $2,500

 TINWARE: Safety glasses

 TIP: You can accomplish this project using jack stands and hand tools. If you have access to a lift and power tools, all the easier.

 PERFORMANCE GAIN:
Ground clearance for off-road driving, more wheel clearance for running taller tires, and permits ability to traverse rugged ground

COMPLEMENTARY PROJECT:
Consider installing bump stops.

Before anything is done, measurements are taken to determine the amount of lift that will be gained. The Chevy HD pickups use a torsion bar suspension that can be adjusted slightly, but requires a lift kit such as the Rancho system to fit larger 33-inch-tall tires. It is also a good idea to measure the install height of the torsion bar cams. Here we measured 1 inch from the cam lip to the bottom edge of the crossmember.

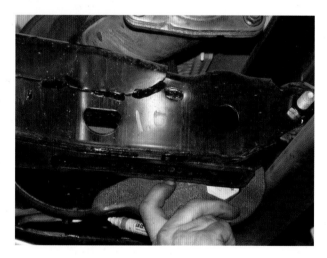

With the pressure relieved on the torsion bar, it can be slid back and the adjustment can be removed. Several of the vehicle's crossmembers will have to be removed, including the front differential mount. In addition, the driveshaft will have to be temporarily removed. The steering is then removed from the factory spindles. The front brake calipers will also need to be removed from the discs and placed aside. What remains is the bare brake rotor and spindle assembly.

These days, everyone seems to like riding high, but getting it's like climbing up the social ladder. Getting to a higher status takes some time and money, and the same goes for your truck. Some trucks, however, rise much more easily than others, but the effect is still the same. A lifted truck not only rides smoother, but also clears the chassis over more rugged terrain; more important, though, a lifted truck allows the owner to use a larger diameter set of wheels and tires, which helps improve the truck's appearance and off-road performance.

The Chevy HD is a popular truck to lift, and although many lift kits are available, we focused in on the Rancho system. We wanted to witness an installation to determine how difficult it was to install a Rancho 6-inch lift. To say the least, it can be done by a seasoned mechanic, but because of some of the specialized tools required and the cutting that is involved, installation should be left to a mechanic who is familiar with the installation.

Nevertheless, the following photos can give you a glimpse of the full day's worth of work that is required to

install the system. Keep in mind that after it is installed, the truck will need to be properly aligned, and the right size tires usually help its overall appearance. In this case, a set of 33-inch-tall tires was used, and the overall effect was one that the truck owner was really happy about.

OFF-ROAD SUSPENSION AND HARDWARE

Rancho provides a new high-quality spindle that also raises the vehicle, but more important, corrects all of the ball joint angles after the lift. With the front differential still bolted into position, the lower bracket is cut according to the instructions. Once everything is out of the way, a couple of stands are used to support the front differential. Then the bolts at the top of the differential bracket are removed. It will take two people to remove the differential from the chassis, and it can be placed on its side until it is reinstalled on to the Rancho cradle. In order to keep the fluid from draining out of the vent, the hose is doubled over and taped shut. The original hub is then bolted to the rear of the Rancho lift spindle. A new lower differential bracket with a urethane bushing is also supplied in the kit and is bolted into position.

The rotor is removed by unbolting the center nut, and the rest of the spindle is unbolted from the top and lower ball joints. To remove the entire spindle assembly, it is easier to unbolt it from the rear of the CV joint carrier. With the driveshaft out of the way, the Rancho technicians began to unbolt and remove the lower control arms from the vehicle. The bottom support bolts at the front differential are also removed. Because the differential will drop down, the factory brackets must be cut and modified.

The Rancho kit comes with new differential brackets that must be bolted into position. The factory hardware is used. To lower everything down, the Rancho kit comes with a differential cradle. This also lowers the mounting point of the lower A-arms.

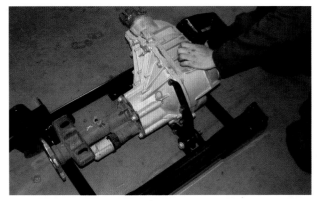

In the meantime, the new crossmember support brackets are placed into position and will be drilled and bolted into place. To improve space, and because it won't be used, the rear differential support is cut and removed from the differential housing.

The front differential is placed on to the cradle and is bolted into position. Once the differential is in place, the driveshaft can be reattached. The torsion bar crossmember is then reattached to the Rancho mounts.

The lower A-arms are also bolted into their new positions on the Rancho cradle. Steel spacers are used to properly position and extend the CV joints when they are reinstalled. Some of the brake line clamps use a sleeve to prevent wear. The sleeves can be easily slid on the line if you crack it open and squirt a bit of WD40. Once the new spindle assembly is bolted together, it can be reinstalled on to the vehicle's suspension.

In order to install the blocks, the rear diff must be dropped a bit. You will have to unbolt the parking brake brackets to do this. With the rear differential properly supported, the U-bolt clamps are unbolted.

The blocks are centered with the factory spring pack pin, and new U-bolts are provided in the kit to reinstall the pack.

This is what the spindle assembly looks like when it is properly bolted back into position between the A-arms. The brake rotors and calipers are then reinstalled and bolted into place. The Rancho shocks are then bolted into position, and the brake lines are checked to ensure that they do not make contact with any suspension part. The engineers at Rancho recommend not to fully tighten all the bolts until all of the pieces are in place. In order to avoid any driveline vibrations, Rancho supplies a carrier bearing spacer that lowers the bearing for proper alignment.

Two torque arms are also bolted into the crossmembers and help support the cradle.

One of the last steps is to reinstall the torsion bars. They can be adjusted to the exact measurements that were taken before their disassembly. New spacers are also provided for the rear differential snubbers. Finally, a pair of Rancho RS9000 adjustable shocks was added. The factory bottom skid plate can also be reused and simply bolts back into position on the new cradle.

TIME: One and a half days

 TOOLS: Full socket set, jack, jack stands, welding equipment, and cutting equipment

 TALENT: ★★★

 APPLICABLE YEARS: Kits for all years, makes, and models of light trucks

 TAB: $1,300

 TINWARE: Access to air-powered wrenches is helpful, but everything can be performed with hand tools.

 TIP: A second pair of hands can make the install go smoother.

 PERFORMANCE GAIN:
Ground and wheel clearance

COMPLEMENTARY PROJECT:
Side steps or rocker bars with foot steps built in to help egress into truck cab

With the truck on the ground, begin by disconnecting the front trac bar at the frame. *Tom Morr*

Unbolt the sway bar links at the axle before jacking up and securing the truck. This hardware is reused. Remove the front shocks. The bushings will be reused. Unbolt the steering stabilizer at its stem end. Separate the drag link from the pitman arm using the appropriate puller. Unbolt the front brake hoses at their coil-tower mounts. Unbolt the brake-hose brackets at the frame. Carefully lower the front axle until the front coils pop loose. The rubber isolators will be reused. The stock pitman arm is indexed on the sector shaft before removing it with the appropriate puller. The Superlift dropped pitman arm restores the factory drag link angle. *Tom Morr*

L ifting coil-sprung Ford 4x4s has been challenging ever since the early Bronco bit the dust in 1977. C-bushings and radius-arm brackets seem simple compared to the Twin Traction Beam (TTB) trucks, which can be difficult to align after lifting.

The new model of Ford Super Duty has its own lifting quirks. However, factory ride and overall drivability don't have to be compromised if camber is properly addressed during the lift: raising the truck causes the radius arms to rotate the axle forward. Therefore, higher lift means more axle rotation, which equals less camber.

CASTER CONSIDERATIONS

Instead of being first to market with 2005–06 Super Duty lift kits, Superlift assessed all of the ramifications while engineering its systems. For example, the new Super Duty loses 3 degrees of caster at about 2 inches of lift if the radius arms remain in their factory mounts. Steering self-centering and shimmy increase, and the truck tends to dart and wander. Adding cargo or trailer tongue weight subtracts even more

caster when the rear ride height drops and items such as heavy snowplows augment the problem.

The most obvious solution is to lower the radius-arm frame mounts with brackets. However, the original equipment (OE) mounts are riveted to the frame and difficult to remove, making drop brackets a viable approach. Superlift's research and development showed that the bracket drop has to equal the lift height to maintain proper caster. So, 8-inch drop brackets would be required for an 8-inch lift kit. Ground clearance compromises and odd appearance undermine this approach.

Superlift's ultimate solution is to use drop brackets for milder

OFF-ROAD SUSPENSION AND HARDWARE

128

lifts and exclusive caster brackets for other kits. Caster brackets bolt to the front of the factory radius arms and fully restore caster without using ball joint cam bushings. The result is correct caster angle and no axle shaft misalignment. Caster brackets are the cornerstones of Superlift's 2- and 2 ½–inch kits for 2005–06 Super Duty trucks. The 8-inch kit shown here combines these brackets with 4-inch drop radius-arm rear frame mounts. (The 4-inch and 6-inch kits include some of the 8-inch system's components, sized as necessary, and use rear drop brackets.)

The standard Superlift 8-inch kit contains additional front components to optimize steering and handling. For one, a trac bar relocation bracket keeps the axle centered, preventing "roll and yaw" and steering-wheel kick. A dropped pitman arm reduces drag link angle, and Superlift even includes a bracket that restores the factory steering stabilizer's OE geometry. The system also contains front anti–sway bar extensions that thread on to the stock units—no cutting or welding required.

To create a ride that most consumers' rear ends will assess as better than stock, Superlift uses engine-specific front coils. Diesel and V-10 applications have a slightly stiffer spring rate than the V-8 models. Two rear-lifting options are offered, each with its own advantages:

Tapered Blocks with Add-A-Leafs: The most cost-effective, this method increases cargo capacity while retaining the factory overload leaf. However, the ride is stiffer, and axle wrap increases under heavy acceleration. Superlift's optional Torque Max traction bars control the wrap.

Replacement Springs: The more expensive option, Superlift's leafpacks are engineered to ride softer than stock. This option combines new springs with a unique hollow-rubber compression–travel control/load-assist system to prevent the springs from overcompressing under load. For its 8-inch system, Superlift recommends a maximum tire size of 38.5 x 13.50 on 10-inch-wide wheels having 5 ¾ inches backspacing.

OTHER OPTIONS

In addition to the Torque Max traction bars mentioned, Superlift offers other ups and extras for its new Super Duty systems. Shock wise, each kit includes standard Superide cylinders: gas-charged fronts and hydraulic rears. Two available upgrades are select series (SS) monotube gas shocks by Bilstein and SSR remote-reservoir monotubes (shown here). Front multi-shock mounts are also available.

Up front, dual and even quad steering-stabilizer kits can be ordered with standard brackets or Superlift's laser-cut "3D" brackets. Stainless-bodied stabilizers are another option. An available brushed stainless-steel skid plate is emblazoned with a laser-cut "flaming" logo, a theme that carries over to the optional Radius Armor and Torque Max SS dress-up plates. Additionally, extended-length bulletproof braided-steel brake hoses with Kevlar linings are offered, as are eXtreme Ring diff cover protectors and the TruSpeed speed sensor recalibrator. All Superlift products are backed by a limited lifetime warranty.

INSTALLATION

PDC Motorsports' Jay Parodi and Ryan Johnson spent a leisurely day and a half installing the Superlift 8-inch kit shown here with all of the various upgrades on a 2005 Ford F-250. Because the Caster Brackets require cutting, Superlift recommends professional installation for this kit.

The photos and captions depict highlights of the job. After all was said and done, the Super Duty now rolls on 38-inch Toyo Open Country M/T tires. Its steering and handling are comparable to stock, and the road ride is actually softer than factory. Superlift's multitude of performance and appearance options make the truck much higher and mightier than run-of-the-mill new Ford Super Duty trucks.

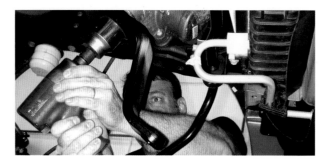

Index the Superlift pitman arm on the steering box, then secure it using copious amounts of thread-locking compound. Remove the factory trac bar bracket from the frame. Scrape any excess undercoating off the frame before mounting the Superlift trac bar bracket. *Tom Morr*

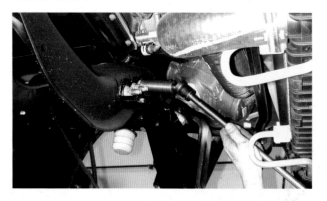

Five bolts securely fasten the Superlift trac bar bracket to the frame. Disconnect the ABS bracket, then unbolt the radius arms from the axle. Unbolt the radius arms from the frame and remove them. Trim off the radius arms' slotted lower tabs. *Tom Morr*

On the driver-side arm, the nut on the upper tab is carefully removed by grinding off the spot welds. This nut will be reused. Place the Superlift caster brackets on the radius arms so that they butt against the pinch welds. Hold in place with factory bolts. Using the caster brackets as guides, drill a ¾-inch hole through the radius arms. Attach the caster brackets to the radius arms using a combination of factory hardware and the kit's bolts and sleeves. *Tom Morr*

Bolt the Superlift 4-inch drop brackets to the OE radius-arm frame mounts. Optional radius armor dress-up panels can be installed now or later. Attach the radius arms rear-first. Don't tighten yet. The axle might have to be shimmied back and forth on the floor jack to align its radius arm holes. Yank out the factory front bump stop snubbers, then unbolt their mounting cups. Use the Superlift bump stop extension brackets as templates for marking and drilling two additional mounting holes per side. Bolt the extension brackets to the truck's frame. Hog out the mounting cups' holes to ⅝ inch. The factory cups and OE snubbers bolt to the Superlift brackets. *Tom Morr*

Remove the springs with the shackles attached. (Don't overextend the vent tube while lowering the axle away from the springs.) For trucks that have two-piece rear driveshafts, the Superlift carrier bearing drop kit is required. It spaces the bearing down to lessen the pinion angle. The Superlift replacement springs have more arch than stock but lack the upper overload leafs. *Tom Morr*

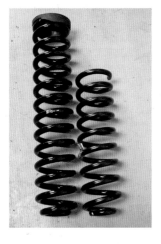

The Superlift 8-inch coil (left) is prestressed to limit sag from spring fatigue. These springs are almost twice as tall as stock. The kit's sway bar extensions thread on to the stock links, spanning the increased distance to the axle. Lower the axle if necessary to make room for the Superlift coils. Transplant the OE rubber isolators and make sure that the coils' pigtails seat in the lower buckets. Raise the axle until the isolators are secure in the upper buckets. Brake line upper extension brackets bolt to the coil towers. The lower brackets attach to the axle in their stock locations. Front SSR shocks and Bulletproof brake hoses are two of the available upgrades. Once the vehicle is on the ground, the trac bar can be reconnected to the Superlift drop bracket, using the kit's notched keys. PDC trimmed the front air dam for extra tire clearance. *Tom Morr*

Insert the bushings and sleeves into the main leaf's eyes. Then transplant the stock shackles on to the Superlift springs, which are marked to indicate the ends that face forward. Inspect the spring perches and repair or replace them if they aren't perfectly flat. Otherwise, the new Superlift springs might not seat properly on the axle. Secure the new springs to the frame and place the kit's blocks on to the axle. The kit's U-bolt and plates secure the new springs to the axle. The factory brake line bracket is bent downward to compensate for the increased space between the frame and axle. The Superlift kit also includes brackets to relocate the E-brake cables on the driver side of the frame. Install new shocks next. Superlift's optional remote-reservoir SSR models are used here. Superlift's load-assist system consists of hollow-rubber springs that mount to the U-bolt plates as well as frame brackets that replace the factory compression travel stops. The kit's extended sway bar links are also installed at this time. The standard Superlift kit includes a bracket that returns the OE steering stabilizer to its factory angle following the lift. Superlift's optional dual-stabilizer kit's outer brackets mount to the tie rod and its adjuster sleeves. *Tom Morr*

The center bracket attaches to the diff cover (optional Superlift eXtreme Ring protector shown) and axle tube. The 3D-effect plate serves as the center attachment point for Superlift's optional stainless-bodied stabilizers. Attach the skid plate's mounting hoop to existing frame holes rearward of the radiator core support. *Tom Morr*

Begin the rear lift by disconnecting the sway bar links (the hardware is reused) and removing the existing shocks. Unbolt the brake line bracket from the diff so that the axle can be lowered to remove the springs. Once the axle is supported with a jack, next off are the U-bolts. *Tom Morr*

Mark and drill the upper holes in the radiator support, then secure the plate to the radiator support and Superlift hoop with the included stainless-steel hardware. Remove the existing diff-cover bolts. *Tom Morr*

TIME: Two hours

TOOLS: Full socket set, jack, jack stands

TALENT: ★

APPLICABLE YEARS: Shocks for all years, makes, and models of light trucks

TAB: $180 per shock

TINWARE: Use new nuts, bolts, washers, and cotter pin

TIP: You don't need cradles to secure the shock reservoirs; the shocks come with rubber spacers so you can secure each reservoir to each shock with hose clamps.

PERFORMANCE GAIN:
Better control running in rough terrain for longer periods of time

COMPLEMENTARY PROJECT:
Consider installing bump stops.

Creating vehicle stability, suspension control, and durability over rough terrain at relatively high speeds is an ever-improving science. Keeping a vehicle under control mile after swift mile while preventing total component failure is a challenge every motor sport contends with. Whether we are talking about NASCAR, CART, Formula One, CORE, or SCORE, one or more monotube shocks are mounted on each wheel to soak up terrain irregularities and provide stability and control.

In the early days of off-road racing, Barry Mancha's (owner of Custom Motorsports in Riverside, California) dad was testing his Class 8 race truck down in Baja, Mexico. Back in the 1970s and early 1980s, most off-road race trucks used at least three mono-tube shocks per wheel (no reservoirs) to distribute the torment that shocks would take in a constant state of piston cycling at high rates of speed over extremely rough terrain. At one point during his prerace testing session, shock failure raised its ugly head.

In those days, all off-road racing savvy was seen through the harsh light of trial, error, and the pain that goes with simply not knowing what to expect from a given situation. So the senior Mancha pulled his truck off to side of the sand wash, popped

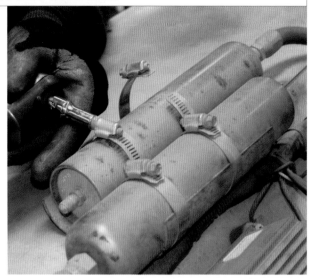

To start, we relieved the shock reservoirs from mounting cradles. If you're truly running reservoir shocks for performance, fabricate cradles like these to secure the reservoir to the engine cage or other solid mounting point. Let some of the nitrogen out of each shock as you dismount it to facilitate collapsing the shock in order to remove it from the shock mounts. As you remove shock bolts, take note of how the washers and spacers are arranged so you can repeat for new shocks. Also note how dry the shock-eye bearing is and its wobbly attitude. That's a potential sign of wear.

When you pull the shock bolt free of the mount, prepare to capture all the washers and spacers when they disassemble. Removing the tire opens up the bottom shock mounts. In the field, you can certainly replace most shocks with the tire in place, but access is much easier with the tire off. Check the position of the spacers and washers as you dismount lower shock assemblies. Remove the shocks and reservoirs. This is the time to inspect each shock for wear if you intend to rebuild or repurpose.

the engine bonnet, and put the full mass of the palm of his hand on one of the shocks. The smell of burning flesh is enough to make anyone wish they understood the consequences of their

131

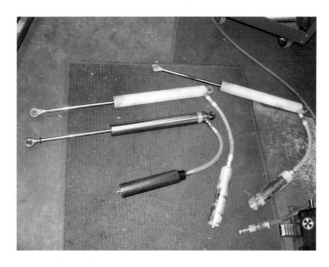

Side by side. The new Bilstein 7100 Series (top) looks identical to the one being replaced. A closer inspection will reveal some wear characteristics to look for.

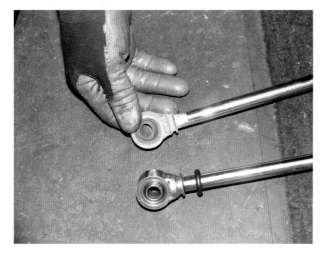

Notice the shock-eye bearing is dry and loose. You should not be able to move a fresh shock-eye bearing with your fingers.

New brass spacers are included with each new Bilstein shock; however, it's sound, off-road vehicle prepping savvy to use all new bolts, washers, spacers, and nuts when you replace certain components such as shocks.

As you load up each new Bilstein 7100 Series shock, have all the bolts and washers next to you to begin assembling each mount.

Mike Mancha prepares to load up the rear, front shock mount. Notice, on this truck, there are shock mounts for three shocks per wheel. Because this truck is not subjected to the rigors of life as a race truck, we used two shocks per wheel. Secure the shock reservoirs. It's not a bad idea to use new hose clamps. The blue rubber mounts in the background are supplied with each new Bilstein 7100 Series shock for attaching the reservoirs to the shock body.

actions before burning a perfectly good flapjack to the bone. The shock's body was intensely hot because the oil inside had heated to extremes, cavitated, and broken down to the point that it was useless, as were the other shocks on the truck. Yes, they would cool down in an hour or more and be useful to some degree, but under race conditions or constant high-speed pre-running, the shock failure would continue.

So Mr. Mancha went to Bilstein looking for some new shocks. The rep at Bilstein asked Mancha if he was using reservoir shocks. "What do reservoir shocks do?" Mancha asked.

"Reservoir shocks have an external body to hold more shock oil," the Bilstein representative says. "As more shock oil becomes available to the shock body, the shock (or shocks) run cooler and are able to cycle constantly for longer periods of time."

The theory that more than one shock per wheel distributes the workload across several shock units is still true. But these days, two reservoir shocks per wheel will allow long stretches of fast speeds over rough terrain. And for you folks who buy big reservoir shocks just to look cool on the street, cool shocks are cool shocks no matter how you use them.

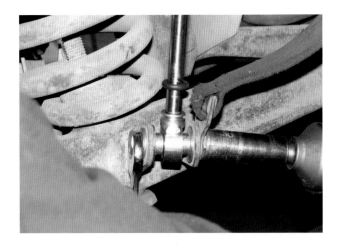

As it is up on top, being consistent with the position spacers, washers, nuts, and bolts is important and repeated for each shock mount.

Up until about a year or so ago, all Bilstein shocks were painted the trademark Bilstein yellow. Now all their reservoir and race shocks are simply clear, clean stainless-steel shock bodies and reservoirs. The Bilstein shocks on this prerunner had served the old hot rod well for a couple years now. With several preruns down the Baja peninsula and some hard miles in the California deserts, the shocks still worked pretty well. But upon inspection, it was evident that a fresh set of reservoir shocks were needed. So with the help of Custom Motorsports and Barry Mancha's brother, Mike Mancha, we'll go through the shock install and point out what to look for in a performance off-road shock to determine if you need to replace it. Mike Mancha has prepped and worked on off-road race trucks for years.

The new 7100 Series Bilstein reservoir shocks we bolted on are for 12 inches of wheel travel. Although this truck is capable of huge wheel travel, the setup with limit straps is geared for about 12 inches up front and less than 10 inches at the rear. When you order reservoir shocks from Bilstein, you can choose the valving best suited for your application. For this set, we went with 235/70 valving for the rear shocks to give us good control and a softer, but not mushy, ride with the truck fully fueled and loaded up for a long prerun.

At the front, we chose one notch less than a race setting for our valving at 275/78. For your understanding, the first number of the custom shock valve setting indicates the rebound force. The second number indicates compression. Thus rebound/compression would tend to increase for more firmness and more control. Less firmness is equated with less control, or softer ride characteristics. Part numbers for the rear shocks are AK7112R05, and rear AK711R04. This is a true application request for a specific performance intention; that would be swift prerunning. Your application might be different, but remember that for shocks to work they must be able to stay cool, and not just look cool.

As expected, these fresh Bilstein 7100 Series shocks provided solid control at the front of the prerunner and good rear end firmness over rough sections of terrain. Because of publishing deadlines, we could not show you this truck duckwalking at high speed over the moguls at the Outlet Center Road near Barstow, California, in the Mojave Desert, but that illustration would miss the point. Fresh shocks are like new running shoes: you must know when to replace them in order to run your best.

Follow along for some insight into shock therapy.

This is the completed front shock install of two Bilstein 7100 Series shocks with reservoirs mounted in fabricated cradles rather than attached to them.

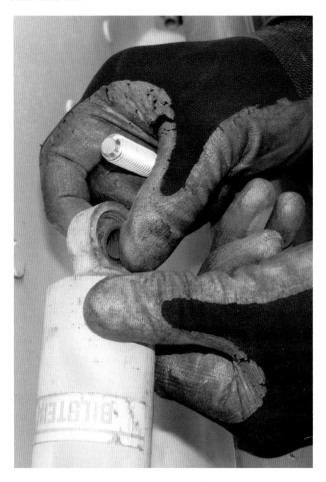

Shock-eye bearings are wobbly and indicative of the need to rebuild or replace.

Each forward shock mount at the top rear of the prerunner required us to use a 90 degree reservoir fitting so the blue reservoir hose cleared the rear roll-cage structure. Note that your application might require a similar adjustment. The fittings and procedure are painless and widely available through Kartek, Off-Road Warehouse, and other automotive sources.

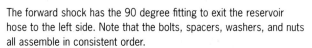

The forward shock has the 90 degree fitting to exit the reservoir hose to the left side. Note that the bolts, spacers, washers, and nuts all assemble in consistent order.

We used the two forward shock mounts at the rear. The third shock mount is there if we really think we are going to get uppity with Mother Earth.

Here's the finished rear shock mounts with fresh Bilstein 7100 reservoir shocks in cradles. Forward of the shock mounts are two 20-gallon fuel cells, caged in and center balanced on the truck.

TIME: Two hours

 TOOLS: Full socket set, jack, jack stands

 TALENT: ★

 APPLICABLE YEARS: Shocks for all years, makes, and models of light trucks

 TAB: $350–$400 for four shocks

 TINWARE: Using new bolts, nuts, and washers for mounting new shocks is a good idea.

 TIP: Inspect shock mount points for cracks or damage.

 PERFORMANCE GAIN:
Increased performance in corners and on uneven highway or off-road terrain

COMPLEMENTARY PROJECT:
Upgrading anti-sway bars, front and back, is a good tag along project for swapping out your shocks.

The front Rancho RS9000X shocks. One boot is installed, the other is not installed. To install the boot, slide it over the top, down to about 2 inches under the top of the cylinder. *Timothy Miller*

This is a view of the Rear Rancho RS9000 installed, with the adjustment valve on the bottom. *Timothy Miller*

First, removal of the bolt on the bottom of the shock was straightforward. Simple wrenches were used to remove them. Then, the same method was used to remove the top nut; only the nut on the top has the anti-backing-out piece welded to it. *Timothy Miller*

One of the easiest modifications you can make to your truck is to upgrade the suspension from stock shocks. This will allow you to change the feel of the ride, thus enabling you to make it a softer or firmer ride. A wide array of shocks and companies exist that you can select from. Here is one way to adjust your suspension for different ride and control characteristics.

We have chosen the Rancho RS9000X nine-position adjustable shock absorber. This shock features a triple-tube construction, a re-engineered design, and nine adjustable settings to maximize off-road and on-highway performance and driver comfort. The Ranchos have a cellular gas design with variable force control for precise flow metering. Each shock has double-welded loops with red urethane bushings and ⅝-inch hardened rods. Each one is double chromed for long wear and comes with a red shock boot for protection. The shocks are warranted against factory defects in material and workmanship (except finish) for as long as the original retail purchaser owns the vehicle on which the shocks were originally installed.

This set of Rancho RS9000X shocks were loaded on a 2003 Dodge Ram 1500 Laramie Off-Road edition 4x4 pickup. This

OFF-ROAD SUSPENSION AND HARDWARE

truck has enough clearance under it to allow the installation of the shocks, without using a floor jack.

We first had to install the red shock boots to the shocks. This is accomplished by sliding the boot over the top of the shock. Drain holes are in the boot, in case moisture gets inside, and those holes are to be lined up at the top of the shock so the moisture will drain properly.

We started with the rear shocks, removing the bottom bolt, then the top. On the top of the Dodge rear shocks is a unique bolt designed to not loosen during driving. There is a piece welded on that will either turn to hit the frame or the bed bottom. This is a safety feature. With the two bolts off, we removed the shock, took the new Rancho RS9000X rear shocks, and held them up to the top-mounting bracket. Make sure the shock adjustment knob is facing outward, as it will be hard to turn the knob later. We slid the bolt in the top, and while holding the special nut, we screwed in the bolt. Then we did the same for the bottom bolt. When both were on, we tightened them. We repeated this procedure for installing the second rear shock.

We then moved to the front. This was a little trickier for the top mount. You need two wrenches, one to hold the top of the shock and another to turn the nut. This is achieved on the 1500 by reaching over the front tire. On the 2500 and 3500, it is easier to come from the top. On the 2500 and 3500, you must remove the air box to get to the top of the shock and nut, on the passenger side. Once the top is removed, you remove the bottom bolt the same as the back shocks. Once the nut on top and the lower bolt is removed, you lower the shock through the A-arm. We took the new shock, slid it up through the A-arm, and connected the top nut, and then we connected the bottom bolt assembly. Again, make sure the shock adjustment knob is facing out and easy to get to. Check the alignment of the bushings when you take the old shock off, as the Rancho shocks have bushings that fit both ways. On the 1500 installation we did, we made the bigger sides face each other, one under the bracket, and one on top before the installation of the nut. This ensured a proper fit and alignment of the shock. Once it is tightened, repeat on the other side.

This is an easy way to change the ride of your vehicle. With the Rancho RS9000X shocks, it gives the driver a chance to vary the ride according to the conditions. These shocks provide a better ride, wherever the road may take you. This was a quick and easy modification that most owners can do themselves.

Installed by Loni Bangert, Colorado Front Range Aviation, 3300 Airport Road, Bldg. F, Boulder, Colorado 80301.

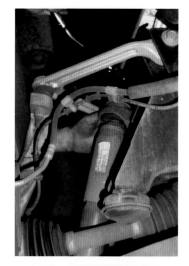

Using the two wrenches, we remove the top nut from the front stock shock. This can be done from over the front tire. Remove the top nut and carefully remove the top bushing to see how the new one is to be positioned. The new Rancho bushing needs to match up with how the old one comes off. There is a different size on each side of the bushings included in the kit. *Timothy Miller*

We feed the new shock up through the A-arm, then up through the top mounting bracket. *Timothy Miller*

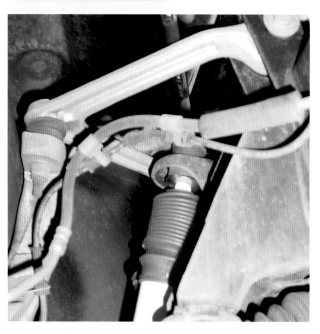

We then put the top bushing and nut on and, with the two wrenches, we tighten it down. *Timothy Miller*

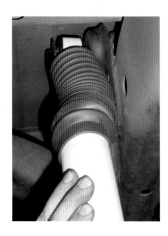

Attach the top of the rear shock to the mounting bracket. Push the bolt through the mounting bracket and shock, then screw it into the special nut. *Timothy Miller*

PROJECT 48 INSTALL HYDRAULIC RAM-ASSISTED STEERING

 TIME: Four hours

 TOOLS: Full socket set, full open-end wrench set, jack, jack stands, Sawzall, Sawzall blades, welding equipment

 TALENT: ★★★

 APPLICABLE YEARS: Kits can be adapted for all years, makes, and models of light trucks

 TAB: $1,000

 TINWARE: Die cutter and fresh cutting wheels, mig welding equipment, and Sawzall

 TIP: If you want to run tall tires, this project makes sense.

 PERFORMANCE GAIN:
Better control for slow-street and rough-terrain driving

COMPLEMENTARY PROJECT:
Install a custom steering wheel, because after this project your leverage will have been increased five-fold.

With the truck off the ground and supported, remove the front wheels and remove the driver's inner wheelwell liner for easier access to the steering box. Disconnect drag link at pitman arm. Remove pitman arm. Disconnect steering box "rag joint" coupling. You'll see the splines protruding from the steering box and entering the unbolted "rag joint" coupling. Disconnect hydraulic lines at the steering box and cap hose ends to prevent excess fluid loss.

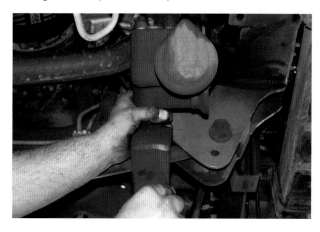

Remove steering box mounting bolts and remove steering box. You'll notice the technician chose to leave the pitman arm on until he removed the steering box. The technician has done many of these kits and prefers to remove the pitman arm at the workbench. The technician's—let's call him Danny—motto here is: "What you remove on the bench, you replace on the bench."

Big, tall tires offer many advantages for off-road vehicles traveling in rough terrain. Big tires look great on trucks that spend time on the street, as well. For folks who have run big tires, from 37 inches on up to say 44 or 46 inches, you know how hard it is to turn those front tires at slow to crawling speeds. At a dead stop, it's all a driver can do to budge the front wheels enough to position the truck for a three-point turn. If you tow a boat or any kind of trailer, maneuvering your rig to launch the boat or spot the trailer demands Herculean efforts to turn the wheels. Things get even more critical if you are locked in four-wheel drive, in low-range, and you are negotiating your rig around boulders, rock ledges, and fallen logs, or find yourself in almost any other scenario you can imagine in a true, off-road situation.

Off Road Unlimited (ORU) in Burbank, California, has been researching and developing off-road hardware for more than 15 years. From the owners and managers to employees in the shops, every person connected with ORU is a lifelong truck and SUV enthusiast. The company builds truck parts to make trucks work better. ORU developed a hydraulic ram-assist steering kit for Ford and GMC four-wheel-drive trucks for models

from 2004 back to the 1980s. The ram-assist exerts greater hydraulic force on the tie rod, making the front wheels turn easier. By distributing more force on the tie rod, the hydraulic ram-assist takes strain off of the steering box and truck frame.

The factory steering box does an adequate job when you are running stock tires or tire sizes up to 33 inches. But as you get into the 35-inch to 37-inch sizes and on up to the really big tires, the stress on the steering box increases. Add four-wheeling

137

conditions or constant low-speed steering requirements, and the steering box is subject to failure. The sector shaft is the component that usually breaks in the steering box, according to Mike Duval, general manager at ORU. Cracks and sheering at the splines of the sector shaft are often the result of the increased stress on the steering box.

A steering stabilizer is not needed because fluid pressure is resistant to movement in either direction, says Duval. Otherwise, this steering kit uses all of your factor steering linkages, making it legal for street use in most states. This ram-assist steering system requires you to swap your factory steering box as a core exchange. With the core exchange, this kit runs about $980. If you are not prepared to do some minor metal cutting and welding, we recommend you have a qualified technician at your trusted off-road shop do this install. It's far easier to be able to put the truck on a commercial-grade hydraulic truck lift and use air-powered tools.

For this publication, an installation was performed on a 2001 Ford F-250 4x4 running a 7.3-liter Power Stroke diesel motor. The truck runs 37-inch BFGoodrich All Terrain T/As, and the owner pulls a shop trailer to promote his Line-X franchise and a toy trailer. His reason for going with the ORU hydraulic ram-assist steering kit is the ability to steer the front tires at slow speeds in tight spaces while spotting his trailers. Before the install, I jumped into the driver's seat, fired the power stroke, and turned the steering wheel with my foot on the brake. Moving the steering wheel was difficult, and even with 37-inchers, the front tires did not want to turn either left or right. Here are the major steps for disassembly and installation that parallel the instructions you will get with your own kit. The end result is to enable the driver to turn 44-inch front tires at a dead stop, with the driver's foot on the brake.

Follow up: after the hydraulic ram-assisted steering system was installed and refilled, I saddled up and fired her up once again. Compared to the morning session, with my foot on the brake, and sawing the steering wheel back and forth, the front wheels turned with little physical effort.

Install new secondary hydraulic lines on new steering box. The shorter hose goes on the inside, longer on the outside. You'll also see L for left and R for right stampings on the steering box. The left "L" is the longer line. Note: Tighten hose nuts down as much as possible and make sure the hydraulic hoses, directionally, pass back over the steering box. Install new steering box. Red Loctite is recommended for use on all bolts. Reconnect "rag joint" coupling. Reconnect factory hydraulic lines.

Reinstall pitman arm and reconnect drag link. Be sure to use a new cotter pin to secure drag link. Remove the four differential cover bolts.

Install ram bracket with new ⅜-inch bolts and lockwashers. If you have a factory steel differential cover, you must use two ⅜-inch flat washers (not included) along with the split washers per mounting bolt as spacers. If you have an ORU aluminum cover, use only the split washers. Remove factory steering stabilizer (if equipped). Disconnect factory trac bar. If you will use the factory trac bar, the welded bracket will need to be modified as seen here. You will remove the steering stabilizer mounting point with a Sawzall (as seen here) and weld in gusseting in order to clear the ram unit. You can use a cutting torch, but a Sawzall provides a cleaner cut to which an end gusset will be welded. The S-shaped inside gusset is welded in between the axle housing and the rear of the trac-bar bracket just behind the Sawzall cut. Cycle the ram unit by hand and mark the center of the rod (approximately 4 inches). Install the Heim joints on the ram unit. Use Loctite on the female Heim when attaching to the ram shaft. Install the ram unit with the body closest to the differential. Install the two short steel spacers at the tie rod. With the wheels facing straight forward, and the ram drive rod at center, locate and mark the mounting position for the weld-on tabs on the tie rod. Use welding C-clamps to secure tab position on the tie rod.

Disconnect the tie rod at the passenger side for better access. Clean the tab-mounting surface and weld the tabs on as seen here. Weld the inside of the mounting tabs. Reconnect the tie rod with a new cotter pin.

Connect hydraulic lines to the ram unit. Then connect ram unit with supplied bolts and spacer. Don't forget the Loctite. Refill power-steering reservoir. Bleed system by loosening the lower ram lines one at a time until some fluid seeps out. Check all connections and clearances, then start engine and slowly cycle the steering. Add power-steering fluid as needed to fill the system.

OFF-ROAD SUSPENSION AND HARDWARE

PROJECT 49 | REDUCE HEAT IN YOUR TRANSMISSION

 TIME: Eight hours

 TOOLS: Full socket set, screwdriver set, torque wrench, transmission jack

 TALENT: ★★★

 APPLICABLE YEARS: All years using the 4R70W four-speed transmission

 TAB: $400 for shift kit, $700 for torque converter, $200 for deep sump transmission pan

 TINWARE: Transmission oil

 TIP: One caveat to be aware of is the requirement of using a different transmission filter than the factory specification for the 4R70W transmission. The filter is a Ford part number for a four-wheel-drive pan (Ford P/N F2VY7A098A or TCI P/N 438505 O-ring and filter). Access to a hydraulic lift is an advantage.

 PERFORMANCE GAIN:
Sharp shifts throughout the power range, longer transmission life

COMPLEMENTARY PROJECT:
Floor-mounted gear shifter, change all drivetrain fluids

Test-fit all new parts. Look up part numbers to be sure they fit the exact transmission you are working with. This can save you a big headache up front.

Remove the transmission pan and let drain as thoroughly as you can. Be alert for any metal shavings or debris at this point.

Remove factory main control assembly. This unit contains all the sensors and, once unbolted, needs to be gently finessed out of its position.

For most of the automotive driving public, a smooth-shifting automatic transmission is a thing of beauty—the smoother the automatic transmission shifts, the better. When you can't even feel the car shifting, well that means you must be driving the ultimate luxury vehicle. Silky-smooth automatic shifts are fine for a vehicle that rarely sees more action than merging on to the 405 freeway northbound from Santa Monica Blvd. in L.A. and getting off at the Getty Center for wine tasting. But if you want performance for extended periods of time, whether it's running up a sand-wash out in the desert, pulling a trailer, or enjoying all the torque and horsepower your little motor can deliver, you need to consider how heat affects your drivetrain.

Smooth shifts in an automatic transmission are, to some degree, the result of clutch slippage. Slipping clutches take longer to lock in the gear, giving a smooth shift but creating an environment where the transmission temperature can rise rapidly if the duration or intensity of the demands you put on it don't allow the transmission to cool itself quickly enough. When heat dissipation is not quick enough, the potential for transmission failure is increased. Big horsepower means big heat

on the transmission and calls for a shift kit to allow transmission gear changes to be more direct.

Some of the things you can do to increase the performance of your transmission as well as help manage the heat buildup are to: increase the capacity of transmission fluid in the system, increase the efficiency of the torque converter, increase the efficiency of the internal components in terms of physical size, increase the intensity of the shifts (shift kit), and install a transmission cooler.

A 4R70W transmission behind a factory V-6 engine is not exactly a bombproof piece of hardware, but it is relatively trouble-free and does a good job. With the Factory Tech C-kit (shift kit), firmer, more direct shifting is induced. The shifting actuators or trigger mechanisms that engage the first-to-second, third-to-fourth gear shifts are designed to allow the gear changes to be firm and direct, thereby reducing clutch slippage and the potential for heat buildup. Even with the mild power and torque produced with the 4.2-L engine, the post-installation evaluation revealed that firm first-to-second gear shifts would chirp the tires easy if the motor had the chops. This endeavor took a couple hours. You need to take your time and be deliberate and organized. We put the factory transmission pan back on while we worked with the transmission jack under the truck so that the original pan would take any punishment that might otherwise be visited upon the new aluminum pan.

Next, we installed a Factory Tech heavy-duty torque converter, a finned aluminum deep sump TCI transmission pan, and TCI Racing transmission fluid to give this F-150 better direct shifts, less clutch slippage, and more efficient use of its torque and horsepower. A transmission cooler is the obvious final addition, but we wanted to install a transmission temperature gauge first and get some baseline temperatures so we could report the effectiveness of a transmission cooler package as if it stood alone.

The Factory Tech torque converter has 45 percent more clutch surface, oversized clutches, a Torrington roller bearing on the thrust surface, Teflon seals, and furnace brazed cooling fins. The cover plates are doubly reinforced, and the lockup occurs at a lower stall speed. These modifications help dissipate heat at the torque converter. This operation involved partially disconnecting the exhaust system to allow room to remove the transmission in order to swap the torque converter. With the transmission removed, you can also check the rear seal of the engine and replace it if needed. By doing the shift-kit first, we had the advantage of draining at least 14 quarts of transmission fluid out, making the transmission a little easier to manage.

A TCI deep sump, finned aluminum transmission pan provides for extra capacity (1.5 quarts more) of transmission fluid. The TCI tranny pan is tapped for a transmission tem-

perature gauge and has a magnet built in to attract any metal shavings that might accumulate over a period of time. One caveat to be aware of is the requirement of using a different transmission filter than the factory specification for the 4R70W transmission. The filter is a Ford part number for a four-wheel-drive pan (Ford P/N F2VY7A098A or TCI P/N 438505 O-ring and filter).

Remove bolts that fasten the two stiffener plates and the bolt that holds down the separator plate to the main control casting. Remove the stiffener plates to expose the main control casting.

Open up the main control casting. Be careful to account for eight black check balls that will be repositioned according to a supplied diagram.

Start reassembly by positioning the black check balls into proper locations on the main control casting.

Install new separator plate.

Install new first-second gear accumulator piston with the supplied brown spring into transmission case. A new retainer and snap ring are supplied with the shift kit.

Here the 2–3 accumulator "bottle cap" piston is reinstalled.

These components are valid performance upgrades no matter what brand or engine type you have in your truck. Whether it's a diesel- or gasoline-powered vehicle, all transmissions are affected by heat. These upgrades are universal for every transmission worth its salt; there are custom shift kits, torque converters, and components to beef them up. You'll need a full day to pull that transmission in order to swap the torque converter, but the shift kit took just a couple of hours. We started with the shift kit, then lowered the tranny and swapped out the torque converter. After we reinstalled the transmission, we bolted the new TCI finned, aluminum transmission pan and filled the system up with TCI Racing transmission fluid. With a big thank-you to Fairway Ford in Yorba Linda, California, and the skills of Brandon Thompson, the photos show the gist of what we did.

Install the new main control assembly using the new supplied gasket. Torque valve body bolts at 80–100 lb-in. Tighten in an even, gradual systematic pattern. Be sure to properly position the manual lever to the manual valve in the valve body. Reinstall all remaining hardware. At this point, we put the factory transmission pan on to protect the tranny bottom in order to remove the transmission for the torque converter swap. With a transmission jack supporting the weight of the transmission, we removed the driveshaft and transmission bolts. We realized it would go more smoothly if we partially disconnected the exhaust system at the factory collector, and disconnected enough hanger points to allow us to work around the exhaust system while it was still largely in place. We removed the transmission crossmember and disconnected all wiring harnesses to allow us to lower the tranny enough to work on it at waist level but still in a position to hoist it back into place.

A socket on the front of the crankshaft will allow you to turn the flywheel to expose the bolts connecting the torque converter to the flywheel. Remove these bolts now so the torque converter comes down with the transmission. We accessed the top bolts on the transmission with some ratchet extensions; with everything loosened, we lowered the transmission jack enough to get a clear shot. The rubber engine mounts allowed the flex and support of the drivetrain at this juncture.

Remove the factory torque converter. This is where unbolting it first is an advantage. We partially filled the new converter with TCI racing transmission fluid to prime it. The Factory Tech converter has a fluid drain plug tapped into it for future convenience.

Carefully install the new Factory Tech converter. Note that the converter must mesh with two series of inside splines before it fully seats. With the transmission reinstalled, check all harnesses and connections. Double-check to be sure the exhaust and all bolts are bolted up.

Now, we install the new TCI deep transmission pan that holds 1.5 quarts more than the factory unit. This pan also has a transmission temperature sensor hole tapped into it as well as a drain plug. The factory pan does not have a drain plug because they want you to remove the pan and replace the transmission filter each time.

TIME: Five to six hours

TOOLS: Full socket set, drill, drill bits, Dremel tool, Dremel bits

TALENT: ★★

APPLICABLE YEARS: Winch applications for all years, makes, and models of light trucks

TAB: $1,200

TINWARE: Gloves and a friend to help will make this project less strenuous.

TIP: A winch is an investment in automotive self-recovery. Don't buy one for looks. If you don't want it permanently mounted, you can install a portable one, though it will have less pulling capacity.

PERFORMANCE GAIN:
Capability to extract your 4x4 and other 4x4s from being stuck.

COMPLEMENTARY PROJECT:
Consider installing off-road lights.

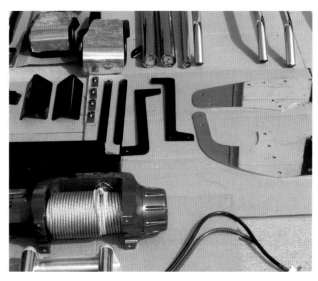

You don't want to preassemble any part of this winch install. Every piece you need is laid out here, with the exception of an enormous bag of bolts sitting off-stage. Remove the front bumper and "paired bolts" that attach the bumper brackets to the frame. Mount the template using the factory "paired bolts" to temporarily keep the template from moving while you locate the bolt holes you will be drilling.

Reeling in the rig of a lost soul mired up to the door handles in swamp coffee is a task no man looks forward to. When you roll up to a potential recovery scene, you've got to wonder whether your motivation to help is altruistic or simply tied to the fact that you have the equipment and know-how to indeed be of assistance. Sometimes all you can do is offer to call for help when your cell phone can lock on to a passing satellite, or you can figure out what channel to dial your CB radio into. In other cases, all you can do is take a photo for a "worst stuck" submission.

Regardless of whether you are the party trying to help, or the four-wheeling guru who got your truck stuck in the first place, having the right equipment and know-how is paramount to getting under way. How do you go about deciding the correct winch for your particular vehicle? The rule of thumb is to determine how much your truck weighs loaded to the gills (say 6,000 pounds), then multiply that by 1.5 times to arrive at the correct line-pull on the winch for your vehicle.

This three-quarter-ton Dodge Ram 4x4 is certainly capable of navigating rough terrain, crawling up steep inclines, creeping down descents, and grappling through a mud hole or soft-bottom

stream. It is also capable of tugging another vehicle out of a sand trap with a tow strap or getting stuck itself. Given the size and load capacity of this 2500 Ram, a good choice of winch is one with about 9,500 pounds of line-pull. The Warn 9.5 installation that we'll walk through also incorporates a full-dress brush guard and light bar finished in stainless steel.

Danny Kempf of Off Road Unlimited in Burbank, California, handled the install. This winch system is a bolt-up operation that can be performed by any truck owner in about four to five hours. It's helpful to study the installation instructions before you tackle the kit to give you an idea of how pieces fit together. You will drill some holes and add some additional superstructure to your truck, but it all keeps the factory bumper in place, and the winch is tucked neatly away, but ready to use.

Drill ⁷⁄₁₆-inch holes through both sides of the frame. Wear safety goggles to protect your eyes from flying metal chips. Pry up the anti-crush brackets from both sides of the frame rails.

Clamp right-hand lower brace (these are specific left- and right-hand braces, not interchangeable) to the bottom of the frame as seen here. The front end of the bracket should be exactly 2 inches from the end of the frame.

Drill a ⁷⁄₁₆-inch hole through each slot into the center bottom of the frame. Position ⁷⁄₁₆-inch nut plates into frame rail.

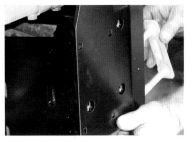

Install frame extensions and push the 3 ½-inch bolts through the frame. Loosely affix all washers, "factory paired" bolts, and nuts.

Fit up the lower brace with the ⁷⁄₁₆ x 1 ½-inch bolts, flat washers, and lockwashers provided. Do not tighten at this time. Hold a spacer tube inside the frame rail, positioned over one of the new holes drilled with the template. Insert a ⁷⁄₁₆ x 3 ½-inch bolt through the new hole and spacer from the outside of the frame. You won't push the bolt all the way through the inside frame wall just yet. Repeat for each hole drilled with the template. Push the anti-crush brackets back into original position. Position the correct upper brace above the frame.

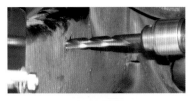

You will have to drill a ½-inch hole for the left-hand upper brace. The right-hand brace uses an existing hole in the frame.

Install the member brackets on both sides. Measure 32 ½ inches between the inner faces of the member brackets. At this point, tighten bolts on this hardware before proceeding. Remove the gray plastic insert of the bumper and slide the bumper-mounting studs through the slots on the frame extensions. Install the original nuts, center the bumper, and tighten it down. Tighten all frame bolts down at this point. Cut two holes in the front air dam to mount the side members. Install the side members at the insides of the side member brackets. With the side members installed, mount the top tube of the brush guard only.

Install the winch carrier with the ⁷⁄₁₆-inch button head bolts supplied with the kit. Tighten all remaining fasteners.

Mount the winch on the winch carrier. Install remaining brush guard assembly. Route positive and negative power cables from winch to battery and connect. Zip-tie the cable to secure its path and keep it from moving. Thread winch cable through lead fairing, attach cable hook, and bolt fairing lead to the winch carrier. Test winch operation with handheld remote control. Double-check all connections.

PERFORMANCE BRAKES

The supplied washers are slipped over each preinstalled stud on the caliper-mounting bracket before the caliper is slipped into place over the studs and rotors. Then the washer and locknut are installed to hold the caliper in place. The caliper bleed screws should be pointing up. *T. J. Miller*

TIME: Three hours

TOOLS: Full socket set, jack, jack stands, gloves, and screwdrivers

TALENT: ★ ★ ★

APPLICABLE YEARS: Disc brake upgrades for all years, makes, and models of light trucks

TAB: $700

TINWARE: Gloves

TIP: Count the cost! If you're going with larger tires/wheels on any big SUV, consider upgrading the brakes.

PERFORMANCE GAIN:
Greater stopping power with less heat buildup

COMPLEMENTARY PROJECT:
Stainless-steel brake lines

The first real task in removing the factory brakes is to unbolt the brake line clamp to free the brake hose and the wiring for the ABS sensor. Then the two bolts that attach the factory caliper to the spindle are removed. Once the bolts are removed, the caliper just simply lifts up off of the rotor. *T. J. Miller*

And with the rotor out of the way, the factory rotor easily slides off of the hub assembly. A thin washer is put on to the factory caliper bolts between the spindle and where the new Wilwood caliper bracket is going to mount. Once the factory caliper bolts are installed, the new Wilwood caliper bracket will look like this. *T. J. Miller*

When the engineers at General Motors were putting together the brake package for the Hummer H2, they knew that a solid brake package was needed. After all, the massive SUV would be built on a three-quarter-ton chassis based on the Suburban platform, and the H2 was projected to be one of the heaviest SUVs that GM produced. So the engineers figured out what was needed for an H2 brake package, and then found the least expensive way to make this happen. And the stock brakes work just fine on a stock H2 with stock-sized wheels and tires.

But the minute a set of larger-diameter wheels and tires are bolted to the corners of one of these bigger-than-life SUVs, it becomes obvious that the factory brake package is no longer adequate. With the larger wheels and tires, a lot more rotating mass occurs, which takes its toll on the factory braking system. The factory system heats up faster, leading to brake fade—and brake fade in traffic in a big SUV is just asking for trouble.

That's where the engineers at Wilwood took over and decided that they could do better. Plus they were not concerned with having to save a nickel here and a penny there when building a brake system for a particular vehicle. They got to use the best of everything right down to the hardware that holds everything together. Plus, they can save weight by using a forged aluminum rotor hat to help eliminate rotating weight for improved acceleration and braking. The Wilwood crew also got to use the company's 16-inch staggered vane-directional rotors for maximum cooling efficiency and increased braking power, which occurred because of the large pad contact surface area. They also went big with the calipers, opting to use huge, six-piston forged billet calipers loaded with Wilwood's own high-friction compound brake pads. And all of that was just for the front!

PERFORMANCE BRAKES

145

Out back, the company replaced the factory brakes with a one-piece directional vane rotor and a forged billet four-piston caliper loaded with those world famous Wilwood pads. The Wilwood rear brake kit for the H2 is a perfect complement for the front brake kit, offering improved cooling as well as a larger pad contact area for more effective stopping power.

But as with every modification to a system as vital to safety as the brakes, the engineers from Wilwood recommended that only experienced professionals should perform the installation of this kit. And, as with all high-performance brakes, they should be checked regularly for wear and fatigue.

After the new caliper bracket is installed, the 16-inch Wilwood rotor and hat assembly can be slipped into place on the hub. Because the lug nuts and wheels are what keep the hats pressed flush up against the hub assembly, a couple of washers and lug nuts are installed at this time. This is just to keep the rotors held in place temporarily. Due to how the brake hoses are routed up and over the top of the spindle, it is necessary to install a 90 degree fitting in the back of the caliper before the caliper is installed. *T. J. Miller*

With the spacers in place, the caliper is slipped down over the caliper mount, and the hardware is snugged down to hold it in place. *T. J. Miller*

There is another retaining clip and a retaining bolt that ensure that the pads don't move around inside the caliper. Here, the retaining bolt is being installed. *T. J. Miller*

With the pads in, the caliper can then be torqued down to the Wilwood caliper mount. Then the caliper mount is torqued down to the spindle. *T. J. Miller*

With the front kit installed, it is time to move on to the rear brakes. First, the pair of bolts that hold the factory caliper to the rear axle housing are removed. *T. J. Miller*

Once the bolts are out, the caliper simply slides off the rotor. And just like with the front, the rear rotor simply slides off once the caliper is out of the way. Then the Wilwood caliper mount is bolted to the rear axle housing using the factory caliper bolts. *T. J. Miller*

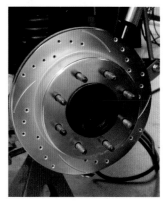

With the caliper mount in place, the new Wilwood rotor and hat assembly is slipped into place over the factory parking brake assembly. A 90 degree fitting is installed into the port in the back of the caliper to help with the routing of the brake hose to keep it out of the way of the suspension components. Then the new rear caliper can be mounted on to the rear caliper bracket. *T. J. Miller*

With the caliper in place, the pads are loaded into the rear caliper just like they were loaded into the front calipers—right down to the clips and retaining bolts. The clearance of the caliper, rotor, and pads are checked, and when all of the spacing is given the green light, all of the mounting bolts are torqued down to the specs in the directions provided by Wilwood. Finally, all of the brake hoses are installed, and the brake system is bled to complete the installation process. Once the SUV is back on its wheels, the process to seat the pads into the rotors detailed in the directions is followed and the job is complete. *T. J. Miller*

PERFORMANCE BRAKES

TIME: Three hours

TOOLS: Full socket set, screwdrivers, jack, jack stands

TALENT: ★★★

APPLICABLE YEARS: Baer brake systems for all years, makes, and models of light trucks

TAB: $114 for front pair

TINWARE: Brake fluid, drop cloth

TIP: Brake systems are critical to safety, but if you have the confidence to tackle a brake project, it will do wonders to help you understand how the system works.

PERFORMANCE GAIN:
More bite for brake pads, firmer stopping power

COMPLEMENTARY PROJECT:
Stainless-steel brake lines

It's very easy to upgrade your rotors. First lift and support the vehicle, and then remove the wheels and tires. *Tony Morrison*

The factory calipers must be removed by unbolting the two bolts that hold it to the spindle. Once this is done, the rotor simply pulls away from the hub. *Tony Morrison*

In order to ensure that the new Baer rotors fit flush with the hub, we removed some of the rust that accumulated with a light sanding. *Tony Morrison*

Replacing the rotors on your truck may seem like a great way to improve its looks and stopping power. But not all rotors are the same. Some rotors are simply made to give your truck a performance brake look, but don't actually improve braking performance.

With the introduction of Baer's new DecelaRotors, the company gives truck enthusiasts a performance rotor that actually looks as good as it performs. The DecelaRotor is designed to be an entry-level upgrade that adds brilliant appearance and impact to your truck. These rotors also enhance stopping power by providing an improved bite compared to the stock original equipment rotors. The design also maintains constant wet weather performance and equalizes the pad wear. Rotational drilling and slotting, the same counter-rotational drilling and slotting used in professional racing rotors, also eliminates gassing while minimizing stress cracks. The DecelaRotors are packaged as pairs, or one axle-set per box. Also, they are covered by a three-year limited warranty against warping and cracking.

Baer offers more than 150 brake system applications that are designed so the enthusiast is not required to do any welding or

147

fabrication to perform the installation. This is evident in the DecelaRotors Baer installed on our 2003 Dodge Ram 1500 Laramie Quad Cab 4x4 truck.

A hydraulic lift was used to raise the truck and remove the wheels to access the factory brakes. If you don't have a lift, a simple floor jack and jack stands will also suffice. Once the tires were removed, the two bolts that hold the calipers were taken out. With these bolts removed, the calipers pulled out from the old rotors. An important note: always have something to support the caliper when it is disconnected so that it is not hanging by the brake line. Allowing the rotors to hang can seriously harm the brake system, making for a costly repair.

With the calipers removed, the old rotors were simply taken off. If you are also replacing your brake pads, you will have to use a caliper piston tool to push the piston back into the caliper so that the new pads will fit over the rotor.

Our test vehicle had some miles on it, so to make sure the new calipers would sit flush against the hub, the accumulated rust was removed with a small grinder, taking care not to grind the lugs.

The DecelaRotors are marked with the side (L or R) and have an arrow showing the direction of the rotation. This is done for the counter-rotation drilling. Care must be taken to make sure the proper rotor is mounted on the correct hub. The new rotors were installed by sliding the lugs through the holes on the rotor, and the caliper is then installed back on the new rotor. Both attaching bolts were installed and torqued. The tire is then placed on, and the proper torque was applied to the lugs. After all four wheels were done, the truck was lowered and the brakes were pumped a few times to set the proper pad distance. No

bleeding was needed on the brakes.

Since the install, the truck has been driven about 3,000 miles. Through hard-driving rain, heavy snow, freeway speeds, and stop and go city driving, the DecelaRotors have performed flawlessly. Compared to the original stock rotors, the DecelaRotors outperform the original equipment with greater consistency and pad bite. The new DecelaRotors also look great, as the slot- and counter-rotational-drilled rotors set off the tires and wheels nicely.

At the rear the factory disc brakes are slightly smaller, but they can also be upgraded with a pair of DecelaRotor rotors. *Tony Morrison*

The rear procedure is done in the same manner as the front, making sure that the direction of the rotor is correct. *Tony Morrison*

The new rotor simply fits over the hub, and the calipers are replaced in the original position. *Tony Morrison*

The rotors are right- and left-side specific, and the direction is important to proper braking operation. *Tony Morrison*

Here you can see the difference in the appearance of the Baer DecelaRotor over the stock rotor. *Tony Morrison*

PROJECT 53 INSTALL PERFORMANCE REAR BRAKE ROTORS AND PADS

TIME: Two hours

TOOLS: Full socket set, screwdrivers, jack, jack stands

TALENT: ★

APPLICABLE YEARS: All

TAB: $750–$1,000

TINWARE: N/A

TIP: If you plan on upgrading your brake line, this is a good time to engage the process because you'll have to bleed the brakes anyway.

PERFORMANCE GAIN:
Better stopping power

COMPLEMENTARY PROJECT:
It's a good time to swap out your shocks if you need them.

The parts are made up of two slotted rotors and larger more-aggressive brake pads. *Lynn Guthrie*

The rear of the truck was lifted and supported with jack stands. Then the rear wheels and tires were removed. *Lynn Guthrie*

Here you can see the factory brake rotor and pads. The stock rotors are not slotted, and although they work well, the SSBC upgrade will provide a better bite. *Lynn Guthrie*

Those of us who have rear disc brakes, know the difference they make on helping a full-size pickup stop quickly and efficiently. But because trucks like the Ford Lightning have the potential of excessive power and speed, stopping becomes even more important. Although this truck also has factory rear disc brakes, these can be upgraded to provide increased stopping power to help tame a performance truck.

We were recently made aware of stainless-steel Brake Company's rear brake system (A2360010), which is designed to improve the stopping power of the Ford Lightning. The rear brake upgrade can be used with the factory front disc brakes, or with the company's Force-10-brake system, which features 14-inch rotors and a four-piston performance caliper.

The system includes two turbo-slotted rotors and high-performance brake pads. The rotors are also available with an optional Xtra Life plating to keep them looking new. The rear upgrade kit is simple to install, and it also improves some of the truck's stability of the front end and minimizes some of the dive associated with the Lightning.

We asked Earl Moorhead of Earl's Automotive to show how

this system is installed, but the process is simple enough for any home mechanic to accomplish with a caliper-piston compression tool.

The two bolts that mount the caliper to the backing plate are removed. This allows you to lift off the caliper. *Lynn Guthrie*

The factory brake pads are then unclipped from the caliper and set aside. *Lynn Guthrie*

The stock rotors are then removed by simply sliding them out. It's also a good time to check the wear on the inner shoes, which are used for the parking brake. *Lynn Guthrie*

Once the area is cleaned with brake cleaner, the new SSBC slotted rotors are installed. *Lynn Guthrie*

In some cases you may need a caliper piston tool to push the piston back into the caliper. This allows you to install the new SSBC brake pads. *Lynn Guthrie*

The pads clip into the caliper just like the factory units do. *Lynn Guthrie*

Once the pads are in place, the caliper is then reinstalled on to the new rotor. *Lynn Guthrie*

Make sure to properly lubricate and tighten the caliper bolts. *Lynn Guthrie*

Perform the same steps for the other side, and the brake install is complete. Now replace the rim and tire assemblies and *hold on* when you apply the brakes. *Lynn Guthrie*

TIME: Three hours

TOOLS: Full socket set, jack, jack stands

TALENT: ★★★

APPLICABLE YEARS: Brake systems for all years, makes, and models of light trucks

TAB: $550–$900

TINWARE: Brake fluid, piston lube, and anti-seize spray will help rusty rotors to dislodge from the axle seating point.

TIP: Think about your complete braking system and consider doing all upgrades within the same project window.

PERFORMANCE GAIN:
Firm stopping power with larger tires, better heat dissipation and braking performance when the brake system is hot

COMPLEMENTARY PROJECT:
Upgrade to stainless-steel brake lines, upgrade brake calipers

The basis of any good brake system is a high-quality rotor. This one from EGR is slotted to improve heat dissipation and pad bite.

The vents on the rotor are designed to aid in cooling and won't cause cracks under severe heat conditions. The direction of the vent is also important to proper cooling and pad service.

PERFORMANCE BRAKES

Although many owners of one- and three-quarter-ton trucks concentrate on adding more towing power, they are at the same time trying to get these big 6,000 pounds–plus trucks to stop. Many owners' trucks have poor stopping power and cracked rotors, and they need chronic changing of front disc brake pads every 8,000 to 10,000 miles.

This may seem ridiculous to many, but the fact is that some of the factory brake systems struggle to stop a heavy vehicle, especially one with 17-, 18-, or 20-inch wheels that are mounted to 35- to 38-inch-tall tires. So, what's the problem? Heat is a major cause, but the type of brake pad materials also influence the amount of heat produced and the amount of friction that is required to stop a vehicle. With the right combination of pad and rotor, and properly functioning brake lines, OEM brake systems can be dramatically improved without resorting to larger, aftermarket systems that range in excess of $3,000.

We contacted EGR Brakes in Corona, California. The company's employees are considered experts at brakes for big trucks and SUVs. Glen Maurer, owner of EGR Brakes, recommends using a high-quality pad and rotor combination. On EGR

brake systems, Maurer uses a gas-slotted rotor that provides improved cooling and helps to provide an initial bite to the pads for improved stopping power. According to Maurer, when a good OEM replacement rotor is used with a performance pad, the combination can dramatically improve stopping power with the factory components.

Much of the emphasis of big truck stopping power is placed on the type of brake pad compound. Many factory pads use a carbon metallic matrix pad that works well but also leaves a lot of carbon dust. EGR uses a specially formulated carbon Kevlar pad that is heat cured to remove any air pockets within the pad matrix. According to Maurer, this process also eliminates brake

151

Your brakes are only as good as the pads you put on them. This Carbon Kevlar pad from EGR eliminates heavy carbon dust, yet has improved stopping power with less heat retention.

The mechanics at Custom Motorsports in Riverside, California, unbolted the calipers and moved them aside. On four-wheel-drive models with independent front suspensions, the rotors must be removed by unbolting the center hub. The rear of the hubs is also unbolted, allowing the rotor to be removed from the factory spindle.

Here you can see the center-bearing hub, which is attached to the rotor by means of the wheel studs. The ABS sensor also must be removed before attempting to remove the rotor. The studs are punched out with a hammer, and the center hub assembly can now be removed from the rotor.

noise and provides improved heat transfer.

"The Carbon Kevlar pads are state-of-the-art brake pad technology," says Maurer. "The fiber strands in conjunction with

The hub is placed into the new EGR rotor, and the studs are pushed back into position with a hammer and punch.

The hub and rotor assembly are then reinstalled on to the spindle with the CV joint attaching through the center.

Once the hub assembly is bolted back in place, the new calipers are bolted into position.

metal particles combine to absorb vibration and dissipate heat." The result is the same stopping power with less pedal pressure and heat. Reducing pedal pressure and heat also reduces wear and provides improved stopping distances.

To further improve upon any stock system, Maurer also recommended blueprinting the factory calipers. Heat can also hinder the operation of the factory calipers and cause the pistons to expand under extreme heat, and thus, stick. This reduces brake pressure to the pads and increases braking distances. The EGR calipers are all blueprinted and feature phenalic or stain-

Here you can see the EGR blueprinted caliper in place, equipped with the Carbon Kevlar pads. At this point, the factory rubber brake hose was removed and replaced with the EGR stainless-steel brake hose. As a part of the EGR system, 1.5 liters of Motul brake fluid are included, along with high-temperature, silicone caliper lube and a brush. The crew at Custom Motorsports used brake cleaner to remove any brake fluid residue or oil from the surface of the new rotor.

This is what the system looked like installed on the passenger side. Note the correct direction of the rotor vents.

The rear of our truck uses an aftermarket disc brake system from Dynatrac. We used a new set of EGR brake pads here as well to ensure that the truck has good front-to-rear proportioning.

less-steel pistons that are hand-fitted into the caliper, with high-temperature silicone seals and boots. This extra effort ensures that there is not sticking or binding of the piston, providing excellent performance even under severe heat conditions.

We wanted to see how well EGR's brake upgrades worked in comparison to the factory system on our 1995 three-quarter-ton truck, using the company's B-package. The kit included a pair of gas-slotted rotors, the company's Carbon Kevlar compound brake pads, a set of blueprinted factory calipers, and 1.5-liters of Motul 600c high-temperature brake fluid. We also went ahead and upgraded the factory brake lines, using EGR's braided hose kit.

We took the kit over to Custom Motorsports in Riverside, California, which managed to install the complete front brake system within a few hours. The EGR instructions indicated proper brake seasoning and bedding procedures. We followed the procedures, and after several stops, noticed that the brakes were seemingly stopping better and better after each use. Once we put about 25 miles on the system, we definitely noticed a dramatic decrease in stopping distance. We also noticed that we used less pedal pressure to stop shorter, and there was virtually no brake squeal.

The EGR components definitely opened our eyes to finding new ways to improve stock brake systems at a reasonable cost. The system for our truck cost about $750. The brake line

upgrade included a complete three- or four-piece kit of UV-protected lines that used Teflon tubing and a stainless outer sleeve. The line kit retailed for an additional $170 but was well worth the cost, considering our old lines were cracked and in need of repair.

A Freezing Proposition

If you continually have a problem with cracked or warped rotors, the problem may be excessive heat buildup in your truck's braking system. Another effective way to combat this problem is to have your rotors cryogenically treated. The process involves freezing the rotors in an enclosed tank that uses liquid nitrogen to bring down the temperature of the parts. The parts never come in contact with the nitrogen, and yet, the parts are slowly brought down to temperatures below –300 degrees F.

"I got into cryogenics as a racer," says Rick Yacoucci, president and owner of NW Cryogenics. "My problem was breaking drivetrain parts on our racing cars." Yacoucci used cryogenics in the past, and when the opportunity came for him to purchase a complete cryogenic system, he began treating his own parts and those of other racers. "We do lots of brakes, especially for motorsports," he says. "Most of the racers are able to double the life of their rotors due to the extreme heat that is applied during the season."

For street vehicles, like heavy trucks, the process can dramatically improve the life of the rotor, as well as reduce or eliminate any pedal pulsation and fade that comes from some areas of the rotor having a harder metal surface than others, called hard spotting.

The cryogenic process takes about 24 hours to cool down and then bring back to room temperature, but the process tightens the molecular structure of the metal, reducing any pores within the brake rotor. The process also strengthens the metal and allows the rotors to dissipate heat much more quickly and effectively than standard cast rotors. The result is longer brake pad and rotor life. Because the process treats the entire rotor, and is not just a surface application, it can never wear, even if you decide to have the rotors turned after extensive use. The treatment is also inexpensive, starting at $25 for treating a single light-duty truck rotor.

Yacoucci also told us that he has had lots of experience with brake rotors and treating them. "It's always good to start off with a high-quality rotor," he says. "Most of the rotors [are] made in the U.S.A. and Canada, and OEM quality replacement rotors are best."

PROJECT 55 | BIG BRAKE UPGRADE FOR LARGE-DIAMETER WHEELS AND TIRES

TIME: Three hours

TOOLS: Full socket set, jack, jack stands

TALENT: ★★★

APPLICABLE YEARS: Brake systems for all years, makes, and models of light trucks

TAB: $1,500–$3,000

TINWARE: Brake fluid, piston lube, and anti-seize spray will help rusty rotors to dislodge from the axle seating point.

TIP: Think about your complete braking system and consider doing all upgrades within the same project window.

PERFORMANCE GAIN:
Firm stopping power with larger tires. Better heat dissipation and braking performance when the brake system is hot.

COMPLEMENTARY PROJECT:
Upgrade to stainless-steel brake lines, upgrade brake calipers

Once the Titan was secured on the lift, the 35-inch-tall tires and 20-inch wheels were removed. *Courtney Halowell*

With the wheels and tires out of the way, the factory calipers are removed and tossed into the scrap pile. With the calipers out of the way, the rotors simply slide off of the hubs. *Courtney Halowell*

If you've picked up some of the recent issues of *Trucks*, you may have noticed a story on a CST suspension lift on a new Nissan Titan. And the owner found out in a hurry what kind of effect a set of 35-inch-tall tires and 20-inch wheels have on stock brakes. The stopping distance from 60 miles per hour got a bit longer, and it was like he had to learn how to drive his truck all over again.

In order to counteract the leverage effect of installing larger-diameter wheels and tires on factory brakes, we contacted Stillen about its AP brake system for the Nissan Titan pickups. The reason we are fans of big brake upgrades is because they decrease the effort it takes to stop your truck or SUV if you have installed large-diameter wheels and tires.

More specifically, the Stillen brake upgrade kit that we just installed has been developed to be compatible with the original equipment master cylinder and ABS system. Stillen's Brake Pros brake upgrade for the Nissan Titan, Armada, and Infiniti QX56 features 51mm dual-piston calipers, made of steel for added stiffness, and massive 14-inch, two-piece, cross-drilled and slotted rotors. The kit comes complete with high-performance brake pads, DOT approved stainless-steel brake lines, and all the necessary hardware for installation.

Due to the massive size of the 14-inch, two-piece discs and calipers, this kit requires 18-inch or larger wheels. Don't worry: the factory Nissan 18-inch wheels will accommodate this kit. And we followed along as one of Stillen's technicians installed this kit on our tech-mule Titan.

After the kit was installed, the Titan actually stopped in a shorter distance than it did right off the dealership's lot—and that's with a wheel and tire combination that is significantly larger and heavier than the factory wheels and tires! But don't take our word for it; feel free to contact Stillen using the information in the resources section for all the specific data about its brake systems and the type of performance increases you can expect to gain by installing one of Stillen's kits on your truck.

Because of the size of the new brake rotors, the factory dust shields have to be trimmed using a pair of sheetmetal shears. *Courtney Halowell*

After the dust shields are trimmed, the new rotors can be easily slipped over the factory Nissan hubs. *Courtney Halowell*

Brake Pros calipers are bolted up to the spindle using the same mounting points that were used by the factory calipers. *Courtney Halowell*

New caliper bolts are torqued to Stillen's specifications. *Courtney Halowell*

The provided brake lines are then installed between the factory hard lines and the new Brake Pros caliper. *Courtney Halowell*

With all of the new parts installed, the front brakes on our tech-mule Titan are really starting to look like they could actually stop those big wheels and tires. *Courtney Halowell*

The stickers that denote what side of the truck the rotors are for are then removed so they don't gunk up the new pads. *Courtney Halowell*

And the next step of the installation is to bleed all of the air out of the brake system. After the pedal is feeling solid and all of the air is out of the brake system, the wheels and tires can be reinstalled. *Courtney Halowell*

TIME: Three hours

TOOLS: Full socket set, screwdrivers, jack, jack stands, gloves

TALENT: ★★★ (Mechanical competency required—this is a major safety item.)

APPLICABLE YEARS: Brake systems for all years, makes, and models of light trucks

TAB: $600

TINWARE: Gloves, drop cloth, anti-seize spray

TIP: Spray anti-seize compound between the wheel hub and brake rotor to make removal easier.

PERFORMANCE GAIN:
Greater stopping power, especially for larger tires/wheels

COMPLEMENTARY PROJECT:
Stainless-steel brake lines

To start the disassembly process, we removed the stock calipers using a T-55 Torx-head socket. Once they were removed, we supported them with a hook. Make sure never to support the caliper by the brake line; it will break. Next comes the caliper bracket itself. *Kevin Whipps*

The new rotors are side specific, and they're labeled L and R for convenience. They slide right in place of the old, small stockers. We used a spare lug to hold the rotor in place. This will make bolting on the new caliper bracket a lot easier. *Kevin Whipps*

The new brake pads we purchased for the install included new hardware, so we installed the new hardware on to the new caliper adapters. *Kevin Whipps*

Everyone wants big wheels. It seems like nowadays you can't go anywhere without seeing a set of 24s on a Yukon, and with sizes getting bigger and bigger every day, it seems like this trend is here to stay.

Often overlooked, however, is the problem that comes with big wheels—that is, a lack of adequate stopping power. Ever seen 26s on an Escalade? Notice how those little, tiny rotors look behind that mammoth roller? Just imagine trying to stop the extra 100 pounds per corner with that puny rotor, and you can imagine what's going on every day on custom trucks all across the country.

Baer Brakes make high-quality big brake kits and six-piston calipers that'll make your high-performance machine stop on a dime. Those kits, although the best of the best, come with a pretty high price tag that can be a little daunting. Fortunately for us, Baer realized this and came up with the new Eradispeed line of rotors.

Eradispeed rotors are the same high-quality cross-drilled and slotted rotors that you can get with their full kits, but they use the stock calipers. They come in a few different types; Eradispeed and Eradispeed Plus use the stock diameter rotors, but

they're slotted and cross-drilled. They match right up with the factory bracketry, no problems. The Eradispeed Plus One and Plus Two models also use factory calipers but include adaptors to mount the new, larger rotors on the spindle. Basically you get the look and advantage of a larger-diameter rotor, but you get to keep your stock hardware. It's a great compromise for those who aren't able to shell out the ducats for new calipers but want to keep their truck safe in the end.

The new caliper adapters bolt on using the same hardware as stock. It's a bit easier to install the outward facing brake pad first; otherwise it can take a bit of work to get it in there. *Kevin Whipps*

Then we installed the inner brake pad, using lots of the lubricant included with our new ceramic pads. The calipers are bolted back on using the stock hardware. You may have to pull the brake line through the stock bracket a bit to gain some room as well. *Kevin Whipps*

Much, much better! Both cosmetically and in terms of stopping performance. *Kevin Whipps*

The stock rear calipers come off the same way as the front, except you may have to use a wrench to hold one of the bolts in place. *Kevin Whipps*

We used an 18mm wrench to take off the caliper brackets. *Kevin Whipps*

After sliding off the old rotors, we slid on the new ones. They're marked so that the arrow points toward the rotation of the wheel, so make sure you use the right side. *Kevin Whipps*

We installed the new caliper brackets the same way as the stockers and installed the new ceramic brake pads at the same time. *Kevin Whipps*

The calipers are installed the reverse of removal, but this time we didn't have to mess with the brake line at all. Now, all that's left is to follow the break-in instructions and we're good to go! *Kevin Whipps*

TIME: Two hours

TOOLS: Full socket set, screwdriver, jack, jack stands

TALENT: ★★

APPLICABLE YEARS: Brake systems for all years, makes, and models of light trucks

TAB: About $700

TINWARE: N/A

TIP: Read instructions several times before the install. Make sure you are familiar with the procedure.

PERFORMANCE GAIN:
Increased stopping power, killer looks with open wheel

COMPLEMENTARY PROJECT:
New tires and wheels

PERFORMANCE BRAKES

Raise the front wheels off the ground and support the front suspension according to the vehicle manufacturer's instructions and remove the wheel. Remove the two bolts that hold the stock caliper-mounting bracket to the spindle. *T. J. Miller*

With the bolts removed, simply lift off the bracket and stock caliper as one unit. Next, remove the cotter pin and the lock ring to allow access to the nut that holds the rotor and hub to the spindle. *T. J. Miller*

Some people have an obsession with brake upgrades. There are a few reasons for that, like the fact that a big brake upgrade is one of the few true performance modifications that can be installed on a truck that actually increases safety. A power adder isn't going to help you stop in any shorter distance when a big rig driver decides to turn out of a driveway right in front of you. A high-end audio and video system won't help to keep your brakes cool and operating properly when you are coming down a curvy mountain road and your family is riding along and your trailer is in tow.

Big diameter brake upgrades also counteract the leverage effect that installing larger-diameter wheels and tires has on factory brakes. Big brake upgrades decrease the effort it takes to stop your truck or SUV in bumper-to-bumper traffic—especially if you have installed large-diameter wheels and tires. And on top of all of those added safety benefits, nothing looks cooler than when you see a truck with 20-inch or larger wheels and the inside of the wheel is just stuffed full of brake.

Follow along as the crew up at Wilwood installs one of the company's new Big Brake kits for 2004 and newer Ford F-150s

(P/N 140-9072). The kit comes with Wilwood's forged six-piston calipers, Wilwood brake pads, machined aluminum hats, 16-inch GT directional vane rotors, new hub assemblies, mounting brackets, and hardware. The stainless braided brake hoses and fittings are available from Wilwood, but because a lot of trucks have lift kits or lowering kits they have to be measured for the individual application and ordered separately.

And remember, only persons experienced in the installation and proper operation of disc brake systems should perform installation of this kit. Before installation begins, please read the complete procedure thoroughly to familiarize yourself with the process to ensure a trouble-free installation.

An air impact is used to remove the hub nut. It takes a little effort, but trust us, the hub nut will eventually come off. Save the hub nut for use during reassembly. Once the nut is off, the hub and rotor assembly simply slides off the spindle. Thoroughly clean and de-grease the spindles while removing any nicks or burrs. Also the factory backing plate can be removed and added to the pile of factory parts that aren't going to be reused. *T. J. Miller*

Slide the new hub assembly into place and secure with original hub nut. Reinstall the hub nut retainer and a new cotter key to hold it in place. Torque the hub nut to the manufacturer's specification. *T. J. Miller*

The caliper-mounting bracket assembly should be installed first with clean, dry threads on the mounting bolts. Install the bracket from the outboard side of the spindle by sliding the stock bolt through from the back side. Place shim washer between the bracket and the spindle. The bracket must tighten squarely against the side of the spindle body. *T. J. Miller*

The hat is bolted to the rotor, and the new assembly is slid on to the spindle. Check to be sure the hat seats squarely against the hub. Install a couple of lug nuts (finger tighten) to keep the rotor/hat assembly in place while continuing with the installation. *T. J. Miller*

The new 90 degree fittings are installed into the back of the calipers before they are installed. The supplied washers are slipped over each preinstalled stud on the caliper-mounting bracket before the caliper is slipped into place over the studs and rotors. Then the washer and locknut are installed to hold the caliper in place. The caliper bleed screws should be pointing up. *T. J. Miller*

Remove the two caliper center bridge pad retainer bolts, nuts, tubes, and anti-rattle clips and slide the brake pads into place. They should install easily without interference. *T. J. Miller*

Check that the outside radius of the brake pad is aligned with the outside diameter radius of the rotor face. Add or subtract shims between the calipers and the mount bracket to gain the proper alignment. Once proper alignment is achieved, reinstall the hardware that holds the pads into the caliper. *T. J. Miller*

OEM rubber brake hoses will not adapt to Wilwood calipers and should not be used. The caliper inlet fitting is a ⅛-27 NPT. Use steel adapter fittings at the caliper and a long enough steel braided line to allow for full suspension travel and turning radius, lock to lock. Carefully route lines to not allow contact with moving suspension, brake, or wheel components. *T. J. Miller*

159

TIME: Three hours

TOOLS: Full socket set and hand tools, floor jack, jack stands

TALENT: ★★★

APPLICABLE YEARS: All makes and models

TAB: $120 per wheel including brake pads

TINWARE: Gloves, drop cloth, mallet, anti-seize spray

TIP: N/A

PERFORMANCE GAIN:
Better braking in all weather, load, and driving conditions

COMPLEMENTARY PROJECT:
Consider replacing shocks if mileage and wear are indicative.

PERFORMANCE BRAKES

Remove both front wheels and set aside. These factory rotors endured more than 65,000 miles on a 2003 F-150. They served well, but would have to be turned and . . . well, it was time for them to go.

Those setups that are larger than stock tire/wheel combinations often cry out for a brake upgrade. Those wheels weigh significantly more and take more braking power to stop the momentum of your truck, load, and extra rolling mass that huge tires bring with them. But many of us, whether we own 4x4s or not, drive our rigs every day, and improved braking is a component of performance all of us can appreciate.

Power Slot rotors are an economic- and performance-based option for you to consider if you need more braking capability. If you want better braking and you don't fully require larger-than-stock rotors or four-piston brake calipers, then consider Power Slot as a solid option. You can also go up in rotor size with Power Slot Plus, but the point of this install is to show you how quick and efficiently you can upgrade your brake system and gain that "slotted" rotor look on your vehicle.

Power Slot brake rotors and Hawk HPS and LTS brake pads are quality engineered and designed to be direct factory replacement rotors of the same diameter. Power Slot rotors will fit in your stock-diameter wheels and offer you increased stopping power in towing, pulling, heavy loads, and daily driving. Hawk

brake pads include benefits such as low dust levels and silent operation. Plus, the pads are easy on rotors and capable of powerful friction, and they bite under any temperature or load conditions.

Those rotor slots serve several functions. Slotted rotors look cool, but they also serve to help the brake pads bite and manage heat. They evacuate brake dust and gases formed as the brake pad wears. Called Vacu-slots, the slots channel-out water and moisture in wet driving conditions as well as provide "bite" for the pads in all weather. Slots are machined to the minimum depth so that when slots vanish, it's time for new rotors.

If you have the confidence and ability to deal with your brake system, installing new rotors and pads that work with your factory brake calipers should be completed in just a few hours. Prices vary, depending upon your source, but you can expect to invest about $120 per wheel with rotors and brake pads. Cost is kept down because you are using your factory calipers and basically installing new rotors and pads.

And basic it is. After a short break-in period recommended by Power Slot to allow the pads to seat on the rotors, braking performance is markedly improved. The break-in simply entails taking the vehicle up to 30 mph and applying the binders until a full stop. Then one or two runs from 50 mph to zero, and you're done. In day-to-day commuting traffic, you might not tell much difference between the factory setup and Power Slots. You can sense the stopping power in rapid slow-downs at freeway speeds and when the truck bed is loaded down with some weight. It's a positive braking action that assures you the truck is scrubbing off speed and will stop you if you need to stop.

We worked with Custom Motorsports and Advantage Performance Center for this install. Both organizations are based in Riverside, California, and serve the light truck and SUV community. With SEMA around the corner, Advantage Performance had time to accommodate only the front rotor install. Lane and Ryan of Custom Motorsports handled the rear rotors.

Bolt up brake caliper bracket.

Remove two brake caliper anchor bolts, set aside, and gently remove brake caliper from the brake rotor. It helps to fashion an S-hook to hang the factory brake calipers on as you prepare to install the Power Slot rotors. Hanging calipers on an S-hook helps to support them while still attached to the brake lines. Remove dust cover, take out cotter pin, and remove spindle nut. As you remove brake rotor, gently catch the inside bearing to dislodge it from its seating inside the front rotor bearing. You will reuse this bearing assembly, so treat it gingerly.

Remove caliper assembly in order to load up new brake pads. Rent or purchase caliper spreader to compress pistons and permit install of fresh brake pads. Position new brake pad into brake bracket.

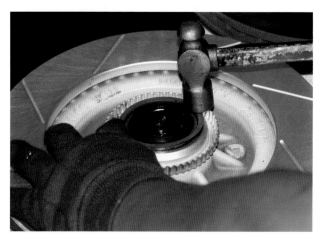

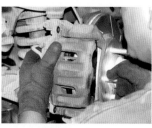

Replace brake caliper assembly on to brake bracket. Bolt down caliper assembly to caliper bracket, and you are finished.

Fully lubricate bearings and rotor cavity with fresh bearing grease. Tap bearing in to seat on new rotors.

Here's the complete installation of Power Slot brake rotors and Hawk Performance brake pads.

Install Power Slot rotor on to spindle. Replace spindle nut and *always* use a new cotter pin. Tap on dust cover.

PERFORMANCE BRAKES

DIESEL

After the factory boost tubes have been removed, the top radiator support must be removed. After unbolting it, it will probably require pry bars to remove it.

TIME: 10 minutes

 TOOLS: N/A

 TALENT: ★

 APPLICABLE YEARS: Check with TS Performance for your specific year/model Cummins.

 TAB: $600

 TINWARE: N/A

 TIP: TS Performance offers programmers for Ford, Dodge, Chevy.

 PERFORMANCE GAIN:
Increased horsepower, torque, and towing capability

COMPLEMENTARY PROJECT:
Project can be enhanced with performance exhaust and intake systems.

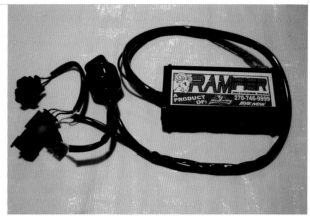

Would you believe that there is 100-plus horsepower in this little box that takes less than 10 minutes to install?

The Dodge Ram 2500 has an updated Cummins engine called the 600. Our test vehicle was equipped with one, and we opted to test the TS Performance Ramifier on it.

If you are part of the growing population of truck owners who take their diesel trucks' performance seriously, then you know the benefits that a good programmer can deliver. In many instances 80–100-plus horsepower is possible with the right type of programming. But just like anything else, there are differences in programs that affect various areas of the engine's power band determining overall performance.

One of the newest programmers to reach the market is the Ramifier, for the Dodge Ram, equipped with the newest version of the Cummins diesel engine, called the 600. These are found on 2004 and 2004½-model year Rams and TS Performance claims that it produces 100-plus horsepower by simply plugging in the module.

We found the Ramifier simple to install as it plugs into two sensors located on the engine's intake manifold. The Ramifier alters fuel pressures that deliver additional fuel with added boost. According to Dennis Perry at TS Performance, the factory fuel rails are capable of handling 29,000 psi of fuel and the Ramifier does not reach those levels to increase the

fuel delivery. Perry explains that the Ramifier reprograms the map sensor signal so that it thinks it is at a different boost level. The sensor then adjusts injection timing to deliver the proper amount of fuel. This is a way that the company avoids raising fuel pressures beyond a safe limit.

We installed the Ramifier in a 2004 Ram equipped with the new 600 Cummins engine. The results were immediately noticeable, and during our test we were able to improve our 0–60 mph times by nearly three seconds and our quarter-mile acceleration times by nearly two seconds.

During our baseline tests, we ran an average of three passes and our 0–60 mph average in stock trim, netted 9.05 seconds. The Ram ran the quarter-mile in 17.19 seconds at 80.1 mph. After plugging in the Ramifier, we drove the vehicle so that the programming would take full effect. We then ran our 0–60 mph test and averaged 6.68 seconds, and our quarter-mile times lowered to 15.52 seconds at 91.3 mph.

The TS Performance Ramifier retails for around $595, and you must be specific as to which Cummins engine your truck is equipped with.

The Cummins 600 engine is installed on 2004 and 2004 ½–model Ram trucks. The engine has different fuel timing calibrations and requires a different programmer than the standard Cummins engine on earlier year models.

These two plugs are removed, and the Ramifier simply connects in between the sensors and the wiring harness. A piece of Velcro holds the Ramifier box to the top of the fuse box, and the installation is complete.

TIME: One hour

 TOOLS: N/A

 TALENT: ★

 APPLICABLE YEARS: Modules for all years, makes, and models of light trucks

 TAB: $500–$800, depending on whether one Edge program component or both are project considerations

 TINWARE: N/A

 TIP: No experience needed for this project, but you do want to follow directions.

PERFORMANCE GAIN:
Increased performance throughout power range

COMPLEMENTARY PROJECT:
Boost and EGT gauges

Attitude installation begins by selecting a visible, reachable mounting location. The kit's swivel arm provides flexible mounting options. Edge also offers an optional pillar-pod mount. The Attitude's wiring cable is routed along the A-pillar weather stripping and into the engine compartment through the slot near the hood hinge.

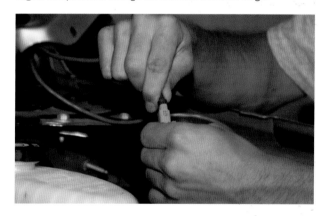

Under the hood, plug the Attitude's cable to the Juice's green connector. Pulling back the front-passenger-side wheelwell splash shield provides convenient access to the exhaust manifold.

ENGINE MODULE

The system's Juice power module mounts under the hood and intercepts signals between the truck's PCM and the engine, constantly optimizing fueling and timing based on the selected power level. The Juice is available as a stand-alone item, although this configuration has only four power levels (maxing out at 90 horsepower and 200 lb-ft torque).

Edge highly recommends adding aftermarket gauges for turbo boost and exhaust gas temperature (EGT) when making any diesel-performance modification. Upgrading to the Edge Attitude provides these functions and much more for only slightly more than the cost of aftermarket gauges. Plus, the Attitude gives the Juice module a fifth power mode and allows the driver to switch between levels on the fly.

DIESEL

By now, most later-model diesel owners know their trucks can easily get 50 percent more horsepower simply by adding a performance module or reprogramming their trucks' Powertrain Control Module (PCM). Making power involves lengthening the fuel-injector pulse, and the diesel engine will continue to pump out power as fueling is increased. But this power is worthless unless it can reliably spin the rest of the drivetrain—high exhaust gas temperatures (EGTs) produced by aggressive fueling require decelerating to avoid engine damage.

Aftermarket manufacturers have mastered the art of altering the factory computer signals to make impressive gains. The main differences among diesel power systems are the additional features and safeguards that permit this power to get to the ground.

Edge Products' Juice With Attitude is one of the most fully featured systems currently on the market. In addition to offering five different power levels tailored to varying driving conditions, the Juice With Attitude monitors powertrain vitals and offers the driver a variety of features that improve performance and reliability.

ATTITUDE POWERTRAIN MONITORING

The Attitude uses a backlit LCD screen to display a variety of powertrain-related information. The driver can select up to four parameters to be displayed at the same time, digitally or as bar graphs that include the following:

Turbo boost
EGT
Actual speed
Throttle position
RPM
Torque converter clutch status
Percent engine load
Transmission clutch slippage
Current gear
Percent back down due to high EGT

SAFEGUARDS AND WARNINGS

The Juice With Attitude system allows the appropriate amount of power to be used as much of the time as possible. For start-up reliability, the Edge system doesn't add fueling or timing while the engine temperature is below 160 degrees F. At 160 degrees F, the Juice module begins delivering fuel at 50 percent of the calculated additional fuel available. The fueling percentage increases as the engine warms up. Once

Edge recommends mounting the EGT probe upstream of the turbo for an accurate reading.

Drill a 5⁄16-inch or a 21⁄64-inch hole. Dipping the drill bit in grease will help trap the metal shavings.

Tap the hole with a 1⁄8-inch NPT tap. Edge then recommends running the engine at idle for 10 to 15 minutes to blow out any small metal shavings. Screw in the kit's fitting.

the engine reaches 174 degrees F, the Juice With Attitude begins delivering 100 percent of the calculated additional fuel and begins to modify timing.

The Attitude also has four safeguard/alert features, EGT included. Edge presets the EGT limit at 1,350 degrees F, but the user can reprogram the Attitude for a different temperature and also for how many minutes to get the exhaust gas temperature back down. Once EGT reaches the specified threshold, the Attitude begins defueling the engine. The defueling percentage is displayed on the monitor and a warning sounds.

Edge says that 1,350 degrees is the realistic consistent limit for a Duramax. Because engine stress is affected by both temperature and time, brief spikes above the limit are much less dangerous than extended pulls above the threshold.

The other alerts and their default values (all of which can be reprogrammed or turned off) include:

Boost—25.0 psi
Speed—70 mph
Engine Temp—210 degrees

Further, the Attitude's low boost fueling adjustment allows five sublevels of "smoke control" within each power level. Sublevel one emits the least smoke and is California Air Resources Board (CARB) friendly; sublevel five is the most responsive but makes the most smoke.

AUTO TRANS CONSIDERATIONS

Edge also controls the Allison transmission to maximize the usable power—and to increase transmission life. The Juice-Attitude monitors the torque converter and automatically defuels when converter slippage is detected. The user can apply this feature to all locked shifts, to only fourth and fifth gear-locked shifts, or can even disable defueling (possibly increasing transmission wear). Percentage of torque converter and trans clutch slippage is displayed on the Attitude's screen. The overall result is smooth torque transfer.

Because GM's Delphi PCM includes adaptive auto-trans learning, shifting is typically rough immediately after installing the Edge system. The trans must be "retaught" by shifting through each gear 20 to 30 times in the course of 100 to 200 miles in the Edge power mode that'll be used most often.

Recommended power modes for various driving conditions are listed later. When towing, however, Edge recommends that the trans always be put in Tow/Haul mode. This provides torque converter lockup in gears two through five, reducing transmission heat. In the process, the shift rpm threshold is raised; Edge advocates engine rpm above 1,800 whenever possible while towing.

Increased Juice-Attitude power also limits auto-trans shifting while towing. The Duramax is able to maintain a higher gear longer, so gear "hunting" is reduced. This helps increase fuel economy too.

POWER LEVELS

Level 1 (40 hp/100 lb-ft): Good for increasing fuel economy and for towing most trailer weights. For trailer weights more than 14,000 pounds GVW on grades more than 6 percent, Edge recommends switching to the stock power level to minimize EGTs.

Level 2 (60 hp/120 lb-ft): Good for increasing fuel economy and for towing trailers weighing less than 6,000 pounds.

Level 3 (75 hp/170 lb-ft): Not recommended for towing, this

DIESEL

is a good level for improving overall drivability and performance of a stock Duramax motor.

Level 4 (90 hp/200 lb-ft): Not recommended for towing or for use on a stock vehicle, this level helps maximize other aftermarket upgrades such as a cold-air intake and performance exhaust system.

Level 5 (125 hp/240 lb-ft): This competition level is designed for use with upgraded drivetrains. It also matches fueling to other engine enhancements such as modified fuel injectors and nonfactory turbos. On a stock truck, it is possible to overstress the engine and transmission while driving in levels four and five.

RECORDING/DATA-LOGGING

Another standout feature is the Attitude's ability to record and store performance and engine values. Performance-wise, Edge taps into the vehicle's speed sensor to capture 0–60 mph and quarter-mile acceleration times (seconds and top speed). The Attitude can also be programmed for nonstock tire diameters, modifying the factory speed sensor to display actual road speed. Other maximum values that can be stored are engine temp, back-down percentage, rpm, and top speed.

FACTORY WARRANTY CONCERNS

Edge reminds its customers that warranty work can't be denied solely because of aftermarket components—the aftermarket part must be responsible for the factory-component failure. Still, Edge recommends always disconnecting and removing the module and monitor before taking the vehicle to the dealer so that the Juice Attitude won't interfere with diagnostic equipment. The system installs easily (see the accompanying photos and captions of the process on a 2004 LLY Duramax) and comes off even faster.

On a somewhat-related note, Edge doesn't recommend "stacking" any other chip or programmer with the Duramax Juice Attitude system. Those other modifications can override Edge's failsafe features.

Diesel performance is currently the hottest segment of the noncosmetic automotive aftermarket. Computer-controlled diesels in light-duty trucks offer enormous performance potential. As demonstrated by the Edge Juice Attitude system, the Duramax can reliably handle dramatic improvements in acceleration and towing power.

Connect the EGT probe to the Juice's connections using the provided screws and self-locking nuts. Then use zip-ties to secure all Edge wiring away from hot and moving parts.

HOT JUICE: UP TO 150 MORE HP/350 LB-FT FOR COMPETITION

Just in case 120 extra Duramax HP and 240 lb-ft of torque aren't enough, Edge Products offers race-ready Hot Juice modules. A 2001–2004 LB7 Hot Juice has been available for a while, and Edge was planning to release an LLY application as this publication went to press.

Edge's Hot Juice uses an even more aggressive fuel curve than the regular Juice. Although the two boxes look the same, the Hot Juice is programmed for diesel drag racing instead of street use—for short bursts of power in Duramaxes that have extensive aftermarket powertrain upgrades.

"We could make a system that produces even more power, but the high EGTs that much fuel and timing produce would blow head gaskets or possibly grenade pistons," says Aaron Stewart, Edge's technical services director. "That's why we recommend that the Hot Juice module always be used with the Attitude controller to defuel the engine before EGTs get too high."

Edge requires its Hot Juice customers to sign a waiver absolving the company from any powertrain damage claims. "We can basically guarantee that the Hot Juice will do transmission damage if the system is run in its upper power levels for extended periods of time," says Stewart.

The existing LB7 Duramax Hot Juice With Attitude offers five power levels: 60 hp/180 lb-ft, 75/220, 90/250, 125/325, and 150/350. Preliminary LLY testing has shown these levels: 50/120, 70/170, 90/200, 120/240, and 145/280.

Edge has an upgrade program that allows customers to exchange an existing Duramax Juice box for a Hot Juice. Or the Hot Juice With Attitude can be purchased outright by adventurous Duramax owners who are willing to sign the waiver and pay about $250 more for the aggressive programming compared to the standard Juice Attitude system.

Insert the EGT probe and tighten its nut to the manifold fitting's threads.

DIESEL

TIME: Eight hours—depending on which components are installed

TOOLS: Full socket set, jack, jack stands, Sawzall, saw blades, gloves

TALENT: ★★

APPLICABLE YEARS: Gale Banks has diesel performance parts for mid-to-late-model Ford, Dodge, and Chevy pickup trucks.

TAB: $600 for speed-loader; $1,200 for inter-cooler/intake; $800 for exhaust

TINWARE: Safety goggles, gloves, drop cloth

TIP: Use new nuts, bolts, washers, and cotter pin.

PERFORMANCE GAIN:
Better performance throughout power range

COMPLEMENTARY PROJECT:
Array of diesel specific gauges, even if redundant

Banks' Big Hoss bundle adds a new Techni-Cooler intercooler, larger boost hoses, and High-Ram intake to its hugely successful Six-Gun bundle. The combination provides 10 percent more charge density roughly translating into 10 percent more horsepower than the Six-Gun bundle.

Removal of the factory boost tubes is the first step to more power. After the factory boost tubes have been removed, the top radiator support must be removed. After unbolting it, it will probably require pry bars to remove it.

A television show got wind of the amazing horsepower and torque that Gale Banks Engineering was pulling out of diesel trucks with its Six-Gun diesel tuner bundles and issued a challenge to Banks: "Beat a new Mustang GT with one of your hotted-up diesels." Banks, of course, jumped at the challenge to prove his company's engineering mettle and installed an off-the-shelf Six-Gun bundle on an otherwise stock 2003 Ford F-250 crew-cab pickup, which had a 6.0-liter Power Stroke Super Duty engine. Banks was ready when the crew showed up at Banks' headquarters in Azusa, California, with a 2004 4.6-liter V-8 Mustang GT. The caravan of vehicles drove the three miles or so to Irwindale Dragstrip, one of southern California's newest and best eighth-mile drag strips, to shoot it out.

To keep everything above board, the Irwindale Dragstrip staff closely monitored the racing. The Banks Six-Gun bundle–equipped F-250 Super Duty legitimately beat the Mustang GT. Nine times in a row. And it's recorded on film for all the world to see.

The truck left the starting line the same way every time—

with a little cloud of tire smoke—and Bam! It was gone. The truck's best run was a 9.93 @ 77.35 mph while the Mustang GT managed a best run of 9.98 seconds @ 76.07 mph. Yeah, it was close. Until you factor in the weight and aerodynamic differences. The truck weighed in at 6,860 pounds—almost double the weight of the Mustang GT's, 3,500 pounds. Almost double! Considering this, it was a slaughter.

Ford's 6.0-liter Power Stroke diesel-powered trucks are, without a doubt, the company's best ever. Brought to market in 2003, Ford put its own spin on variable-geometry turbocharging and delivered the new Power Stroke V-8 diesels with the new Electronic Variable Response Turbocharging (EVRT) system. EVRT turbos have variable vanes inside that allow the turbocharger to react like a small turbocharger at low rpms and like a larger turbo at higher rpms. It makes the truck a pleasure to drive at both low speeds and freeway speeds.

Banks' engineers have tested many of Ford's 6.0-liter Power Stroke diesels on their chassis and engine dynamometers. They know everything about them. They've learned that, from the factory, real-wheel horsepower peaks at 269, and torque at 467 lb-ft. They've also learned that, although it's a great truck, Ford left plenty of room for improvement in the horsepower and torque departments. Maybe the Blue Oval folks did that to make Gale Banks happy, or maybe they did it to save production costs.

Although Ford did a pretty good job on the air intake side of things, Banks was able to make huge gains in fuel delivery and exhaust flow. The Banks crew spent more than a year designing, engineering, and testing its Six-Gun bundle before releasing it to the public, and it was worth the wait: best gains of 138 additional rear-wheel horsepower at 3,600 rpm and 231 lb-ft of rear-wheel torque at 2,400 rpm were the results.

Banks technician Kevin Hannah is shown removing the stock intercooler. Banks' Big Hoss bundle can be installed by a mechanically competent enthusiast and a buddy in about a weekend.

To make room for its High-Ram intake, Banks includes a template with its Big Hoss bundle to show where to cut the plastic fan shroud. Hannah is shown using a cutting wheel to neatly trim the plastic shroud. With the factory components out of the way, Hannah can begin installing the Big Hoss bundle components. With the Techni-Cooler in place, Hannah replaces the boost tubes with the larger Banks boost tubes.

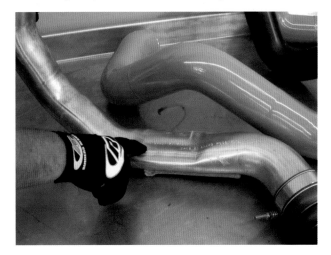

Factory boost tubes often have crimps or flattened areas to provide clearance for accessories. This reduces airflow considerably. Banks' boost tubes are engineered from larger-diameter tubing that has a constant diameter (no flat spots) for increased airflow. After the passenger battery has been removed, this bracket requires trimming to make room for the larger boost tube on the right side. The unused bracket is a leftover from the coolant overflow tank on earlier models. The coolant overflow tank on 6.0-liter Power Stroke diesel models was moved to a different location, but the bracket remains, so there is no problem with trimming it. Banks includes this spacer for under the left-side battery box. The spacer neatly moves the battery box up and away from the larger left-side boost tube.

With the Techni-Cooler, boost tubes, and High-Ram in place, Hannah will move under the truck to begin installing Banks Monster exhaust system.

To be able to accurately measure exhaust gas temperatures, a bung must be drilled and tapped into the left-side exhaust manifold for the thermocouple probe. Detailed instructions for this process are available in the Six-Gun owner's manual. It is highly recommended that the exhaust manifold be removed for this process as *any* metal shavings can do catastrophic damage to the turbocharger. After drilling and tapping the exhaust manifold, it should be thoroughly cleaned and blown out with air to remove all traces of metal shavings.

The next step is to install the thermocouple probe into the previously installed bung in the exhaust manifold. This will provide accurate exhaust gas temperatures to the Six-Gun and DynaFact pyrometer gauge. The factory catalytic converter is the only part of the stock exhaust that is not replaced with Monster exhaust pipes. After the head pipe is installed, the factory converter can be replaced. After installing the Banks Monster muffler, Hannah has only the tailpipe and tailpipe tip to install before moving on to installing the Six-Gun diesel tuner and Speed-Loader upgrade and DynaFact gauges. Banks' Six-Gun diesel tuner mounts under the hood on the driver-side inner fender on 2003–2004 Ford 6.0-Liter Power Stroke diesel models (consult Banks' Six-Gun diesel tuner owner's manual for information on mounting the Six-Gun on 2005 models). Hannah will remove a small clip that attaches the hood latch cable to the inner fender, and then push the cable out of the way to clear a spot for the Six-Gun.

How does a peak of 384 rear-wheel horsepower and 691 lb-ft of torque at the rear wheels sound? This is 58 percent more horsepower and 51 percent more torque! The Six-Gun bundle has the power to turn the Super Duty from a mild-mannered work truck into a weekend track warrior and everything in between. It comes with a Six-Gun diesel tuner that provides six levels of horsepower improvements at the turn of a knob. With each click, you gain 20 percent more power.

So, how is all of this power made? Well, it starts with the Six-Gun diesel tuner, which adjusts not just one, but three parameters—fuel injection pulse width, fuel timing, and fuel pressure. By tuning all three parameters, it can provide more horsepower and torque without overturning any one parameter. As of press time, we couldn't find another diesel tuner that tunes all three parameters—most tune fuel pressure or pulse width alone.

Banks' software suite, dubbed AutoRate, adds five safety features to the Six-Gun diesel tuner. These include turbocharger overspeed protection, transmission shift protection, converter clutch lockup protection, cold engine protection, and high coolant temperature protection. This is a lot of safety packed into one unit, and it says a lot for peace of mind.

Banks also includes a Speed-Loader upgrade in its Six-Gun bundle. When the Speed-Loader is plugged into the Six-Gun, it increases the power output by another 23 hp and 25 lb-ft of torque. It's like turning the Six-Gun up to level 7. Another great thing the Speed-Loader does is to back off on fuel delivery when exhaust gas temperatures (EGTs) reach a preset temperature (1,400 degrees F on the Ford 6.0-liter Power Stroke diesel).

As you probably know, diesel engines run more efficiently and economically when exhaust gas temperature is kept low. It's important to keep an eye on it so you can ease up on the throttle to bring your EGT back down. Without a gauge, it's a guessing game whether EGTs are high, low, or normal, so the Six-Gun bundle includes an electronic Banks DynaFact pyrometer that measures and displays EGTs. But remember, if you're running the Speed-Loader, you don't have to worry about it because the software will back off the fuel delivery for you.

Also included in the kit is an electronic boost gauge that measures turbocharger performance. Boost—or the amount of pressure above atmospheric pressure the turbocharger is building—is pretty easy to understand: the higher the number, the greater the performance. Banks' DynaFact boost gauge measures boost in pounds per square inch (psi). An under-the-dash mounting bracket holds both gauges and is included in the bundle. Other optional gauge mounts are available, including dash-top and A-pillar mounts.

Six-Gun bundles also include Monster exhaust systems that do their part to add power and reduce back pressure (according to Banks, up to 85 percent less back pressure in the Ford 6.0-liter Power Stroke application). Banks was also proud to point out that unique to this exhaust system is the 4-inch turbine outlet pipe. It removes the stock restriction from the turbo to the exhaust pipe and has a "resonating chamber" that gets rid of the screechy turbo noise. From there, 4-inch mandrel bent stainless-steel exhaust pipes replace the often semi-flattened, smaller-diameter factory pipes for greater exhaust airflow. Banks

Besides the large connector, which plugs into the powertrain control module (PCM), there are several wires that must be spliced into with "T-taps" (included). Banks provides detailed wiring installation instructions in its Six-Gun diesel tuner owner's manual. Banks provides a template for locating its Six-Gun control switch knob on the Ford's dashboard. After installation, the Six-Gun control switch knob provides six levels of power at your fingertips.

Detailed wiring instructions to install Banks DynaFact electronic gauges are also in the Big Hoss bundle. Hannah is shown here buttoning up his installation on a customer's truck. After a quick test drive to make sure everything is working correctly, he will hand the keys back to the lucky Banks customer.

designed the Monster muffler with the specific requirements of diesel engines in mind: it has a straight-through design with an expansion chamber that eliminates the drone common to a lot of straight-through diesel mufflers. And it has a great sound. To finish it off, the system has a polished stainless-steel 5-inch exhaust tip, which is dual-walled to resist discoloring from exhaust heat.

Monster exhaust systems typically add 8 to 14 horsepower to a stock truck. Although this might not sound like much, this is honest, rear-wheel horsepower that would be quite noticeable. Where Monster exhausts really shine is when they are used with a Six-Gun diesel tuner, which provides the proper amount of fuel to go with the added airflow, as in this case. Their efficiency increases and the horsepower gained directly from the Monster Exhaust system probably becomes closer to 20 to 25 horsepower.

Since its Six-Gun bundle–equipped F-250 dusted the Mustang GT a few months ago, Banks released a new top-of-the-line system for the 6.0L: the Big Hoss bundle. It's based on the Six-Gun bundle but adds several new components engineered to provide a cooler, denser intake air for maximum power output—a new Banks Techni-Cooler intercooler, larger boost tubes, and a High Ram intake.

The Techni-Cooler for the 6.0-liter Power Stroke has a 20 percent larger core than the stock intercooler and is built entirely of aluminum for strength and durability (the stock intercooler has plastic side tanks). Banks Techni-Cooler has a high-flow tube-and-fin design, larger (3 1/8 inches) inlet and outlet, and comes with larger (3 1/2 inches) boost tubes for the most efficient airflow possible. Last, but not least, Banks includes a new cast-metal High Ram intake that features higher intake airflow due to the larger-than-stock chamber and 3 1/2-inch-diameter inlet.

Together, the Techni-Cooler, larger boost tubes, and High Ram intake take full advantage of Gale Banks' philosophy that "increasing charged air density increases power." According to Banks, these products combined produce roughly 10 percent more dense air charge. When you increase air density, the added increase in power is roughly the same percentage. So, in this case, the 10 percent increase in air density would directly translate into 10 percent more power. The 6.0L Powerstroke with a Big Hoss bundle, as tested on a chassis dyno, produces a whopping 156 more rear-wheel horsepower and 275 lb-ft more rear-wheel torque (versus 138 hp and 231 lb-ft with the Six-Gun bundle).

Given that much added power, you'll be able to hunt down the Mustang GTs in your own neighborhood and give them a run for their money. Follow along as we install one of Banks' new Big Hoss bundles on a 2004 Ford 6.0-liter Power Stroke diesel pickup.

DIESEL

PROJECT 62   IMPROVE YOUR DIESEL'S TOWING PERFORMANCE AND FUEL ECONOMY

 TIME: One hour

 TOOLS: Full socket set and hand tools

 TALENT: ★★

 APPLICABLE YEARS: All

 TAB: $250

 TINWARE: N/A

 TIP: Read and understand the instructions before you begin any project, including this one.

 PERFORMANCE GAIN:
Better cool air intake

COMPLEMENTARY PROJECT:
Large bore exhaust

DIESEL

Under the hood, the first thing to do in the disassembly of the factory air intake system was to remove the air temp sensor from the air box outlet. The hardware that attaches the air box to the core support and fender are removed. Next, the attachment collar that attaches the OEM air tube to the turbo inlet is removed. This bolt is kind of hard to reach. The easiest way to get to it is from the firewall side. Once the lower collar clamp is removed, the entire factory air intake assembly can be removed in one piece.

Leave the turbo inlet clamp in place on the inlet tube as the new S&B performance intake tube will attach directly to it like the factory one did.

The aftermarket performance air filter and intake market is serious business and—rightfully so—it should be. Performance begins with the air intake system. Companies such as S&B Filters, Inc. have spent years developing air filter kits for most makes and models of vehicles. Intense research, designing, and endless testing takes place for every filter design the company is challenged with producing. The goal isn't to just make a replacement filter for your truck. No, the challenge is to allow you, the consumer, to be able to easily install a replacement air intake system, which will definitely improve the towing, performance, and fuel economy of your truck.

One of the most difficult things for air filter system manufacturers to do is to convince consumers that just simply replacing the OEM air filter or system with an aftermarket version doesn't always guarantee the results they were looking for. Some kits are just to make the engine compartment look good. Some are aimed at making a vehicle perform well, based on experience on a totally different type of engine. As most know by now, each and every engine type has different breathing requirements. What works well for one doesn't necessarily work the same for another, different

application. This is where those companies that rely upon technical research and testing rise to the top and actually guarantee their products will work as advertised. Big money is spent to ensure that a product is better. After all, that is what you want, right?

Some of you might have never heard of S&B Filters. But there is a good chance you probably have used a filter they developed and manufactured. For more than 30 years, S&B Filters has been focused on supplying the most technically advanced high-performance filters on the market. A commitment to the racing community allowed the company to develop products that feature the incredibly high efficiency ratings and tremendous low airflow restrictions. S&B has succeeded at keeping its production capabilities on the front edge of technology, always focused on a goal of producing a high-performance air filter that tests better than any other manufacturer. Today the company is pushing other manufacturers to test to their high standards. One of the most important of these standards that S&B employs includes designing and testing to meet the ISO 5011 Air Filtration Test Standard. These tests reveal that S&B's filters meet OEM requirements for filtration yet greatly surpass the OEM filters in airflow through reduced restriction.

Although S&B has long and quietly been one of the major private label manufacturers recognized worldwide for air filter products, its goal today is to provide the company's intense research technology directly to the consumer with S&B's own line of performance kit. One of the more popular at the moment is S&B's diesel performance intake kits. Each kit features a washable, eight-layer premium cloth gauze filter to maximize airflow and filtration for diesel engines. A custom high-performance air box isolates the filter from engine heat, drawing in cooler outside air to boost engine performance. The design of the diesel intake system streamlines airflow, allowing the engine to ingest more air, which translates into more power. Diesel trucks generally are used in a dirty environment, which makes it that much more important that the filter system continue to provide clean air to the engine without sacrificing performance.

To show you just how easy it is to install one of S&B Filter's new diesel air intake packages, we visited the S&B manufacturing facility in Ontario, California, to document the installation of the diesel intake system into a Dodge Cummins diesel. The airflow

dyno results revealed that the S&B filter kit was nearly identical to the OEM diesel filter in its ability to filter out debris, while improving airflow by almost 40 percent! That translates to the ability for the Cummins engine to produce additional horsepower, without sacrificing quality air intake protection. Like what you have read so far? Good. Then check out the following photos which detail the step-by-step installation of the S&B Filter diesel performance kit for the Dodge Cummins diesel.

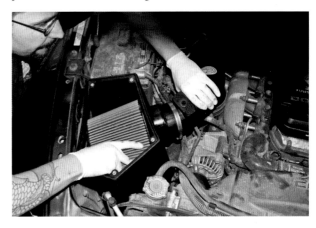

The exit end of the filter installs into the box with the exit end going through the box and sliding over the intake tube. A new stainless-steel clamp is then installed over where the air filter boot mates with the intake tube and then is tightened to secure the assembly. There is a small gap around the filter boot to accommodate the movement of the diesel engine while running.

Next, we tackle the easy installation of the S&B air box installation. This custom-made box was designed to house the more efficient S&B filter and fits perfectly into the original box location. The box even uses the factory mounting locations and installs with new, provided hardware. Over on the assembly bench, a provided rubber grommet is installed into the hole on the air box exit tube where the ATS will be mounted. The new S&B intake tube is a one-piece design. The tube installs similarly to the factory tube with one end fitting into the new air box and the other attaching to the turbo inlet. The new tube fits perfectly on to the turbo inlet where the OEM clamp is snugged down to hold the tube. You'll come back later in the installation and permanently tighten the clamp. Next comes the installation of the S&B air filter.

The new intake tube features a raised boss for the factory air temp sensor. The sensor is inserted into the tube and mounts just like it did on the factory tube.

Five stainless-steel screws with rubber washers are used to permanently attach the clear cover to the box.

There you have it: a quick and easy way to install the S&B diesel performance intake system on the Cummins diesel engine, an improved air filtration system that can be cleaned routinely, allowing the engine to take in more air, which equates to more power. And we all know—we can always use more power!

PROJECT 63 | INSTALL A TORQUE CONVERTER

TIME: Two hours

TOOLS: Full socket set, screwdrivers, jack, jack stands, transmission jack

TALENT: ★★★

APPLICABLE YEARS: Converters for most makes and models of light trucks

TAB: $1,000

TINWARE: Safety glasses, gloves, extra pair of hands, transmission fluid

TIP: Seating the new torque converter into place is crucial. Be certain you have it right.

PERFORMANCE GAIN:
Smooth acceleration and lower transmission temperatures

COMPLEMENTARY PROJECT:
Deep sump finned aluminum transmission pan.

DIESEL

The Ford 4R100 transmission in our truck was a rebuilt Ford unit, replaced sometime in the truck's life. The odometer read 86,000 miles, but there was no telling how many miles were on the transmission.

Step 1 was removal of the transmission wiring harness. Novice transmission folks should label the connectors to make certain they go back in the original places. Then, we removed the torque converter inspection cover and shifter mechanism from the side of the transmission. Remove the six torque-converter-to-flex-plate bolts. One bolt at a time can be accessed in this manner by turning over the engine with a crankshaft socket.

When you think about bolting on performance parts, typically items such as air intakes, exhaust, nitrous, and more come to mind. Rarely does the thought of a torque converter seem like a performance upgrade that will actually help your truck's acceleration and torque capacity. Yet, the right torque converter can actually demonstrate improvements that you can measure.

Torque converters are thought of as drag-racing items that allow your engine to freely rev up to the desired launch rpm before take-off. However, in truck applications, especially diesels, a performance torque converter can increase mileage, operate cooler, and provide additional torque to the ground.

So, what does it take to install one and how well do these converters perform? We asked TCI Automotive in Ashland, Mississippi, to help us with this question. TCI manufactures a line of truck converters that add performance and mileage, but we were not ready for the results that we achieved with this test. We opted to perform a TCI diesel truck torque converter swap to see the installation process and to conduct a before and after test on the truck. For this application, we also sought the help of

a reliable transmission installer, and we used Oliver's Transmissions in San Fernando, California. After the installation, the results were dramatic. We were able to shave two-tenths of a second off the truck's quarter-mile time and improved fuel economy by two miles per gallon. We also experienced an overall improved "feel" eliminating that slow-off-the-line diesel start-up according to Jeff Souter, owner of the 2002 F-350 Powerstroke diesel we tested.

TESTING THE BEAST

Our test began at Los Angeles County Raceway. In tests performed on the track, we netted a best of 17.20 seconds and 78.9

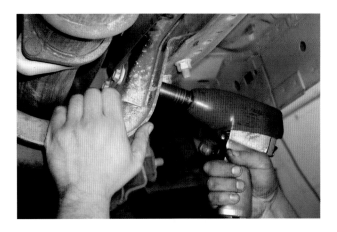

With the transmission supported, remove the entire crossmember. Next, remove the driveshaft, making certain not to lose the U-joint cups. This device holds the cups in place.

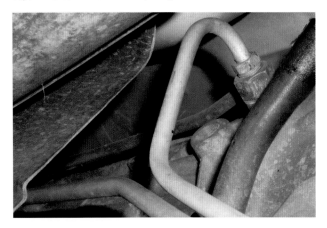

Above: Remove the oil cooler lines and plug them to avoid losing fluid.

Left: Remove the remaining transmission to engine bolts and lower the transmission with a transmission jack. Watch for this shield at the back of the transmission.

mph. Fuel mileage was approximately 18 mpg on an engine that had just recently turned its 86,000th mile. This was real world stuff from a well broken-in engine.

At Oliver's Transmission we began the tear down. Our first revelation was the fact that the truck was equipped with a Ford replacement transmission, the original unit having left the premises some time earlier in the life of the truck. No matter, according to Oliver, the process of removing the transmission was unchanged from any regular OE operation.

The TCI diesel torque converter we were installing is a heavy-duty unit incorporating a heavy-duty forged steel case in place of the factory thin walled unit. In addition, it features a steel stator unit, which is much stronger than the factory piece. Upgraded internal bearings and fully welded housing fins complete the high-performance enhancements.

OUT WITH THE OLD

Removing the transmission began by taking out a series of wiring harness clips that attach to the transmission. Most of the clips simply squeeze or pry off, the bigger picture here being the need to remember where everything goes to ensure it goes back together correctly. Using a socket wrench, we removed the shifter bracketing systems as well.

The driveshaft must be removed next, making certain not to lose the U-joint cups. A rear transmission cover was used to avoid losing fluid from the transmission. The hardest task of all (actually the entire process is not that hard) was removing the torque converter bolts. Once the torque converter inspection cover is off, you can move to remove one torque converter attachment bolt at a time. By turning the engine with a proper crankshaft socket (making sure the transmission is out of gear), the engine can be rotated and the torque converter turned so that each of the six diesel torque converter bolts can be reached. Remember, diesel torque converters have six bolts as opposed to gas engines, which use four bolts.

The Ford transmission used here weighs about 200 pounds, so a transmission jack is advised. Once the two transmission-cooler lines had been unhooked and plugged, the remaining transmission-to-engine bolts were removed. Being careful not to catch the thin metal shield at the rear passenger side of the transmission, the entire transmission was lowered out slowly.

REMOVAL AND INSPECTION

The factory torque converter was pulled out of the front of the transmission and compared to the new TCI diesel truck converter. There was a big difference. The TCI unit was much stronger looking than the factory unit, which looked like it was made from stamped steel rather than the forged steel of the TCI unit. Oliver, our transmission specialist, noted the wear marks on the front of the case of the OE unit. Clearly the toughness of the case is an issue with diesel application torque converters and the rationale behind TCI making such a big deal about beefing up the case. As the truck's owner, Jeff Souter, noted, he was looking for an improvement in not only fuel mileage, but due to the fact that he often tows cars in his enclosed trailer, having a reliable torque converter is significant.

We put two quarts of TCI Max Shift automatic transmission

DIESEL

175

fluid in the torque converter and slid the new TCI unit in place on the transmission. Oliver stressed the point that the torque converter must properly seat fully into the transmission. If it does not go completely into place, it will burn up the torque converter, and you will have to do this entire operation over again and purchase a new converter as well. If you are not certain you have done this right, seek professional help. Retracing our steps, we re-installed the transmission, filling it with 11 quarts of Max Shift fluid and started breaking in the transmission on the way back to Los Angeles County Raceway.

INSTANT RESULTS

As we left Oliver's transmission shop, we received a call on the cell phone from Jeff Souter, owner of the F-350. He was elated. "I can already feel a big difference in the way the truck drives," stated Souter. "That diesel off-idle stutter is gone. The truck seems as though it has much more torque. It feels like we picked up a lot more power too. I like it already."

At the drag strip, we backed up his claims. After several break-in runs, we put it to the wood for some real numbers. The best run: 16.98 seconds at 80.45 mph—slightly more than two-tenths of a second improvement over stock. As we were to learn in coming weeks, we added 2 mpg as well. But the most gratifying improvement continued to be the better seat-of-the-pants feel for the truck. Souter stated several times during subsequent drives, "It feels like a new truck, very different and much better."

We put 2 quarts of Max Shift transmission fluid in the new TCI diesel torque converter before installing it into the transmission. A total of 11 quarts is required.

Fully seating the torque converter in place on the input shaft is critical to proper performance. If you don't, you'll be doing this operation again and buying a new converter.

The factory torque converter simply slips out of the front of the transmission.

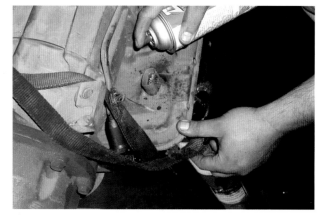

The electronic transmission plugs need to be free of transmission oil. Oliver cleans the connections and then blows them dry with compressed air. Oil-filled connections will lead to shorts and ultimate transmission failure.

Before reinstalling the transmission, make certain the dowel alignment pins are in good shape. With diesel applications, they are commonly broken or cracked.

Our F-350 not only improved in quarter-mile time but also picked up 2 mpg and drastically improved driver satisfaction levels.

TIME: 30 minutes

TOOLS: Plug and play

TALENT: ★

APPLICABLE YEARS: All

TAB: Max Micro-Tuner: $360–$400

TINWARE: N/A

TIP: This is a plug-and-play project.

PERFORMANCE GAIN:
Higher performance across power range

COMPLEMENTARY PROJECT:
Install boost temperature and EGT gauges.

Here we see Superchips, Inc. technician Jim Ferraro "rigging up" our 2005 Ford Excursion for dyno testing at the company's Sanford, Florida, facility.

Superchips thoroughly tests all of its products in this state-of-the-art dynamometer facility, which is equipped with a total of three Superflow two- and four-wheel dynamometers.

To say that not all power tuners are the same would be an understatement. Yes, they all reprogram your vehicle's computer, but in a turbodiesel application, a variety of options exist that differ among various tuner manufacturers. The idea is to get as much power as possible out of the engine while maintaining the integrity of the drivetrain components such as transmission, differentials, and bearings.

A search for an optimal program that provides benefits to both the engine and drivetrain is what most programmer manufacturers are diligently searching for. One of the latest is from Superchips, which recently introduced its MAX Micro-Tuner for the Ford 6.0-liter Powerstroke. The programmer is different from most as it does not momentarily enhance performance or fuel economy. Nor does it circumvent your factory engine management system by fooling it into "thinking" that it is operating within certain parameters inside the OE program.

Superchips' exciting new MAX Micro-Tuner model 1704 does function as a dedicated tuner that locks into your 6.0L Powerstroke-engine-equipped Ford truck or SUV with OBDII engine management system, allowing the owner/operator to be able to

actually reflash or reprogram the computer. This process is what Superchips engineers refer to as a "select tuning program."

MAX Micro-Tuner allows for three individual programs. The "high-performance" setting provides the most aggressive performance gains. This level of performance permits towing up to 6,000 pounds maximum, which is ideal for the light-duty cross-country towing of something like a racecar trailer or a boat.

On the other hand, Superchips' "tow safe" level should be selected when your Powerstroke diesel is routinely being used for towing payloads up to 8,000 pounds. This setting is great for workhorse activity like towing cattle trailers out on the ranch and hauling heavy payloads around town.

Superchips' "economy" tuning level optimizes your 6.0L Ford diesel engine for maximum fuel economy. This level can be selected for around town driving or for when your truck is being used for towing up to 8,000-pound payloads. "All three calibrations can be changed upon demand," says Superchips'

A number of initial dyno pulls were conducted with the stock engine tuning. A 15 percent load was applied through the dual eddy current brakes on the dyno to create a resistance to the truck's acceleration curve much like a loaded trailer would create.

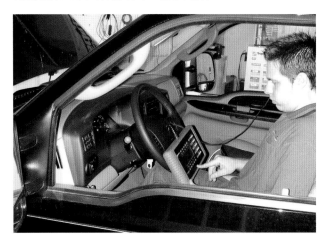

Because power output is directly related to fuel, boost, rpm, injector timing, and so on, and because all of these parameters are dependent on load, it was vitally important to test these varying loads to realize an accurate power output under all driving conditions.

Next, plug the Superchips MAX Micro-Tuner Model 1704 into the diagnostic connector located under the dash.

Once powered up, the MAX Micro-Tuner Model 1704 "VIN locks" into the Ford OBDII processor and identifies the vehicle in question.

It then begins with the "Ign. OFF Press >" prompt. It will then instruct you to turn ignition switch on, but do not start the vehicle. Once the MAX Micro-Tuner detects that the ignition switch has been turned on, it will then ask you to wait.

At this juncture, you will enter the "selecting tuning phase." At this juncture, the MAX Micro-Tuner will ask: A=Tune Vehicle or B=Diagnostics?

Next, the MAX Micro-Tuner will flash "establishing communications," with the identifying vehicle computer. This will be followed by the prompts to inform you what it is intending to do. First, "2 files are used for tuning." Then, "one for the engine, one for the transmission," then "the stock files will now be read," then "turn ignition switch 'off'." And finally, "press >." For the sake of time and space, the remaining steps are outlined in the MAX instruction manual and were executed according to MAX Micro-Tuner instructions.

Across-the-board testing of a number of 6.0L Ford Powerstroke-engine F-Series and Excursion vehicles yielded an overall average of 75 horsepower at 4,000 rpm and 100 lb-ft of torque at 4,000 rpm.

calibrations manager Jay Payson. "The reason for creating this product is that we've recognized a broad customer base out there. Simply put, the function of the Superchips MAX Micro-Tuner is to make the driving experience all the more enjoyable across the board!"

Payson continues, "For example, it's very irritating to tow a boat or a racecar trailer up a hill and have the transmission inside your Ford truck search for the right gear with the torque converter intermittently locking and unlocking. We try to optimize the (engine) powerband and set up the shift schedule (points) in the right place. We find that sweet spot where the engine and transmission are fully functioning as one and not working against each other while searching for the right gear."

Payson went on to relate that in most applications, the Superchips MAX Micro-Tuner also increases fuel economy due to the fact that engine and transmission efficiency are increased. "This is all done through calibration without changing any hard parts. The bottom line is that we're able to run less rpm through our optimized towing program at the same engine speed while increasing the boost and horsepower," Payson says. "With a standard transmission–equipped vehicle for example, we are within a 10 percent increased torque and horsepower 'gain range'. However, the drivability below the 'performance curve' is (also) noticeably increased through advanced ignition timing and optimization of power enrichment at both wide-open throttle and in power reduction between shifts."

According to Payson, with the introduction of a Superchips' MAX Micro-Tuner featuring the company's proprietary VXD Strategy, a couple of things on your Ford Powerstroke 6.0L diesel are altered. Power enrichment is brought in sooner at wide-open throttle, which means more horsepower when you

need it. Power reduction during a shift is also reduced by increasing power immediately upon making the gear transition. "We have seen up to two to three tenths gained in the quarter-mile just by altering the spark curve and power reduction between shifts," says Payson.

Ergonomically designed to comfortably fit in the human hand, Superchips' MAX Micro-Tuner measures approximately 3½ x 8 x 2 inches in size. These units are equipped with what is known as a "DTC code reader," which allows the operator to either troubleshoot, via a supplied list of DTC interpretation codes, or reprogram your OBDII processor to optimize and achieve the aforementioned performance, towing, or economy.

"We've added a number of user-friendly options, which our customers will immediately recognize for the added side benefits," says Payson. "For example, a lot of guys install larger size tires and wheels on these trucks. It's very important for us to be able to recalibrate the electronic speedometers on these vehicles based on the real tire and wheel size so that the speedometer not only reads accurately, the vehicle also shifts correctly, and so on."

Last April, we were able to sit in on the preliminary testing of a 2005 6.0L Diesel Powerstroke-engine Ford Excursion. The following parameters were constantly monitored: rpm, mph, engine oil temperature, coolant temperature, intake air temperature, load (measured as a percentage), loop (it is important to make sure that the engine management system on a diesel is operating on closed loop. Unlike gasoline engines, a 6.0L Powerstroke will run "open loop" in a fail-safe situation), gear (the transmission must be monitored to make sure power is accurately measured at a 1:1 ratio), torque converter lockup (or, percentage of full lockup), and injector timing, which is vitally important to power output, mileage, and EGT.

However, due to the time constraints and vehicle availability, the team at Superchips was not able to drill the manifolds on the Excursion to monitor exhaust gas temperatures. However, when it came to power measurement, that was another story. "The dyno itself creates many challenges when working with an automatic transmission," commented Ferraro. "In order to accurately measure power, the transmission must be 'locked' in whichever gear yields a 1:1 final drive ratio. In this particular test case, it is the fourth gear reach when up shifting, which is actually labeled '5' in the stock Ford program. This was not the only challenge. The Ford Powerstroke also has a unique 'Torqueshift' transmission, and the torque converter has some issues locked at very low rpm locked in a high gear."

Ferraro continues, "In short, in the real world you will never be at low rpm (under 2,000) in a higher gear at wide-open throttle because the transmission will immediately downshift to get the engine at a higher rpm level where it makes peak power. This is why the torque converter creates low rpm issues on the dyno when testing the vehicle locked in fifth gear. However, to make dyno plots readable as a single curve, the vehicle must be locked in a single gear.

"Any way you look at these locking issues, a compromise is necessary, which is why we make pulls in single gear; more dyno pulls through the gears, and more pulls locked in every individual gear under every possible load percentage. This makes sure the truck develops max power and torque in every gear, running empty or loaded, uphill or downhill, under any situation the driver can create. It is important to see loaded runs to ascertain what type of performance gains are realized while pulling a trailer, which matters the most to 6.0L Powerstroke-engine Ford F-Series owners."

DIESEL

PROJECT 65

SELECT AND INSTALL AFTERMARKET AIR INTAKE SYSTEMS, PERFORMANCE MODULES, AND FREE-FLOW EXHAUST SYSTEMS

TIME: Eight hours

TOOLS: Full socket set, screwdriver set, appropriate jack, Sawzall

TALENT: ★★

APPLICABLE YEARS: All

TAB: $600 for exhaust; $400 for intake; $800 for downloader

TINWARE: N/A

TIP: Make sure you and your family members like the sound of performance exhaust systems.

PERFORMANCE GAIN:
Cleaner running and more-responsive throttle experience

COMPLEMENTARY PROJECT:
Spark plug wire change and fresh plugs

One of the items installed was the MBRP stainless-steel exhaust system. The kit comes completely polished and clamps on using the factory exhaust hangers. The MBRP exhaust is a free-flow muffler that adds a performance sound but does not restrict any of the exhaust flow. Some of the tubing had to be trimmed as it is manufactured for various body lengths. Proficient simply measured the system and marked where it needed to be cut. Using a Sawzall, the tubing was cut, and the rest of the system could be easily bolted together.

The turbo down pipe was bolted to the rear of the factory turbo. This was fairly easy to install relative to other exhaust systems Proficient has used in the past.

By now, most late-model turbodiesel owners know that the easiest and most-effective way to coax massive amounts of horsepower and torque from their engines is by installing an air intake system, performance programmer or module, and a free-flow exhaust system. Although this may sound easy, a problem arises when one begins to investigate and weed through the abundance of products available. This ultimately leads to the question of how do all of these different products work together? Does one manufacturer's intake work well with another manufacturer's exhaust and a third manufacturer's programmer?

In an effort to help curb many of these questions, Proficient Diesel began combining intakes, exhaust, programmers, and downloaders to come up with viable combinations that provide excellent performance numbers from reliable products that it sells through Proficient Diesel.com. After many years of doing this same type of testing with superchargers, Proficient Diesel compiled a combination of name-brand performance products that should work well together for turbocharged diesel applications.

One of the company's many attempts at grouping performance products was to find a power combination for the popular Ford 6.0-liter Powerstroke turbodiesel. Proficient selected a Volant cool air intake system P/N19860, and combined it with a free flowing, MBRP polished stainless-steel, dual-exit performance exhaust system P/N S6210304. Proficient then selected the newest Bully Dog Triple Dog Power Pup to complete the system and to use the benefits of increased air intake and exhaust flow.

DIESEL

181

The tubing slips together and uses C-clamps to hang it from the factory hangers.

The muffler is then installed, as is the Y-pipe to direct the exhaust out of both sides of the truck for the dual tips and to help reduce EGTs.

On the intake side, the factory air box was removed and replaced with the Volant cool air intake system. The inlet tubing from the filter box to the throttle body is also removed.

Proficient found a stock 2005 Ford F-250 as its test truck to bolt the combination to. After acquiring all of the products from the three manufacturers, Proficient employees bolted on the products at their facility in Irvine, California, with the exhaust being the most difficult, but still within the limits of someone doing it at home with adequate tools.

To begin with, the Volant cold air intake was a welcome improvement to the restrictive factory intake system. Volant replaces the filter box with its own larger box that gathers air from two sources so that it has a larger volume of cold air available. This, in combination with a cotton-gauze filter, allows the engine to take in more air and have the potential of additional horsepower.

After the Volant cool air intake was installed, Proficient took a close look at the MBRP diesel exhaust system. This particular kit for the Powerstroke features a dual exhaust exit from the muffler, a high-flow down pipe, and an optional catalytic converter test pipe. Although several exhaust manufacturers offer test pipes, it is wise to check with local state laws as to the legality of their use. In many cases, the test pipes are useful in off-highway and racing applications where the system can eliminate excess heat, especially when using it with a power programmer that adds additional fuel. For testing purposes, Proficient included the MBRP down pipe and cat test pipe, but reinstalled the catalytic converter once it was able to see the overall power gains without it.

The MBRP exhaust system was easy to install, especially when it came to bolting up the new down pipe. On many other systems, the down pipe requires several attempts to fit it up from under the engine and between the frame rails. Yet, the MBRP pipe bolted in without any problems. Some trimming of the MBRP head pipe is required, as it fits a variety of cab applications, but the rest of the system bolted together easily. The MBRP system also features a high-flow muffler that uses a straight-through-style inlet and outlet. The entire system is polished and uses a high-flow Y-pipe at the muffler's outlet, which separates the exhaust so that it can exit out of the right and left sides of the truck, giving it a dual exhaust appearance. This unique feature on the MBRP exhaust is one of the main reasons why Proficient selected to use it on this application. Not only does the dual exhaust look great, but, from the company's experience, the added dual exit tubes actually lower exhaust gas temperatures, further increasing the benefits of this system.

Finally, Proficient added the Bully Dog Triple Dog Power Pup. This new programmer features three levels of diesel performance from a towing mode to a performance and an all-out power mode. The unit easily downloads into the vehicle's factory computer through the diagnostic port under the dash, and this particular system allows the owner to switch from one program to the next without having to stop and reprogram the vehicle. Bully Dog also offers a trial version of the Triple Dog Power Pup that can be downloaded into your vehicle from one of various Bully Dog dealers across the country.

In theory, the Power Pup should provide most of the performance gains, but the addition of the Volant intake and the MBRP exhaust system will also allow the combination to flow the proper amount of air and exhaust to make the most of the programmer's ability to make power. Most important, however, is that the use of an aftermarket intake and exhaust on a diesel will curb the heat that is typically generated by adding a programmer to a truck that is constantly under load or used in performance applications.

Once all of the components were installed, it was time to test the truck and look at all of the data. To do this, Proficient took the Ford over to Autowave Inc. in Huntington Beach, California. It was here that Mike Lapier aided Proficient with the dyno tests on the company's rear-wheel dynamometer.

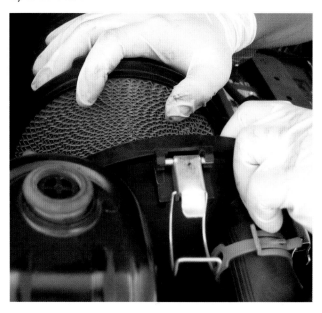

The filter must be removed first by unlatching the cover from the housing.

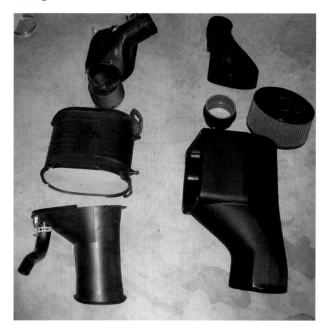

Here you can see the difference between the factory intake on the left and the Volant unit.

The truck previously visited the shop where Proficient asked Lapier to perform a baseline dyno test on the truck. In stock configuration, the rear-wheel dyno showed that the engine made approximately 250 horsepower and 475 lb-ft torque. The next dyno test was with all of the products—Volant, MBRP, and Bully Dog units—installed.

Because the Triple Dog Power Pup features three stages of power, the first test was with the Power Pup in the Towing/Economy mode. The F-250 showed some encouraging gains, improving the truck's performance to approximately 311 horsepower and 630 lb-ft torque. In the Performance mode, the power shot up to 320 horsepower and torque jumped to 660 lb-ft. In the Extreme mode, the horsepower peaked at 339 horsepower and the torque reached 690 lb-ft of torque.

Although the power in the Extreme mode is definitely a wild ride for this truck, the gains we made in the Towing/Economy and Performance modes were impressive and well within the limits of the diesel's powertrain to be used on a daily basis. Proficient put together a potent combination with these products, and the Bully Dog's Power Pup is probably capable of more power with additional tuning that is available by contacting Bully Dog.

As we also suspected, the EGTs were lower on the Performance and Extreme modes, proving that the addition of the Volant air intake and MBRP exhaust are well worth the effort when adding a power programmer.

The Volant kit uses a slightly smaller air filter, but it features larger pleats that make up for the surface area. It also flows much more air than the factory unit and allows for a greater volume of air into the engine.

The remainder of the factory air box is removed, and the Volant unit is installed.

We found out that the elbow on the intake tube should be installed first before the rest of the unit, and you must have a smart torque's head to remove the stock mass airflow sensor from the stock unit.

This is what the Volant intake looks like installed on the engine. The lid is held on with four screws and also takes in air from under the hood and between the radiator core support, providing somewhat of a ram effect.

The Bully Dog Triple Dog Power Pup allowed three power functions that can be changed on the fly.

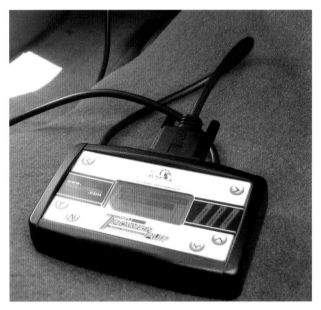

The Power Pup is simply plugged into the vehicle's diagnostic port, and the program is downloaded into the factory ECU.

DIESEL

TIME: Five hours

 TOOLS: Full socket set, jack, jack stands

 TALENT: ★★

 APPLICABLE YEARS: All three upgrades available for most years, makes, and models of light trucks

 TAB: $450–$500 for exhaust; $250 for air intake; $500 for Granatelli Tuner

 TINWARE: N/A

 TIP: Read the instructions the night before you tackle the project.

 PERFORMANCE GAIN:
More than 100 horsepower is obtainable with this combination.

COMPLEMENTARY PROJECT:
Install exhaust gas temperature, transmission temperature gauges.

The factory intake sits next to the battery and is completely sealed. It houses a restrictive filter that limits airflow. By loosening the retaining clamps, the factory air duct is removed from the turbocharger inlet. Unplugging the factory mass airflow sensor is necessary as it will be removed and placed on to the new Airaid unit. Once everything is loosened, the factory air intake is removed from the vehicle.

The factory filter-box bracket is left with the rubber grommets. The Airaid intake features two studs that fit into these grommets to hold the box in place. We removed the factory mass airflow sensor and replaced it on to the inlet tube of the Airaid unit, using the hardware provided.

More power, better fuel economy, and greater towing capabilities are some of the more popular elements that diesel truck owners desire for their vehicles. But many don't exactly know how to get these. Popular blues guitarist Kenny Wayne Shepherd is one of those diesel owners who wanted increased performance from his 2004 Ford F-350, which he uses to tow his "Extreme Lee" Dodge Charger and to pull a general car hauler and horse trailer.

Shepherd asked us to help him select the right components to improve his truck, which is equipped with a 6.0-liter, Powerstroke turbodiesel. We opted to improve the air entering the engine with a high-flow air intake system as well as remove any restriction on the exhaust side with a large-diameter, stainless-steel exhaust. These two modifications would improve the breathing characteristics of the truck and also provide a better platform for adding a performance programmer or module that would boost horsepower and torque for improved performance and towing capabilities.

We asked Joe Granatelli of Granatelli Motorsports to help us install and dyno test the products we selected in an effort

to see if Shepherd's truck would end up playing a different tune. We began by placing the long-bed, crew-cab F-350 duallie truck on to the Mustang Dyno at Granatelli Motorsports and performed a baseline run. The truck made 217 horsepower at 3,400 rpms and 334.2 lb-ft of torque at 3,300 rpms to the rear wheels. We then let the engine cool a bit and decided on an Airaid intake system for the Powerstroke. The intake kit replaces the factory air filter and includes a new filter housing that fits into the factory location.

The top of the intake box uses this frame and seal, which allows air to enter from between the hood and radiator core support but seals the rest of the system to the hood of the vehicle.

The new air inlet tube and filter box have to be installed in the vehicle before it can be bolted to the unit. Here you can see how the new inlet tube bolts together from the inside of the new filter box. The factory bellows, which feeds air into the turbocharger, is reinstalled using the factory clamps.

The top of the housing seals directly to the underside of the hood, allowing more air to enter from the factory location and from between the hood and grille area. Airaid uses a cone filter with larger pleats for increased surface area. The factory mass airflow (MAF) sensor, which also includes the air temperature sensor, is removed from the factory filter housing and is inserted into the new Airaid duct that attaches to the inlet tube of the turbocharger.

Once the installation of the Airaid intake was completed, the truck went through another dyno run to see the results. In this case, the truck's power increased to 225.2 horsepower at 3,400 rpms and 353.7 lb-ft of torque at 3,300 rpms. The Airaid intake resulted in an increase of 8 horsepower and 19.5 additional lb-ft of torque. From here, we went on to installing a performance power module that would help in both towing and delivering optimum power if needed.

We asked Granatelli to install and demonstrate the Granatelli Motorsport Big G power module. The module has three power modes: Towing, Performance, and Race,

This is what the completed installation looks like. Not only did the Airaid intake look good, it delivered an additional 8 horsepower and 19 lb-ft of torque. Airaid supplies a high-flow, cotton-gauze filter that is inserted and clamped into the air filter box. The filter is washable and reusable and has larger pleats for increased surface area. Finally, the top seal is added to the lid of the box to prevent engine heat from entering into the box.

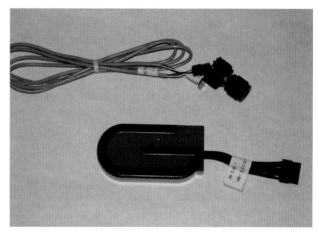

The next step was to dramatically increase the F-350's power by installing the Granatelli Motorsports' Big G module. Installing the Big G is as simple as following the instructions and plugging in the wiring harness into key areas in the engine.

Key sensors are used to feed the Big G engine information, which it regulates and modifies to provide increased horsepower and fuel economy. Granatelli Motorsports prefers to install the module under the dash to protect it from heat and vibration. To do this, a small hole was drilled in the firewall so the harness could be routed to the interior of the cab.

which can be accessed by simply turning a dash-mounted dial. The Big G comes with its own wiring harness, and by following the instructions, it easily attaches to key areas on the Powerstroke engine. A small hole is drilled in the vehicle's firewall to pass the wiring from the engine to inside the cab. This allows the installation of the power switch and the module itself, which prevents it from being exposed to excessive vibration and heat.

After 30 minutes, the Big G was installed, and again the truck was run on the dyno with the Big G set on the Tow mode. The horsepower jumped to 279.3 hp and 430 lb-ft of torque; an increase of 54 horsepower and 76.3 lb-ft of torque. When we placed the Big G in the Performance mode, the horsepower jumped to 321.6 hp and 471.3 lb-ft of torque, which added another 42.3 horsepower and 41.3 lb-ft of torque. Finally, we set the Big G into the Race mode and recorded 384.4 horsepower and 573.3 lb-ft of torque, adding another 62.8 horsepower and 102 lb-ft of torque on top of what we already made.

The Big G definitely added the towing and performance power that the F-350 desperately needed. Granatelli pointed out that because exhaust temperatures can rise quickly, it is not recommended to tow in the Performance or Race mode. Nevertheless, the power potential is there if Shepherd ever wanted to out-accelerate Mustangs or Corvettes with the truck, before reaching for his Xtreme Lee Dodge Charger.

The final step in this installation was to improve the exhaust on the truck, which would not only increase its power potential, but also effectively reduce any restriction from the factory exhaust and decrease temperatures. We wanted to install a high-end system and decided on a B&B exhaust. B&B manufactures a 4-inch-diameter system that has mandrel bends and includes a highly polished muffler. The system can be mounted with or without the factory catalytic converter, but you should check your local laws to find out what the legalities are of doing so.

Because we were curious as to how much power the combination of the Airaid, B&B exhaust and Big G module would make, we decided to install the exhaust system without the catalytic converter, but reinstalled it after we concluded our testing. The B&B system has the appropriate flanges to do so and comes with an adaptor to slip-fit the exhaust system to the rear of the factory converter.

The factory exhaust can be unbolted and removed but we found it necessary to use a Sawzall to cut the tailpipe section behind the muffler in order to ease its removal. The B&B system easily bolts together and is hung on the factory hangers and includes heavy-duty band clamps. The end of the tailpipe, muffler, and the 5-inch tip are highly polished. And after approximately 30 minutes, the B&B exhaust was on and we were anxious to see the results of how much power can be made with the entire combination installed in the truck.

To make some kind of comparison dyno runs, we opted to switch the Big G into the Performance mode and compare the results of the new exhaust with that of the dyno run of the truck with the stock exhaust, Airaid intake, and the Big G set on Performance mode. The dyno run with the B&B exhaust yielded 348.7 horsepower and 537.8 lb-ft of torque. This meant that the B&B exhaust alone added an additional 27 horsepower and 66.5 lb-ft of torque. We did not have enough time to test the B&B exhaust with the factory catalytic

converter placed back in the truck, but we would imagine that the performance gains would suffer only slightly.

Our final test was to place the Granatelli Big G in the Race mode to see what the maximum power would be with the entire combination. The dyno results were impressive, showing that the combination made 427.2 horsepower at 3,600 rpm and 625.9 lb-ft of torque at 3,600 rpm. Compared to our stock, baseline run, we added a total of 255 horsepower and 291.7 lb-ft of torque. This was quite an impressive combination, and, once the transmission was adjusted to take advantage of the engine's new-found horsepower and torque, we also noted a 1.2-mpg increase in fuel economy as well and found that passing power and acceleration with the Big G in the Performance mode was more than enough to handle freeway and city driving.

We're sure that once Kenny Wayne Shepherd gets his truck back and steps on the throttle, he'll be extremely pleased with the results and switch his tune from blues to rock.

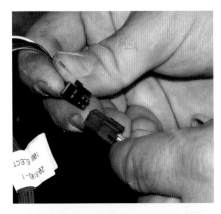

With the harness inside the cab, the Big G and the dash-mounted knob are plugged in. We also drilled a small hole in the dash to mount the adjustment knob. This area is out of the way and still easily accessible to the driver.

The OEM exhaust system is long and restrictive because it has kinks in the bends and does not have a high-flow muffler. We began its removal by unbolting it from the front flange at the catalytic converter.

The muffler is hung on the factory hangers, and the rest of the system is clamped together with the provided band clamps. The result of this combination is incredible, making a maximum of 255 additional horsepower and 291.7 lb-ft of torque to the rear wheels.

TIME: Eight hours for all components

TOOLS: Full socket set, jack, jack stands

TALENT: ★★

APPLICABLE YEARS: All

TAB: $600 for Speed-Loader; $1,200 for inter-cooler/intake; $800 for exhaust

TINWARE: Loctite blue, gloves, safety glasses, drop cloth and fender cloth to prevent scratching

TIP: Gale Banks Engineering makes diesel performance products for Ford, Dodge, Chevy.

PERFORMANCE GAIN:
Increased performance via greater horsepower and torque

COMPLEMENTARY PROJECT:
Exhaust gas temperature gauge, other relevant diesel-powered gauges

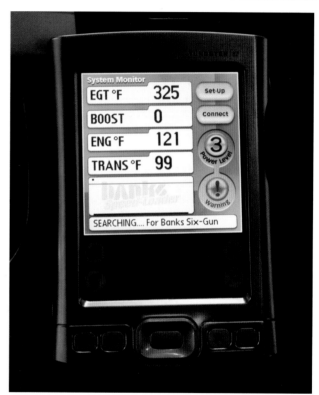

The Power PDA will display exhaust gas temperatures (EGT), boost, and two other engine vital signs of your choice. You will have as many as 15 different parameters to monitor, but you will always have EGT and boost on the display screen as constants.

So, what's it going to take to free up and outfit your 24-valve 5.9-liter Cummins diesel to put down about 500 honest horsepower and a solid 1,000 lb-ft of torque in your Dodge Ram? It will take less than you might think and deliver more than you thought possible. If the idea of keeping the versatility and drivability of your daily driver in good health with added capacity for robust performance sounds enticing, then consider the software and hardware components engineered at the Gale Banks campus in Azusa, California.

This red 2005 Dodge Ram 1500 4x4 is a Banks Sidewinder All-Terrain tuner truck. It's a packaged power pack of performance components for the 5.9-liter Cummins diesel that you can buy as a complete system or invest in, choosing any of the cohesively designed pieces one at a time. If you own a Dodge Ram with a Cummins diesel motor, then here are a few performance enhancements you should be aware of. The first of these power-makers is brand new and cutting edge.

POWER PDA
With the ever-advancing progress engine tuners are making

these days with the onboard engine management computers, it's not a huge leap to think that one day you'll be able to control your Cummins diesel with a personal digital assistant (PDA). It would be a window into the mind of your motor. If you could just adapt the parameters and functions that are controllable to the software capabilities of what is essentially a handheld computer that can manage, map, and adjust performance characteristics, what a breakthrough.

In fact it is a breakthrough, and Gale Banks Engineering is

DIESEL

The Six-Gun diesel tuner box is located on the driver's side of the engine bay.

Compare the size of the factory intercooler on the left with the heavyweight Banks Techni-Cooler charge-air cooler on the right. You are looking at approximately 25 percent difference in actual core surface area. Cool.

bringing it to market. They're calling it the PowerPDA, a handheld interface for the Banks Six-Gun diesel tuner. This interactive portal is designed for the 2003–2005 5.9-liter Cummins diesel motor (also the 2001–05 Duramax and 2003–05 6.0-liter power stroke diesel). The PowerPDA stations on a dash-mounted recharging holder and is essentially a fully operational PDA with a 64-megabite memory card. Eliminating the need for analog gauges, the PowerPDA will display exhaust gas temperatures (EGT), boost, and two other engine vital signs of your choice. You will have as many as 15 different parameters to monitor, but you will always have EGT and boost on the display screen as constants.

Instead of using the selector dial to choose one to six levels of performance built into the Six-Shooter program, you

This Sidewinder diesel is running a Banks Shape Shifter Turbo and a Banks Big Hoss exhaust manifold and injectors in addition to the Banks High-Ram intake from the intercooler.

Here's the split chamber directing exhaust from the single can out to the rear of the truck.

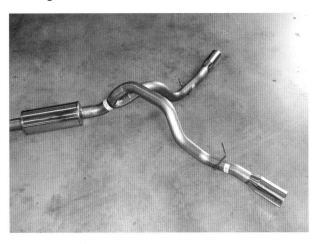

The new dual Monster exhaust is all stainless steel and runs from the cat . . . back.

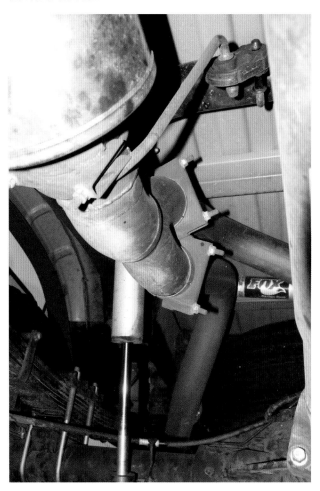

The installed system in the Banks Sidewinder Ram shows how the 4-inch tubing routes out of the can, up over the rear axle, and out to respective exits to the rear.

will select your power levels on the fly and on the PDA. In addition, you will be able to choose how the information is displayed, such as in the form of the traditional gauge face or digital readout. You will also be able to record 0–60 mph and quarter-mile runs with EGT and boost readings logged so you can view the data at a later time.

Furthermore, the software can compensate for oversized tires and give you corrected vehicle speed, always an asset while crossing the great state of Montana on a clear blue-sky day with dry roads and unlimited visibility and nary another vehicle in sight. You can read and clear any diagnostic trouble codes that crop up in the course of an expression session. Inputs to the PDA include using the touch screen or a handheld scribe. The value-added feature to this system is the versatility of the PowerPDA as a fully functional digital assistant compatible with Microsoft

Exhaust tips are double-walled, 5-inch polished stainless steel.

With all that performance under the hood, the dual Monster exhaust will look just like this on your Ram.

Word, Excel, and PowerPoint software. The PowerPDA synchronizes with Outlook so you can transfer and access your e-mail, calendar, contacts, and task roster in addition to managing your diesel. This Tungsten E PDA is completely scalable; it can expand, as you need, with additional memory added.

SPEED-LOADER

Adding the optional Banks Power Speed-Loader module to the Six-Gun diesel tuner adds an additional level of power to settings two through six, leaving setting one at the factory power level just as it would be with the Six-Gun tune alone. The additional horsepower increase is above what the Six-Gun tune brings on its own.

BIG BORE INTERCOOLER

No doubt the factory intercooler provided for your diesel motor is designed for most any task. However, increased cooling capacity is an asset when you find yourself staring down a quarter-mile run or approaching an eight-mile dead-pull over the top of the Great Divide with a four-place horse trailer loaded with gear and feed. The Banks Techni-Cooler charge-air cooler system offers more overall mass in physical dimensions and width of the unit. The radiator end tanks are broader in surface area leading up to the boost tubes, and cooling surface is larger. End tanks are made from aluminum, rather than plastic, and optimize airflow while maintaining complete integrity under heavy

boost conditions. The core area is 25 percent larger than the factory unit.

BANKS HIGH-RAM INTAKE

Greater physical size and less restriction in the shape enables the Banks High-Ram intake to deliver cooler, dense air into the engine. The High-Ram is designed to increase airflow and boost without increasing back pressure at the turbine. As a result, the engine is more fuel-efficient and responsive while providing increased torque at any EGT.

MONSTER EXHAUST

There's something about dual exhaust that strikes a cool cord with automotive enthusiasts wherever they reside across the country. This dual Banks Monster exhaust is the latest exhaust configuration for Dodge Ram trucks. The Banks Sidewinder is a four-door Ram outfitted with all stainless-steel construction, 4-inch, heavy-wall tubing with constant diameter bends to mitigate back pressure. The polished stainless-steel muffler can is a straight-through design using high-temperature spun ceramic packing around the 4-inch diameter exhaust flow passageway. The 4-inch Monster exhaust starts from the catalytic converter into the single muffler can, then into the dual directional chamber that splits the exhaust flow out behind each of the rear wheels. Each exhaust side exits through a 5-inch, polished, stainless-steel, double-walled tip.

TIME: Two hours

TOOLS: Electrical pliers

TALENT: ★

APPLICABLE YEARS: Available for most diesel-powered makes and models of light trucks

TAB: $500

TINWARE: N/A

TIP: Consider installing a boost pressure gauge and fuel pressure gauge to complement this project.

PERFORMANCE GAIN:
More responsive acceleration

COMPLEMENTARY PROJECT:
Intake and exhaust systems are obvious step-up projects.

DIESEL

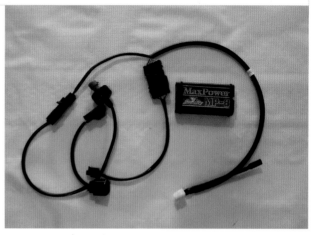

The MP-8 module from TS performance comes with the module, wiring harness, and complete set of instructions.

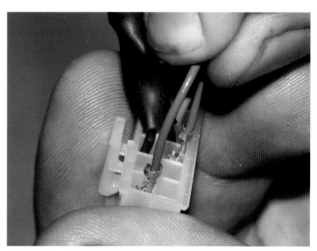

Because the module can work with many other diesel applications, the instructions call for jumping two of the connectors. This allows the MP-8 module to activate the correct program for the specific application.

Most of us know that it's pretty simple to add significant power to our diesel pickup trucks. Plug in a module or download a program, and you've got an additional 100 horsepower and 200 lb-ft of torque. The problem is that most of us who are new to diesel trucks don't exactly know what the modules do and how they affect the engine.

It's definitely not magic, but a programmer does reprogram or modify the vehicle's computer to produce more power. We contacted Dennis Perry of TS Performance to tell us how this is done on his company's MP-8 performance module.

Perry explained that many modules and programmers modify the vehicle's computer fuel tables to add fuel pressure. Additional fuel pressures typically make additional horsepower gains. Although this is okay in most situations, some programmers and modules can exceed the factory recommendations for what the factory fuel rail can handle.

Perry told us that in the case of TS Performance's MP-8 module, TS also adds a small amount of fuel pressure but keeps it well below the factory limits. This, according to Perry, adds about 60 more horsepower. Additional horsepower is obtained

by improving the injector pulse timing, thus adding additional fuel without increasing pressure. According to Perry, this adds the extra 40 horsepower to make a total horsepower gain of about 100 horses.

A module like TS Performance's MP-8 also plugs into the manifold absolute pressure (map) sensor. This is done to determine the maximum boost the engine can handle. By setting a value to that setting, additional horsepower and proper fuel delivery can be obtained.

All of this may seem simple, but decoding the factory programs and knowing how to alter them correctly are what separate the various products that are available for diesel engines. To demonstrate how simple it is to plug in a module, we installed one of TS Performance's MP-8 modules on to a 2005 Dodge Ram with a Cummins diesel. The MP-8 module can also be upgraded with new downloads from TS Performance, and the unit can be used on just about any other diesel engine with the correct harness attached to it.

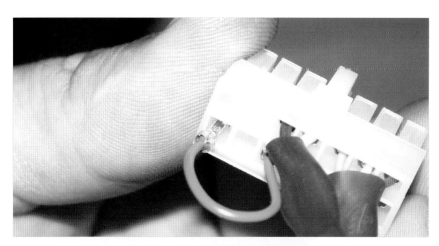

Here you can see how the wires were jumped. The kit comes with appropriate jumper wire and you simply look to the instructions to find out where to plug it in.

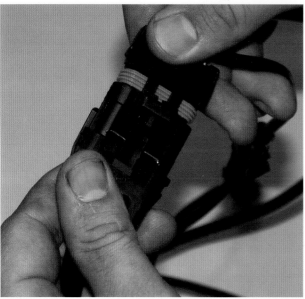

The wiring harness is then assembled by plugging it together. This attaches the engine leads to the main harness.

One end of the harness lead plugs into the MAP sensor. The other plugs into the fuel pressure regulator.

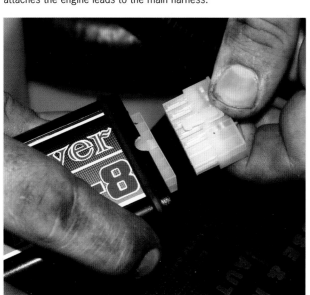

The other end of the harness plugs into the MP-8 module.

Some Velcro is used to attach the MP-8 module on to a safe surface that is away from heat.

TIME: 10 minutes

TOOLS: Hands only

TALENT: ★

APPLICABLE YEARS: 2002–2006 GMC diesel-powered pickups with overhead storage compartments

TAB: $79

TINWARE: N/A

TIP: Carefully follow instructions. Some projects look easy, yet they are just as easy to mess up. Read the directions.

PERFORMANCE GAIN:
Secure mount position with good access to programmer controls

COMPLEMENTARY PROJECT:
Exhaust gas temperature gauge

DIESEL

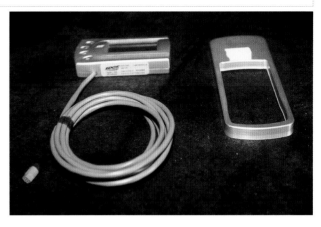

To fit the monitor into the first-generation faceplate/bracket at right, the label must be removed and the unit unscrewed and opened.

Four screws, one at each corner, must be removed to open the monitor. When the unit is opened, the label on the side must be removed and the manufacturer's warranty is, thereby, voided. Each half of the unit is fitted into the faceplate/bracket.

Nobody wants to admit how it happened. It's one of those business screw-ups for which no one is ever responsible. Here's the deal. Edge Manufacturing of Ogden, Utah, created an Attitude monitor for controlling its computer chip for diesels. As fate would have it, the monitor was just the right size to fit in the standard opening in the overhead console of '01 to '05 GMC and Chevrolet pickups. To secure the monitor in that overhead console, the unit needed a special faceplate/bracket. The bracket that suddenly appeared on the market required that the monitor be separated into its halves by removal of four screws, one at each corner of the unit, to mount it securely into the faceplate/bracket. Unfortunately, Edge, the manufacturer, did not want the monitor opened for fear of tampering. To prevent unauthorized people from unscrewing the monitor and opening it, Edge affixed a stick-on label on the side of each unit. Removal of the label would immediately void the manufacturer's warranty.

These labels put a serious wrinkle in the plan to use this technology on these GMC and Chevy pickups. None of the existing faceplate/brackets on the market for positioning the monitor

neatly into the overhead console of a late-model GM pickup could be mounted without separating and opening the monitor. No Edge Attitude monitor could be unscrewed and opened without removing the stick-on label. And no label could be removed without voiding the manufacturer's warranty. Are you still there? If so, you've got the picture.

Enter Jesse Garcia, a front office full-timer at Rolling Big Power, the diesel performance specialists in Corona, California. In his spare time, Garcia designed a new faceplate/bracket that incorporates a groove into the design that holds the Edge Attitude monitor securely without the need for opening the unit. Problem solved? Indeed.

At first glance, it doesn't appear to be a big deal. But think about the number of '01 to '05 GMC and Chevy diesel pickups on the road. Then think about how many of those are equipped with an Edge Attitude monitor. Then consider how many of those owners would like to tuck their monitor safely, easily, and neatly into the standard overhead console. And finally, guess how many of those owners would like to do that tucking without voiding their Edge warranty. Suddenly, it's a big deal after all.

The accompanying photos illustrate the problem with the old-style faceplate/bracket and how the new RBP bracket works.

The halves are then screwed back together with a screw at each corner to secure the monitor into the faceplate/bracket.

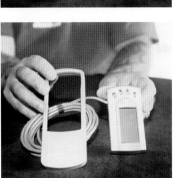

Our technician prepares to demonstrate mounting the Edge Attitude monitor into the new RBP faceplate/bracket.

With no disassembly required, the monitor is fitted securely into the groove in the new RBP faceplate/bracket.

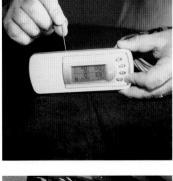

To complete the assembly, all that remained was tightening four tiny set (or Allen) screws, two on each edge of the monitor.

Inside the truck, the overhead console had been removed. Previously, the monitor had been mounted on the mirror, so the wires for the monitor were already run under the headliner. The wires are moved under the headliner and connected to the monitor.

Now the console can be reattached to the headliner with the wiring, and the monitor can be run through the front opening of the console.

The new RBP bracket housing the Edge monitor will then fit right into the opening very nicely.

And there you have it, a quick way to install your Edge monitor into a factory location that has a much cleaner appearance and is still in a nice viewing range.

TIME: Five hours

 TOOLS: Full socket set, jack, jack stands, transmission jack

 TALENT: ★★★

 APPLICABLE YEARS: Available for most diesel-powered makes and models of light trucks

 TAB: $1,000 (allot $200–$500 for programming upgrade)

 TINWARE: N/A

 TIP: Recruit a friend to help you with the transmission.

PERFORMANCE GAIN: Smoother acceleration and cooler transmission temperatures

COMPLEMENTARY PROJECT:
A deep sump finned aluminum transmission pan will hold more transmission fluid and look great. Also consider a shift kit upgrade while you have the transmission unplugged.

DIESEL

Our first step to installing the Precision torque converter was to take our truck to Inglewood Transmission Service where they began by unbolting the driveshaft from the transmission. The transmission was supported with a trans-jack and the vehicle's crossmember was removed.

All of the transmission's linkage and harnesses were disconnected from the main body.

In most situations, adding performance will put a strain on the vehicle's transmission. Nevertheless, people like Mike Lovrich at Inglewood Transmission Service see folks adding performance to their vehicle's transmissions all of the time. Lovrich's trans shop is a favorite among local southern California diesel truck owners who love to race their trucks at local drag-racing events.

Lovrich explained that the problem with adding big power to the late-model turbodiesel engines is that the factory torque converter clutch assemblies cannot handle the amount of horsepower and torque. In essence, the torque converters are too loose, and they slip, forcing the transmission to handle the extra power. The result is excessive heat buildup and eventually entire transmission failure. Lovrich also explained that, in addition to installing a torque converter that can handle the abuse, it is also necessary to reprogram the vehicle's transmission electronic control unit (ECU) to compensate and operate within the new levels that a performance converter can deliver.

Terry Hedrick of Precision Industries, which manufactures high-performance torque converters for street, racing, and diesel

truck applications, understands why factory torque converters fail. Hedrick has come up with some solutions that require building a converter from scratch, and not just from combining internal components from factory and aftermarket parts. These solutions have led to the development of Precision Industries Stallion Power Stroke converter.

Hedrick told us that this converter is uniquely designed to handle the extra stresses of a performance turbodiesel. In this case, the Power Stroke converter is for the Ford 6.0-liter engine, but the fact that the torque converter features a one-piece steel billet housing makes it almost indestructible and less prone to leaks, compared to two-piece converters that have the cover welded together and are prone to this problem. In addition, including a multiple-clutch pack that would not fit into a standard factory converter housing was necessary.

Furthermore, we found out that the Stallion Power Stroke converter also has a larger clutch surface area that measures 130 square inches compared to the standard torque converter clutch surface areas of 39 square inches. The larger surface area, with a

The access hole between the transmission bell housing and the oil pan allows the technicians to unbolt the torque converter by rotating it as each bolt is removed.

Rotating the transmission end-shaft allows access to each of the torque converter's bolts to free the transmission from the engine.

Finally, the bell housing bolts are removed from the transmission allowing it to be separated from the engine block.

unique clutch assembly that Precision designed, can survive the abuses of high-performance, late-model turbodiesel vehicles. This larger surface area combined with an impeller and turbine is fully furnace brazed, not stitch tacked. The surface area adds maximum vortex fluid flow and strength to the converter, and the unique friction materials in the clutch can also handle higher operating temperatures.

So, can a performance torque converter really add that much performance to a turbodiesel? We wanted to find out and had one installed on a 2004 Ford F-350 that was equipped with a Granatelli Motorsports Inc. Big-G performance module, and a B&B stainless-steel exhaust system. Switching the Big-G into the Performance mode allowed the F-350 to produce nearly 800 lb-ft of torque and 400 horsepower. Although the acceleration is impressive, we did notice that the shifting was slow and there was too much time between shifts, indicating that the transmission is slipping and forcing the vehicle's torque-management system to take away power.

We obtained a Stallion Power Stroke converter from Precision Industries and took it and the truck over to Inglewood Transmission Service where the entire process of installing the torque converter took about 30 minutes. Because both Hedrick and Lovrich recommended upgrading the transmission ECU to

The factory Ford transmission is then lowered from the chassis using the trans-jack.

Here you can see the factory torque converter and the six studs that must be unbolted to release the unit from the engine.

a performance level, we also contacted Brian's Truck Shop in Leadhill, Arizona, which was recommended by Precision and has been working on a program to improve the shifting parameters of the Ford Powerstroke transmission. After a discussion regarding the truck's components' power output and average driving conditions, Brian's Truck Shop sent us a programmer that was simply downloaded via the diagnostic port on our truck. The programmer was custom tuned to improve the shift points and line pressure of the system to further handle the power and torque generated by our test truck.

Once both were in place, the results were impressive. First, we noticed that the vehicle would begin to accelerate right from idle, without any hesitation. When we stood on the throttle, the hesitation of the torque-management system still remained, but after a few weeks of driving, it completely went away to provide smooth acceleration every time. We also noted a slight increase in fuel economy as well as a decrease in transmission temperature while towing vehicles in traffic or lugging a load up a steep grade.

Although these benefits were great results from a simple torque converter change, we can't help but admit that one of the best benefits is the peace of mind, knowing that the occasional fun of a big duallie blowing the doors off a Corvette or Mustang will not result in having to tow the truck home with the transmission in the bed. Considering that the cost of the Precision Stallion Power Stroke converter is about $1,043, and the programmer can cost in the $200–$500 range depending on the application, adding the converter and programmer is much better than the cost of installing a new transmission on your truck, knowing that it can blow at any time again if you're too hard on the throttle.

The Precision Stallion Power Stroke converter is made from one-piece billet steel and is incredibly strong with superior clutch force.

New hardware is also included with the torque converter and is used for various applications.

DIESEL

198

With the factory torque converter removed, the transmission input splines are checked for wear; in this case they were in perfect condition.

T-bar handles are included in the kit to ease the installation of the Precision torque converter on to the input shaft.

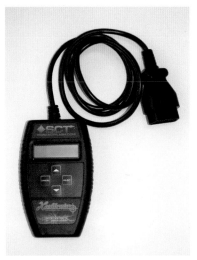

Brian's Truck Shop works closely with Precision and installs Precision's transmission programming into the SCT programmer. This is simply installed by plugging it into the data port and downloading the new program.

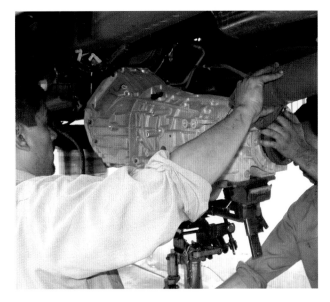

With the new torque converter in place, the transmission is reinstalled into the truck's chassis.

We finished off our installation by adding Royal Purple Max ATF to our Ford. This allowed for smoother operation and helps reduce heat.

EXTERIOR

It takes quite a bit of time, talent, and effort to complete the designing and masking steps for a quality custom paint job.

TIME: One hour

 TOOLS: Socket set, screwdrivers . . . basics

 TALENT: ★

 APPLICABLE YEARS: Most years, makes, and models of light trucks

 TAB: $200–$500; depends on type of grille and whether you change the surround

 TINWARE: N/A

 TIP: This is an easy way to change the appearance of your pickup truck.

 PERFORMANCE GAIN: Cosmetic only, but cool looks appear faster and louder than stock

COMPLEMENTARY PROJECT: Driving lights and color-matching bumper cover

In order to install one of the two new billet pieces for the 2005 Super Duty, the surround must be removed. This is done by pushing up on the clips that hold the surround to the core support. The screws at the top of the core support are also removed, and the factory grill/surround can be removed from the truck.

The billet pieces are inserted; once they are in place, the factory grille/surround is replaced on the truck for a nice upgrade.

EXTERIOR

Many Ford truck enthusiasts eagerly anticipate the availability of the next model-year Super Duty pickup trucks. Although the truck has a slightly new appearance, some eager owner will want to be the first on the block to customize one. Fortunately, some aftermarket components are already being developed for the new Super Duty. We were offered an exclusive look at Stull's new grille for the 2005 Super Duty, as well as a new, less-expensive grille and surround that will fit on to the 2004 and earlier models. Stull designs aftermarket components for earlier model trucks as well as next year's model and the model year after that.

Ford engineers did a great job in upgrading the appearance of the 2005 Super Duty, but for those of us who can't leave well enough alone, two aftermarket pieces are available that can quickly change the truck from stock to custom. The first is Stull's billet aluminum inserts that fit into the five factory grille openings on the original grille. In this application, no cutting is necessary because the billet pieces fit over the egg-crate sections of the grille and are held in place with easy-to-install brackets that secure the billet inserts from behind the factory grille.

The second option offers enthusiasts a more custom appearance. Stull's offers a full-face billet grille that replaces the factory unit and comes with its own surround. The surround is a premolded plastic piece that can be painted to match the body color. This option requires drilling a couple of brackets into the Super Duty's radiator core support in order to hold the full-length billet grille in place. The new surround snaps into the factory clip holds at the bottom of the core support and is bolted to the top of the support with the factory screws. The results are exactly what many Super Duty enthusiasts love, a clean custom appearance that is easy to install and offers a different look over the large factory grille.

For the current and earlier model trucks (2004 and earlier), Stull's also offers a billet insert system that has the same full-billet grille appearance that utilizes the factory surround and does not involve any cutting. The billet insert fits into the factory grille and surround and clamps into place with the provided brackets. Although there is no need to cut out the original grille from the surround, Stull's recommends masking and spraying the inside portion of the factory grille with flat black paint. This prevents any of the chrome on the factory grill from showing through the billet overlay. The result is a custom full-billet appearance that many Super Duty owners prefer. Earlier versions of this style grille required a separate insert and used a metal surround. The cost for this kit was about $400–$500. Stull's new full-grill insert gives you the same appearance for less than $200.

Both grill treatments are made with Stull's precision billet extrusions that are powder-coated and come with a fully polished edge. We've illustrated the installation procedures here, and depending on the look you want for your Super Duty, it takes only about 30 minutes to install the insert.

Stull's highly polished grille fits perfectly within the factory surround. Some Phillips screws are used to secure the grille to the surround; they are inserted from the front.

The top of the surround is unbolted from the radiator core support, and similar clips are used to secure the bottom.

This shot from the rear shows how the grille is supported with brackets and long Phillips screws.

Once the bottom clips are released, the grille/surround can be removed from the truck.

The customized grille is then installed by pushing the bottom clips into the radiator core support. The factory screws are reinstalled on to the surround to complete the installation.

This full billet grille look is also less expensive, as it does not require a new molded surround. The $200 suggested price reflects the savings that many enthusiasts will love.

Here's how a properly masked and painted Super Duty grille looks when it is done.

TIME: Two hours

 TOOLS: Full socket set and hand tools

 TALENT: ★

 APPLICABLE YEARS: Mostly late model, but check with manufacturer

 TAB: $400

 TINWARE: Auxiliary lights

 TIP: It's a simple install, but instructions are still needed.

PERFORMANCE GAIN:
Some protection from a low-speed impact and as a porous barrier in front of the radiator

COMPLEMENTARY PROJECT:
HD lights or additional driving lights mounted on the grille guard

The two black bolts on each side of the bumper must be loosened just enough to slide the grille guard brackets into position beneath the bolts. This is easy, because the nuts holding these bolts in place are fixed and do not require a wrench on the other end. Loosen only one side of the bumper at a time.

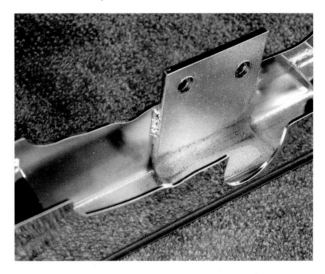

The grille guard uprights are laser cut from 11-gauge steel and finished with nickel-chrome plating that is backed with a six-year warranty.

When push comes to shove, bigger is better. In many off-road situations, many vehicles often need a push to get out of a sticky situation. In this case, a truck with a good push bar will do the trick. But if you are looking for a real grille guard that doesn't wobble or is merely added on for looks, then you may want to check out the Go Industries Big Tex grille guard. Not only is the Big Tex larger than most other guards, but it uses sturdy factory mounting points so that it is actually functional.

The Big Tex guard is manufactured from 14-gauge steel and features a one-piece tubular frame that measures 1.9 inches in diameter. The guard is available in a chromed or black powder coat finish and features light tabs to mount multiple off-road lights. With external welds and a sturdy design, the Big Tex is definitely heavy duty, and Go Industries claims that the Big Tex is simple to install.

We looked into what it would take to install a Big Tex grille guard on to a Ford F-150 Super Duty and found that the installation was as simple as Go Industries claimed. The brackets included in the kit were easy to install near the factory tow hooks

of the truck. Once these were in place, the upright bars were bolted on to the brackets. It's a tight fit but it goes together without any problems. Once the upright bars are in place, the one-piece crossbar is installed and bolted in behind the uprights.

After we bolted together the guard, we noticed that it was solid and that there was still plenty of room between it and the front grille of the truck. The mounting points even allowed us to still use the truck's factory tow hooks. In addition, the chromed finish looked great on this vehicle, giving it an improved look.

EXTERIOR

203

Because the grille guard bracket holes are threaded, attaching the uprights is easy. At this point, do not tighten the bolts. We'll save that for a later step to allow for adjusting the grille guard's fit.

The heavy-duty push pads are firmly attached and thick enough to absorb relentless abuse throughout the course of their lifetime.

After adjusting the Big Tex grille guard to its proper position, tightening the bolts is made easy by the ample space between the grille guard and the grille.

The Big Tex bar not only looks good, but it protects the front of this Ford Super Duty and provides a solid platform to lend aid to any stuck vehicle.

The crossbars are then bolted into position on the upright brackets. The crossbars come preassembled and simply bolt in at the rear.

EXTERIOR

TIME: Two hours

TOOLS: Hand application

TALENT: ★

APPLICABLE YEARS: Available for all years, makes, and models of light trucks

TAB: Depends on extent of graphic application you want. Estimate: $150

TINWARE: Gloves, clean room

TIP: Consider vinyl graphics as an alternative to paint. Both have advantages and challenges.

PERFORMANCE GAIN:
N/A

COMPLEMENTARY PROJECT:
N/A

Emigdio Perez "weeds" the black vinyl section, separating the perfectly trimmed design from the excess vinyl.

Perez extracts the finished graphic carefully and skillfully from its vinyl base.

One of the easiest ways to add some graphics to your truck is by using vinyl. But if you remember vinyl graphics only as large triangles and stripes that are made from neon colors that are prominently displayed on mini-trucks, you haven't kept up to date. Vinyl graphics are now used on new vehicles from the manufacturer, including the Ford Harley Davidson Edition trucks and several others.

Vinyl graphics have been around for a long time but have evolved with thinner materials that have a wider range of colors. Computer-generated vinyl graphics also allow for more intricate designs that could not be done in the past. Furthermore, some vinyl products also adhere better and resist fading from exposure to the sun.

In addition to all of the advances in vinyl graphics, these materials are as diverse as the people who can come up with the designs. Everything from flames to tribal designs is possible. We wanted to upgrade a truck with vinyl to see how drastically it

EXTERIOR

can alter the truck's appearance. We took a bright red 2002 Ford F-150 to Permanent Impressions, a graphics studio in Huntington Beach, California. The owner wanted a tribal band design applied to the truck in a combination of black and silver. The results were impressive, and the steps it took to create the design will give you an idea of the process.

Perez encases the finished black vinyl section in transfer tape so he can apply the graphic to the vehicle.

The company's applicator, Matt Murphy, begins the tedious task of applying the black section of the tribal band graphic.

Murphy and Perez painstakingly lay the vinyl section on the passenger-side front fender so it is level and positioned exactly.

Satisfied that the graphic within the transfer tape is perfectly positioned, Spencer Watzke begins to peel the black section of the graphic.

Perez carefully trims the graphic around the truck's emblems and door openings.

The vinyl graphic is massaged permanently and smoothly into place, and all air bubbles are removed.

The silver section of vinyl is permanently positioned above the black section.

Although it is impossible to see both sides at the same time, great pains are taken to be sure the graphics are positioned exactly the same on both sides of the truck.

Unlike custom paint, vinyl graphics can appear exactly the same on several vehicles, however, the customer can specify whatever colors he desires so he can be different from the next guy.

TIME: Eight hours

TOOLS: Metal-cutting snips, tin, tack welding gear, bodywork tools

TALENT: ★

APPLICABLE YEARS: Available for all years, makes, and models of light trucks

TAB: $50 in materials

TINWARE: Body filler

TIP: Once you have completed this project, you have the ability to shave any automotive component you want. The process is similar for each door handle, radio antenna, and so on.

PERFORMANCE GAIN:
Strictly aesthetic

COMPLEMENTARY PROJECT:
Line up roll-pan installation

After the tailgate handle relocater is installed, body-man Emo Torrez begins the shaving procedure by preparing the surface around the handle depression.

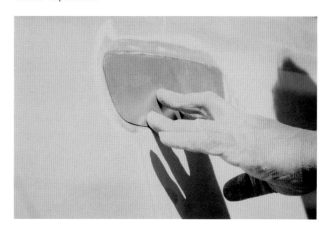

He then test-fits a precut section of metal specially designed to fit the stock handle depression.

Torrez then carefully tacks the filler piece into position to fill the depression.

EXTERIOR

Some conversion procedures have become traditional in the creation of a quality project vehicle. Among these are tinted windows, big custom wheels with fat tires, a tonneau cover, altered suspension (either raised or lowered), custom grille, rolled pan, and so on. Although some of these items simply bolt on, modifying the truck's sheet metal involves much more knowledge and technique.

One of the most popular and simple to install upgrades is the addition of a shaved tailgate. Simply stated, the stock tailgate handle is relocated to the inside surface of the tailgate via an easy-to-install tailgate handle relocator. The depression and hole in the tailgate left by the removal of the stock handle is what takes the skill of a professional body man, but saving some money by doing most of the work yourself can still make this upgrade an affordable one.

After relocating the tailgate handle to the inside (bed) portion of the tailgate, the hole that is left requires welding in a steel plate, applying filler, and smoothing it for paint. There is more than meets the eye in shaving a tailgate. The fact is that the surrounding sheet metal wants to buckle as heat is applied to weld the hole. It

requires a body man with experience, talent, and finesse to carefully fill the handle depression and hole with just the right amount of heat from the welding torch and apply the heat in exactly the right spot so that the surrounding sheet metal doesn't buckle.

Body specialist Emigdio "Emo" Torrez at Continental Auto Body, in Huntington Beach, California, has been shaving tailgates as long as he can remember. He's a master at it. In the accompanying photos, Emo shows us how it's done on this Dodge Ram. As you can see, the result of this small body modification makes a huge difference in the overall appearance of any truck.

He then removes any traces of the letters and the factory adhesive with a polishing wheel that does not hurt the paint.

Once the filler piece is in place, Torrez fills the spot with a "Bondo-like" acrylic filler and smoothes it.

Although traces of the handle depression are still visible, the depression is almost smooth and, with a little more filler, will be ready for paint.

The Ram's tailgate is beginning to look shaved. Torrez gives the tailgate a little love here and there, but the final smoothing of the filler can't happen until the filling material is thoroughly dry and well hardened.

Torrez applies additional coats of filler to the depression to make the area perfectly smooth.

In the paint booth, painter George Valle gives the tailgate extra attention.

He then smoothes the filler while it is still soft to eliminate any signs of the welding depressions. After the soft filler is as smooth as possible, Torrez continues the shaving process by removing the factory lettering and dislodging the letters with plastic banding material.

Valle applies coats of primer and paint to ready the tailgate to be reinstalled. When the tailgate is thoroughly dry, it is reinstalled on to the Ram.

TIME: Depends on project complexity

 TOOLS: Creativity

 TALENT: ★★★★

 APPLICABLE YEARS: Available for all years, makes, and models of light trucks

 TAB: Depends on design (case by case)

 TINWARE: Paintbrushes, paints, solvents, drop clothes

 TIP: It's easy to mess this one up. If you have the money, pay for an expert's time.

 PERFORMANCE GAIN:
Strictly aesthetic

COMPLEMENTARY PROJECT:
New tires and wheels always look trick with fresh flames flowing.

EXTERIOR

G raphics featuring flames have been popular on customized vehicles for years. The idea stretches back to the early 1950s and has been prominent on everything from hot rods to full custom trucks. Recently, custom paint jobs featuring flames have enjoyed resurgence in popularity, especially on trucks. The larger, wider hoods allow for a larger canvas from which the artist can add a multitude of flames that dazzle the imagination.

The new automotive flames are bigger and better than ever, more elegant and colorful. And they're not only in painted-on graphics, but flames are also used in aftermarket gauge faces, license plate frames, shirts, and more. Applying the new generation of painted flames is more of a science than ever. The available paints have been improved with time and technology. Painters and pinstripers have developed new techniques and procedures that go from a traditional freehand layout of flames to precut vinyl stencils and even realistic-looking airbrush techniques.

We followed the application of a traditional-style flame paint job on a well-customized 2003 GMC Sierra. Like many painters, the one who did this job designed his paint job right

Our painter began by outlining the flames with tape and completely masking the surrounding area with a combination of blue and green tape. The hood is masked so that the exposed surfaces can be sprayed with chameleon paint to form the flame design.

The design is then carried to the front fenders and doors.

The painter prepares to complete the masking on the driver's door.

Satisfied that the truck is masked exactly as he wants it, the painter carefully hand-sands the surfaces to be painted so that the paint will adhere.

on the vehicle. He did some careful sanding to prepare the "cleared" surface to accept his customizing paint. He thoroughly masked the areas surrounding the flames to protect them from his paint. He then sprayed that trick chameleon paint that seems to change color depending on how the light hits it. When the area was completely dry, the painter color-sanded the entire area before it was buffed out to a brilliant shine. Then the pinstriper took over and accented the flames with pinstripes in a vivid color, and the job was done. The accompanying photos and captions show the highlights of the application.

The sanded surfaces are wiped down with a solvent.

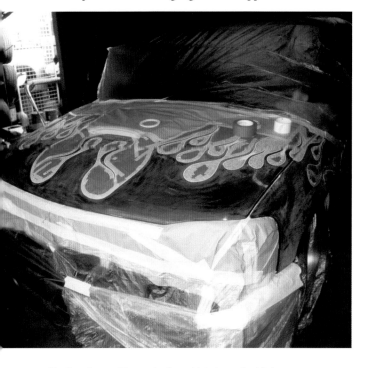

He then thoroughly masks the vehicle to protect it from overspray.

Spraying the chameleon paint smoothly and evenly requires a steady, experienced hand.

Careful attention is paid to applying paint to all of the truck's surfaces.

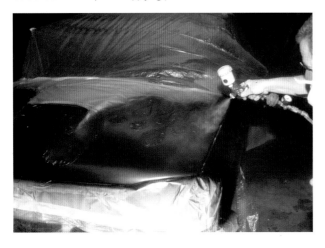

Once the first coat is dry, a second coat of paint is sprayed to the hood.

The masking tape must be carefully removed so it doesn't disturb the hard edge of the chameleon paint.

When the paint is thoroughly dry, remove the masking tape. This is a tedious job that requires care and time.

"Soft" paint is very fragile, especially in a complex design such as this, and must be handled gingerly.

The painter then color-sanded the freshly painted surface and buffed it to a brilliant shine.

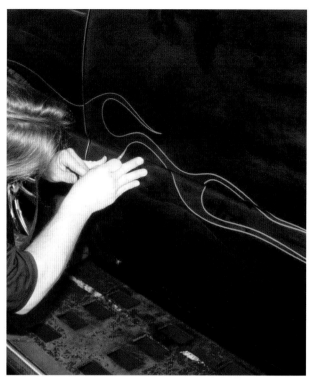

A vivid pink paint is selected for the pinstriping. This acts to accent the flames with a contrasting outline and provides a nice transition between the flames and the body color.

Because the painted flame design was clear-coated, the pinstriper had to scuff it once again to "break" the clear coat so the pin-striping paint would adhere.

When the pinstriping was thoroughly dry, the Sierra was once again polished, clear-coated, and detailed.

TIME: One hour

TOOLS: Small socket set

TALENT: ★

APPLICABLE YEARS: All

TAB: About $700

TINWARE: N/A

TIP: Allow the hood to settle in place several days before you have it color-matched.

PERFORMANCE GAIN:
Aesthetic benefits only

COMPLEMENTARY PROJECT:
Bumper cover and driving lights

The old hood is unbolted by removing the two bolts on the factory hinges. There are two bolts on each side of the hood. You should have someone help you support the hood as you unbolt it.

With all the bolts removed, two people can carefully remove the hood from the truck. Make sure to keep the factory latch, as it will be used on the new hood.

O ne of the simplest ways to improve your truck's appearance is with a custom hood. Hoods come in a variety of styles that can be both functional and aggressive in appearance. Seldom is one hood both functional and aggressive, but the fact is that cold air can produce additional horsepower if the air path can connect to the engine's air intake system.

Hoods vary not only in styles but also in the materials they are constructed from. Most are manufactured from either steel or fiberglass. Although both have distinct advantages, one material may be better for your particular truck than the other.

Steel hoods have the advantage of being ready to paint and are a simple bolt-on application. Steel hoods also tend to fit better than fiberglass hoods, but they are also heavier and are typically not functional. Their rigidity allows them to be sturdier than fiberglass, but they cannot be sanded or modified to ensure a perfect fit.

Fiberglass hoods can be sanded and smoothed to give an exact fit if they are molded properly. Good fiberglass hoods will also feature a smooth, gel-coat finish on both the outer and inner portions of the hood. This allows the hood to have a smooth look underneath that, when painted, enhances the engine compartment.

Furthermore, many fiberglass hoods can come with a functional hood scoop that adapts to the factory air intake system. This can provide cool air into the engine and can increase horsepower and torque. Although fiberglass hoods do need to properly cure, most body shops recommend that you leave the hood bolted on the truck for a few days to a week to allow the hood to shrink and set before attempting to paint. This eliminates any shrinking after the paint has been applied, which can result in small cracks in the finish.

Let's see how simple it would be to install a high-quality, aftermarket, fiberglass hood. Our truck was one that was in dire need

EXTERIOR

of attention: an older 1998 Ford F-150 that had a thin carbon-fiber hood that has long since deteriorated past the point of use.

We opted to use a Cobra-style hood that incorporates a cowl to improve the appearance of this truck. APM is one manufacturer of quality fiberglass hoods that bolt on using the existing factory hardware. The hood came with a finished gel coat that simply needs to be sanded and prepped for paint. Unfortunately, our model truck did not accept one of APM's functional scoops, but the style would definitely allow us to easily change the truck's appearance by simply unbolting the old hood and bolting on the APM hood.

It takes two people to support the hood and to bolt it into position. Once this is done, the bolts are left relatively loose, allowing the hood to be adjusted from side to side and from front to rear. Once the correct alignment has been made, the hood's hinge bolts are tightened, and the hood is ready to be prepped for paint.

Once this hood is installed, you will see the difference it can make in the overall appearance of the truck, turning it from stock to custom with one simple modification.

This APM hood features steel inserts so that it can be easily bolted on to the factory hood hinges with the original hardware.

It may take several tries opening and closing the hood, but if the hood's hinge bolts are snug, the hood can be adjusted. Also make sure to adjust the hood's bump stops to ensure it sits at the proper height in comparison to the fenders.

In most cases the factory hinges with the hood struts are sufficient to supporting an aftermarket fiberglass hood and don't need to be changed.

The original hood latch mechanism is removed from the old hood and is bolted on to the new APM fiberglass unit.

The finished installation looks good and will dramatically improve the appearance of the truck. The hood will be left on the truck for several days to reduce shrinking before it is sent to the paint shop.

TIME: Eight hours

TOOLS: Cutting wheel, power source for cutting wheel, marker pen, body working tools

TALENT: ★★

APPLICABLE YEARS: All

TAB: $10.50 to whatever price you are willing to pay to acquire the scoop

TINWARE: Masking tape, primer paint, template material, color-matched paint, sandpaper

TIP: Test-fit the scoop unpainted and color-match after install.

PERFORMANCE GAIN:
Potential great source of cool air if you take the time to channel (duct hose) the air into your filter housing

COMPLEMENTARY PROJECT:
Routing duct hose from each vent into the air filter housing

EXTERIOR

If a suitable donor vehicle is unavailable, try other sources. This '72 GTO fender vent was purchased on eBay for $10.50.

It was then sanded down to bare metal and primed to prepare it for attachment to the host vehicle.

Ram-Air or cold-air induction hood scoops have been in use on factory musclecars for decades. Aside from helping the engine breathe in cool air, they also look great. This has resulted in the proliferation of both functional and non-functional hood scoop options on virtually any vehicle that's a high-performance model or a "Hi-po wanna-be." The shift from carbureted engines to fuel-injected engines has moved the typical air intake/air filter location away from the top, center of the engine and over to one side or the other. Many of the fuel-injected Chevy trucks use one of the fenders as the cold air intake chamber. There are probably a dozen aftermarket sources that attempt to improve on this air intake setup with high-flow air filters, smooth air ducting, low-restriction mass airflow (MAF) sensors, and even improved throttle bodies, but very little has been done to help get the air into the fender in the first place. Take a close look at your truck to see how air gets into the fender chamber, and you'll find a disappointingly small opening. This represents an airflow restriction that's been practically ignored. Adding your own fender scoop can give your truck the same performance and aesthetic benefits as the Ram-Air or cold-air

induction hood scoops that we're all still so fond of.

There aren't many add-on fender scoops available through normal sources, but there is another option, which is to take a fender vent from a 1960s or 1970s musclecar, reverse it so it becomes a scoop instead of a vent, and mount it on to the air intake fender of your truck. Thumb through any musclecar magazine and you'll see various sizes and styles of vents and side scoops on cars from Buicks to Trans Ams.

We got this idea from Rick (alias Rickman2K and 89Sierra) on the Chevy Truck World.com Forum, who installed a pair of Trans Am fender vents on his Chevy truck. Because many of us prefer not to "cross-breed" components from two different manufacturers, we stuck with General Motors and grafted a reversed fender vent from a 1972 GTO on to a 1996 GMC Z71 pickup. The method of affixing the scoop to each fender should reveal itself. Some will use backing bolts as part of the scoop; you may acquire correct bolts with the scoop or, if necessary, you can rally up a couple from the auto parts store.

Most auto parts stores carry spray paint that's close to matching the common factory colors. Next, paint it to match and patiently wait for at least a day before you mount it. Apply gobs of wax along the cut edges of the fender to inhibit rust, and then bolt on your new Ram Air Fender scoop from the inside. Your completed project is not only as functional as the popular Ram Air hood scoops, but it definitely looks cool too.

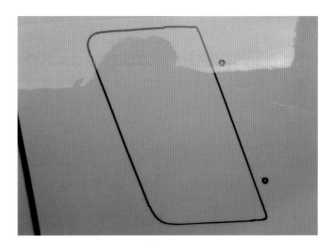

Then use the template to draw your cutout and mounting holes.

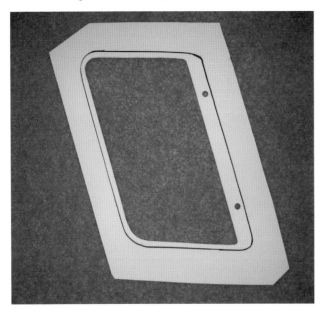

Draw and cut out an accurate cardboard template of the vent/scoop. This will help position it correctly on your truck's fender.

This is the scary part (it's sort of like doing surgery on a family member). Use a small cutting wheel to cut and trim the hole.

Pick a functional, good-looking location for the scoop where you have some access from the inner fenderwell and the contour of the fender is close to the shape of the new scoop.

File and sand the edges of the cut until they are smooth. Then trial-fit the scoop. This one was made of metal, so a few whacks with a rubber mallet (off the truck, of course) resulted in it having the same curve as the fender of the truck.

TIME: Two hours

TOOLS: Full access to tools and bodyworking equipment

TALENT: ★★★

APPLICABLE YEARS: Body kits and components for all years, makes, and models of light trucks

TAB: About $1,500 for complete kit as seen in this publication. Price reduced when broken into component parts.

TINWARE: N/A

TIP: Fit parts before you paint.

PERFORMANCE GAIN:
Aerodynamics may improve due to downforce created by the ground effects.

COMPLEMENTARY PROJECT:
New tires and wheels

First order of business was to open the boxes and get a look at the Extreme Dimensions Platinum aero kit made up of six pieces and an optional hood. John's Customs & Performance had worked on the development of the product, but this was its first look at production pieces.

EXTERIOR

For many years, racers have installed and tuned ground effects to master the flow of air to literally punch a hole through the wind at high speeds. The idea is to channel the resisting air around and over the vehicle, as well as eliminate much of it from being forced underneath, which causes lift and a loss of traction. In the world of trucks, installing ground effects is probably 80 percent form and 20 percent function. In short, ground effects, in this instance, are installed primarily to enhance the overall appearance of a Ford F-150 pickup.

I'm sure that everyone who has watched any form of racing has heard the phrase "The track came to us." In this world of ground effects, the market changed and came to Extreme Dimensions (ED). What changed the market? Big, bigger, and then huge diameter wheels! The owner of this Ford F-150 would settle for nothing short of 24-inch "bling" for his new ride. But he also desired the best of both worlds and searched for a way to lower his truck as well . . . or at least a method to make it look as if it were clamped down to the asphalt. The answer came in the way of a six-piece Platinum body kit from Extreme Dimensions.

Although Extreme Dimensions primarily targets the import, performance, and luxury car markets, a portion of its 6,000-plus products are targeted at the truck/SUV marketplace as well. Launched in the summer of 2000, the company has raced to the forefront of the ground effects market, providing one of the largest varieties of high-quality aerodynamic products at a self-described affordable price. What sets Extreme Dimensions apart from competitors is that the company is a manufacturer, importer, and distributor of fiberglass and carbon composite products.

The new-bodied Ford F-150 debuted in the fall of 2004. Following a marketing plan, Extreme Dimensions began the task of developing an aerodynamic package for this truck after one year of production. What came as a surprise to me, though, was learning that the company literally scrapped the initial designs even though it meant not being able to debut it at that year's SEMA show. These pictures are the very first to show this aero kit!

What you can't see is a Valor 6.5-inch Double Din fully motorized in-dash monitor featuring components from MA

Audio installed by Rezonates Creations. And also hidden from view is the DJM 2/4-suspension drop installed by IMZZ. What you can see are the huge 24-inch wheels and tires from American Racing and BFG, respectively. Snugtop stepped in with one of its latest bedcovers while Magnaflow installed a cat-back exhaust system with a polished tip. Modern Image handled the show roll call. But the key ingredient to the show looks of this ride is the Extreme Dimensions aero package.

Several things happen with the installation of huge wheels. You get more chrome flash than anyone on the highway, and the wheelwell openings are filled with nothing but wheel and tire. For us custom types, though, the suspension drop has to be modest if any at all. This is where the Extreme Dimensions ground effects come into play. By extending the body down closer to the ground, the truck not only becomes a standout from the crowd, but it creates the visual illusion that it is slammed. Because its products are actually race influenced and aerodynamically functional, particular and unique lines had to be engineered into all six pieces of this Platinum kit. The most dramatic lines to be found are on the nose and hood, which was not installed on the final version of this particular truck.

Leigh Guarnieri, ED's sponsorships and special events coordinator, practically lived with the folks at John's Customs & Performance as the kit went from drawing board to reality. This process also included a very tedious test involving the design and redesign process. It is one thing to design and attach boxy

The crew at JC&P had to hang the nose, set the hood into place, and temporarily mount the side skirts just so everyone, including yours truly, could have a look. Once all components have been given a final fit, they will be removed for painting, as they are now only in white gel coat.

First order of business was a test fit of the side skirts. Each side is made up of two components, one for the cab and another to extend on to the bed, with a small gap in between.

With the tailgate removed, you can see how the rear aero kit component will mount behind the rotation of the stock tailgate. The hitch assembly had to be removed as well.

The rear bumper cover was removed from the truck, painted to match the white finish, color-sanded, and then buffed to a glossy finish. You also get a clear view of the rear panel and how it seals underneath the tailgate. The sides have hidden mounting tabs.

EXTERIOR

components to a square van or SUV and quite another task when it comes to extending and enhancing the swoopy styling of the very aerodynamic Ford F-150. The photo sequence documents the final product, which showcases the end product involving months of work by several parties. If you love big wheels but desire the looks of a lowered truck, Extreme Dimensions just may have the aerodynamic kit you desire to personalize your truck or SUV!

As mentioned previously, the side skirts are made up of two separate pieces, one for the cab, one for the bed. Now that the pieces are finished and painted, each is aligned and permanently mounted on to the body. A mesh screen is included in the kit and must be formed over the brake duct openings to complete the cosmetic appeal of the nose. Likewise, the large fish-mouth opening of the nose piece can be left this way or fit with a large section of aluminum mesh to form a custom grille. Fit is important at this stage. Using body filler as a glue, they used it to install the wire mesh grille. Mix it hot, and it dries in a minute!

This is where the skinny guy at the body shop team comes into play. Once the grilles were in place, someone had to go under the truck to install the mounting bolts.

The front wheels are the same size, 24-inch American Racing units, but now they truly tuck and fill the wheel openings without giving this Ford a lifted look. Extreme Dimensions achieved its goal of making this truck look like it is going 100 mph while standing still.

TIME: Two hours

TOOLS: N/A

TALENT: ★

APPLICABLE YEARS: All years, makes, and models of light trucks

TAB: $500–$700

TINWARE: N/A

TIP: Plan on dropping off your truck and picking it up at the end of the day.

PERFORMANCE GAIN:
Great truck bed protection that won't scratch, gouge, or fade

COMPLEMENTARY PROJECT:
Install a bed cap or tonneau cover

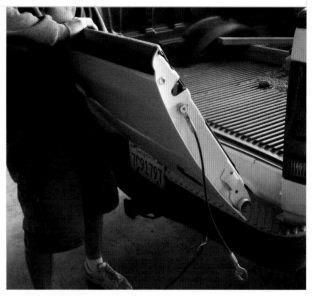

Truck bed sides are protected with construction paper and plastic. Tailgate is removed.

Detail tape outlines the area to be sprayed. After the Line-X is applied and the protective masking plastic comes off, the fine wire embedded in this white tape will be pulled, and it defines the clean separation between the paint finish and the protective liner.

The tailgate's exterior is protected and only the surface that receives the spray-in liner is exposed. Screws and bolts anchoring the drop-in bedliner are removed. Once freed, the entire drop-in bedliner is removed. Anchor bolts fastening the truck bed to the truck frame are removed so that the spray-in material coverage is complete.

For the guy restoring the classic pickup truck, a hardwood bed kit all smoothed and polished with glistening stainless-steel runners is a trick way to finish the truck bed flooring. The truck bed sidewalls are color-matched with the rest of the truck, and nothing more than a couple of weekend getaway suitcases will likely ever be used as cargo. That's a fine way to go for a hot rod or show truck.

However, if you haul gear with your pickup, that painted surface on the truck bed is going to get worked. Even when you order your late-model pickup with a drop-in plastic bedliner from the factory, you might experience rust buildup between the plastic bedliner and the sheet metal of the truck bed after a few years. Dirt, leaves, and moisture immediately start to collect under the plastic bedliner. And we have all seen the occasional entire drop-in plastic bedliner crumpled up against the freeway retaining wall that a rogue gust of wind picked up, threw high into the air, and enjoyed some hang time in front of oncoming traffic like a maple leaf dancing in the wind.

A spray-in bedliner is an option that offers protection without the risk of gouging sheet metal or corrosion between the drop-in liner and the truck bed. Line-X is a product that is sprayed on to the truck bed floor, sidewalls, and inner tailgate at 200 degrees F. The bond is instantaneous, and you can drive your truck away almost immediately. The process is quick and the protection is permanent. Check out the photos to see what is involved.

EXTERIOR

221

Once the drop-in bedliner is removed, the bedrails are masked off. Late-model Ford trucks have a more permanent plastic top rail protector, so it is more logical to leave it in place. Other trucks lend themselves more readily to extending the Line-X coating over the top bedrail.

Line-X is sprayed on to the truck bed, and in a matter of minutes, the material is applied at 200 degrees Fahrenheit. The bond is instant.

With the truck in the spray booth, the truck cab is covered with plastic sheeting.

Here's the complete install, clean and simple.

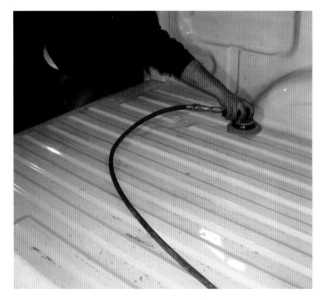

The truck bed is cleaned up with compressed air, then scuffed with a power disc to create a bonding surface for the Line-X. Denatured alcohol is used to wipe down and clean the truck bed surface.

Bed bolts, screws, and anchors are all reinstalled, and the truck is ready to roll.

TIME: Two hours

TOOLS: Full socket set, screwdrivers

TALENT: ★

APPLICABLE YEARS: All years, makes, and models of light trucks

TAB: $1,300–$1,700

TINWARE: N/A

TIP: N/A

PERFORMANCE GAIN:
N/A

COMPLEMENTARY PROJECT:
Tailgate lock if not installed from factory

The roll cover is shippable by common carrier and comes complete with every piece of hardware you will need. Place the roll cover canister on the edge of the tailgate and recruit a helper to heft it up toward the front of the truck bed. Walk on the outer sides of the truck bed rather than in it.

Position and center the roll cover canister from side to side. Measure the space between the inside of the truck rails and the canister housing. Next, you will position the curtain guides on the left- and right-side bed rails. The curtain guides lock into the curtain canister.

EXTERIOR

That big box attached to every pickup truck is one of the most versatile spaces in the automotive nation. You can fill it up, cover it up, or collect wind samples until an acquaintance promotes you to a friend on moving day. However you use your truck bed, there are many times when you wish you could protect valuable gear such as your work tools or goose decoys from theft and weather. With a single-panel tonneau cover, the look is great, but to transport anything taller than the bed rails means the cover is lifted to clear the object. That looks awkward. Forget about hauling the dirt bikes or snowmobile. A camper shell also has its advantages, limitations, and lockable space.

A high-quality alternative that will allow you to cover your truck bed and secure the contents is the roll cover by Truck Covers U.S.A. A roll cover permits you to open up your truck bed to accommodate and transport large objects, and keep it covered with a hard surface that cannot be penetrated with a knife or pointed object. The long-bed cover installs with eight heavy-gauge aluminum clamps (six clamps for a short bed) that guide the aluminum curtain. Each aluminum panel or slat that makes up the roll cover would remind some folks of an aircraft aileron

because of the high-end construction and almost seamless fit. The curtain is powder coated black to ensure a durable finish.

Installation is fairly quick, about two hours, and straightforward. Two people are recommended to perform the install. While one friend helps align and hold sections of the guide rails and curtain in place, the other bolts it down. You will drill holes for four drainage outlets that provide a flexible and well-designed system to get water and moisture out of the truck bed when the curtain is closed.

There are some variations and tapering, from the front of the truck bed to the tailgate, depending upon which truck manufacturer and model you are dealing with. To custom fit each application, high-density nylon shims are included with each application. These shims will not crush or deform under the load of the clamp bolts.

223

Take a measurement from side to side at the cab end of the truck bed and again at the tailgate as seen here. Any taper in the truck bed from front to rear will be revealed through this measurement and you will compensate, if needed, with shims. Have your helper pull the side rail tight against the truck bed rail while you place shims and snug down the clamps. You can tighten these Grade-8 bolts until they are cinched without fear of pulling through the clamp or stripping. With the help of your partner holding the rail fast against the truck bed, walk your way down each rail side positioning all eight clamps and shims where needed.

Grab the tether and draw the tonneau curtain back to the tailgate. Check the clearances, the fit, and the ease of locking the cover. You can adjust the spring tension easily if the curtain does not pull back at a comfortable pace. With the cover alignment squared away, tighten down all clamp bolts.

You will drill drain holes through the double-walled sheet metal just below the drain spigot along the side-rail drain channel. Spray the raw drain hole with corrosion preventative and insert rubber grommet. Measure and cut the flexible hose supplied, and then install.

Here's how the drain assembly looks up at the front of the truck bed under the roll canister. You can also see how much useable space you have beneath the canister.

Pull the curtain taut and flush over the lip of the tailgate, then test the lock and fit once more.

Install final locking screws to secure entire rear assembly in place.

Install canister roll cover plate. You can stand on this plate.

Install finishing canister cover screw caps. And there you have it!

TIME: Two hours

TOOLS: Full socket set and hand tools

TALENT: ★

APPLICABLE YEARS: All

TAB: About $1,200

TINWARE: N/A

TIP: N/A

PERFORMANCE GAIN:
N/A

COMPLEMENTARY PROJECT:
Bed rug kit

Cargo caps are recognized for their ability to add security and for weatherproofing a truck's bed, but our test revealed a 2-mpg increase in fuel mileage due to reduced drag!

Prior to the bed cap being installed, the wiring harness is ported through the bed and is readied for connection to the cap's lighting. The truck's door seal is removed to allow access to the pickup's remote door locking system, which will be attached to the rear glass latch system of the Leer cap.

John Collins took note of the growing popularity of the pickup truck back in the late 1960s and the need for truck caps. After all, trucks haul cargo and freight, and pickup owners needed a truck cap for recreational use, both requiring security and protection from the elements. Makeshift camper shells fabricated of wood and aluminum just weren't going to cut it with the lack of styling and quality. Fiberglass arose as the preferred material to meet the new demands for style proving to be remarkably strong and lightweight.

Collins' eventual bed cap company became known as Leer. The Leer name is a spin on Lear, a major Shakespeare character and a close spelling to a very popular, sleek private jet. Collins' timing to introduce a stylish fiberglass bed cap to the pickup industry could not have been better as what began as a dream quickly matured into a dominant industry in the truck accessories category. Truck owners discovered the benefits of adding protection and security to their pickups. The added benefits are found in protecting the bed itself from the elements, including the sun, and other hazards.

Research studies indicate that more than one out of every five pickups in the United States and Canada are now fit with a bed cover or bed cap! While we were looking to increase the secured hauling capability of this pickup through the installation of a Leer bed shell, the first long-distance trip revealed a clean two-plus mpg increase in fuel mileage! In other words, the installation of this Leer bed cap will pay for itself in less than a year's time!

Bonuses proved to be numerous. The convenience of an automatically locking cap made the use of the bed simple, and the owner knew that each time he used his key fob to lock his truck doors, the shell was locked simultaneously! What a convenience. Although ventilation is a positive, the new owner raves about the ceiling-mounted gear net; everything stays dry and nothing gets crushed. Being on a roll, a Thule roof rack was also mounted, just in case anything bigger than the bed needed to be hauled. This addition made the bed cap totally useful for the secured hauling of cargo!

For installation, we visited El Monte Campers in El Monte, California, one of hundreds of authorized Leer dealers nationwide. As you will soon see, no drilling is required to mount a Leer bed cap, which is color-matched and manufactured to fit your truck. Visit www.leer.com for a complete fit chart, picture gallery, features, and options, as well as information on how to locate a Leer dealership near you. Not only does a bed cap add style to your truck, but it will improve fuel mileage. Imagine that!

EXTERIOR

With the wiring complete, the cap is prepared for installation on to the bed. This cap can be removed just as easily for a larger load. A fat tape seal is applied to the bed rail top, which will weatherproof the cap and prevent damage to the paint.

Following a test fit and the installation of the seal tape, the Leer bed cap is slowly guided into position for the final install. Leer caps and bed covers are sold and serviced only by authorized dealers nationwide.

This installation requires no drilling. Mounting bolts penetrate the cap, then clamp to the truck's bed rails, and it doesn't move—ever.

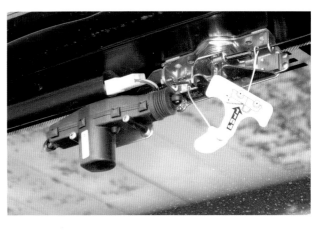

The single most favorite feature of this Leer cap install for the owner is the solenoid locking system, which works off of the stock truck's key fob. One push of the button and the truck and shell are secured!

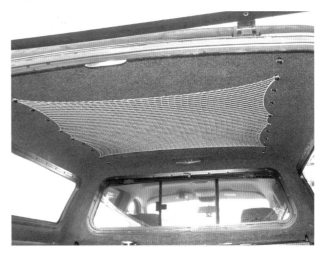

A trick accessory is this ceiling-mounted cargo net, which is ideal for protecting lightweight objects from being crushed!

With the Leer bed cap installation complete, Bill Lee was ready for his chase truck to follow the F-100 SuperTour coast to coast, and back. The secured and weatherproof bed storage proved invaluable—and the truck picked up more than 2 mpg as an added bonus!

TIME: One hour

TOOLS: Full socket set and hand tools

TALENT: ★

APPLICABLE YEARS: All

TAB: About $200

TINWARE: N/A

TIP: N/A

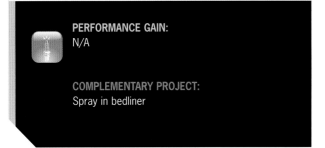

PERFORMANCE GAIN:
N/A

COMPLEMENTARY PROJECT:
Spray in bedliner

The first step is to remove the tailgate. Drop the tailgate, then lift up on it just enough so that tension on the cable is released. Once one cable is removed, remove the other cable while carefully supporting the tailgate so that it does not drop down. Lift the tailgate up and remove it. Next, remove the cable post bolts from both sides and install the AMP Research latch brackets.

One of the reasons we love our trucks is because of the versatility they provide. With comfortable interiors and all the amenities of some of the best automobiles, as well as a bed to stow cargo, tools, or toys, America's once-humble pickup truck has become the vehicle of choice for people with active lifestyles. It then makes sense that anything we can do to further increase the versatility of our trucks is naturally appealing—especially when it involves a product that is relatively inexpensive and can be installed at home in just a few minutes.

The Bed X-Tender from AMP Research is just such a product. This cleverly engineered device attaches to your truck bed just in front of the tailgate, using brackets that are installed with existing hardware (in most applications). By lowering the tailgate and swiveling the Bed X-Tender down into place, you've effectively lengthened your truck's usable bed length by more than a foot, while at the same time prevented any cargo from falling out. Close the tailgate and swivel it toward the front of the bed, and it's a handy cubby that secures small items between the tailgate and Bed X-Tender to keep them from rolling around. It's simple, it's genius, and most important, it works.

The Bed X-Tender is one of those "Why didn't I think of that?" products, for sure. Developed by AMP Research's founder, Horst Leitner, the Bed X-Tender was designed to address a re-occurring problem that he and his friends had experienced from time to time. See, Horst is a motocross racer and former European motocross champion, but also an innovator who has designed numerous products for both motocross bikes and mountain bikes. He's just one of those guys who is constantly thinking of better ways to do things.

Well, one weekend, he and his friends were out motocross riding and they started talking about one of the guys who had the misfortune of having some of his gear fall out of the back of his pickup truck. Seems the unfortunate fellow had the tailgate down to accommodate his bike, and the smaller stuff sort of slipped by and ended up on the highway. "Horst thought there must be something he could do about this," explained AMP Research's marketing director, Mark Wronski, "so he went home, penciled out a design, and that's pretty much the same product that we're selling today."

Understand that when the Bed X-Tender was invented, AMP Research was in the mountain bike business, not the truck busi-

EXTERIOR

227

ness. "We knew it was a good idea, a good product, but it wasn't until we took it to the SEMA show that it really took off," says Wronski. "Some guys from Ford came by and seemed very interested in the product. As it turns out, they were working on the Explorer Sport Trac, which wasn't due out for another year, and they were looking for a solution to make the truck's short cargo box more useable." The rest, as the saying goes, is history. "We were still offering the product to the aftermarket, but once word of the Ford deal came out, it kind of moved us into a whole new ball game."

Kind of? That's the understatement of the decade; the Bed X-Tender is not only a factory offering with Ford trucks, but also Chevy, Dodge, Toyota, Nissan, Mazda, and others. It's also available through Westin Automotive, 4 Wheel Parts Wholesalers, truck accessory shops, warehouse distributors, and even auto parts chains like Pep Boys.

We have a 2000 Chevy Silverado extended cab short bed that we use to haul the occasional dirt bike or two, and it was in desperate need of a little extra bed length. We ordered up a GM-specific "truck bed extender" (automakers used the generic name, "bed extender") through GM Parts, but AMP Research now makes a universal Bed X-Tender that fits all popular truck bed sizes. It also has a neat, new feature: a spring-loaded latch makes it possible to install or remove the Bed X-Tender from any angle, rather than just in its vertical position (like previous models and our particular model).

Follow along with the photos to see how we installed our Bed X-Tender.

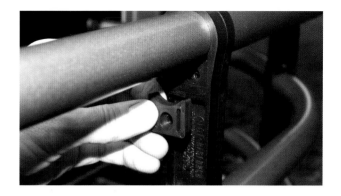

AMP Research provides a selection of small plastic wedges of different sizes and some stainless-steel screws that tighten the center tubes in the plastic support brackets. The wedges go into pockets on both sides of the center supports. For the top tube, the wedges go immediately underneath, as shown. For the lower tubes, the wedges go above and below. Place one wedge on either side of the center support, hold them together with your fingers, then insert and tighten the screw. This action draws the wedges together, securing the tubes.

One of the cool things about AMP Research's Bed X-Tender is its versatility; when folded forward, with the tailgate up, it makes a great place to put small items in the bed that you don't want rolling around, such as grocery bags. When the tailgate is lowered and the Bed X-Tender is folded rearward, you've got more than a foot of extra bed length. Tilt the Bed X-Tender to its upright position, and it can be easily lifted out; newer, universal-fit applications can be installed/removed from any position thanks to a new, spring-loaded latch mechanism.

Take the three center tubes and slide them into the center support bracket so that the assembly looks like this. Then, slide the tubes of the center section into the corner assemblies. With the Bed X-Tender loosely assembled, lower it in place over the latch brackets. You may have to slide the assembly farther apart or closer together to get it to the correct width. If you do, be sure to check the center section tubes to make sure they are still centered between the corner assemblies.

The Bed X-Tender comes with these cleverly engineered straps that click into the stock tailgate latches. Simply give them a push on each side until the latch clicks into place; this prevents the Bed X-Tender from flopping around over rough terrain or even potholes. To release the straps, just pull up on the tailgate handle. The only exception to this retention system is the Bed X-Tenders available through Ford and Mopar Parts.

TIME: Two hours

TOOLS: Socket set, floor jack, jack stands

TALENT: ★

APPLICABLE YEARS: Tanks are available for most late-model applications.

TAB: Call shop for price on your application

TINWARE: N/A

TIP: Empty fuel out of stock tank before starting the project.

PERFORMANCE GAIN:
Provides protection and ground clearance for lowered trucks and any truck that benefits from having heavy-gauge sheet metal on bottom of the fuel tank.

COMPLEMENTARY PROJECT:
Upgrade fuel lines to braided hose and M-8 fittings

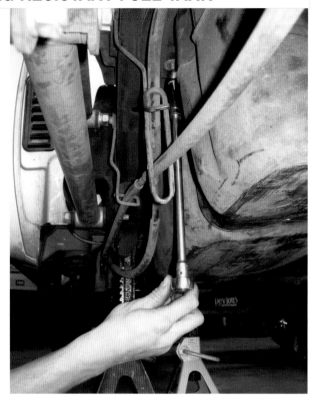

The first step after draining all of the fuel out of the tank into approved containers is to remove all of the electrical connections that connect to the sending unit/fuel pump. The first thing to be unplugged is the fuel-level sending unit. Next, the connection for the fuel pump is unplugged. Finally, the fuel hoses that connect to the top of the tank are disconnected. Next, we move over to the outside of the fuel tank where the fuel filler hose is removed. A floor jack is used to support the weight of the tank, and the rear tank strap is unbolted. Then the front fuel tank strap is unbolted.

This story is dedicated to those folks who have carried a bar of soap around with them in their glove box in case they needed to plug that pesky pinhole in their fuel tank. And for those individuals who have had to park their truck out in the dirt so that the gasoline leaking ever so slowly out of their fuel tank wouldn't puddle up on the concrete driveway or eat a hole in the blacktop. And for folks who have had someone get into their truck and ask "Do you smell gas?" And it is especially for those people who read any one of these previous sentences and thought that we had been following them around with a van full of surveillance equipment.

The guys over at Devious Customs can feel your pain. Well, that and they got tired of having to park their customers' leaky trucks outside, so they designed a new line of fuel tanks for trucks of all shapes and sizes that bolt into the stock location but offer greater ground clearance. These tanks are ideal for both ground-scraping lowered trucks as well as those who use their trucks as weekend rock crawlers.

The new tanks are all designed so that they don't hang down below the frame rails, keeping them up and out of harm's way. The

With both straps removed and all of the hoses and electrical connections removed, the tank can be lowered and removed.

design of the tanks allows the tough frame rails to take the brunt of the punishment while still retaining the factory filler location and using the stock fuel level sending unit and in-tank fuel pump. These tanks come with all of the installation hardware as well as any other parts necessary to complete the installation (straps, clamps, and so on). And installation is straightforward with no cutting or welding necessary. In fact, you don't even have to remove the bed to complete the installation, but we did to make it possible to shoot photos of the top of the fuel tank where the sending unit and hoses have to be unplugged. To find out if Devious Customs has a fuel tank for your truck, or if you have questions about the installation, feel free to contact the company using the information listed in the resources at the back of the book.

Just like they came off, the fuel hoses are reattached.

The ring that holds the sending unit and fuel pump assembly into the factory fuel tank simply spins and unlocks, and it can then be removed. Once the ring is out of the way, the factory fuel sending unit and fuel pump assembly can be simply lifted out of the tank.

The new Devious Customs fuel tank comes with a new clamp ring to hold the stock sending unit in place in the new tank. A dab of red Loctite is applied to all four of the bolts that hold the new clamp ring in place before they are installed into the top of the fuel tank.

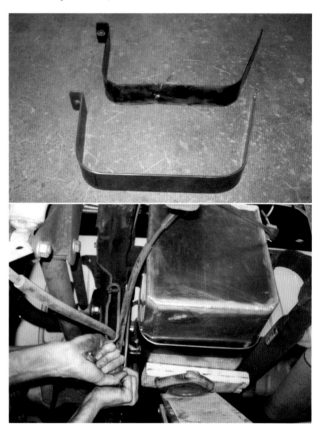

The new fuel tank is slipped into place under the truck, and a floor jack is used to lift it into place. Up top, the first order of business is to install the fuel filler hose on to the new Devious Customs fuel tank.

The new shorter fuel tank straps are unpacked, and they are installed under the tank to hold it into place under the truck to finish up the installation.

Then the electrical connections for the fuel pump and sending units are plugged in to the top of the sender assembly.

If you compare this photo to the one at the beginning of the process, you will notice that the new Devious Customs fuel tank doesn't hang down under the frame nearly as far as the factory tank did.

TIME: Two hours; painting and curing will take its own time

TOOLS: Power drill, Phillips screwdriver, ⁵⁄₁₆-inch drill bit, 5mm Allen wrench, 10mm open-end wrench

TALENT: ★ on roll pan install;
★★★★ on paint application

APPLICABLE YEARS: All years, makes, and models of light trucks

TAB: $300

TINWARE: N/A

TIP: N/A

PERFORMANCE GAIN:
Cosmetic only

COMPLEMENTARY PROJECT:
Front bumper cover or ground effects

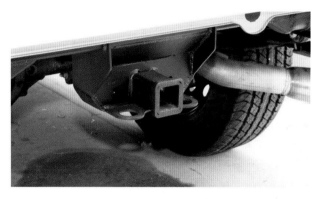

We actually pulled the rear bumper off of this truck before we installed the hidden hitch setup purchased from the local truck accessory shop. Because there are so many different hitch manufacturers out there, and they all seem to bolt right into the factory bumper mount locations, we figured we could forego the hitch install this time around.

The first thing we did once we started shooting photos was remove this truck's tailgate so we could easily access the tailgate jamb to mount the new Street Scene roll pan.

Although a lot of popular modifications require welding and fabrication or even special skills that are above and beyond the average truck enthusiast, a lot of other modifications can be performed right in your own driveway. Then there are others, like the installation of this Street Scene roll pan, in which the actual installation of the roll pan is really easy and can be done in less than an hour with pretty standard hand tools.

Unless you're an experienced automotive painter, though, you are going to have to rely on someone to spray the paint on the parts after the fact. This is especially true considering the way that today's automotive colors are filled with metallic flakes and pearls, making them almost impossible to match unless you have years of automotive painting experience. And let's face it, if you care enough about your truck to invest the time and money to make it look a certain way by adding accessories like a roll pan, the last thing you want is for parts of your truck to be a different shade or color than the rest of the truck.

So, after you have found a shop to paint your roll pan for you, there are two ways you can go about installing it. You can have the roll pan painted first, and then attempt to install it without

scratching the fresh paint. Or you can install it first—that way if you slip with the drill it isn't that big of a deal. We decided to go ahead and install the roll pan before we took it back off and dropped it off, along with the freshly shaved tailgate, at the painter.

The only tools we used were a power drill, a Phillips screwdriver bit to install the screws that hold the roll pan in place, a ⁵⁄₁₆-inch drill bit to drill the holes for the license plate as well as a 5mm Allen wrench and a 10mm open-end wrench to install the license plate and frame. To hook up the license plate light we used a pair of butt connectors and some hand crimpers. Here is what the installation looked like from start to finish.

EXTERIOR

231

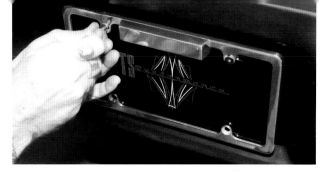

Next, the new Street Scene roll pan is set into place. It is pretty obvious where the pan should be affixed to the bed. Line the sides of the roll pan up with the bed sides and apply a little masking tape to hold it in place.

After you are satisfied with the fit and position of the roll pan, screw the roll pan into place using the provided self-taping screws.

To ensure that the bottom of the roll pan isn't flapping in the wind, a couple of the self-taping screws are installed in the side flange of the roll pan down near the bottom of the bed side.

After the roll pan is secured to the bed, four holes are drilled to mount the lighted billet license plate frame into the new roll pan; it is installed using the hardware that was provided with the license plate frame.

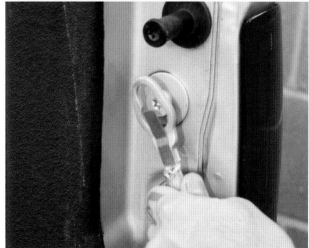

Once all of the work is finished, all that's left to do is reinstall the tailgate—a task that takes all of 15 seconds on today's modern pickups.

This is what the truck rear looks like less than an hour after we started. In fact, there was still time to drop the truck off at the body shop that afternoon to paint the new roll pan and the area of the tailgate where the handle had been shaved.

TIME: Two hours

TOOLS: Small socket set (half-inch socket), half-inch open-end box wrench

TALENT: ★

APPLICABLE YEARS: Steps are available for all years, makes, and models of light trucks

TAB: $300

TINWARE: N/A

TIP: N/A

PERFORMANCE GAIN:
Easier ingress (vehicle entry)

COMPLEMENTARY PROJECT:
Install a grab handle in the cab.

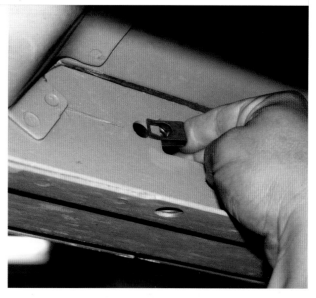

You'll mount three primary brackets on each side of the truck first. Note that a ½-inch wrench is all you'll need for this process. Install TPI clip nuts in the factory locations designed for the mounting brackets.

Starting at the front of the truck, hang the mounting brackets from the factory locations. Use the 5⁄16-inch bolts, washers, and nylon nuts to attach the brackets to the vehicle. Leave all the bolts relatively loose so you can adjust the fit.

Most trucks that come from the factory are fairly easy to get in and out of if you are of average height and health. But when you want to run taller tires, which often require a suspension lift, you may need to accommodate yourself and your passengers with some help climbing aboard regardless of how tall you are.

For example, when Debbie Rodriguez, director of operations at the Fender Guitar Center in Corona, California, bought her 2004 Ford F-150 Super crew-cab, she was all for the 35-inch tires and suspension lift that gave her truck the off-road look that she wanted. Rodriquez is a tall lady who has no trouble getting into her truck. But her daughter, who was eight months pregnant at the time of this Auto and Truck Specialties step installation, needed some assistance getting into the truck when Mom came by to take her shopping for baby clothes.

We took this opportunity to show you just how straightforward and quick it is to install your own side steps. The project can be done in about two hours. These ATS side steps, or their running board if you like, are of solid, yet light construction and come with all the hardware you need. The kit number is C810-BRK-90. With as little fanfare as we can muster, let's show you how quick you can install these side steps—and you can count on them even when the snow level rises and the temperatures drop.

EXTERIOR

233

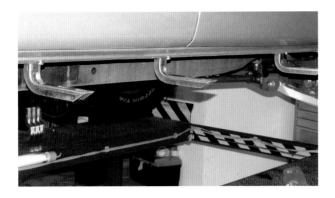

Three mounting brackets are installed, yet intentionally left loose until everything is correctly positioned.

Use a Uni-bit to open the hole up to 5/16 inch.

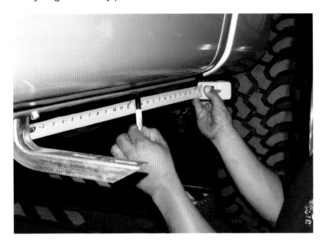

Measure about 12 inches from the rear brackets that use the factory mount point. Mark the point on the pinch weld of the rocker panel to begin your starter hole. This mount will support the rear of the running board and allow you to stand on it while reaching into the truck bed to load or unload cargo.

Install the rear-most mounting bracket and leave loose.

Place the 5/16-inch square head bolts into the I-beam slots on the underside of the running boards. Line them up in pairs that will coincide with the mounting brackets: five bolts on the inside slots and five on the outside.

Mark and drill a pilot hole with a 1/8-inch drill bit. Be certain to center it from top to bottom.

Position running board over brackets as to allow the square head bolts to pass through bracket holes. Attach running boards to the brackets and install SAE washers and nylock nuts. Center the running boards and adjust fit from side to side.

Check that the rear of each running board is in about the same relation to the rear of the truck cab and allow proper clearance from the rear tire.

Snug the bolts down and cinch them down. Make sure to tighten the inside bolts.

This install is an excellent way to start personalizing your rig and making it more user friendly.

TIME: One hour

 TOOLS: T-30 Torx-head wrench

 TALENT: ★

 APPLICABLE YEARS: This full-size Chevy truck application fits 1999 and newer Silverado, Suburban, Tahoe, and Avalanche models. Applications for Ford, Dodge, and Hummer H2 are also available.

 TAB: About $165 for billet aluminum

 TINWARE: N/A

 TIP: N/A

 PERFORMANCE GAIN:
N/A

COMPLEMENTARY PROJECT:
Billet door sill plates

The first step is to remove the two fasteners at the top of the opening that secure the black plastic filler neck cup to the body sheet metal. This will require a T-30 Torx-head socket, which we obtained from the tool department at Sears for about $6.50. Next, use the same socket to remove the two fasteners that secure the fuel door hinge. With the cup and hinge fasteners removed, push the plastic cup back and pull the fuel door and hinge assembly free, as shown. Next, position the mounting bracket in between the plastic cup and the body sheet metal, and align the holes. Note that the top hole lines up with one of the plastic cup mounting holes, while the other holes line up with the original fuel door hinge mounting points. Install and snug down the top-mounting hole first, as this will make it easier to line up the two hinge mounting holes.

Before installing the new fuel door, make sure to remove the rubber bumpers from the stock fuel door assembly.

EXTERIOR

Pumping gas has never been considered one of the most joyous things we do with our trucks. True, popping that door and lifting that handle is indeed symbolic of a few more hundred miles of fun, but the actual task certainly leaves something to be desired.

If you'd like to put a little more fun into this humdrum affair, then consider an alloy fuel door from AMP Research. AMP Research has a reputation for developing innovative products that not only work well but also add functionality to your vehicle, and this billet aluminum fuel door is no exception. Unlike some cheap "one size fits all" fuel doors you may have seen in auto parts stores or swap meets, each AMP Research alloy fuel door is computer designed and manufactured at the company's facility in Irvine, California, to ensure a perfect fit and the right look for your application.

In fact, this fuel door is of such high quality, it is used by OE manufacturers such as Chevrolet, Ford, Mazda, and Mitsubishi, either as factory equipment or as a factory-authorized accessory. Perhaps best of all, the AMP Research alloy fuel door requires no drilling and installs in minutes using readily available hand tools.

A lot of aftermarket products out there are designed to improve the look of your vehicle, but few things are better than a product that not only looks good but is functional as well. The Alloy Fuel Door from AMP Research fills the bill. You can get yours through Westin Automotive Products, the exclusive North American distributor of AMP Research products.

Line up the alloy fuel door assembly with the mounting holes and install the two supplied hex-head fasteners, which match the simulated fasteners around the perimeter of the fuel door bezel. We found the top fastener went in easily but the bottom one was a little trickier, because the bracket would move away from the fastener as it was installed. We solved this problem by opening the fuel door and holding the bracket in place while we installed the lower fastener. The opposite side of the fuel door assembly is secured to the body with a single piece of high-strength two-sided tape, located under the bezel.

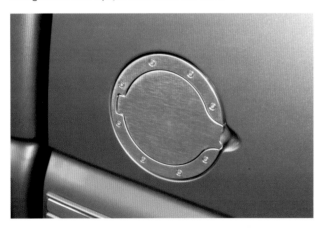

With its brushed aluminum, anodized finish, the AMP Research alloy fuel door looks great and will maintain its rugged appearance for years to come.

A spring-loaded cam makes for smooth operation and a refined, solid feel when the fuel door is opened and closed.

SECTION 8

INTERIOR

We improved the appeal of this cab with custom seat covers.

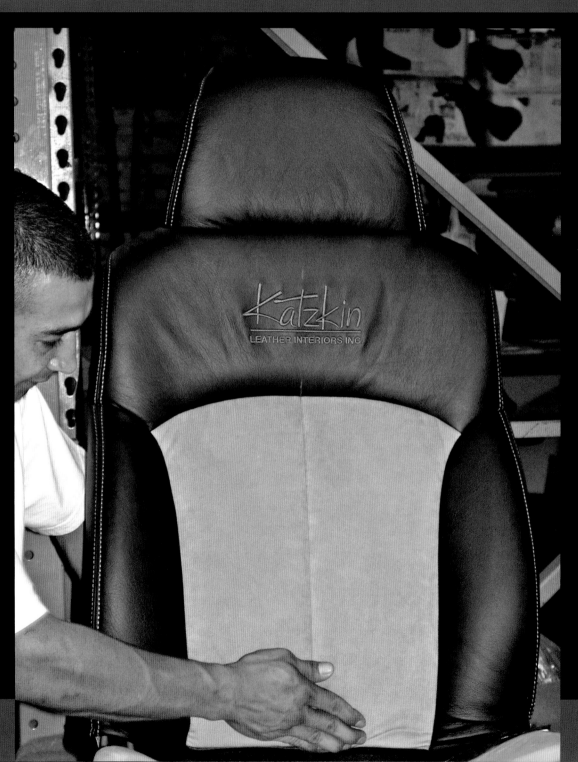

TIME: Two hours

 TOOLS: Hand tools, Torx-head wrenches

 TALENT: ★

 APPLICABLE YEARS: Most years, makes, and models of light trucks

 TAB: $150

 TINWARE: Loctite

 TIP: N/A

 PERFORMANCE GAIN:
Cosmetic only

COMPLEMENTARY PROJECT:
Think about the complementary interior billet pieces you want your truck to have and change it all as one project.

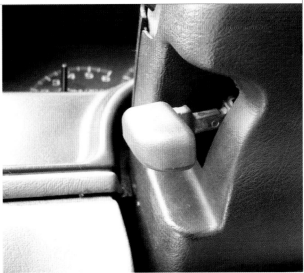

First step is to lift the tilt upward so you have an easier access for the following steps. Grab hold of your tilt knob and pull outward toward the driver's door. The knob should pop out with some force applied.

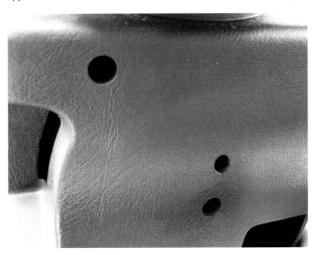

Next, take a T25 screwdriver or bit and remove the top left and bottom right Torx-head screws (as shown in photo). This will allow the bottom half of the column cover to drop away from the upper half in the following steps.

Our collective search to find the "one more piece" of billet aluminum or stainless steel to add to the interior of our prize possession—our trucks—continues. And companies like TRENZ have stepped up to give yet one more option to those of us with the creature comforts of the automatic transmission.

Most of you know there are a lot of modifications out there that can intimidate the beginner truck builders and even intimidate some of us who might have the knowledge and know-how of the trade. A lot of aftermarket products are somewhat taxing and can test the patience of the calmest of men and women. Not all of us as truck enthusiasts were born with a wrench in our hands, but through how-to publications like this, some of the less-gifted truck addicts will be able to say to buddies and family "I did this," or "Do you want me to show you how it's done?"

This is my experience with the installation of the TRENZ billet aluminum shifter handle on a 1998 C/K 1500 GM truck with a 4L60E automatic overdrive transmission.

INTERIOR

239

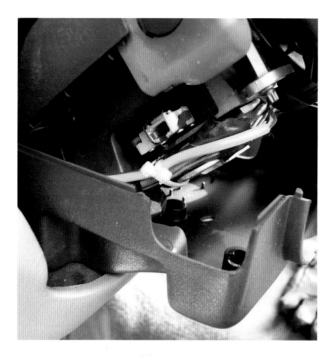

This is as far as you need to remove the bottom half of the shell at this point. Be sure not to "reef" on this plastic, because it will break with too much force.

Now, pull the factory shifter boot upward on the shifter handle to reveal the factory Torx screw.

This close-up simply gives you a better idea of a Torx screw.

Next, remove this Torx-head screw (may take some torque to remove this due to factory Loctite). Then move shifter slightly to remove it from sleeve. *Do not remove the roll pin to release the shifter handle.*

This is when you will remove your shifter boot from your factory shifter handle and place it on the new billet version. Note the placement relation on the shifter boot. There is only one way this boot is supposed to mount.

Slide the new shifter (with the shifter boot slid up the handle) into position. Before installing the Torx screw, put some thread locker on the threads. We suggest using only the blue Loctite as red is overkill. This is for safety, so please do so.

INTERIOR

Next, sandwich your two column covers together paying close attention to clips and shifter boot location before completing. You will have to do this while sliding the shifter boot into position. Then reverse procedure by putting the Torx screws back in.

This is what your tilt knob will look like when removed from its position.

Finally, place the tilt knob back into the slot and push (toward column) firmly into position.

And—*voilà!*—you're done. With parking brake applied, run vehicle through the gears once or twice to be sure that everything works fine. Check your tilt to be sure it is working as well.

TIME: Two weeks

TOOLS: Upholstery tools

TALENT: ★★★★

APPLICABLE YEARS: Custom upholstery for all years, makes, and models of light trucks

TAB: Price depends on scope of completeness requested

TINWARE: N/A

TIP: Use this level of project as a high-water mark in custom upholstery. It's more than seat covers and may be a consideration if you are doing a high-end custom job.

PERFORMANCE GAIN:
Superior workmanship

COMPLEMENTARY PROJECT:
Install new carpet, headliner, and dashboard to match.

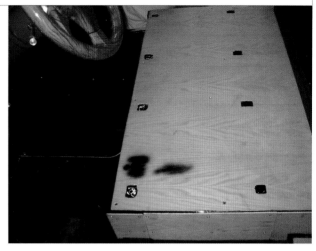

Like a raw canvas, the 1951 Ford F-1 was delivered to LB Threads, ready for a custom interior. Bucket seats had been mounted to a platform and Rod Doors door and cab panels fit. To compensate for Bonnie Lee's stature, Bill Lee stacked two by fours until the seats were high enough for her to see over the hood. He then fashioned a seat frame out of 1-inch tubing, then powder coated it before encasing the assembly in door skin paneling.

Dense foam bolsters were carved to fit the seat sides to improve thigh comfort and enhance the seats' cosmetic appeal. The tops of the seats fit like envelopes over the seat frames, then modifications were performed on the cut portion of the seat frames, done by the owner to lower the seat backs.

Ironically, truck enthusiasts will inevitably find a rusted piece of what's left of an old war horse and immediately envision it with a brightly colored finish and a complementing interior. So, it comes as no surprise there was little doubt in Bill Lee's mind concerning the interior color selection to be used in his wife's purple 1951 Ford F-1 long before it was purple. In his wheeling and dealing, Lee had come across a flawless, gray leather hide. Matched up with a set of modified 1990 Ford Aerostar buckets, gray would prove to be perfect for Bonnie's Ford, he thought.

Lee's truck building continued; he then asked Bonnie to test-fit the seats. He continued to pile two by fours under the driver's seat until Bonnie was able to see over the F-1's hood. However, with the rails raised 5 inches, the seat back was way too tall. A pass by a Sawzall blade and some welding lowered the seat back's frames down so they no longer blocked the rear window. Lee's specialty is automotive truck and car wiring, so he swapped a wiring job on a custom car for upholstery work. The modified buckets were soon covered in the dark leather and complementing tweed, but the rest of the upholstery job stalled.

Months passed; Lee progressed until the truck was drivable,

with final paint work within sight. That's about the time he got in touch with Mike Sutton of LB Threads (formerly Long Beach Upholstery). Lee was searching for someone to finish the headliner, door panels, carpet, and dash, but in a street rod level of quality. Sutton advised Lee that he could make his interior high tech, but he would not do the job if he had to use the dark leather and tweed. "I took a look at the upholstery and sat down. The edges gave no support and a bracket hit me between the shoulders when I leaned back. The only way to fix them was to start over," added Sutton.

This convinced Lee to ditch the seat covers and turn him

INTERIOR

loose on a light gray interior design. Quite a change in direction for Lee, but he wanted it done and done right. With a "See you in a couple of weeks," Lee departed, leaving the leather- and tweed-covered seats and a bare purple F-1 in the hands of LB Threads! What was to come was nothing short of amazing. We'll let the pictures do the talking as this interior went from rags to riches in less than three weeks!

The original seats had headrests that had been removed, however, the hardware was retained and you felt comfortable when you leaned back. The brackets were eliminated, and this cutting-edge design was fashioned for both comfort and appearance.

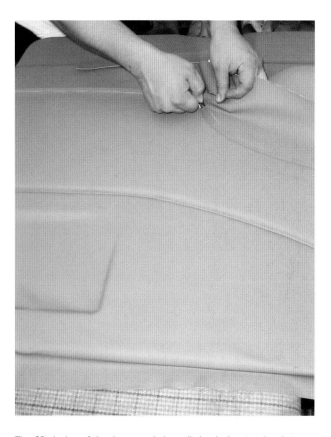

The 3D design of the door panels is really beginning to take shape. A piece of chrome trim, found in the shop, was added to the door panel along with a map pocket. Stitched panels add contrast without relying on color changes.

With the seats upholstered, it was time to move on to the door panels. You can see the designs, which were created to match the seats. Note the armrest.

Bill Lee had purchased molded interior panels from Rod Doors. These trick panels are formed to fit all the curves of the inside of the cab, which cuts down on upholstery immensely.

Like the headliner, the rear panel was sprayed with adhesive glue, then a thin, low-density foam was applied. It will be rolled into the pattern to create a unique look. The completed rear panel now features contrasting designs and is padded through the addition of the light foam.

INTERIOR

A unique addition to this upholstery job was wrapping the dash with the Shadow Flake vinyl material, starting out with an even application of upholstery adhesive.

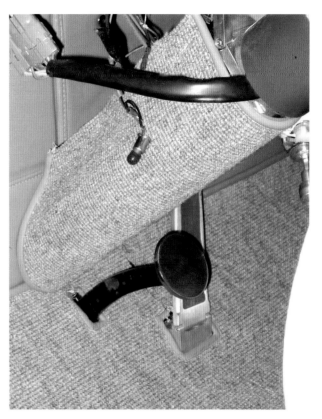

Gray German wool carpet was then selected, cut to fit, trimmed, and installed to cover the floor and firewall. An added bonus was a carpet wrap to cover the lower portion of the steering column.

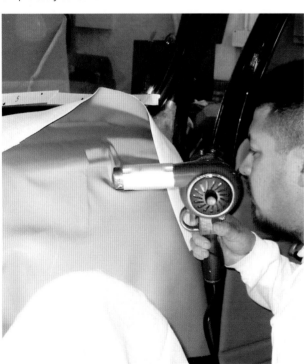

Using a heat gun and a lot of talent, wrap the dash in the same materials used to upholster the seats and panels. You know a craftsman really knows the upholstery business when a metal dash featuring many contours can be wrapped with one piece of material!

With the addition of complementary gray seatbelts from J&J Auto Fabrics, Bonnie Lee's bright purple 1951 Ford F-1 escalated to the show class. LB Threads did awesome work on this upholstery job!

TIME: Five hours

TOOLS: Hands

TALENT: ★

APPLICABLE YEARS: Kits for all years, makes, and models of light trucks

TAB: $300 and up, depending on how many seat rows you are covering

TINWARE: Staple gun, spray glue, scissors

TIP: Place the seats out in the sun after covers are installed so the foam can warm up and fill out the covers.

PERFORMANCE GAIN:
Comfort

COMPLEMENTARY PROJECT:
N/A

With the seats removed from the vehicle, locate the two main clips (front and back) that hold the factory upholstery to the seat's frame. Using a long, flat-head screwdriver, pry the clips away from the seat frame. After the clips have been unattached from the frame, it is time to remove all seat mechanism hardware. Because the original upholstery was put on before the seat sliding hardware, it is necessary to cut the corner sections of the bottom upholstery in order to remove it.

It is necessary to remove the seat adjuster hardware to remove the seat cover. The upholstery utilizes a Velcro system in order to properly attach to the seat. The seat covers are clearly marked in order of installation.

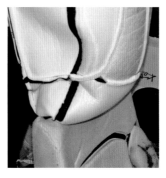

Install the new seat covers exactly opposite to how the old ones were removed. Simply roll from top to bottom. Be sure to thoroughly smooth out and stretch cover to the contours in the seat.

There is nothing quite like the feeling of sliding into the soft, supple confines of an accommodating piece of furniture. The welcoming feel invites you back every time you depart. And why not plan the very best for your seating material as you would any other aspect of your vehicle? It is, after all, where you will spend your entire time while with the vehicle, and if you are like many of us, you will be seated there, in traffic, for quite some time.

Customization, like the rest of a personalized truck, is the centerpiece to the entire design of the plan. If every dial and gauge has been modified or customized with a certain amount of style and originality in mind, it goes without saying that the interior will make as big a statement as those oversized wheels and tires.

Once only seen as exclusively a luxury vehicle option—and still is for the most part—custom leather interior is available for virtually any make or model vehicle. The styles and patterns are almost endless and are limited only by your imagination, or lack thereof. Come with us as we walk through a typical install on a 2001 Chevrolet Blazer. The photos will give you a good idea how high-quality seat covers are installed.

A good tip while applying the seat cover is to trim the excess material from the seam so as to remove the apparent bulge that is created when the cover is fitted. After installation of the cover, massage along the seam lines to place the extra edges evenly so that the actual stitches will not be as visible. When you have completed all of the seats, set them in the sun so that the foam has a chance to expand and properly fill out its new cover.

INTERIOR

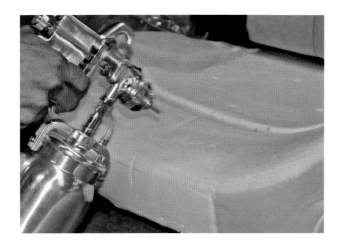

A light coating of glue is sprayed to the foam seat and the underside of the seat cover in order to keep all areas of the cover adhered firmly to the seat and prevent bunching or shifting.

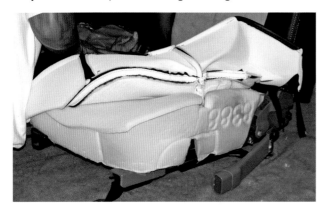

The seat cover is reapplied so that the Velcro seams meet to further create a more secured cover, and the clips at the bottom are reapplied. The original cover had to be cut in order to remove it because seat assembly was finished after the cover was applied; Katzkin came up with zippers to overcome this. All hardware is reapplied. Holes are cut into the tops of the seat covers in order to allow the headrest installation. The headrest cover is simply rolled on and a clip underneath the opening provides a hidden attachment.

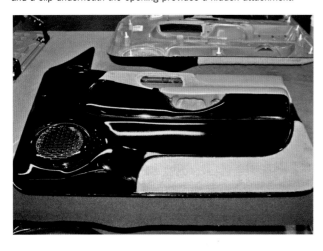

Seen here, the upper portion of the door panel will be removed in order to reupholster.

To remove, the stapled clips adhering the padded upholstery to the door panel are removed.

A sheet of suede is laid out and cut to reupholster the section that has been removed.

The panel's seams are sprayed with glue to better adhere the suede to its new home. After the material has received a light coating of glue, it is laid on to the panel and the seams are retraced for better adhesion.

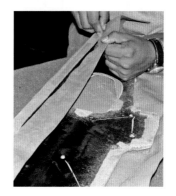

The panel is then turned upside down and the outer edges are again sprayed in order to wrap the edges over the panel. Then the excess material is cut away. After the material has been trimmed with a razor blade to fit and glued to the panel, it is then stapled for further stability.

The freshly upholstered panel is reattached to the door panel, and the hardware is adhered.

TIME: Five hours

 TOOLS: Hands

 TALENT: ★

 APPLICABLE YEARS: Seat covers for all years, makes, and models of light trucks

 TAB: $300 and up

 TINWARE: Staple gun, spray glue

 TIP: Place the finished seats out in the sun for a few hours so foam can expand and fill out the seat cover

 PERFORMANCE GAIN:
Comfort

COMPLEMENTARY PROJECT:
Install a fresh carpet kit while the seats are out of the vehicle.

An essential part of the installation process is to remove the seats from the cab of the truck. This may take awhile, as door sill plates and seatbelts must sometimes be removed to release the seat brackets. In this instance, the rear seat will also be covered, so it too was removed, revealing the subwoofer system underneath. The front seats are also unbolted from the cab, leaving the interior bare. The factory covers are held on with Velcro and in some cases zippers. They literally fit over the seat cushions like a glove.

The seat bottom cushions can be unbolted from the seat frame, making the installation easier. The sensors and adjustment motors must also be unplugged from the seat.

One of the easiest ways to transform your interior from a mild-mannered truck to an eye-catching showstopper is with the installation of a custom leather interior. Many interior kits are available in a variety of colors and materials that can easily transform your stock interior into one that looks like custom upholstery work. These kits simply slip over the factory seating, allowing anyone to dramatically change his or her vehicle's interior in a matter of hours.

One manufacturer of leather seat kits is Classic Soft Trim. The company allows the customer to choose from an almost endless selection of different color and material combinations. Options range from a simple two-tone leather cover to a wild carbon-fiber-style vinyl with contrasting stitching and custom embroidered logos. The kits come ready to install, utilizing the factory foam and fasteners. Most interiors can be installed in four to five hours depending on the application. Installation can be a do-it-yourself job if you are experienced with the technique. However, it is recommended that installation be done at one of Classic Soft Trim's nationwide installation centers if this is a first-time application for you.

Classic Soft Trim allowed us to see the procedure of installing one of its custom leather seat kits. Here, the company installs a two-tone seat cover on to a 2002 GMC Sierra. The owner thought the vehicle needed a custom interior to match its unique exterior. Black leather was chosen as a base for the seats to match the black carbon-fiber interior. Yellow perforated leather was used as the seat and door panel inserts, to bring in the yellow from the powder-coated exterior parts.

For added effect, yellow stitching was used to complement the seat and door panel inserts. For the installation, the seats must be removed from the vehicle, and the OEM covers must be stripped off the seats. Once the seats are bare, the new custom leather covers are installed in no time. It was obvious how much of a change was made when the new seat covers were added.

In these pages, you should get an idea of how the professionals do an install to get a job done right, including modifying an existing pattern to fit a custom stereo. For more information on leather combinations and installation centers near you, contact Classic Soft Trim at www.classicsofttrim.com.

INTERIOR

This installation also replaced the factory door panel inserts so the panels had to be removed.

To make the leather more pliable for installation, the installers sometimes use steam. This allows the leather to slip over the factory cushion more easily. The new covers simply slip over the existing seat foam. In many instances it is a tight fit.

New door inserts are glued in place and tucked into the existing insert. The edges are cut away, and the rest is tucked in behind the insert.

There are plastic lips and clips that hold the seat covers to the frame in various locations. These must be pulled tight and connected to the frame.

The cushions are then bolted back to the seat frames after they have been covered with the new leather covers.

In order to complement the new seat covers, items such as the center console door had to be reupholstered. This requires a different technique that is best left to an experienced upholsterer.

The center console is bolted back into the cab, along with the newly covered seats. Once the passenger seat was covered, it too was bolted back into the truck's cab.

The finished installation looks great and offers a continuous color scheme from the outside of the truck to its interior.

TIME: Five hours

 TOOLS: Medium socket set, hand tools

 TALENT: ★

 APPLICABLE YEARS: Seat belt restraint systems for all years, makes, and models of light

 TAB: About $220

 TINWARE: N/A

 TIP: N/A

 PERFORMANCE GAIN:
Safety

COMPLEMENTARY PROJECT:
Install new seat covers (Katzkin) or have seats reupholstered.

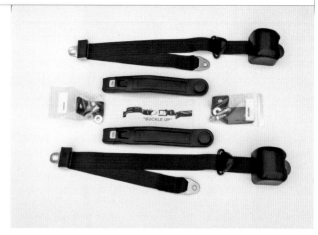

Truck Stop Specialty Conversions (of Fullerton, California) "Buckle Up" brand three-point, inertia reel safety belt restraint system for both ¾-ton and ½-ton 1967–1972 Chevrolet and GMC light-duty trucks is 100 percent bolt-on using the factory pickup points and is available in a total of six OE colors. This product retails for $220. One of the modifications carried out during Jimmy's restoration was the addition of a 1971 Chevrolet CSK "bench/bucket seat." Because this one-piece unit features a combination fold-down armrest and "sissy seat" (which required a new set of Buckle Up's reproduction OE lap belts), the seat had to be unbolted and slid forward in order to gain access to the factory seatbelt mounting points. This was accomplished with the removal of a series of four ⅞₆-inch nuts.

Speaking of seatbelts, Truck Stop Specialty Conversions based in Fullerton, California, offers a complete line of OE fitment seatbelts marketed nationwide under the "Buckle Up" brand name. These belts are available in all of the popular factory GM colors. And a total of three buckle styles are available. First you have the nostalgic aircraft-style buckle. Then you have the "GM-style" deluxe push-button metal buckle, ideal for either the restorer or those desiring that OE look. And lastly there's the standard black push-button buckle, which is ideally suited for classic street trucks with custom interiors.

All of the Buckle Up brand seatbelts are manufactured in conformity with all applicable federal motor vehicle safety standards and codes, specifically DOT numbers 208 and 309. In this day and age, nothing short of a three-point, inertia reel safety belt restraint system will satisfy most insurance underwriters much less the law. Obviously, either faction can justifiably quote a ton of statistics generated by the National Traffic Safety Council (NTSC) showing you that a three-point, inertia reel safety belt restraint system is effective in restraining both driver and passenger while engaged in some form of traffic mishap. However, you may be asking yourself, how are you going to install a three-point, inertia reel safety belt restraint system in that classic 1967–1972 Chevy of yours without drilling a bunch of holes inside the cab?

GM equipped all 1967–1972 Chevrolet and GMC half- and three-quarter-ton cabs with a ⅞₆-inch weld nut located inside the rear door pillar, placed eye level, right where the cab curves, between the rear door jamb and rear window opening. Apparently, the general and his army of designers must have original-

INTERIOR

Truck enthusiasts just love GM's 1967–1972 Chevrolet and GMC light-duty trucks. With classic looks and great performance, these little haulers have got real "staying power," and the DMV has the statistics to prove it. Would you believe there are more 1967–1972 Chevrolet/GMC light-duty trucks registered and on the road throughout the good old U.S. of A. than any other make or model of vintage light-duty pickup manufactured from the years 1950 to 1980?

It also should come as no surprise that an extremely healthy aftermarket parts base exists for these little haulers. All you have to do is thumb through the accompanying advertisements in any automotive enthusiast magazine and you'll be able to fill out your "wish list" in record time. You'll quickly discover that it's possible to purchase just about anything and everything needed to restore or modify one of these trucks ranging from the more obvious items such as reproduction pickup beds and exterior sheet metal to items such as exterior trim molding, ID badges, grilles, and door handles, as well as "soft trim" items such as rubber weather stripping, carpeting, upholstery kits, and yes, even seatbelts.

ly intended on installing a swiveling three-point seatbelt restraint system on these trucks when they were first introduced (you should find a plastic mushroom trim button covering said weld nut), but then elected to shelve the option until the introduction of the later series "CST" models.

Buckle Up brand three-point, inertia reel safety belt restraint system fits all 1967–1972 Chevrolet and GMC light-duty trucks and uses 100 percent of the stock factory mounting points. These seatbelts are user-friendly regardless of whether you are dealing with a bench or bucket seat or whether the truck is a half- or three-quarter-ton vehicle.

A total of six OE colors, including black, blue, burgundy, gray, red, and tan are available. And each of these three-point inertia reel systems (Buckle Up offers a multitude of applications including one for the Tri-5 Chevies, 1967–1972 Chevrolet El Camino and Chevelle, and 1966–1967 Chevy Nova/Chevy II to name a few) comes with its own specific application mounting brackets and a full set of fully detailed instructions. The retail price for one of these systems is approximately $220 plus shipping.

The vehicle used in this particular installation is somewhat unusual in its own right. It's a fully restored or "restified" Hugger Orange, 1968 three-quarter-ton GMC utility bed belonging to Phil West, owner of Phil's Electric Service, which is based in Norco, California.

Along with installing a set of Buckle Up's three-point, inertia reel safety belts, our installer will also be upgrading the CST's "sissy seat" with a pair of Buckle Up's reproduction lap belts to boot. Last winter we all rendezvoused at Truck Stop Specialty Conversions shop in Fullerton, and the pictures show how things go together.

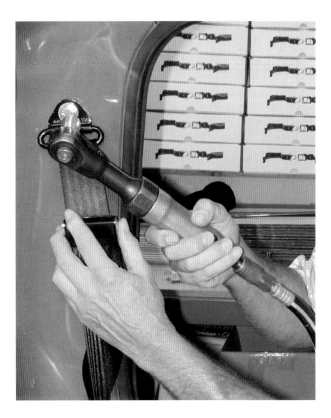

Installation of the driver-side upper seatbelt swivel bracket comes next using the shouldered 7⁄16-inch bolt provided with the kit. At this juncture, our installer checks to make sure that the bracket swivels freely. This is *very* important.

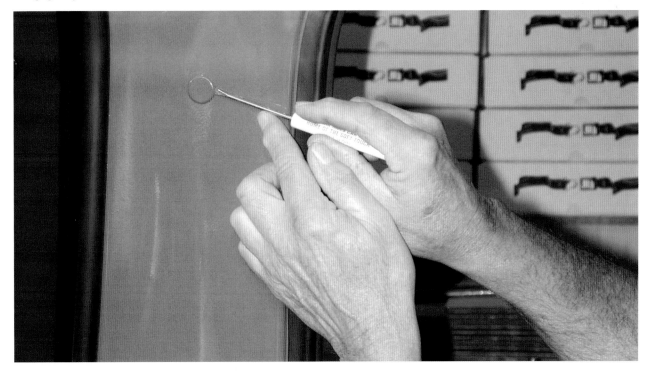

Remove the passenger-side outer retractable lap belt assembly using a 7⁄16-inch socket and air wrench. Next, take hold of the inner portion of the OE lap belt and use a 7⁄16-inch socket and air gun to remove it from the floor pan. The next order of business is tackling the driver's side with the removal of the OE retractor assembly using an air gun and 7⁄16-inch socket. Again, the OE bolts are saved for reuse. Removal of the factory plastic mushroom button comes next. This is easily removed using a pick, pocket knife, or fine blade screwdriver.

Next comes the installation of the Buckle Up seatbelt retractor, which is bolted to the new bracket using the provided ⁷⁄₁₆ x 20 nut, bolt, and washer. To install the passenger-side seatbelt retractor swivel bracket, simply repeat the process.

Here we see the installation of the special inside seatbelt extension L-bracket using the supplied ⁷⁄₁₆-inch bolt, which comes with the kit. With that done, install the driver-side push-button latch assemblies for both sissy seat and driver's side and using the provided ⁷⁄₁₆ x 20 nut, bolt, and washers provided. Because space is tight, the use of hand tools is necessary.

INTERIOR

Now, it's on to the passenger side. First comes the installation of the special L-bracket, which is installed in the very same manner as the driver-side bracket was. Installation of the passenger-side L-bracket (which differs slightly from the driver-side bracket) comes next, using the previously removed OE ⁷⁄₁₆-inch bolt. Installation of the passenger-side belt retractor assembly comes next, using a ⁷⁄₁₆-inch socket and air gun.

Here is the fully installed, Buckle Up brand three-point, inertia reel safety belt restraint system prior to bolting the CST bench/bucket seat back in place.

TIME: 12 hours

 TOOLS: Hand tools

 TALENT: ★

 APPLICABLE YEARS: Weather-strip molding kits for all years, makes, and models of light trucks

 TAB: About $100, depending on the size cab of truck you are working on

 TINWARE: N/A

 TIP: It's helpful to have a friend assist you. Weather stripping is designed to fit the structure of the door frame. Once you see how weather stripping seats itself, weather stripping project will go smoothly.

 PERFORMANCE GAIN:
Proper door and window seal; keeps weather out

COMPLEMENTARY PROJECT:
New window and door glass if needed

This is a great-looking door seal installation. If the weather stripping is fit properly, it is tight to the door, and there is no visible adhesive. This door is going to be wired for both power door locks and power windows. The wires will be routed through a length of braided steel line for looks and protection. The first order of business is to mark and drill a hole for this hose to penetrate the doorjamb.

A nyone who has ever tackled a classic truck–building project knows quite well that the fitting, weather proofing, and wiring of power windows is really no easy task. On the other hand, there are pro building tips that are worth their weight in gold to a novice who has just acquired Dad's, Uncle's, or Grandfather's old truck and is trying to make something reliable out of it. And trust me, even someone who doesn't know the difference between a lug nut and a radiator cap can tell you when the doors open, close, and seal properly.

FITTING THE DOOR

On a classic truck, you will want to fit the doors to the truck before you paint it, and especially before you remove the door from the truck. When I go shopping for a classic truck, I always grasp the bottom, outer corner of the door and give it a slight lift. If it moves slightly, it is repairable. If it rocks, the hinge, door pin, or pocket has problems, which need to be resolved and may be more of a job than you are willing to tackle. But let's just say that the hinge is in good working order. By using a friend's help and a few wooden door shims, you can get it

adjusted to where all the gaps are even and it closes without interference.

Tighten down the door hinge bolts. The big question is, how in the world will you even get this big, heavy door with adjustable top and bottom hinges back into place, especially after it is painted, without a big ding? Simple, there may be a cover over them, but three to four bolts will hold the hinge on to the door. To ensure the door goes back in the same, exact location, drill a ⅛-inch hole through the hinge as shown, through the backing plate right behind it. I used a short section of gas hose over the drill bit to ensure it did not go through and hit the door skin. Drill both the top and bottom hinges in this manner. When you go to reinstall the doors, use the same drill bit for alignment purposes. Line up the holes, and then retighten the bolts. Your door will be in perfect position every time!

WIRING

Power window and power door locks are wonderful for eliminating cranks and buttons but have to be properly wired. One trick is to run the wires from the doorjamb into the door

Drill a ⅛-inch hole through the center of the door hinge and backing plate on a properly adjusted door. Once removed, a heavy classic truck door can be reinstalled while being perfectly adjusted by using drills as alignment pins! The door was then marked to ensure the wiring tube was properly aligned, then the door hole was drilled. A square of metal was removed to create access to the back side of the stainless tube. A hole was also drilled through the door brace and a protective grommet was installed.

Wires are then pulled from the kick panel, through the stainless-steel tube, and up to the upper door pocket. These wires will feed the power window switch.

through braided steel tubing (which is lined with a plastic tube). Wonderful little kit, but installing it can be a big pain in the butt. Because we will have these F-100 doors off to add new weather stripping, now is the time to add an easy wiring system. Once you have determined a logical wiring path that will not interfere with any truck structure, mark a parallel line between the doorjamb and door. We used a Uni-bit to make a large hole for the braided tube. Then we reached through from the back side to mark the door where the hole will be made.

REMOVING THE DOOR

Now, the door can be removed from the truck. A shipping blanket and large table serve as a good working area. Just be sure no metal filings get between the door and blanket as you work or the paint will be marred. Moving right along, we drilled a big hole to accommodate the large braided steel tube for the wiring.

Reaching inside the F-100 door reveals a serious bulkhead panel that seals off the hinge area. What to do? The answer is to mark and drill four holes just inside the door panel mounting holes. Then you can cut out that small square area. You now have access to the back side of the wiring and can add a clamp to the braided line to hold it in place. In the photos you will see a grommet hole where the wiring will be fed up to the power door lock and window motors and solenoids. The door panel will cover this hole. Snake the wiring up to the devices and add the appropriate plug ends to complete this task.

ADDING NEW WEATHER STRIPPING

This tip is a little out of order, but before you even begin this project, lay the weather stripping out in the sun. The good stuff, such as weather stripping from Dennis Carpenter Ford Reproductions not only fits the door but also has memory. Once out of the bag, it will return to the shape of the door if you let it warm a bit.

Wipe the area of the door where weather-strip adhesive will be applied with an appropriate prep solution. I like 3M

With the door removed from the truck and resting on a shipping blanket, the door seal can be test-fit to the perimeter of the door, making sure it fits all corners and the dog leg for a tight fit!

weather-strip adhesives and I follow the instructions. But, before we glue it in place, do a dry run with the weather strip, tackling the trouble areas first. On a 1956 Ford F-100, this will be the dogleg area just above the hinges. The pros tell me that weather stripping cannot be applied properly without removing the doors and laying them flat, as shown.

Also, it is a good idea to do a dry fit of the weather stripping; tape it in place to ensure it fits all corners and bends at that dogleg area! You also need to identify the area to be glued and ensure the sealing lip is facing the doorjamb.

Adhesive is available in black or yellow. The yellow seems to have a more immediate tack, but can become unsightly whereas the black will disappear on a black paint job. We went with the black 3M adhesive. Apply a medium line of adhesive, working it into the door corners with a latex-gloved finger. Working about 6 inches at a time, the weather strip is depressed into the adhesive, and then taped into position with masking tape. Do not stretch the weather stripping, as it is formed to fit the shape of the door. Do not allow the weather strip to roll or twist! Again, the fit at the corners and dogleg are of utmost importance! Once the weather strip has been glued to the door, allow it to dry per the manufacturer's instructions. Don't get in a hurry to hang the door back on to the truck. I gave it 12 hours.

HANGING THE DOOR

With the weather stripping secured to the door and dry, two people should hang them back on to the truck. I put a pad atop a floor jack to support the heavy door, and then slid the top and bottom hinges into place, aligned the ⅛-inch drill bits, then tightened the mounting bolts. We had marked and removed the doorjamb latch mechanism and slowly closed the door for the first fit test. It fit perfectly, but the new, fat weather stripping resisted. I hated to slam the door closed (with the window down), but I did. It took several days before the rubber began to fit, and the doors were somewhat easier to close. Guess what, though? If you use the fat ones, there are no wind whistle noises!

While we are on the subject of classic truck doors, I threw a few more tips at you. Hope this helps to make your classic truck rebuild somewhat simpler.

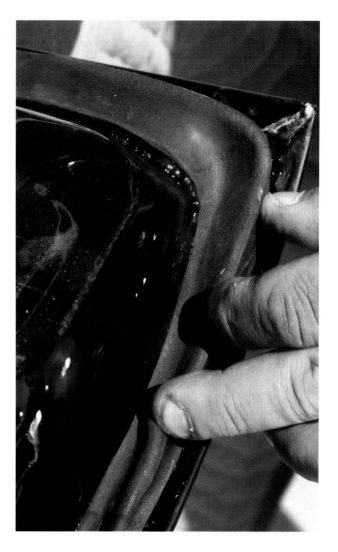

Make sure you have identified the door seals as right and left and that the actual seal is facing toward the doorjamb. Masking tape can be used to hold the weather stripping in place after the adhesive has been smeared into the corner.

It is extremely important to ensure the corners are properly positioned and glued into place. We used a black 3M weather-stripping adhesive to ensure adhesion.

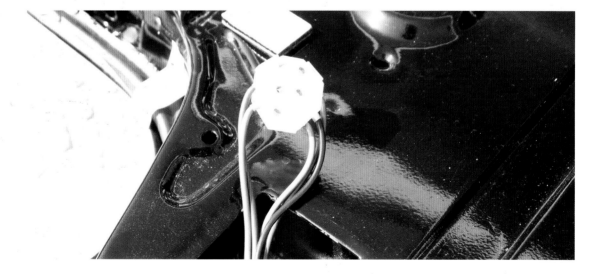

The hot ticket is to work the installation of the rubber gasket on to the door about 6 inches at a time, then apply tape to keep it into position. With the weather-stripping adhesive glue drying, now is a great time to install those power window switch plugs. The switches will be mounted into the door panels, which will align with these holes.

Now is a great time to replace all those wing window seals and gaskets. We used Dennis Carpenter Ford Reproduction Parts for this application as well. This also will eliminate wind noise.

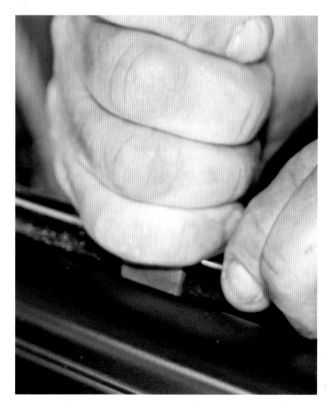

Window rattles are yet another matter that can be eliminated by installing new fuzzies. In Ford trucks, they simply snap into place by using a large flat metal bar. Some guys use a file. Remember that braided steel line that houses the door wiring? Here it is in a finished truck, and it simply slides within those aluminum grommets while the wires never kink or short out.

The finished job will not reveal the wiring or door seals; however, the great part is no wind noise and no door rattles, even on your old classic truck. And you have power door windows to boot!

TIME: Eight hours

TOOLS: Full socket set and hand tools

TALENT: ★★★

APPLICABLE YEARS: Air conditioning systems for all years, makes, and models of light trucks

TAB: $1,100 base cost for a system. Additional costs depend on add-on items and what kinds of hardware you want.

TINWARE: Locate pro-shop to bend your coolant lines.

TIP: Ensure that the correct size of O-ring is oiled and installed into the correct connection, or the system will leak!

PERFORMANCE GAIN:
Greater comfort and weather control

COMPLEMENTARY PROJECT:
Billet accessories on dashboard to upgrade

The Vintage Air Gen-II A/C system will chill the cab of a classic truck in minutes or provide heat and dehumidified defrosters as well. This under-dash panel mounts the louvred vents and control panel. Vintage Air's Sure Fit air conditioning, heating, and defrost systems for 1953–1956 Ford F-100 trucks are designed specifically for each application. The kit is complete from evaporator and condenser to hoses, brackets, lines, and hardware!

The evaporator will be hung under the dash, almost out of sight, utilizing supplied brackets, which attach to the firewall, cowl vent housing, and the bottom of the dash. More than half of the evaporator unit will be under the dash, which means you lose two-thirds of the glove box. This is a test fit of the brackets, as vent hoses will be attached before final installation.

If the mystery of how air conditioning works has kept you from installing it into your truck, then let me introduce you to Vintage Air. This company has an air conditioning unit for your truck, probably in an all-in-one kit form, which is almost simple to install. I say almost because you may need to have hoses and/or lines fabricated and refrigerant added; otherwise it is 90 percent a bolt-on kit!

Vintage Air targeted the street rod industry as it flourished but soon took notice of the huge void in the classic and pickup truck industry. The company's Ford F-100 kit has been around for years but received an update with the release of the Gen-II technology system. Marketed in all-in-one kits, you can purchase just the evaporator kit, or the complete kit. The base evaporator kit comes with an air conditioning, heating, and defrosting combination evaporator designed specifically for your vehicle. It includes an original deluxe control assembly for your dash that connects to and controls the evaporator functions. Designed to mount on existing holes and brackets, it comes with all mounting brackets, hardware, louvres, duct hoses, wiring harness, and installation instructions. The next

step is the complete kit, which comes with all of the above plus the condenser, brackets, standard drier, and preformed aluminum lines. You provide belts, refrigerant, and any required additional engine pulleys with either unit.

Once you have received the complete air conditioning unit from Vintage Air, here are a few hints to make the installation easier. The under-dash vent hoses will block access to a number of cab and dash functions, so get them in good working order first. This includes under-dash wiring, gauges, radio, wipers, linkage, lights, and your cowl vent operation! I highly recommend you remove the seat for access, especially if you have expensive upholstery. Next, remove the passenger kick panel, glove box (which you will lose most of), heater, control panel, and those old defrost hoses. You will also need to remove the passenger-side defrost duct. (The neck will need to be shortened if you intend to hang the evaporator as high as possible.)

The instructions give precise length measurements for the duct hoses, so they should be cut to length. Also, install the hoses to the top of the evaporator at this time and place them to the sides. Supplied brackets and hardware are then used to mount the evaporator under the dash using the cowl, firewall, and dash. A binary (pressure) safety switch is mounted at this time, and any exposed hard lines should be wrapped with insulating tape. Feed lines are routed through the firewall opening before brackets are totally secured. The firewall cover must go on before lines are attached under the hood, and I suggest you install some insulation around this area, even if it is foam tape to weather seal this cover. The first major step is now accomplished!

The best time to install air conditioning is during the building of the truck, otherwise the grille will have to be removed for the condenser mounting. The condenser resembles and functions much like a small radiator, however, it must be positioned in front of the truck's radiator. Templates, clamps, and such are all supplied for mounting.

Refer to the photos to walk you through the making and installation of all the air conditioning and heater hose plumbing. We used the original Ford air conditioning compressor, which eliminated the bracket and belt problem, the swap-out being that the hard lines and muffler have to be modified. Although it is possible to cut and crimp your own hoses, I felt it best to work with a professional and went to Lorenzo at Tempco in Signal Hill, California. After seeing the modifications needed to create the plumbing, I'm glad I did! Moving inside the cab, Vintage Air has a number of options when it comes to in-dash louvres as well as an under-dash panel that mounts the louvred vents and the control panel. The under-dash panel fits as if it is a factory piece and gives you the option to upgrade to billet or in-dash louvred vents in the future.

Basic mechanical skills are all that are needed to mount the majority of components, which is the way we handled this installation, relying upon a pro to form the hoses and modify the compressor's hard lines. I went without air conditioning in my classic trucks for years and did not know what I was missing. Adding air conditioning can make your old truck a pure pleasure to drive during those hot, muggy summer months!

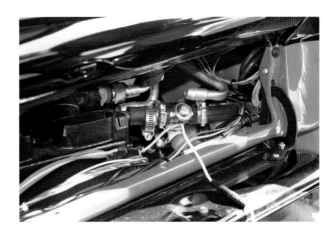

Once the heater control valve is attached to the evaporator, it will be connected to the aluminum feed line in the background. The other is the heater return line. Both are attached with short lengths of ⅝-inch heater hose. A thermocouple feeds temperature information to the control panel to provide the proper cab temperature for heat or air conditioning.

Complete, detailed instructions are provided for the proper wiring of the back side of the temperature control panel, which is now mounted into the under-dash panel as shown. Brackets and hardware are supplied for the mounting of the Vintage Air condenser, which must be installed in front of the truck's radiator. Hoses are then attached per factory instructions.

This is one of two connections for hot engine coolant to provide heat for the heater and windshield defrosters. The heater control valve allows hot engine coolant to flow into the evaporator when needed and shuts it off when not required. Flow direction is marked.

The condenser installation is now complete, and it must be mounted in front of the truck's radiator so that the engine fan cools it. Supplied aluminum lines are then attached to the condenser and routed through a template-positioned hole in the core support leading to the inside of the engine compartment.

The stock compressor and muffler will be used; however, the original lines are not compatible with the Vintage unit. The stock air conditioning muffler and the hard lines leading to the stock air conditioning compressor will have to be modified for use with the Vintage Air unit.

A special fixture is then used to form and attach compression fittings on to the ends of several lines in preparation for hose installation. These new hard lines then have to be formed to clear engine components and flow along the inner fenderwell lines.

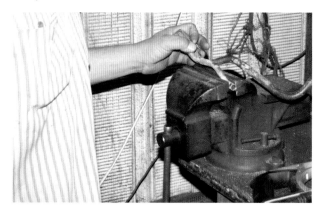

The stock compressor is fit with a hard line manifold, which will not attach to the new lines. Ends are trimmed in preparation for new fittings. The key to altering the new air conditioning plumbing comes in the form of adding Schrader valves for filling and bleeding the system.

This is one of the fabricated high-pressure hard lines that connects the condenser to the under-dash-mounted evaporator. High-pressure lines are then cut to length and fit to the hard lines, which will feed the compressor and the attached muffler.

A hole is located and drilled. Next, a Schrader valve (much like a car tire valve) is torch welded to the aluminum muffler. A new air conditioning line will be attached to the end of the muffler, so the appropriate line fitting is also torch welded to this end. Likewise, the air conditioning compressor hard lines have to be fit with new ends, which must also be torch welded into place.

With the hoses cut to length, they can now be installed on to the hard lines and muffler utilizing this crimping tool. A key here is to ensure the lines are positioned correctly as they will not swivel! Lines and hoses finally make their way to the engine compartment and are loosely positioned prior to permanent installation.

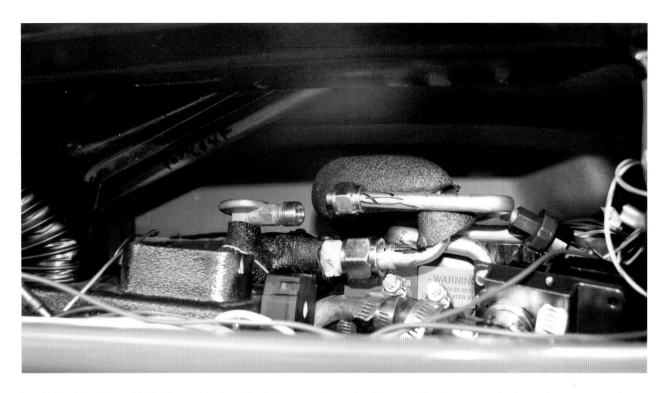

Installation of the air conditioning lines on to the under-dash evaporator requires large wrenches in a very confined area. A vacuum pump is attached on to the custom-installed Schrader valve, and the whole system is evacuated for some 40 minutes!

A final look at the view glass located behind the truck's grille indicates the system is filled and functioning. And the very cold air blowing out of the ducts tells us the install is now complete!

Section 9

ELECTRICAL

The new Sony upgrade speaker fits perfectly into the door's existing speaker hole. It is connected to the wiring and installed back into the door panel.

TIME: One hour

 TOOLS: Small-socket socket set

 TALENT: ★

 APPLICABLE YEARS: Most years, makes, and models of light trucks

 TAB: $150

 TINWARE: N/A

 TIP: N/A

 PERFORMANCE GAIN:
Brighter illumination at night, better looking day-to-day

COMPLEMENTARY PROJECT:
Install grille insert

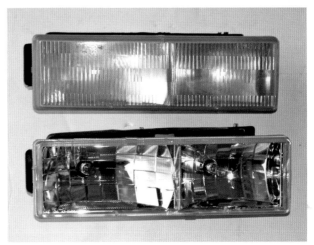

Here's the difference between oxidized old headlights and those of the new Crystal Clear set that we ordered from LMC Truck.

In this application, the headlights are held into the grille with two long studs that are unscrewed and removed.

Several aftermarket replacement headlight lenses feature brighter bulbs, HID units, and even projection head-lamps. The decision on which one to use is up to you, but for the most part many will feature a clear lens that resembles the same appearance on European cars and trucks.

Whatever set you decide to use, swapping out your headlights is a simple task that takes only a matter of minutes. As an example, we decided to upgrade the old headlights on our 1995 Chevy pickup truck. The factory headlights were oxidized, and aside from not looking their best, they also limit the amount of light intensity during nighttime driving.

We took the easy route and contacted LMC Truck, ordering the company's Crystal Clear Headlight Set, P/N 37-7350 for our application. The headlights featured a clear lens and bright white bulbs for both the headlight and high beams. The lights are D.O.T. approved and come with a certificate. They are a stock replacement headlight assembly and fit in the factory headlight sockets perfectly and plug into the original factory wiring harness.

The installation was simple: removing the two long studs that hold the housings in place on the factory front grille releases the assembly. Once the lights are replaced, we strongly recommend taking your lights to a service technician to have them properly aimed. Lifted trucks should have the lights aimed down slightly to avoid shining them directly into the rearview mirrors of the vehicles in front of you. Lowered trucks should also have their lights adjusted accordingly as well.

Once the installation was complete, we really noticed the amount of light that was being blocked by the old, oxidized headlights. The crystal clear set was noticeably brighter, and it also gave our old truck an updated look.

ELECTRICAL

The headlight assembly can then be removed from the grille. Note how in most cases the entire assembly includes the beam adjusters.

Holding the headlight steady, we unplugged the factory wiring harness leads to the headlight's regular and high-beam bulbs.

The Crystal Clear units come individually boxed and are ready to be installed with new hardware.

We held the new headlight in position and connected the harness leads to the appropriate bulbs on the Crystal Clear units.

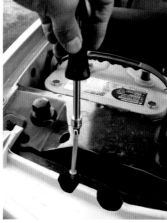

We inserted the new hardware into the headlights and screwed them back into place.

The difference between the old and new headlights was dramatic in both appearance and brightness at night. Make sure to have the lights properly adjusted by a technician.

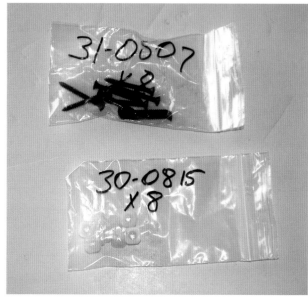

LMC has a parking light grommet and screw kit that is excellent for replacing the worn factory units that often get loose over time.

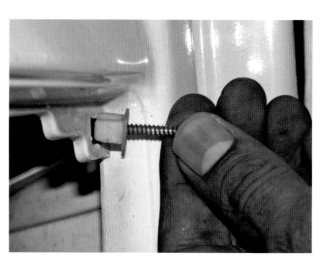

We simply removed the parking light and inserted the screw to pull out the old grommet. The new grommets are pushed into place and the parking lights are now secure.

TIME: Two days

TOOLS: Access to body shop tools, die cutter, gas welder, tin snips, and so on

TALENT: ★★★

APPLICABLE YEARS: Brake lights for all years, makes, and models of light trucks

TAB: About $100

TINWARE: N/A

TIP: N/A

PERFORMANCE GAIN:
Cosmetics, visibility

COMPLEMENTARY PROJECT:
Shave door handles.

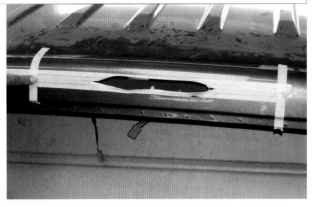

With the factory third brake light removed from the top of the truck cab, lay down masking tape to draw the horizontal template you will use to guide your cuts on the sheet metal. Carefully measure the radius of your end cuts with a protractor.

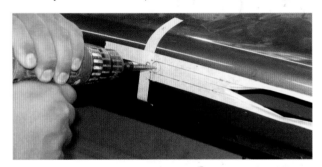

This will be your first invasive cut into your own truck's skin. With the end-radius holes cut, razor cut and remove excess masking tape to leave only the metal to be removed.

The body man makes the horizontal incision from the opening of the factory brake light up to the radius endpoint. Next, you'll measure and cut a filler section out of a similar gauge of sheet metal. This filler section will take up the gap space left from the boxier factory brake light. Prep the area where the sheet metal filler inserts will be tack welded in. Use a Dremel bit to smooth out the radius cut at the ends of the brake light cutout.

A s sure as automotive manufacturers introduce a new standard in design such as the third brake light, people will find ways to customize and make a unique statement that's not so easy to follow. This installation will demonstrate the highlights of installing a third brake light that sits flush to the sheet metal when finished.

When Joe Carrillo, of Starbucks Customs in Corona, California, started cutting and customizing automotive sheet metal, it took awhile before he had the skills and confidence to fire up a pneumatic saw to surgically remove otherwise healthy metal. That was eight years ago, and Carrillo has performed many custom operations on untold cars and trucks no more than a few hours old. Only you can determine if you have the skills and resources to tackle a project like this on your own. The instructions are simple enough; it's the intuitive know-how and precision measurements, and tack welding thin sheet metal without warping your new truck's finish that are the challenge. Your call.

Our intention here is to give our readers an idea they may want to incorporate in their truck mod plans as well as what it takes to achieve that trick-looking long and horizontal third brake light.

Bear in mind this kind of customizing is similar to the processes you would go through if you wanted to shave door handles and badging, or relocating, the tailgate handle. It's also a procedure you might plan for if you are going to do a complete makeover with new body modifications, paint, and/or graphics. This flush brake light install is not intended to be a start-to-finish how-to on every step. Heck, this truck won't be finished with all the graphics, body mods, paint, and other custom work for months. We just want to show you the nuts and bolts.

ELECTRICAL

265

Test-fit the brake light bar to ensure correct clearance at the radius ends and along the edge where the filler inserts will be located. Magnets hold the sheetmetal filler inserts in place.

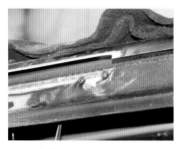

Here are the first weld tacks to secure sheet-metal inserts in place. Use tack weld procedure only, as a continuous weld bead would warp the sheet metal.

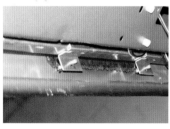

This is a cut made on the truck interior to provide room for the long-bar brake light mounting bucket and mount studs. Note how many spot tack welds were used to secure the sheet-metal filler inserts. Mounting studs for the brake light bucket are tack welded in place.

The metal surface is smoothed and prepped for Mar Glas (Bondo). Mask off the inside of the brake light opening so Bondo doesn't flow inside.

Apply well-mixed body filler to the area, smooth out, and let it set up.

Carrillo block sands excess filler down to the paint line. Bondo inside the brake light slit is removed with pneumatic cutting wheel and shaping files. One thinner coat of filler will be applied to fill any pockets.

Test fit the horizontal third brake light again to note where any gaps or additional shaping needs are.

The sheet metal is modified, filled, and primed. When the rest of the truck sheet metal is prepared for paint and graphics, the third brake light will be mounted, wired, and then sanded flush to the sheet metal for that one-in-a-million look. Now you know what it takes to get that look.

TIME: Two hours

TOOLS: Hand tools, electrician's wire cutters

TALENT: ★★★

APPLICABLE YEARS: Late model; can be adapted to any vehicle

TAB: $280–$350

TINWARE: N/A

TIP: N/A

PERFORMANCE GAIN:
Rearward vision improvement

COMPLEMENTARY PROJECT:
N/A

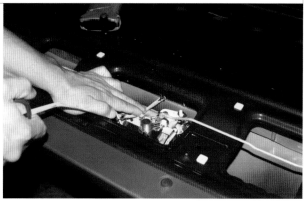

For our installation, we started with the camera mount first. Make sure to place tape over the area of the tailgate in which you will be drilling the hole for the camera to protect the paint. Once we decided on the location of the camera on the tailgate, just below the handle, we verified that our placement would not interfere with any of the mechanisms for opening the tailgate itself. This was simply removing the back panel on the tailgate and checking for clearance.

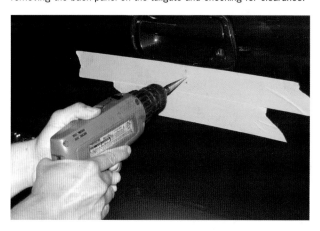

Once everything was checked, we drilled out a 27mm-diameter hole in the tailgate. Once drilled, we checked to make sure the camera would fit properly and snug in the hole. The camera and shroud, once installed on the tailgate, take up only a small amount of room and will almost disappear at a distance.

One of the first things you notice when you get your first truck or SUV is that backing the thing up in a normal parking lot is an interesting experience. Ever notice how many rear bumpers on trucks out there have a small ding, dent, or are slightly tweaked? Most of the time it is hard to judge distances or see directly behind you when backing your truck, which leads to bumping into walls, bushes, low posts, boxes, or even the occasional fire hydrant. These are just stationary obstacles. If you have kids, then you have to worry about toys, bicycles, and of course the kids themselves running behind the truck where you can't see them. According to a recent survey, more than 25 percent of all accidents occur when the vehicle is in reverse. Unless you are very good or very lucky, you need another set of eyes in the back of the vehicle.

First out in the market were the radar-style sensors that simply told you visually or audibly how close you were to an object behind the vehicle. This is simple technology to install, and the kits for these systems are relatively inexpensive. The only problem is that if something is below the radar beam level, it is not picked up. The technology also wouldn't pick up another car or

other moving object or person who runs behind your truck or SUV while you are backing up. To solve this minor glitch in these rear-sensing systems, many manufacturers developed mini camera systems that turn on only when needed or when the vehicle is in reverse. Initially, you had to install a large monitor to view the image, but this technology has since come a long way.

Rostra Precision Controls, Inc. (www.rostra.com) has been one of the industry innovators of these rear-sensing systems for many years. The latest systems include a rear-mounted camera with a complete shroud plus a rearview mirror replacement that includes a 3.5-inch LED screen built-in. The quarter-inch color camera features an electric auto iris, auto brightening adjustment, and a waterproof case. The rearview mirror is a direct replacement for the OEM rearview mirror. The mirror and kit come with a brightness adjustment, reverse override switch to

ELECTRICAL

turn the camera on when not in reverse, and a total of three inputs for other cameras in the vehicle (baby monitoring cam, navigation). This is one complete kit, and the instructions, although rather long, are very detailed and well illustrated. Rostra Precision Controls, Inc. also makes other camera models for various vehicles and situations.

We took a 2006 Toyota Tundra Deluxe Cab Limited that was destined to have a large ARE shell on it, which would seriously reduce our rear-end visibility from the driver's seat and installed Rostra Precision Controls, Inc.'s 250-8005 shrouded camera with rearview mirror kit specifically designed for the Toyota truck. For our install, we used the expertise of the technicians at Toyota of Glendora because all Toyota dealers carry and routinely install these systems as an option for new vehicles.

As you can see from the final photo of our truck, the camera is very small and unless you know what you are looking for, you won't notice it. Operating the system is very simple. There are three buttons on the face of the mirror: REV, CAM, and MAP. The system will automatically turn on when the truck is put into reverse, and the camera stays on for 10 seconds after you shift into drive. You can turn on the camera to see what your boat trailer is doing while not in reverse by pressing the REV button. The other two buttons are for additional inputs for such things as a baby camera for the rear seat area and your navigation system input. You could also install a second camera in your front bumper to watch the trail directly in front of your 4x4 when you are on the trails.

This system was easy to install, and it took only two hours for the technician to complete the task. Even if you are experienced installing electronics on your truck or SUV, for warrantee purposes it would still be best to let a dealership or other professional take care of the installation of these types of systems. The system is very user-friendly and provides that additional margin of safety to not only protect your truck but also anything behind it.

Another hole had to be drilled in the side of the tailgate for the camera feed to connect up to the wiring harness for the system. The wiring actually ends up going up the tailgate support cable and behind the left rear taillight. To keep the wiring snug to the tailgate cable, we used a piece of heat-shrink tubing over the cable and wiring harness.

Now that the tailgate and camera were taken care of, another hole was drilled in the cavity behind the taillight for the rest of the wiring harness and connectors. The main camera connection was placed in the cavity with a screw-on connector in case you need to remove the tailgate later. With our camera connected to the main harness, the main connectors were held in place in the taillight cavity with special clips included with the installation kit. With all the work done on the rear of the truck, the wiring harness was wrapped in black electrical tape and run along the frame rails to the cab of the truck. The harness was pushed through to a stock wiring harness hole in the cab under the driver's seat.

The wiring harness was pulled through the access hole and out under the driver's seat. We punched the camera wiring harness through a hole and sealed our damage to the watertight grommet with a hot glue gun. The side pillar of the driver's side and the lower kick panel were removed to run the wiring harness for the camera system up the side and into the headliner to get it to the rearview mirror location.

The stock rearview mirror and overhead console were removed and disconnected from the electrical harness of the truck, and the new wires were routed through the headliner to the location. Once the new mirror was attached and all the wiring was connected and wrapped, it was time to put the overhead console back in place and finish the connections.

With all the wiring completed, you can see that the actual camera mounted on the tailgate is not as noticeable as you might think. This is a great setup.

PROJECT **97** ADD A SUBWOOFER AND ENCLOSURE

 TIME: One hour

 TOOLS: Small appliance electrician's tools

 TALENT: ★★★

 APPLICABLE YEARS: For all years, makes, and models of light trucks

 TAB: $300

 TINWARE: N/A

 TIP: N/A

 PERFORMANCE GAIN:
Better sound quality

COMPLEMENTARY PROJECT:
Upgrade stereo wiring to MTX Streetwires while you are dealing with sound system connections.

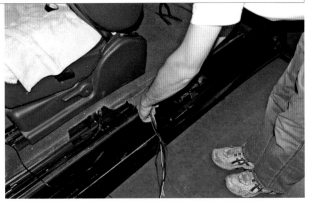

Remove the driver-side threshold trim to gain access to the factory wire loom beneath it. Next, Abo Gulkarov, owner of South Coast Speed & Sound, lifts and locks the rear seat out of the way and clears the area so the wiring can be run to the area where the ThunderForm will be placed later in the installation. You will still be able to use the factory location for the spare tire jack. The wiring, including the right and left speaker leads, trigger, EBC, and 10-gauge power wire, are then placed into the factory wire track and run forward to the dash. MTX's instructions ask for the speaker leads to be spliced into the rear factory speaker wires at the rear of the truck, but instead we chose to run them forward to the head unit and splice them there.

Automotive audio has come a long way in recent years. While often we find ourselves eyeing the latest and greatest gadget to hit the scene, we tend to forget that some products are still as useful and popular as the day they were engineered. And one of those products is the time-tested ThunderForm subwoofer enclosure from MTX Audio.

In the past, all subwoofer enclosures had to be custom made to fit into a vehicle. This was always in accordance with a "custom" sound system, which completely replaced the factory model. Of course, in those days, factory sound systems were not all that great to begin with. But such is not the case with modern factory sound systems. Many trucks today come equipped with very good sound systems featuring numerous speakers, and in some cases, amplified systems. MTX is one of the companies that realized some consumers wanted to add some thump to their system, without the cost of completely replacing their stock setup. They developed what has become the time tested ThunderForm enclosure, which is engineered to fit specific models of trucks.

The 1.9 cubic foot ThunderForm enclosure comes with either one or two 10-inch Thunder4500 subwoofers, and has an option for an amplified version serving up 200 watts of power. The enclosures are generally designed to fit under the rear seats of the trucks so as not to take up much of the important cab space. They also come in every factory color to properly blend into a stock interior. But with all that, what makes the MTX ThunderForms so popular is that they easily integrate into the factory sound system. Basically all that is required is to mount the enclosure, then run the wires to the dash. Then you need to run the power wire to the engine power supply and the speaker leads to the head unit, where they are spliced into the existing rear channel wires.

On the amplified model that we had South Coast Speed & Sound install for us, the enclosure features its own amplifier, which also includes an EBC (electronic bass control) and pre-amp station. A 10-gauge fused power wire provided in the harness is more than ample to handle the demands of the amplifier. In addition, our 2004 Silverado had the factory-amplified Bose system. Rather than splice into the speaker leads from the head unit, we were required to splice into the leads at the factory amplifier located in the center console.

In about an hour, the guys at South Coast Speed & Sound had completed the installation of the MTX ThunderForm, showing us just how quick and easy it is to put some bass in the factory sound system. And when you consider the amplified enclosure features its own pre-amp with adjustable gain controls, along with the EBC, you can turn the bass signal down on the head unit to make the factory mids sound better. At the same time, this installation allows the new pair of 10-inch subs to take care of the low-end frequencies.

For folks looking for some extra kick in their tunes without the high cost of a custom sound system, the ThunderForm is definitely something to check out.

ELECTRICAL

Before we finished with the dash, the last thing to do was to install the EBC into the panel we modified earlier.

Make sure you have a good ground. Gulkarov grinds away the paint from a small area on the cab floor near the seat bracket and installs the ground cable there using a self-tapping screw. Moving forward, the harness is run through the track to where the dash kick panel has been removed. The wires will run behind the kick panel and up through to the dash. The wires that will run through the dash are taped so they stay together as they travel through the under-dash landscape. To feed the power wire into the engine compartment, Gulkarov uses a special tool that pokes a hole through the steering column boot. The power wire is then fed through the tool into the compartment where it is easily acquired.

The 20-amp fuse is removed from the power wire. The wire is then attached to the power post located on the driver's side of the engine. Back into the interior, the dash bezel is removed to gain access to the head unit along with running the needed wires to that location. We had to decide on a location to mount the EBC (electronic bass control). We chose the blank panel next to the air bag on/off switch. In order to install the control in that location, the panel assembly had to be removed. The small, blank panel was then removed from that assembly and on to the back side, and the plastic cross-structure was cut out to clear a path for the control assembly. The EBC comes with a min/max sticker overlay, which was placed on the blank panel.

Using a drill bit, a small ¼-inch hole was drilled in the center, which will allow the control shaft to extend through and be secured to the panel. With that complete, we then move back into the truck where the lower dash panel is removed so the wires can be routed.

Here we see the provided RCA high-level input wires spliced into the appropriate speaker wires on the output side of the factory amplifier. The RCA wires are designed to accommodate the power from the amplifier and will not interfere with the amplifier inside the ThunderForm enclosure.

Now comes the part you've been waiting for. The MTX ThunderForm enclosure is installed into the truck. The box is designed to form perfectly to the floor to the point that it is nearly impossible to install it wrong. Once positioned correctly, the RCA inputs, ground/power connector, and trigger are plugged into the preamp located in the center recession of the enclosure. The amplifier will not power up until the 20-amp fuse is installed into the power wire inside the engine compartment.

The ThunderForm also comes with two locations that allow you to screw the box down to the cab floor. It is advised that you mount the box, as it will slide forward in the event you have to brake hard when driving.

And there you have it: a quick and easy way to add 200 watts of bass to your factory system without losing your rear seating area. The MTX ThunderForm fits perfectly under the rear seat, and the finish nicely matches the interior.

ELECTRICAL

PROJECT 98 BUILD A SUBWOOFER CABINET

TIME: Five to eight hours

TOOLS: Woodworking tools

TALENT: ★★

APPLICABLE YEARS: All years, makes, and models of light trucks

TAB: $100 in materials

TINWARE: N/A

TIP: Measure twice, cut once.

PERFORMANCE GAIN:
Custom enclosure, sound quality

COMPLEMENTARY PROJECT:
Upgrade total sound system.

The first step was to build a mounting point for the subwoofer. This one is a Kicker L7 10-inch-square subwoofer, so the mounting frame is square. The rear seat was removed, and the carpet was lined with duct tape. The subwoofer-mounting frame was inserted to see where it sits on the bottom of the cab. The sides of the subwoofer frame are built so that it can be attached to the inside of the enclosure. The three sides of the enclosure are placed in the cab again with the subwoofer mocked in place. The subwoofer will be exposed to air at the bottom of the enclosure, so the remainder is sealed. This is done to begin forming the bottom with fiberglass. Layers of fiberglass and resin are added to form the floor of the subwoofer enclosure. The tape that was placed down before will help form the mold of the fiberglass without hurting the carpet.

You can see how the mold is taking form and the fiberglass is left to dry.

One of the biggest problems with pickup trucks is that no room exists in the cab for a nice subwoofer. However, this doesn't mean that you will have to do without ground-pounding bass and limit the type of music you can listen to. If you have the time and patience to do so, you can build a custom enclosure that is designed to fit perfectly into your truck and has the ability to pound the windows out of the cab.

Although a simple box can be fabricated out of wood or medium-dense fiberboard (MDF), professional installers know that the interior of your truck isn't made up of right angles. There are many curves and crevices in your truck that a custom box needs to conform to in order to fit properly. This is one of the reasons why many like to use a combination of MDF and fiberglass. The fiberglass conforms to the various contours of the cab while the wood sections provide a solid platform for mounting the subwoofer and reflecting bass tones.

To get a better idea of what this process involves, we looked on as the professional installers at Sound Advice in Mission Viejo, California, installed a pair of custom subwoofer enclosures into an SS Silverado. The intent was to mount two subwoofers under the rear seats and to provide this truck with extreme bass.

ELECTRICAL

271

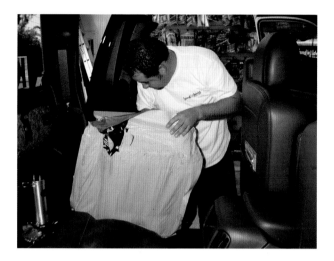

Once the extra tape is removed, the entire subwoofer and fiberglass form can be carefully removed.

In order to let the air move with this subwoofer, a router is used to cut down a section of the enclosure.

The exterior of the subwoofer is sanded to have a smooth finish. The inside edges of the enclosure are also sealed with silicone.

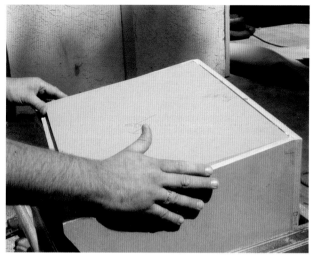

A top is then measured and cut from MDF and inserted into the enclosure. Keep in mind that the subwoofer will surface mount on the frame at the bottom. The top is glued and screwed into place ensuring that everything is square and flat.

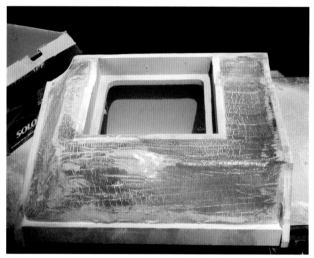

Here is the finished, ported subwoofer. Now it will have to be dressed up.

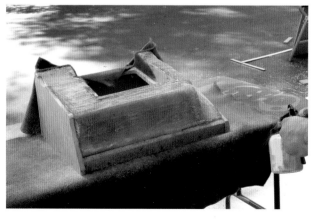

Some adhesive is sprayed on to the inside of the carpet so that it will stick to the enclosure.

Here's what the finished product looks like. Because the bottom will be facing down, there's no need to cover this area.

A small hole was drilled to allow the wiring for the subwoofer to run through the inside of the enclosure.

The subwoofer is then inserted and screwed into the enclosure.

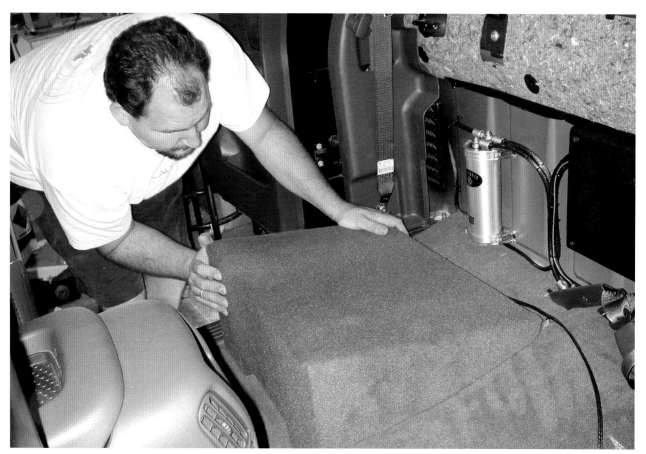

The finished installation looks great, and the subwoofer wires are routed to the amplifier.

TIME: Two hours

TOOLS: Electrician's tools

TALENT: ★★★

APPLICABLE YEARS: All

TAB: $2,000

TINWARE: N/A

TIP: N/A

PERFORMANCE GAIN:
Better sound

COMPLEMENTARY PROJECT:
N/A

The dash-trim housing is removed from the vehicle to expose the radio and the factory wiring harness. Sony's replacement Xplod speakers are coaxial and replace the factory door speakers to improve the sound quality. Sony's NV-900 DVD overhead console features a 9-inch screen and built-in DVD player. Properly crimping the wires and high-quality connections are what separate a good installer from a bad one. These guys made sure that the connections were well made to avoid any problems in the future. Aside from the wiring connections from the amplifier to the head unit, a harness is used to connect the head unit to the factory wiring system.

The brain of the entire system is the Sony XAV-A1 head unit, which provides plenty of power and is upgradeable to incorporate additional components. The factory wiring harness and audio/video upgrade wiring has been run and zip-tied for a clean look.

A cool SUV should have a modified suspension, custom wheels and tires, and some DVDs playing on the entertainment system. Although it may seem like adding a high-quality entertainment system in your SUV takes a custom installer and plenty of fiberglass molding, the fact is that many aftermarket manufacturers have compiled a host of products that work in synch with each other to produce high-quality video and audio at a reasonable price . . . one that you can also afford to have installed.

Such is the case with Sony's new Specialty Series system, which includes a variety of components that are meant to work together. When combined, the system provides optimum-quality sound and video from a few components that can be easily bolted to your vehicle.

Sony invited us to Auto Sound & Security, a mobile-audio installation facility and Sony dealer where we could see the company's newest system installed and see and hear its overall performance.

The installers at Auto Sound & Security made it clear that you don't need any special cutting or modifications to install these components to the vehicle. They demonstrated this by first installing the Sony XAV-A1 head unit, which features a radio tuner and a built-in 7-inch monitor. This unit replaced the factory head unit on a 2004 Ford Expedition and was easily put into place with a new dash fascia and wiring harness that simply plugged into the factory harness. The unit comes with 17 watts of power (RMS 50 x 4), which is plenty to power the Sony front coaxial front door speakers.

Sony also provided a set of door speakers that replaced the factory units with coaxial pieces and are powered with a single

Sony XM-SD46X, four-channel amplifier. The amp provides 60 watts rms per channel and has a variable high/low pass filter and a 10db at 40 Hz bass boost.

With the audio portion of the system installed, Auto Sound & Security moved on with an additional overhead monitor and DVD player unit that fits as an overhead center-console. The Sony NV-900-SDS is an all-in-one unit that contains a 9-inch, fold-down monitor and DVD player. The monitor also swivels 180 degrees, and the system features additional audio and video inputs for game consoles. It also has a memory stick slot for mpeg, jpeg and MP3 playback.

The system was mocked to ensure that it was centered in the cab, and a small hole was cut into the headliner to route the wiring. The system comes with a mounting kit that allows the unit to be easily bolted to the vehicle's roof, and once this is done, it is properly wired into the vehicle's power and ground and is connected to the head unit.

The installation took only a few hours, and once completed, the system turned an ordinary SUV into an extraordinarily cool vehicle. The large monitor of the Sony NV-900 unit allows plenty of viewing angles for rear passengers, and the audio can be played through the XAV-A1 head unit instead of through an FM modulator. This made the sound much better. The system even allows dual system operation, which allows the front passengers to enjoy music while the rear passengers can play a video game or enjoy a movie.

The system, although easy to install, costs about $2,000 plus installation. Nevertheless, the completeness of the system allows for a greater enjoyment of your SUV, and it will definitely thrust you into the highest realm of the coolness factor.

The Sony head unit was then inserted into the dash. Note how the extra space is taken up with a slot to hold extra stuff. Once the head unit was wired and ready, the factory dash panel/housing was fitted back on to the vehicle.

Finally, it was time to replace the factory door speakers with the Sony Xplod units. To do this the door panels were removed. The factory speakers are easily unplugged and removed from the doors. The new Sony upgrade speaker fits perfectly into the door's existing speaker hole. It is connected to the wiring and installed back into the door panel.

This is what the Sony speaker looks like once it is installed using the factory hole and mounting holes.

This system required a Sony XM-SD46X power amp for increased quality of sound throughout the vehicle. We opted to install the power amp behind the driver-side quarter panel.

Finishing off the installation is the Sony overhead DVD console. We opted to move it up as forward as possible for both sets of rear seat passengers to enjoy.

The overhead console looks like a factory unit, but it is clean and high-tech in appearance. The DVD head unit also looks and operates great and enhances the overall appearance of this SUV.

TIME: Four hours

TOOLS: Socket set, razor blade knife, electrical hand tools

TALENT: ★★★

APPLICABLE YEARS: DVD players for all years, makes, and models of light trucks

TAB: $2,200

TINWARE: N/A

TIP: N/A

PERFORMANCE GAIN:
Entertainment for the kids and other freeway motorists

COMPLEMENTARY PROJECT:
Upgrade sound system.

Begin by unlatching the factory seat back upholstery. Unhook it from the bottom of the cushion. Starting from the front, the factory cloth cover is slowly pulled upward, making sure not to rip or damage the upholstery in any way. Vehicles with vinyl or leather upholstery are removed in the same manner.

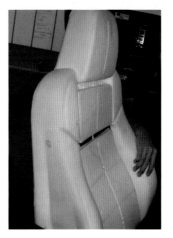

Work both front and rear a bit at a time until enough of the seat cover is lifted to remove it from the cushion. That black strip in the center of the factory seat cushion is Velcro that secures a fold in the seat cover. Once the cover is off of the cushion, it simply slides up and out from the steel seat frame.

Those days of singing songs or keeping children busy with coloring books during a long trip have been replaced with GameBoys, Playstations, and DVD movies. Yes, it's easy to convince your spouse that adding a DVD player to your sport utility vehicle will keep the kids quiet, but the real reason is that it turns your "family vehicle" into a cruise mobile. The only thing left would be adding a set of chromed 22-inch wheels and tires to finish off the look.

Deciding on a DVD system for your vehicle is not an easy task. In the past, many vehicle systems had to be custom installed. Nowadays, complete systems come with everything you need, including several monitors and a compact DVD player that can be installed without any custom upholstery work or extensive wiring. On many vehicles, the easiest way to install monitors is in the factory headrests. Aftermarket manufacturers offer pre-assembled headrests with monitors built in, so that the consumer simply has to push them in place and wire them up to their existing DVD system.

In some cases, however, sport utility vehicles don't have detachable headrests. We found an SUV that fit this situation

and instead of having to custom mount and upholster a monitor into the seat back, we discovered that Visualogic manufactures a complete seat cushion replacement that has the framework to fit an LCD monitor into the back.

The Visualogic system also came with a compact DVD player and control box that makes the wiring much simpler. The system also uses a wireless remote control, and in this installation, the owner also wanted a passenger sun visor monitor included in the installation.

We observed as Wired For Sound in Murrieta, California, installed the Visualogic DVD system on to this 2005 Ford Expedition. From start to finish, the installation took about three to four hours to install and no custom wiring or upholstery was necessary. In the end, this modification gave this family vehicle a high-quality video system that would keep the kids entertained while making the owner look "fly" on his way to the office.

ELECTRICAL

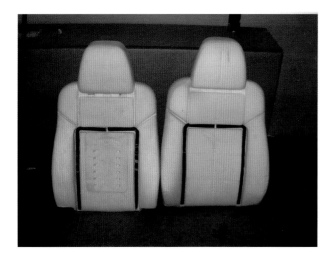

The factory and Visualogic seat cushions are almost identical. The only difference is that the Visualogic seat cushion also has a cutout for an aftermarket heater as well as the cutout for the monitor on the back of the headrest. Placing the Visualogic cushion on the floor, the factory upholstery is reinstalled. This is done by turning it inside out and starting at the top of the headrest.

The monitor is then plugged into the harness, and it simply snaps into the frame. You may need to trim away more of the seat cover, but it is best to cut too little than too much. If you get it right, it will look like a professional installation.

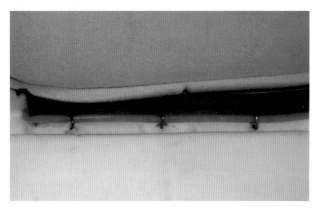

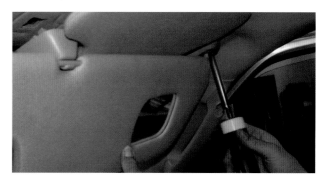

Here you can see a close-up of how this was done. It may take some practice to use the hog-ring pliers, but it is simple once you get the hang of it. With the upholstery secured on to the cushion, it is simply slipped over the steel frame.

To install the sun visor monitor, the factory sun visor is unbolted from the headliner. Then the window pillar is removed by accessing the screws from the handle.

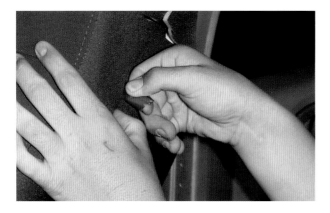

You can feel where the opening is for the monitor and begin cutting the cover for the monitor. It is best to start with an X shape. The system includes a wiring harness that goes into the seat back and comes out of the bottom. This then plugs into the monitor.

The sun visor monitor replaces the factory mirror, and the wiring is routed through the headliner and down the side of the window pillar cover. The wiring for the sun visor monitor is routed alongside the vehicle underneath the factory sill plate.

The Visualogic DVD player also plays CDs and MP3s. It is a small unit, so we had enough space to mount it under the front passenger seat. The wires are labeled as to where they attach, and some of the cables were routed under the carpet.

Because this system uses an FM modulator to transfer sound through the vehicle's stereo system, a switch is installed in the glove box to turn the modulator on or off for a better signal when the DVD system is on. The FM modulator must be attached to the factory stereo, so the dash is removed to access it.

The modulator plugs into the radio antenna and is wired to the rest of the DVD system. The owner simply has to tune into a preset radio station to listen to the DVD's soundtrack. The installation took about four hours. Although a professional installer put this system in, an experienced home mechanic could install the Visualogic DVD system.

TIME: Three hours

 TOOLS: Full socket set, hand tools

 TALENT: ★

 APPLICABLE YEARS: For most years, makes, and models of light trucks

 TAB: $1,300

 TINWARE: N/A

 TIP: Use new nuts, bolts, washers, and cotter pin.

 PERFORMANCE GAIN:
Easy entry for all passengers

COMPLEMENTARY PROJECT:
Suspension lift, tires/wheels

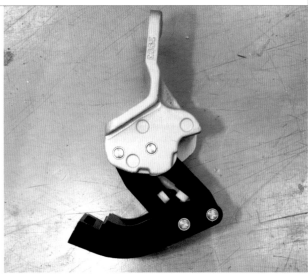

When it is retracted, it is amazing how compact the linkage assembly becomes.

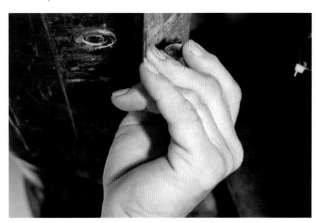

The Titan has threaded mounts and mounting studs in the factory rocker panels for the installation of different factory options, and AMP Research takes full advantage of this, using them to mount the front and rear linkage assemblies. Here, the plastic plugs are being pulled out of the threaded mounting points. The front and rear linkage assemblies are then simply bolted into place using the provided hardware.

A lot of us have walked up to a lifted truck or SUV and wondered how to go about getting inside without the use of a ladder—or at least a friend willing to give us a boost. There are those truck owners who have bolted on big tubular steps or running boards, but honestly some trucks just don't look right with a big set of steps hanging down off the sides of the truck.

That's where the folks from AMP Research can help. They have taken all of the experience and creativity that they use developing trick parts for various OEMs and brought it to the truck and SUV aftermarket with their power steps. The AMP Research crew developed a retractable full-length running board that everyone from moms and dads to tots and teens and even grandmas and grandpas can use to easily enter and exit even the tallest truck cabs. When the door is closed, the full-length running board automatically retracts under the truck, out of view. And unless you actually crawl up under the truck, you would never know that the power steps are even there.

The power steps employ a patented multi-link design to achieve its extended range of motion. And in the case of the power steps for the Titan, they reduce the threshold height by a

full 12 inches. That's right, that first step needed to gain access to the interior of a Nissan Titan is a full foot lower than it would be without the power steps!

And once the door is closed, the electric motor is activated to quickly retract the boards back under the rocker panels of the truck. In fact, the power step mechanism goes from fully retracted to fully extended in less than 1.3 seconds after a door is opened.

Typical installation time for the AMP Research power steps takes less than two hours. Each package includes left- and right-side running board assemblies, mounting hardware, OEM quality wiring harness, control module, and detailed installation guide. And although it can be done at home with a pretty basic assortment of tools, professional installation is recommended.

ELECTRICAL

After the linkage assemblies are snug, the boards are slipped on to the end of the linkage assemblies. The bolts that hold the linkage to the boards are installed but not tightened. That's because the position of the boards has to be adjusted so the back of the step board overhangs the position of the rear linkage assembly by 11 ½ inches. Once it is in position, the bolts are tightened up.

Once the control unit is mounted, the wiring harness in the kit is plugged in and the wiring is run as per the instructions. Two parts of the harness run down the frame rails and simply plug into the electric motors that were mounted to the rear linkage assemblies. Then there are two sections of the wiring harness that run up through the floor on both sides near the front kick panels.

The electric motors are lined up with the large upper shafts on the rear linkage assemblies. To get the bolt holes in the electric motor to line up with the mounting holes in the assembly, the boards have to be moved up or down slightly before the bolts can be installed.

The last step is to hook up the section of wiring harness that connects the control unit to the battery.

As soon as the doors are closed, the power steps retract up under the truck for the first time.

When all of the bolts are in place and tight, this is what the rear assembly looks like with the electric motor installed. The control unit for the power steps comes with a mounting bracket that allows the unit assembly to be easily bolted to existing mounting points on the inner fender between the air box and the ABS unit.

To give everybody an idea of exactly what kind of difference the AMP Research power steps can make, we enlisted the help of the owner of this particular Titan to demonstrate exactly how much lower that first step is now.

A+ Performance
17571 Griffin Lane, Building A
Huntington Beach, CA 92647
(714) 841-0101
Fax: (714) 848-5997
www.performanceexhaust.net
www.aplusperformanceauto.com

Advantage Performance Center
1253 W La Cadena
Riverside, CA 92501
(951) 684-8483

AEM
2205 126th Street, Unit A
Hawthorne, CA 90250
(310) 484-0512
www.aempower.com

Airaid
2688 E Rose Garden Lane
Phoenix, AZ 85050
(602) 443-3333

Airaid Filter Company
14840 N 74th Street
Scottsdale, AZ 85260
(800) 498-6951
www.airaid.com

Air Lift Company
2727 Snow Road
Lansing, MI 48917
(800) 248-0892 ext. 244
www.airliftcompany.com

Alcoa Wheel Products
1600 Harvard Avenue
Cleveland, OH 44105
(800) 242-9898
www.alcoawheels.com

AMP Research
2552 McGaw Avenue
Irvine, CA 92614
(888) 983-2204
(949) 221-0023
www.amp-research.com

Amtech Corp.
3120 Venture Drive
Las Vegas, NV 89101
(888) 880-8949
www.amtechsprings.com

APM Automotive
17490 East Street
North Ft. Myers, FL 33917
(239) 731-3838

Auto & Truck Specialties (ATS)
11110 Business Circle
Cerritos, CA 90703
(562) 924-7757

Auto Accessory Warehouse
68-390 E Ramon Road
Cathedral City, CA 92234
(760) 202-9766

Auto Sound & Security
12171 Central Avenue
Chino, CA 91710
(909) 364-0494

Autowave, Inc.
17122 Gothard Street
Huntington Beach, CA 92647
(714) 841-2433
www.autowaveinc.com

B&B Exhaust
23045 15th Avenue
Phoenix, AZ 85027
(623) 581-7600

Baer Brake Systems
3108 W Thomas Road, Suite 1201-Q
Phoenix, AZ 85017
(602) 233-1411
www.baer.com

Barry Grant Incorporated
1450 McDonald Road
Dahlonega, GA 30533
(706) 864-8544

Bassani
2900 E La Jolla Street
Anaheim, CA 92806
(714) 630-1821
www.bassani.com

Billet Specialties
Department 10
500 Shawmut Avenue
La Grange, IL 60526
(708) 588-0505
info@billetspecialties.com

Bilstein of America
Department 10
14102 Stowe Drive
Poway, CA 92064
(800) 537-1085

Brian's Truck Shop
14991 Industrial Park Road
Leadhill AR 72644
(870) 422-3673

Bully Dog
2854 W 2200 South
Aberdeen, ID 83210
(208) 397-3200
www.bullydog.com

CAGE Off Road
200 Port Avenue
St. Helens, OR 97051
(503) 397-3169
www.cageoffroad.com

Central 4 Wheel Drive
9240 N Whitaker Road
Portland, OR 97217
(800) 829-9599

Continental Auto Body
18651 Beach Boulevard
Huntington Beach, CA 92648
(714) 847-1241

Corsa Performance
140 Blaze Industrial Parkway
Berea, OH 44017
(800) 486-0999

CST Performance Suspension
115 W La Cadana Drive, Suite 100
Riverside, CA 92501
(909) 328-9902

Custom Motorsports
12150 Severn Way
Riverside, CA 92503
(951) 549-1740
www.custommotorsports.com

Devious Customs
Department 10
915 E Grevillea Court
Ontario, CA 91761
(909) 947-1800

Earl's Automotive
232 N Maclay Avenue
San Fernando, CA 91340
(818) 831-7154

Edge Products Inc.
1080 S Depot Drive
Ogden, UT 84404
(888) 360-3343
(801) 476-3343
Fax (801) 476-3348

EGR Brakes
(800) 468-2279
www.egrbrakes.com

El Monte Campers
10927 Garvey Avenue
El Monte, CA 91733
(626) 443-7913

Extreme Dimensions, Inc.
586 N Gilbert Street
Fullerton, CA 92833
www.extremedimensions.com

Factory Tech Transmission Performance
6818 Midnight Sun Drive
Mainville, OH 45039
(513) 677-5358

Flex-A-Lite
P.O. Box 580
Milton, WA 98354
www.flex-a-lite.com

Flowmaster
100 Stony Point Road, Suite 125
Santa Rosa, CA 95401
(707) 544-4761
www.flowmastermufflers.com

Gale Banks Engineering
546 Duggan Avenue
Azusa, CA 91720
(626) 969-9600
www.bankspower.com

Gear Vendors Inc.
Department 10
1717 Magnolia Avenue
El Cajon, CA 92020
(800) 999-9555
www.gearvendors.com

Gibson Performance
1270 Webb Circle
Corona, CA 92879
(800) 528-3044
(951) 372-1220
www.gibsonperformance.com

Go Industries
420 North Grove Road
Richardson, TX 75801
(800) 527-4345

Granatelli Motorsports
1000 Yarnell Place
Oxnard, CA 93033
(805) 486-6644

Ground Force
Department 10
P.O. Box 149
Mt. Braddock, PA 15465
(724) 430-2068
Fax: (724) 437-0705
www.groundforce.com

GS Motorsports
1251 Beach Boulevard, Unit B
La Habra, CA 90631
(888) GSM-HEMI
(562) 947-0753

Hellwig Suspension Accessories
16237 Avenue 296
Visalia, CA 93292
(800) 435-5977
(559) 734-7451
www.hellwigproducts.com

Hoffman Group/Stellar
Vehicle Security
11981 SW Pacific Highway
Tigard, OR 97223
(800) 873-4036
www.thehoffmangroup.com
www.stellaralarms.com

Holley Performance Products
1801 Russellville Road
Bowling Green, KY 42102-7360
(270) 781-2783

Inglewood Transmission Service
4919 W Century Boulevard
Inglewood, CA 90301
(310) 674-4400

JET Performance
1749 Apex Circle
Huntington Beach, CA 92647
(714) 848-5515
www.jetchip.com

Johns Customs & Performance
20022 Normandie Avenue
Torrance, CA

Katzkin Leather
6868 Acco Street

Montebello, CA 90640
(323) 725-1243

LB Threads
2730 Cherry Avenue
Signal Hill, CA 90755
(562) 989-3422

Leer Corporation
www.leer.com

LMC Truck
Box 14991
Lenexa, KS 66285
(800) 562-8782

Mac's Springs
26746 E Baseline
Highland, CA 92346
(909) 862-4811

MBRP Diesel Exhaust
315 Old Ferguson Road, RR #1
Huntsville, ON P1H 2J2
CANADA
(705) 788-2845
www.mbrp.com

McGaughys Suspension Parts
Department 10
5680 W Barstow
Fresno, CA 93722
(559) 226-8196
www.mcgaughys.com

MSD Ignition
1490 Henry Brennan Drive
El Paso, TX 79936
http://msdignition.com/

MTX Audio
Department 10
One Mitek Plaza
Winslow, IL 61089
(800) 225-5689
www.mtx.com

Nitrous Supply
5482 Business Drive, Suite B
Huntington Beach, CA 92649
(714) 373-1986

Nitto Tires
Dept. Ten
6021 Katella Avenue, Suite 250
Cypress, CA 90630
(800) 648-8652
www.nittotire.com

No Limit Engineering
Department 10
455 S D Street
San Bernardino,
CA 92401
(909) 386-7637
www.nolimit.net

NWCryogenics
35820 77th Street East
Littlerock, CA 93543
(661) 944-3468
www.nwcryo.com

Off Road Unlimited
300 N Victory Boulevard
Burbank, CA, 91502
(818) 848-2020

Performance Distributors, Inc.
Department 10
2699 Barris Drive
Memphis, TN 38132-1202
(901) 396-5782
www.performancedistributors.com

Performance Steering Components
PSC (Pump Kit)
901 Finney Drive
Weatherford, TX 76085
(817) 270-0102

Permanent Impressions
5985 Engineer Drive
Huntington Beach, CA 92649
(714) 899-9810

Precision Differential & Chassis/PDC
Motorsports
570 W Lambert Road, Unit F
Brea, CA 92821
(714) 671-9752

Precision Industries
80 Pierce Road
Oakland, TN 38060
(800) 649-7866

ProComp Wheels
(866) 232-0665
www.procomptire.com

Proficient Performance
18 Technology Drive, Suite 168
Irvine, CA 92618
(949) 872-2444
www.proficientdiesel.com

Rancho Suspensions
Tenneco Automotive
6925 Atlantic Avenue

Long Beach, CA 90805
(734) 384-7805
www.gorancho.com

Rancho/Tenneco Automotive
One International Drive
Monroe, MI 48161
(734) 384-7804
www.gorancho.com

Ranch Truck Accessories
27499 Commerce Center Drive
Temecula, CA 92590
(951) 676-4043

Robby Gordon Off-Road
2980 East Miraloma Avenue
Anaheim, CA 92806
(714) 632-0166
www.robbygordonoffroad.com

Rolling Big Power
Department 10
1655 W 6th Street, Suite 106
Corona, CA 92882
(951) 272-9090

Rostra Precision Controls, Inc.
Laurinburg, NC
(800) 782-3379
www.rostra.com

Roush Performance
28156 Plymouth Road
Livonia, MI 48150
(800) 597-6874
www.roushperf.com

S&B Filters, Inc.
Department 10
787 Wanamaker Avenue
Ontario, CA
(909) 947-0015
www.sbfilters.com

Skyjacker Suspensions
212 Stevenson Street
West Monroe, LA 71292
(318) 388-0816
www.skyjacker.com

Smeding Performance
3340 Sunrise Boulevard, Unit E
Rancho Cordova, CA 95742
(916) 638-0899
www.smedingperformance.com

Sony Electronics, Inc.
16450 W Bernardo Drive
San Diego, CA 92127
Sound Advice

28641 Marguerite Parkway, Unit C-1
Mission Viejo, CA 92692
(949) 364-6464

South Coast Speed & Sound
Deptartment 10
1746 W Katella Avenue
Orange, CA 92867
(714) 628-0400
www.teamscss.com

Squires Turbo Systems
165 N 1330 West, Suite C4
Orem, UT 84057
(801) 224-3477
(866) WE-TURBO
www.ststurbo.com

St. Andre's Automotive Accessories
7128 Garden Grove Boulevard, Unit C
Westminster, CA 92683
(714) 891-1002

Stainless Steel Brake Corporation
11470 Main Road
Clarence, NY 14031
(800) 448-7722

Steve Millen Sportparts, Inc.
Department 10
3176 Airway
Costa Mesa, CA 92626
(866) 250-5542

Stillen Motorsports
3176 Airway Avenue
Costa Mesa, CA 92626
(714) 540-5566

Street Scene Equipment
Department 10
365 McCormick Avenue
Costa Mesa, CA 92626
(888) 477-0707
(714) 426-0590

STS Performance
Department 10
6285 E Spring Street #270
Long Beach, CA 90808
(562) 531-6328
www.stsperformance.com

Stull Industries
1315 W Flint Street
Lake Elsinore, CA 92530
(800) 227-9206
www.stullindustries.com

Superchips, Inc.
1790 E Airport Boulevard

Sanford, FL 32733
(407) 585-7000
Fax: (407) 585-1926
www.superchips.com
Superior Axle & Gear
1477 Davril Circle
Corona, CA 92880
(888) 522-2953
http://www.superioraxle.com

Superlift Suspension Systems
300 Huey Lenard Loop Road
West Monroe, LA 71292
(800) 551-4955
Fax: (318) 397-3040
www.superlift.com

TCI Automotive
151 Industrial Drive
Ashland, MS 38603
(662) 224-8972
www.tciauto.com

Tempco, Inc.
Department 10
1505 E Burnett Street
Signal Hill, CA 90755
(562) 427-5569

Texas Auto Gear
(281) 448-4371
www.texasautogear.net

Toyo Tires
(800) 442-8696 (West Coast)
(888) 444-8696 (East Coast)
www.toyo.com

Toyota of Glendora
Auto Centre Drive
Glendora, CA
(909) 305-2000

The Truck Stop Specialty Conversions
Department 10
1889 West Commonwealth Avenue,
Unit B
Fullerton, CA 92833
(714) 870-7920
Fax: (714) 870-5715

TS Performance
1025-B Lovers Lane
Bowling Green, KY 42103
(270) 746-9999
www.tsperformance.com
Vintage Air, Inc.

Department 10
18865 Goll Street
Garden Ridge, TX 78266
(210) 654-7171
www.vintageair.com

Visualogic
1493 Bentley Drive
Corona, CA 92879
(800) 624-7960

Volant Performance
8759 Lion Street
Rancho Cucamonga, CA 91730
(909) 476-7225
www.volantperformance.com/

Warn Industries, Inc.
Department 10
12900 SE Capps Road
Clackamas, OR 97015-8903
(503) 722-3038

Westech Performance Group
11098 Venture Drive, Unit C
Mira Loma, CA 91752
(951) 685-4767

Westin Automotive Products
5200 N Irwindale Avenue, Suite 220
Irwindale, CA 91706
(800) 345 8476

White Motorsports
1160 Sterling Avenue, Suite A
Riverside, CA 92503
(909) 324-8242

Wilwood Disc Brakes
Department 10
4700 Calle Bolero
Camarillo, CA 93012
(805) 388-1188
www.wilwood.com
sales@wilwood.com

Wired For Sound Motorsports
41604 Date Street
Murrieta, CA 92562
(909) 696-2200

Wrangler NW Power Products
810 N Graham Street
Portland, OR 97227
(800) 962-2616
www.wranglernw.com

INDEX

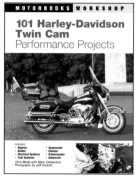
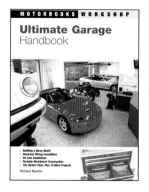